BIBLIOTHECA HISTORICO—ECCLE

Church and People in Britain and Scandinavia

Editor: Ingmar Brohed

Lund University Press

Lund University Press
Box 141
S-221 00 Lund
Sweden

© The Authors

Art nr 20440
ISSN 0346-5438
ISBN 91-7966-387-7 Lund University Press
ISBN 0-86238-454-0 Chartwell-Bratt Ltd

Printed in Sweden
Studentlitteratur
Lund 1996

Contents

Contents	3
Hugh McLeod (University of Birmingham) Introduction	7

Part I Christianisation

Lesley Abrams (University of Cambridge) Kings and Bishops in the Conversion of the Anglo-Saxon and Scandinavian Kingdoms	15
Torstein Jørgensen (Mission College, Stavanger) From Wessex to Western Norway: Some Perspectives on one Channel for the Christianisation Process	29
Hjalti Hugason (University of Reykjavik) The Acceptance of Chritianity in Iceland: An Attempt at a New Interpretation	45
Dawn M. Hadley (University of Sheffield) The Vikings' Relationship with Christianity Reconsidered	59
Per Beskow (University of Lund) Runic Inscriptions, Liturgy and Eschatology	77

Part II The Reformation

Robert N. Swanson (University of Birmingham) Late Medieval England: Road to Reformation or Road to Deformation?	93
Martin Schwarz Lausten (University of Copenhagen) The Contradiction between Evangelical Faith and Political Aims by the Danish Exiled King Christian II with reference to his Relations with King Henry VIII	109

Simo Heininen (University of Helsinki)
The Early Reformation in Sweden   123

Marianne Jensen-Broby de Perez (University of Copenhagen)
The Genesis of the Reformed Danish Ordination Ritual of 1537   131

Ingun Montgomery (University of Oslo)
A Reformation without a Reformer: The Realisation of the
Reformation in Norway   147

Jeremy Gregory (University of Northumbria at Newcastle)
The Making of a Protestant Nation: "Success" and "Failure" in
England's Long Reformation, c.1530-c.1830   159

Part III Free Churches and Revival Movements

R.W. Ambler (University of Hull)
"Building up the Walls of Zion" - The Development of the New
Connexion General Baptists in Lincolnshire 1770-1891   181

Myrtle Hill (Queen's University, Belfast)
Assessing the Awakening: The 1859 Revival in Ulster   197

Anders Jarlert (University of Lund)
The Oxford Movement and Group Revivalism in Britain and
Scandinavia   215

Samuel Rubenson (University of Lund)
Church between Society and Association: The Case of the Syrian
Orthodox Church in Sweden   231

Part IV Religion and National Identity

Dag Thorkildsen (University of Oslo)
Church and Nation in the 19th Century   249

Petur Petursson (University of Reykjavik)
Clergy and Nation-Building in Iceland 1830-1850   267

Callum G. Brown (University of Strathclyde)
Religion and National Identity in Scotland since the Union of 1707   283

Mika Nokelainen (University of Helsinki)
The Orthodox and the Lutherans in Finland 1809-1923   301

Aila Lauha (University of Helsinki)
Foreign Relations for Nationalistic Goals: The Activity of Finnish
Theologians Abroad during the Years of Russification between
1908-1914   315

John Wolffe (Open University, Milton Keynes)
To Die is Gain? Religion, the Monarchy and National Identity in
Britain 1817-1910   333

Introduction

Hugh McLeod

The papers in this volume were presented at the first joint meeting of British and Scandinavian church historians, held at the University of York from April 6-9, 1995. The conference was organised by the British and Norwegian Commissions of the international organisation of church historians, CIHEC (Commission Internationale d'Histoire Ecclesiastique Comparee). Beautiful spring weather added to the pleasure of an event attended by historians coming from all of the Nordic countries and all parts of the United Kingdom. Apart from the papers collected here, three were delivered at the conference but not subsequently submitted for publication: by Alicia Correa on "The Anglo-Scandinavian Conversion: Liturgical Evidence and Impact", by Brenda Bolton on "England and Scandinavia in the 12th Century", and by Stuart Mews on "Archbishop Nathan Soderblom, British Church Leaders and European Unity".

The theme of "Church and People in Britain and Scandinavia" was chosen because it seemed likely that there would be many interconnections and parallels. The interconnections were most obvious in the early medieval period. The volume appropriately begins with Lesley Abrams' overview of the conversion of the Anglo-Saxon and Scandinavian kingdoms - the only paper to adopt a comparative framework. The papers on Christianisation point repeatedly to the crucial importance of the traffic across the North Sea in the period from the eighth century to the eleventh. The role of English missionaries in the conversion of Scandinavia is repeatedly emphasised. Torstein Jorgensen also notes the significance of Hakon the Good of Norway, who had been educated at the court of Wessex, and stresses the relevance for the Christianisation of Norway of the fact that Scandinavian settlers in England were moving towards Christianity in the second and third generations. Dawn Hadley, in a well-documented piece of revisionism, argues that the Viking influence on the English church was much less negative than has been generally alleged. Per Beskow indicates the importance of Anglo-Saxon influences on the religious vocabulary, prayers, and distinctive forms of belief of the early generations of Scandinavian Christians.

The triumph of Lutheranism in the Nordic countries ensured that their strongest international links would in future be with oneanother and with Germany, as is illustrated, for instance, by Aila Lauha's account of the attempts of Finnish nationalist churchmen to win support abroad. However, direct links with Britain have remained, both because of the affinities between some Anglicans and some Lutherans, and also because of the importation from the British Isles in the nineteenth and twentieth centuries of a variety of forms of sectarian or undenominational Protestantism. A notable example of the latter is explored by Anders Jarlert in his analysis of the impact of the Oxford Group in Scandinavia in the 1930s and '40s. Stuart Mews, in detailing Nathan Soderblom's close links with many Anglican bishops, gave an example of the former. Another point of direct contact, the Porvoo Declaration, happened shortly before the conference, and played a part in at least one of the discussions, though it is significant that it seemed to arouse stronger feelings among the Scandinavian than the Birtish participants.

But very often in the modern period, the church histories of Britain and the Nordic countries have parallelled oneanother without touching directly. One of the most striking features of the post-Reformation era in Scandinavia was the precocious achievement of mass literacy. This achievement was parallelled, though in lesser degree, in Scotland. England and Sweden have both at times believed themselves to be chosen nations, whose victories over Catholic enemies were willed by God. In the nineteenth century Protestantism also played a part in the development of a distinct national consciousness among the various smaller peoples on the "periphery", such as the Welsh, and as is shown by Petur Petursson, Dag Thorkildsen and Mika Nokelainen, the Icelanders, Norwegians and Finns. In the same century religious revivals, often associated with temperance and often leading to the foundation of free churches, flourished in most parts of the British Isles, and also in several of the Nordic countries - though in the latter they were a mainly rural phenomenon, whereas in the British Isles they also affected industrial areas and cities, as is shown by Myrtle Hill in her account of the 1859 revival in Ulster. One of the most interesting parallels, unfortunately not discussed at the conference, lies in the fact that in the period from about the 1880s to the 1950s, both Britain and the Nordic countries saw a rapid drop in religious participation, and in the eyes of many were pace-makers in secularisation - until in the 1960s and '70s they were overtaken by some of their European neighbours. Perhaps because of the decline in public concern with religious issues, England, Scotland and the Nordic countries remain among the last European countries to retain the link between church and state. Recently, both regions have seen considerable immigration from non-Christian countries, or from those where the forms of Christianity practised are widely different from those prevailing in northern Europe. Samuel Rubenson's account of the Syrian Orthodox Church in Sweden provides a graphic account of the sometimes rather drastic religious changes consequent on transplantation to a very different social and political environment.

The conference attracted an impressive number of papers of high quality. It also revealed that research in church history in Britain and the Nordic countries is often focusing on different issues and using different methods. This partly reflects different institutional environments. The Nordic participants were generally working in Departments of Theology or Religious Studies, often with a strongly Lutheran ethos. The British participants were predominantly members of Departments of History, and those attached to Departments of Theology or Religious Studies were generally working in a pluralistic situation where no religious denomination had a dominant influence. But the differences and similarities between the British and Nordic approaches also varied as between the areas of research represented here. The common ground was apparently greatest among those working on the early medieval period, where the same themes recur in the contributions from different countries. For instance, speakers from all sides stressed the relatively slow pace of Christianisation and the complexities of a process, which may have proceeded in some areas of religious life than others. All agreed that too much stress has been placed on particular turning-points - for instance, 999/1000 in Iceland, the focal point of Hjalti Hugason's argument. They all stressed both the ways in which the ground was prepared before, and the step by step process by which change continued afterwards.

All of this would probably make sense to Jeremy Gregory, who approaches the processes of Protestantisation in a similar spirit. On the whole, however, the Reformation period sees the greatest contrasts between British and Scandinavian approaches. The contrasts are most evident in a comparison between the papers by Robert Swanson and Jeremy Gregory and those by Simo Heininen, Martin Schwarz-Lausten and Marianne Jensen-Broby Perez. The British lay more stress on popular religion, on local evidence, and on long-term change. The Scandinavians give more attention to poltical and/or theological factors, and provide a more intensive analysis of a shorter period. Ingun Montgomery, in her study of the implementation of the Reformation in Norway, comes nearest to combining elements of both approaches, though in focusing more on the intentions and methods of the refomrers than on the factors determining the popular response, she is closer to the other Scandinavian contributors than to Jeremy Gregory. The papers in this section provoked some of the liveliest discussion in the conference. One debate focused on Robert Swanson's paper and the question of whether it would be possible to conduct research of a similar kind in Scandinavia. Some participants argued strongly that it could and should be done, while others contended that the sources did not exist in sufficient abundance. The second focused on Marianne Jensen-Broby de Perez's paper, the theological assumptions underpinning it, and its implications for the current negotiations between the Church of England and the Lutheran churches.

The papers on free churches and revival movements also revealed fascinating differences of approach. Rod Ambler, in his study of the Lincolnshire Baptists, and Myrtle Hill, in her analysis of the 1859 revival in Ulster, get closer, perhaps, than any other contributors to the volume to the religious experience of the "ordinary person". On the other hand, Anders Jarlert, in his account of the international religious networks of the years around World War II, and Samuel Rubenson, in his examination of the legal constraints affecting the development of the Syrian Orthodox Church in Sweden, open up topics that British scholarship has scarcely begun to explore.The papers on national identity indicate again the parallels between British and Scandinavian developments, even in an area where there were few direct influences. All the papers stress the complexity of the relationship between religion and national identity and the ways in which this relationship varied over time. The tendency also is to suggest that religion has been less important than other factors in constructing this identity. For instance, Dag Thorkildsen's carefully argued account of the history of nineteenth-century Norway stresses the fact that the conservatism of the church leadership limited their political influence. Callum Brown's powerful polemic highlights the continuing importance of sectarianism in modern Scotland and the extent to which religious divisions have been a major barrier to the development of an effective nationalist movement. Finland in the early twentieth century differed from Scotland or Norway in that nationalism was mainly directed against rulers who were conspicuously different in religion - in this case,

Orthodox Russia. For a relatively brief period in the later nineteenth and early twentieth centuries, Lutheranism and the Lutheran Church played a significant part in Finnish nationalism. Yet, as Aila Lauha shows, the church's attitude to the national movement was mainly rather cautious. And as Mika Nokelainen suggests, the Orthodox minority soon won acceptance in independent Finland, and attempts to define Finnishness in exclusively Lutheran terms were repudiated. John Wolffe, in one of the most strikingly original contributions to the volume, offers a rather different perspective on these issues. In focusing on the public mourning for members of the British Royal Family who died in the nineteenth and early twentieth centuries, he is able to bring together many themes that are handled in detail or in passing in other parts of the book - for instance, the relationship between religion and patriotism and between the various branches of Christianity, and also the tendencies towards secularisation in the nineteenth century. On the one hand, he argues, "the churches remained an essential medium for expressing the nation's shared sense of identity and loss". On the other hand the increasingly bland and uncontentious observations made by churchmen on these occasions tended to become "the religious icing on the cake of national secular consciousness". This suitably ambivalent conclusion offers a fitting end to the volume.

Part I
Christianisation

Kings and Bishops and the Conversion of the Anglo-Saxon and Scandinavian Kingdoms[1]

Lesley Abrams

The conversion of Scandinavia seems to have occurred at a strikingly unhurried pace: almost three hundred years separate the first known mission, that of St Anskar in the first half of the ninth century, from the effective end of the pagan cult at Uppsala.[2] This long, drawn-out period of transition from paganism to full-fledged Christianity can be judged in different ways. Some have attributed a die-hard heathenism to the Scandinavians, a religious conservatism resistant to the influence of Christianity. Others have identified the operation of an admirable Nordic "detachment", "coolly balanced between the two religions, examining the merits of both, and in some cases trying to get the protective benefits of both".[3] Still others have pointed out the difference between accepting the faith and developing centralized institutions to support it. This phenomenon of apparently leisurely Christianization seems to me to be worth considering, both as a chapter in the history of ecclesiastical institutions and as an aspect of a wider subject, the way in which Viking-Age Scandinavia absorbed the religion of western Europe and the Mediterranean. I hope to show here that even a brief comparison of the evangelization and Christianization of the English and Scandinavian kingdoms can bring out some noteworthy contrasts between the two societies.

There is a difference, of course, between conversion and Christianization. The former may be achieved in a moment and by an act, such as a baptismal ceremony or the formal prohibition of pagan rituals. Christianization on the other hand is not an act but a process, less quantifiable and inevitably more drawn out, even where the new religion has been received with enthusiasm. The progress of Christianization is

---

[1] This paper was originally prepared for oral delivery. In order to observe the imposed word-limit, references to secondary literature have been kept to a minimum, thereby neglecting – regrettably – the wealth of material on this subject.
[2] King Sverker *ca* 1138 represented the demise of the pagan cult by building a great new church at Uppsala, allegedly using material from the temple in its construction.
[3] Christine Fell, in *The Viking World*, ed. James Graham-Campbell (London, 1991), p. 186.

awkward to judge. Even with good source material, there is room for debate about how to measure the assimilation of Christianity by a converted society. There is almost always residual paganism, where private pagan practices continue after the public exercise of a pagan cult has ceased, but this does not generally jeopardize or reverse the act of conversion. Most converted peoples experience a syncretistic phase, a period of cultural and spiritual elision between the old and the new. As is well known, even missionaries and churchmen as rigorous as Pope Gregory the Great not only recognized that syncretism was inevitable but advocated it as a means of making the transition less painful.[4] The development of ecclesiastical institutions fosters and may even be seen to complete this transition, and the early history of the Church in Scandinavia particularly invites us to assess the role of an institutional Church in changing beliefs and practice. Before doing so, however, I should like first to consider more generally the pace of Christianization in early Anglo-Saxon England and in Viking-Age Scandinavia.

In Anglo-Saxon England missionary activity is well recorded, thanks in part to the achievement of Bede in his great work of ecclesiastical history, completed in 731.[5] Although his account downplayed the very considerable Irish contribution to the story, Bede provided a narrative of conversion campaigns in individual kingdoms, from the start of the Roman initiative in Kent in 597 under Augustine, through the mission to Northumbria from Iona beginning in 634, and ending with the violent conversion of the Isle of Wight in the 680s. Bede preserved Augustine's requests for instructions on practical matters as well as Pope Gregory's letters to several of his missionaries and to a number of royal converts. Corroboratory and supplementary evidence comes from various other sources. For example, the change in burial practice displayed by a series of so-called transition cemeteries, which lack grave goods and lie near earlier pagan burial grounds, has been taken to indicate a convert population.[6] These cemeteries begin in Kent in the first half of the seventh century and in other kingdoms from *ca* 650, reflecting the spread of both Roman and Irish missionary activity outside the Kentish orbit from the

---

[4] *Bede's Ecclesiastical History of the English People*, ed. and trans. B. Colgrave and R.A.B. Mynors (1969; rev. ed. 1991) (hereafter HE), I.32.
[5] See note 4.
[6] Apart from some earlier examples in Kent, these date, according to the archaeologists, from *ca* 650-750. See M. Hyslop, "Two Anglo-Saxon Cemeteries...", *Archaeological Journal* 120 (1963), 161-200, and A.L. Meaney and S.C. Hawkes, *Two Anglo-Saxon Cemeteries at Winnall* (1970).

630s. Written evidence apparently confirms this physical suggestion of missionary success. King Æthelberht's laws from the early 600s announced the immediate extension of royal protection to the Church and, by the end of the century, King Wihtred's legislation expressed at least the ideal (if not the reality) of very extensive ecclesiastical control over the life of the laity.[7] Penitentials, also based on late seventh-century texts, likewise reveal a concern for the proper ordering of society according to the principles of Christianity, from serious matters of social and sexual conduct (murder, theft, drunkenness, adultery, and abortion) to the trials of everyday life – if a mouse falls into a container of liquid, for example.[8] Although the laws and the penitentials by their prohibitions reveal the existence of continuing pagan practice, they nonetheless demonstrate that Anglo-Saxons of the seventh century were being asked to live their lives according to a series of new rules defined – and often administered by – the Church. They also were asked to pay dues to support it.[9]

In addition to this textual record of the Church's efforts to penetrate and regulate lay society, there is impressive evidence for the proliferation of a professional religious class and the growth of ecclesiastical institutions in Anglo-Saxon England. Augustine was empowered by Pope Gregory to consecrate bishops as required, and although the first came from his team of imported talent, the succession of native Englishmen to episcopal office soon followed: in 655 a West Saxon, who took the name Deusdedit, was consecrated archbishop of Canterbury.[10] In 597 Augustine had founded a monastic house on land given to him by King Æthelberht, and this example was followed repeatedly over the succeeding years, as surviving charters attest. Initially as centres of missionary enterprise and then as monuments of personal piety established by kings and their aristocracies, monasteries multiplied, so much so that by 734 Bede was expressing concern over their numbers as well as their quality.[11] Monastic

---

[7] *Die Gesetze der Angelsachsen*, ed. F. Liebermann, 3 vols (Halle, 1903-16); *The Laws of the Earliest English Kings*. ed. and trans. F.L. Attenborough (Cambridge, 1922). Æthelberht's code specifies royal protection of the Church in its first clause but otherwise reflects a society as yet untouched by Christianity. Eorcenberht of Kent (640-664) was the first to forbid the worship of idols, and he also enforced a forty-day Lenten fast (HE III.8; no text survives). Only one clause of Hlothere's and Eadric's code (670s-680s) refers to Christianity, but by the time of Wihtred (690-725) every clause reflects the Christian impact. The laws of Ine, king of Wessex (688-726) continued the process.
[8] *Medieval Handbooks of Penance*, trans. J.T. McNeill and H.M. Gamer, pp. 179-215 (esp. 191).
[9] *Ibid.*, p. 213; *The Laws*, ed. Attenborough, p. 36.
[10] HE III.20.
[11] *English Historical Documents c. 500-1042*, ed. D. Whitelock, 2nd ed. (London,

and episcopal communities founded schools (attested from the early seventh century),[12] and by the 670s the products of their learning began to appear in manuscripts and in the work of such ostentatiously learned men as Aldhelm, abbot of Malmesbury (from *ca* 674) and bishop of Sherborne (*ca* 705-9). Religious houses quickly became wealthy and powerful, some of them developing into the dominant economic institutions of their regions and wielding powerful political influence at court. Right from the start they built religious, domestic, and industrial buildings, developed their estates, practised large-scale husbandry and exploited other natural resources, produced manuscripts and metalwork, and probably engaged in trade. At least from the time of Theodore, archbishop of Canterbury from 669, abbots and bishops from these communities across the Anglo-Saxon kingdoms gathered together at synods which formulated and encouraged the implementation of church policy.

It has been said that "by the time of Theodore's death in 690 missionary efforts in England were no longer necessary".[13] Although this statement doubtless overestimates the effect of the new religion on the mass of the population, it seems that during Theodore's period in office at least the organization of the early Anglo-Saxon Church was completed, and stringent measures for the discipline of the converted peoples were devised, if not always implemented. There had been a number of setbacks with the second generation of converts in the first half of the seventh century, but these had been routinely overcome. It is therefore possible to suggest on the basis of the evidence that the apparently thoroughgoing Christianization of at least a significant proportion of Anglo-Saxon society was achieved in a relatively short period of time after the first arrival of missionaries. Some have gone so far as to say that Christianization was so successful that, although pagan practices may have endured (especially in the countryside), the Anglo-Saxon upper classes had by the eighth century left paganism so far behind that they could be described as suffering from collective religious amnesia.[14] It may be that the surviving evidence of Bede and the laws, charters, and penitentials – concerned as they are with

---

1979), no. 170 (pp. 799-810).
[12] When King Sigeberht founded a school in East Anglia *ca* 630, he did so with the help of Bishop Felix and masters and teachers *iuxta morem Cantuariorum* (HE III.18). For the later seventh-century school at Canterbury, see M. Lapidge, "The School of Theodore and Hadrian", *Anglo-Saxon England* 15 (1986), 45-72.
[13] R. Sullivan, "The Papacy and Missionary Activity in the Early Middle Ages", *Mediaeval Studies* 17 (1955), 46-106, at 63.
[14] P. Wormald, "Bede, Beowulf and the Conversion of the Anglo-Saxon Aristocracy", *Bede and Anglo-Saxon England*, ed. R.T. Farrell (Oxford, 1978), pp. 32-95, at 60.

legislative, tenurial, and social control and administration – exaggerate the change. They do illustrate, however, in the words of C.H. Talbot, the role (in southern England especially) of "diplomats, lawyers, and architects, who wove Christianity into the framework of the State" and in so doing guaranteed its success and speedy assimilation.[15]

Before introducing the Scandinavian comparison, I should like to consider one aspect of how this apparently rapid Christianization was achieved. Before he sent Augustine to England, Gregory the Great's missionary initiatives in Italy show that he expected Christian landowners there to take responsibility for their unbaptized tenants and forcibly compel them to convert.[16] Clare Stancliffe has argued that Gregory took for granted a Roman tradition of the responsibility of leadership and that his decision to send Augustine to Æthelberht, and his assumption that a king had the power to control his subjects even in these matters, derived naturally from that Roman tradition.[17] Directing a religious campaign at rulers was not an exclusively Roman habit, however, and Irish missionaries chose the same approach (on the Continent as well as in England). With some exceptions, it worked extremely well, and, in Clare Stancliffe's phrase, "Anglo-Saxon paganism... collapsed at the top as soon as Christianity arrived".[18] Bede may be misleading us when he represents the decision to convert as voluntary and not a result of coercion. Æthelberht, for example, who had initially been told by the pope to suppress pagan cults, later received milder instructions; he is said explicitly to have forced no one to be baptized, though he favoured those of his court who joined him in conversion.[19] Bede's subsequent reference to those of Æthelberht's subjects who had accepted Christianity "either out of fear of the king or to win his favour" may offer insight into the kind of pressure brought to bear on those making this "voluntary" decision.[20] Yet there is also Anglo-Saxon evidence that the king's decision was not always an autocratic one: Edwin of Northumbria consulted his counsellors before agreeing to accept baptism.[21] Boniface, the eighth-century Anglo-Saxon missionary to Germany, was explicit about the practical importance to a

---

[15] C.H. Talbot, *The Anglo-Saxon Missionaries in Germany* (London, 1954), pp. ix-x.
[16] Robert A. Markus, *Gregory the Great and Missionary Strategy* (London, 1970).
[17] C.E. Stancliffe, "Kings and Conversion: Some Comparisons between the Roman Mission to England and Patrick's to Ireland", *Frühmittelalterliche Studien* 14 (1980), 59-94.
[18] *Ibid.*, p. 69.
[19] HE I.26.
[20] HE II.5.
[21] HE II.13.

mission of a king's authority: "Without the protection of the king of the Franks I can neither rule the people of the Church nor defend the priests, clerics, monks or female servants of God; nor can I forbid the practice of heathen rites and the worship of idols... without his orders and the fear he inspires".[22]

Kings had religious influence not just over their people but over other rulers. It is well known that the Anglo-Saxon kingdoms succumbed to the new faith by a combination of clerical endeavour and political pressure: some nine seventh-century rulers were converted and baptized thanks to the efforts of fellow kings, whose spiritual motives cannot be disentangled from considerations of secular power. The marriage of Christian queens to pagan husbands likewise had the potential of extending both religious and political influence.[23] Further, the bond created by overkingship clearly allowed, if it did not require, dominant kings to persuade lesser ones to join the new club. Conversion was one way of consolidating dominance. Michael Richter has argued that Bede in all likelihood exaggerated the role of the professional missionary in the conversion of the English peoples, and that royal dynasties were "an agent of Christianization of paramount importance".[24]

After the initial conversion, the responsibility of kings for law and the administration of justice allowed them to encourage the extension of Christian influence. In addition, royal control of the kingdoms' landed resources enabled the Church to develop an economic identity. After the conversion kings increasingly transferred tenure of lands and their dues and other income to the Church, thereby providing a perpetual means of support for ecclesiastical communities. Anglo-Saxon kings of the conversion period, therefore, not only received and encouraged the first missionaries but thereafter provided the Church with the economic means to flourish and lent royal authority to the attempt to impose a new social order.

Turning to consider the conversion and Christianization of Scandinavia we are faced with a far more daunting task. This derives primar-

---

[22] *Die Briefe des heiligen Bonifatius und Lullus,* ed. M. Tangl, MGH Epistolae selectae 1 (Berlin, 1916), no. 63; Talbot, *The Anglo-Saxon Missionaries,* p. 117.
[23] Stephanie Hollis has argued that Bede was "hostile to female influence, especially in ecclesiastical matters", and therefore downplayed the role of queens as active proselytizers: *Anglo-Saxon Women and the Church. Sharing a Common Fate* (Woodbridge, 1992), esp. pp. 226-34.
[24] M. Richter, "Practical Aspects of the Conversion of the Anglo-Saxons", *Irland und die Christenheit,* ed. P. Ní Chatháin and M. Richter (Stuttgart, 1987), pp. 362-76, at 366-7.

ily from a serious dearth of source material. There is no Bede and no Ecclesiastical History of the Scandinavian Peoples; and there is little help from the other types of written source which illuminate the Christianization of Anglo-Saxon England. Extant laws are late (beginning to be recorded in the twelfth and thirteenth centuries, although incorporating some earlier material), as are most charters. There is virtually no contemporary correspondence and, with one exception, no early hagiography. The one contemporary missionary *vita*, that of Anskar, is consequently crucial in its representation of pagan society in Denmark and Sweden in the first half of the ninth century;[25] it is, however, the record of an ultimately unsuccessful mission. Those which did succeed are much less visible: in particular, English missionaries who evangelized in Norway perhaps from the mid-tenth century and in Denmark and Sweden throughout the eleventh are shadowy, almost invisible, figures. Some of them can be glimpsed in the other great work on which we rely, Adam of Bremen's *Gesta Hammaburgensis ecclesiae pontificum*, written in the 1070s for the archbishop of Hamburg-Bremen who, since the time of Anskar, had by papal order a mandate for the conversion of the North.[26] Adam, however, had no interest in recording the work of churchmen not subject to Hamburg-Bremen, and his history of the German archbishopric's missionary ventures, invaluable though it is, tells only a partial story. Adam's omissions are very difficult to fill in. There are no house-histories or chronicles of Scandinavian ecclesiastical foundations of this period. Some scraps of information (which I have assembled elsewhere) can be salvaged from contemporary English sources.[27] The few, precious, contemporary native sources include skaldic poetry, runic inscriptions (which Dr Beskow has discussed), and liturgical imports (the subject of Dr Corrêa's research).[28] Otherwise, indigenous evidence is late, retrospective, tendentious, and, in the case of the Kings' Sagas, which feature the first Christian kings of Norway, a rich (and inseparable) mixture of fact and fiction. A further disadvantage is that all of this material is spread unevenly across the Scandinavian lands. This reinforces the im-

---

[25] *Vita Anskarii auctore Rimberto*, ed. G. Waitz, MGH, Scriptores rerum Germanicarum in usum scholarum (hereafter SRG) (Hannover, 1884).
[26] *Gesta Hammaburgensis ecclesiae pontificum*, ed. B. Schmeidler, MGH, SRG (Hannover, 1917).
[27] L. Abrams, "The Anglo-Saxons and the Christianization of Scandinavia", *Anglo-Saxon England* 24 (1995), 213-49.
[28] See Beskow's contribution to this volume..

pression that development was significantly different in Norway, Sweden, and Denmark, but does not allow those differences to be drawn in detail.

We should, I think, first consider the connection between this comparative poverty of written evidence and our impression that the progress of Christianity in Scandinavia was slow. Might it be that the sources which could have detailed conversion campaigns and social regulation – as in Anglo-Saxon England – have simply not survived, thereby obscuring what went on and consequently misrepresenting the pace of Christianization? How substantial a picture of Anglo-Saxon conversion could we draw without Bede? Despite the danger of arguing from negative evidence, I would suggest that although the paucity of source material doubtless derives in part from losses, the lack particularly of native testimony is nevertheless real and significant. I am not arguing that it indicates an absence of Christian belief or even of missionary action; but it seems to me to testify to the absence of certain kinds of ecclesiastical activity, which suggests something about the development of ecclesiastical institutions, and perhaps something else: an enduring oral culture, strong enough to assimilate Christianity but resist the full force of its gift of literacy for some time.

I shall not rehearse here the details of the conversion of the Scandinavian countries, as far as they are known. It seems, however, that missionaries from both Germany and England followed the pattern of their predecessors in Anglo-Saxon England and aimed their efforts initially at kings. Anskar's first posting was to the court of Harald Klak in a diplomatic arrangement with Louis the Pious. On his subsequent missions to Denmark and Sweden, Anskar addressed himself in all cases to the local kings and is explicitly said to have asked for and received their permission to evangelize.[29] However, Rimbert, Anskar's biographer, set down a conversation between the missionary and the Swedish king Olof on the occasion of the second mission to Birka which suggests that the relationship between king and people was not quite what it had been in seventh-century England. Olof received Anskar (and his gifts) with pleasure but claimed to be unable to grant Anskar's request to evangelize before first consulting the gods and then ascertaining the will of the people on the matter: "it is our custom", he said, "that the control of public business of every kind should rest with the people and not with the king".[30]

---

[29] *Vita Anskarii*, ed. Waitz, chs 11, 14, 17, 19, 24, 25, 26, 28, 31, and 32.
[30] *Ibid.*, ch. 26.

Although the gods and the people alike decided in favour of Anskar at the assembly, the king explained that he "could not give his full consent until, in another assembly which was to be held in another part of his kingdom, he could announce this resolution to the people who lived in that district". "This assembly subsequently declared that they too would give their entire and complete assent". The king allowed those who so wished to become Christian (and a *prefectus* of the king was among those who did), but he did not tell them to or even encourage them. In fact, not one of the kings among whom Anskar and his missionaries evangelized was converted. Their tolerance of missionary activity was, it seems, largely a gesture of goodwill towards the empire; their disinclination to accept the new religion was perhaps on the other hand a sign of their distrust of imperial ambition.[31] Christianity probably continued to filter in through merchants and returning converts, but as far as we can see paganism suffered no collapse.

Kings did not remain aloof when missionary activity revived after a lengthy pause. Some time after 960 Harald Bluetooth proclaimed his role in the conversion of the Danish people on an elaborate rune-stone at Jelling. In Norway, English missionaries, probably sent by Æthelred, king of England, joined the entourages of Olaf Tryggvason and Olaf Haraldsson. These "apostle-kings" actively directed the process of conversion, and their religious campaigns doubled as campaigns of conquest and unification. This, at least, is the message of the later medieval sagas. From the late tenth century, therefore, according to Adam of Bremen, missionary bishops were associated with Christian kings in Norway, Denmark, and Sweden. How did they compare with Augustine and his companions?

That question is, of course, almost impossible to answer, given the bleak state of the evidence. But two types of activity are discernible: preaching in the field (often across very wide areas), and ministering to the king and his court. What the bishops may *not* have done may in fact be easier to specify, as several elements which were intrinsic to the conversion process in Anglo-Saxon England seem to be missing here. Most noticeable is the absence of episcopal and monastic communities. Although bishops were associated with certain towns in Denmark – possibly all of

---

[31] H. Mayr-Harting, "Two Conversions to Christianity: the Bulgarians and the Anglo-Saxons", *Stenton's "Anglo-Saxon England" Fifty Years On*, ed. D. Matthew *et al.* (Reading, 1994), pp. 1-30 (esp. 5-9), has emphasized the point that some kings avoided taking Christianity from a powerful neighbour.

them royal centres – as early as 948, none of the many bishops named in connection with Scandinavian kings throughout the tenth century and most of the eleventh is known to have had a fixed episcopal seat and a community to serve it. Adam of Bremen is explicit about the situation: even in the 1070s, he says, "[outside Denmark] none of the bishops [was] as yet assigned to a fixed see"; "on account of the newness of the Christian plantation among the Norwegians and the Swedes, none of the bishoprics has been assigned definite limits, but each one of the bishops, accepted by the king or the people, co-operates in building up the Church and, going about the country, draws as many as he can to Christianity and governs them without objection as long as they live".[32] Exactly how such a bishop could have "governed" the people is not specified. Nor did this collection of bishops have its own organization: they were royal officers, tied to their patrons, and there was no Canterbury to pull this weak and dependent episcopate together into a Church. Hamburg-Bremen would have liked to play that role in the eleventh century, but as so many of the bishops then active in Scandinavia did not acknowledge the authority of the German see, its efforts at control were doomed. In earlier phases of missionary activity throughout Europe, the papacy had offered itself as the authority on correct religious observance where rival missionaries came into conflict, and it had been instrumental in instilling the crucial principle that an independent episcopate was of the utmost importance in the conversion process.[33] After 900, however, papal intervention in missionary activity had drastically declined. When in the later eleventh century the papacy revived and renewed its interest in the North, it established direct links with Scandinavian kings and their clergy and bypassed Hamburg-Bremen. This led, at last, to the creation in 1104 of a Scandinavian archdiocese, but even then the archbishop of Lund at first lacked effective overall control. Papal legations in the 1150s led to the for-mation of Norwegian and Swedish national Churches with their own archbishops. Full-scale institutionalization had finally arrived.

The absence of an ecclesiastical co-ordinating agency (before the late re-entry of the papacy) seems, therefore, to have been a key element in the tardy institutional development of the Scandinavian episcopacy. In addition, there was in Scandinavia no lapsed Roman infrastructure or

---

[32] *Gesta*, ed. Schmeidler, II.26 and IV.34.
[33] For example, when King Boris of the Bulgarians complained of differences introduced by Eastern and Western missionaries, the pope offered himself as the final authority: R. Sullivan, "The Papacy", p. 93; see also p. 105.

earlier ecclesiastical pattern to reorganize or resume, as there had been in England. This, combined with the size of the Scandinavian lands – immense compared with the Anglo-Saxon kingdoms – would surely also have impeded communication and retarded centralization. The small number of towns likewise may have been a factor: Richard Morris has argued that the growth of urbanism may have done more than the efforts of churchmen to weaken paganism in England.[34] Dioceses did indeed develop first in Denmark, the most urbanized Scandinavian kingdom. Monasteries, so tied up with the missionary enterprise in Anglo-Saxon England, are conspicuously absent, as we have seen. Two points can perhaps be made about the dearth of Scandinavian monastic houses before the twelfth century. David Knowles gave credit for the initial English missionary interest in Scandinavia in the tenth century to the advocates of ecclesiastical reform. It may be more likely that those churchmen in England who were not supporters of reform were in fact forced to turn their attention elsewhere, and that it was these men who went to Scandinavia.[35] There may have been few monks among them, especially in view of the stricter application, from the tenth century, of the principle of *stabilitas*. It is striking that during Cnut's reign as king of England from 1016, the monastic party, which had been dominant at the Anglo-Saxon royal court for so long, was in decline; the most powerful men in the Anglo-Saxon Church of Cnut's generation were secular clerics.

The apparent absence of early monastic houses in Scandinavia may therefore be a sign of something no more significant than trends in ecclesiastical fashion. The absence of cathedral chapters and endowments is another matter. Anglo-Saxon episcopal *familiae* were supported by the estates granted to bishops by kings. On this wealth rested their independence. It is unlikely that Scandinavian bishops did not desire land, so it may be reasonable to infer that it was somehow unavailable – that kings were not in a position to grant it. The weakness of the Scandinavian episcopate may have been due, therefore, not to the overweening dominance of kings, but on the contrary to the limitations on royal power. Unfortunately the nature of landholding in Scandinavia in this period is quite obscure, but the striking dearth of ecclesiastical communities – both monastic and episcopal – before the twelfth century makes sense if we deduce that kings did not hold or could not alienate the kind of landed re-

---

[34] *Churches in the Landscape*, p. 62.
[35] Abrams "The Anglo-Saxons", p. 245.

sources granted to the Church in Anglo-Saxon England. The earliest known surviving record of a Scandinavian grant is that of Estrith, Cnut the Great's sister, to Roskilde after 1047.[36] The earliest charter-text extant (also Danish) is from 1085.[37] Grants may of course have gone unrecorded, but the situation does suggest that royal donations of land were not a significant feature of the missionary phase. Nevertheless, kings typically were concerned to expand their royal powers, and there is evidence that they seized the lands of their followers in order to enlarge the royal demesne. This was the accusation (retrospectively) levelled at Harald Fairhair, for example; more reliably, in the 1030s Magnus the Good was criticized by the skald Sighvat Thórðarson for appropriating land from local chieftains.[38] There is other evidence both for the weakness of Scandinavian kingship (despite the legendary fierceness of individual kings) and for popular resistance to attempts to strengthen it. Niels Lund recently has argued that Viking-Age military organization reflects not a strong central authority but a society which depended on personal ties between the king and his leading men.[39] Public military obligations, according to Lund, were not introduced into Denmark until King Cnut the Holy attempted to do so in the 1080s. Cnut aimed also to impose a set of laws (*edictum regale*, according to his biographer), possibly like the early Kentish codes, to regulate the life of the laity according to Christian practice.[40] The resultant rebellion cost the king his life. This evidence may be added to that for the ninth century, which, as we have seen, presents kings as acting in concert with their assemblies, not commanding them. Because seventh-century Anglo-Saxon and tenth- and eleventh-century Scandinavian kings shared the same Germanic background, we might expect their conditions of rule to have been fundamentally the same; it is likely, however, that the relatively recent experience of migration and kingdom formation had significantly strengthened Anglo-Saxon kingship. A difficult issue remains unresolved, however, if the evidence for strong royal power in eighth- and tenth-century Denmark – first the Danevirke and other defensive structures and the establishment of towns,

---

[36] *Scriptores minores historiae danicae*, ed. M.C. Gertz, 2 vols (Copenhagen, 1917-22), p. 23.
[37] *Diplomatarium danicum*, 1st ser., 2, ed. L. Weibull and N. Skyum-Nielsen (Copenhagen, 1963), no. 21 (pp. 43-52).
[38] *Den norsk-islandiske skjaldedigtning*, ed. F. Jónsson, 4 vols (Copenhagen and Christiania, 1912-15), B.1, pp. 234-9.
[39] "Danish Military Organisation", *The Battle of Maldon: Fiction and Fact*, ed. J. Cooper (London, 1993), pp. 109-26, at 126.
[40] *Vitae sanctorum Danorum*, ed. M.C. Gertz (Copenhagen, 1908-12), p. 101.

and later the fortifications of Harald Bluetooth – is raised in this connection. Some distinction between strong kingship and a strong king may help to resolve the problem. Did Viking-Age rulers have great military and/or sacral status and prestige but no great executive power? And did they accrue power to themselves only personally, an opportunistic supremacy which dissolved at their death as there was no institutional structure to carry it?

The nature of Scandinavian kingship and the relationship of the Church to secular authority were evidently crucial factors in the progress of Christianization. Until kings developed the relevant secular mechanisms, the institutional Church could not use them to extend its influence among the people. Anglo-Saxon kings apparently could and did harness these mechanisms without delay; in Scandinavia, ecclesiastical demands themselves seem to have helped to create the apparatus of central control. There was clearly a close relationship between secular and ecclesiastical government and they developed together.

C. H. Talbot dismissed the efforts of early Irish missionaries on the Continent with the following criticism: "the practice of consecrating bishops with no fixed responsibilities, no jurisdiction, no ties, and no superiors... was not conducive to the establishment of Christianity on a lasting basis among the pagan population".[41] Could the same judgement be made of the missionaries to Scandinavia who operated under some of the same conditions? How much did they actually achieve? Their accomplishments are difficult to assess, as no reliable source chronicles their activities and measures the results. Under the circumstances, it is not always possible to distinguish between lack of Christians and lack of Christian organization. The presence of so-called "missionary bishops" does not necessarily mean that there was an endless supply of pagans or back-sliders. Rather, it signifies that there were bishops who had no chapters, held no synods, consecrated no other bishops, and had no territorial dioceses to administer. The extent of their flock is another matter, however, as is the force of Christian belief within it. The size of the Christian population is something to discuss with the archaeologists, who are better equipped to assess numbers, through analysis of burials and church-building. The question of belief doubtless will remain obscure. In view of the difficulty, it may be unwise to proceed, but it could be asked how great a role these

---

[41] *The Anglo-Saxon Missionaries in Germany*, p. ix.

apparently weak kings and dependent bishops actually played after the initial act of conversion. Without religious communities, a territorial Church, and jurisdictional powers, could the bishops really penetrate the countryside and achieve much beyond the widespread baptism of the population? If so, how was it done? If not, who did Christianize the population, and when?

From Wessex to Western Norway: Some perspectives on one channel for the Christianisation process

Torstein Jørgensen

The version deduced – an "elephant in Malmø"?

The Norwegian author, Cora Sandel, once said that when reading presentations of historical persons she often came to be thinking of a visit she once paid to The Historical Museum in the Swedish town of Malmø. The zoological department of this museum contained the most parodised exhibition of peculiar creatures that she had ever seen. And the worst of them all was the elephant. This figure appeared as a stiff, clumpy monster totally out of proportion, with the skin of what had once been an elephant stretched around it. Presentations of historical persons very often remind me of that strange, unreal stuffed being, the famous author said.

As a historian dealing with historical persons and processes living and taking place some one thousand years ago it is not difficult to feel sympathy with the technicians of the Malmø museum. As for them also my situation is that the sources I have are very scarce. And their informative value very often is not in correspondence with the questions I find the need to ask. As often as not I find myself left with some pieces of skin that will hardly suffice for the covering of a whole body.

In this presentation I will make an attempt to put together some pieces from different sources, hoping that the figures of my reproduction will bear as much similarity as possible to the historical originals. What I want to do is to draw attention to what seems to have been one rather marked channel for the christianisation of Norway and the establishing of an organised Christian church in the country, and one that lasted approximately 130 years. I am speaking of the connection between the Wessex kingdom, the more or less only remaining free political unit outside Viking control on the British Isles during the 10th century on the one hand, and reigning monarchs of Norway and their supporters from the time of the last years of king Harald Fairhair in the 920's until about 1050 on the other. I will especially focus on the beginning and early phase of this line.

The complexity of the story

The christianisation process in Norway is, like similar processes elsewhere, a *complex story*. It is complex with regard to the time-aspect. It is complex with regard to the aspect of the different levels of society at which the process took place. It is also complex with regard to the question of the sorts of information that can be drawn from the different sources at hand. And finally it is complex in respect of differences between different traditions of scholars and disciplines being occupied with the matter. The particular channel to be dealt with here must therefore be seen as *one* line within this complex and variegated framework of events, efforts, and processes leading up to the change of faith and customs in Norway. But before going into details on this particular channel we shall have to throw a glance at some of the more general elements of this complex framework.

Some interpretative perspectives on the contact between Norway and Britain up to the 10th century – a general outlook

The process of interrelation between the peoples of Scandinavia and the peoples of the British Isles and the north-western coasts of the continent has very old roots. Archaeological excavations both in Eastern England and Norway bear witness of intercultural contact already from Roman times and onwards. Findings of Roman warrior equipment in graves both in the eastern and western parts of Norway are now being interpreted as a sign that Norwegians have been serving as assistant soldiers – auxiliarii – in the Roman army, most likely on the British Isles. In fifth century graves in Eastern England brooches with a Norse style of ornamentation have been found. A fairly recent analysis of 6th to 9th century graves in the county of Rogaland on the south-western coast of Norway, has shown that of a total number of approximately 35 graves, 15 proved to contain what the archaeologist Per Hernæs has labelled "Christian indicators", i.e. they contained crosses and other signs reflecting influence from Christianity, and 7 so-called "poor graves" which are all "younger" graves from the 10th century. The clothes of the persons buried in this latter category show that they were rich people, and the fact that people of such high social rank were buried so poorly, is taken as an indication of Christian influence.[1]

A number of different sources now bear witness that the Viking ship-traffic criss-crossing the North Sea, Skagerac, and the Baltic Sea waters increased considerably during the 8th, 9th and 10th centuries. Viking vessels were in this period improved and made more fit to stand the powers of the winds and waves of the North Sea.[2] Excavations at Kaupang on the Norwegian south-eastern coast[3], and the famous visit paid by the Norwegian Hålogalandian merchant Ottar at the court of king Alfred the Great in the late 9th century, are in different ways testimonies of trade lines that seem to have been of considerable importance.[4]

One important element of the contact between Norwegians and Britons during this period was, of course, the many brutal Viking attacks on Britain starting with the well-known attack on the Lindisfarne monastery in 792. For a period of more than two hundred years Norwegian and Danish raids seem to have occurred as more or less regular annual events in different parts of the British Isles.

However, it is of vital importance for the understanding of how the process of interrelation between Norwegians and Britons came to develop, and in the next instance for the understanding of the process of religious change, to note that the occasional and transitory Viking attacks very soon turned into conquering and colonization of land, more permanent settlements, and the subjugation of the local population under Viking rule. This colonization process is known to have been well in progress in the early 9th century. Already in the 1950's Haakon Shetelig documented that Viking graves on the British Isles comprise *"the burials of men and women in fairly equal* numbers". And he is very definite in his conclusion that these graves cannot be regarded only as *"reminders of the*

---

[1] P. Hernæs, "Tidlige kristne impulser i Rogalands vikingtid", *Frá Haug ok Heiðni* (1994) No 1, pp. 17-22.

[2] B. Myhre, "The beginning of the Viking Age: Some Current Archaeological Problems", *Viking Revaluation: Viking Society Centenary Symposium 14-15 May 1992*, London 1993 pp. 182-205 + fig. 1-11.

[3] C. Blindheim/R.L. Tollnes, *Kaupang: Vikingenes handelsplass*, Oslo 1972, C. Blindheim, "A Collection of Celtic(?) Bronze Objects found at Kaupang (Skiringssal), Vestfold, Norway", *Proceedings of the seventh Viking Congress Dublin Aug 1973*, Dublin 1976 pp. 9-27.

[4] J. Hines, The Scandinavian Character of Anglian England in the pre-Viking Period, *BAR* 124(1984).

Norsemen's occasional descents upon and battles in the British countries", but were *"evidently left by Norse colonists permanently established on the land"*.[5] The women buried in these graves most likely came over from Norway and Denmark together with the Viking men, but some of them might very well also have been British or Irish women taken into the Norse settlements as part of the early assimilation process.[6]

Another noteworthy characteristic of the Norse settlements on the British Isles is the fact that they fairly soon seem to have started to bury their dead in the churchyards of the native population. In the 9th and 10th century settlements north and west of Scotland and in the countries surrounding the Irish Sea this seems to have been the case already among the second generation settlers. As a consequence the Norwegians from Dublin and other older colonies who invaded Northumbria in the 10th century did not observe traditional Norse burial customs, and the same also applies to the Danish invaders of Central and Northern England in the latter half of the 9th century who mostly seem to have been recruited from the Continent (Normandy and Brittany). The Norse burials in churchyards seem to have represented a transitional stage between pagan and Christian burial customs showing the gradual penetration of Christianity among the Norse settlers as early as during the 9th century.[7] Generally speaking the pagan burial system did not survive the first generation of colonists. On the whole the traditional Norse worship seems never to have been firmly established among the settler communities in Ireland, on Man or on the British mainland.[8] One rather special and distinctive indication of this is the well-known inscription on one of the stone crosses at Kirk Michael, Man, saying that a person with the Nordic name *"Gaut made this cross and all in Man"*. Shetelig was of the opinion that Gaut was operating in the latter part of the 9th century[9], but David Wilson and others have later established that this and other cross-stones with connection to the Viking

---

[5] H. Shetelig, "The Viking Graves", *Viking Antiquities in Great Britain and Ireland*, ed. H. Shetelig, Vol. VI, Oslo 1954 p. 68.

[6] A. Stalsberg has delivered convincing documentation that Viking women acted as merchants on an independent basis. A. Stalsberg, "Women as Actors in North European Viking Age Trade", *Social Approaches to Viking Studies*, ed. R. Samson, Glasgow 1991 pp. 75-83.

[7] H. Shetelig, 1954 pp. 86,96.

[8] F.M. Stenton, *Anglo-Saxon England*, Oxford 1947 pp. 499f, A. Mawer and F.M. Stenton, *Introduction to the Survey of English Place-Names*, p. 56.

[9] P.M.C. Kermode, *Manx Crosses*, London 1907, H. Shetelig, The Norse Style of Ornamentation in the Viking Settlements", *Viking Antiquities in Great Britain and Ireland*, ed. H. Shetelig, Vol VI, Oslo 1954 pp. 125-127.

settlements are early 10th century products.[10] Gaut's activities, and with this I am referring both to the very fact that he acted as a sculptor, and to the way in which he made use of Norse ornamentation on stone-crosses in Britain, is a remarkable example of how the relation between the Norse and the native population could develop, and how the traditions that the two groups were representing could melt together.

Thus, what appears from these very brief observations are the contours of an assimilation process which seems to have been triggered already at the very starting point of more permanent contact between the two population groups, and which very soon developed into an active interrelative process. Of course, the process also involved severe tensions, conflicts, and open fighting. The source materials almost swarm with evidence to testify that. But the testimonies of conflict must not overshadow the fact that the relationship between Vikings and indigenous inhabitants of the British Isles in the 9th and 10th centuries to a great extent also consisted of a process of more peaceful assimilation. One main tendency, however, seems to be clear: Although the Viking settler population certainly came to put their imprint on the way of life, customs and general behaviour in the new communities, *their religious faith and cult seems not to have been exportable to new settings and surroundings outside Scandinavia*, except into the areas in which the Norse settlers constituted the majority population.

A theoretical perspective

At this stage in our presentation it could be useful to draw the attention to a theoretical perspective based on modern sociological approaches to processes of religious change. Some sociologists today speak of religious change processes as something that normally takes place as a result of the emergence of what they call *"new plausibility structures"*.[11] With this term they refer to the emergence on the historical stage of some sort of

---

[10] D.M. Wilson, *Viking Art*,...and O. Klindt-Jensen, 2nd ed. London 1980, *The Viking Achievement*,...and P.G. Foote, London 1970/80, *Three Viking Graves in the Isle of Man*,...and G. Bersu, London 1966 (The Society for Mediaeval Archaeology. Monograph Series 1), "The Art of the Manx Crosses", *The Viking Age in the Isle of Man*, ed. C. Fell et al., Ninth Viking Congres Publications, London 1983. On the development in Scotland see B. Crawford, *Scandinavian Scotland*, Leicester 1987.

[11] P.L. Berger, *The Sacred Canopy : Elements of a Sociological Theory of Religion*, NY 1969, R. Jackson, "Religious Education and the Arts of Interpretation", *in* Starkings, D. (ed.), *Religion and the Arts in Education*, London 1993, pp. 157-166.

new elements, perspectives, and questions with regard to reality, existence, and life itself, to which the old religious explanations and structures no longer correspond. Openness towards religious change will, according to this model, presuppose some sort of incongruity, or, as the sociologists prefer to say, asymmetry, between the established religious patterns of explanation on the one hand and the new life-situations and life-questions on the other. It seems to me that this theoretical perspective renders a very plausible explanatory point of departure for the understanding of the rapid religious change among the Norse settler groups on the British Isles in the 9th and 10th centuries.[12] The traditional Norse religious ideas and cult were strongly connected to family, place of residence, traditional structures of society and ways of life, and when these factors came to be radically changed in the new settler communities on the other side of the North Sea, the old Norse religion proved not to have posessed the potential to relate in a meaningful way to the new structures and ways of thinkung and behaviour that the Vikings encountered there. This by no means implies that the Norse religion in itself and within its own place and setting should have been weak or dying. I agree with the Norwegian religious history professor, Gro Steinsland, who has emphasized the vitality of the Norse religion in the Viking age,[13] but in my opinion this vitality only applied to the traditional societies in Scandinavia, and not to the Viking emigrant communities in Britain and France.

Scenario at the entrance to the 10th century

Our observations so far should now provide the basis for the following scenario at the entrance to the 10th century:

1) *On the British Isles*, in Ireland, and along the coasts of Northern France Viking communities and settlements were established. The people in these communities seem to have found themselves in a fair way in their transition towards and conversion to Christianity, and the assimilation process with the local population seems to have been well in progress. Some of these societies were even strong

---

[12] T. Jørgensen, "Religionsskifteprosesser: Noen teoretiske overveielser," forelesning ved Senter for studiar i vikingtid og nordisk mellomalder, Universitetet i Oslo, 20 feb. 1995, *Norsk Tidskrift for Misjon* 49 (1995) 169-176.
[13] G. Steinsland/P.M. Sørensen, *Menneske og Makter i Vikingenes Verden*, Oslo 1994.

enough, if we can believe what Snorre writes in his Harald Fairhair saga, to represent a threat against the population on the Norwegian west-coast by raiding these areas in the summer season.[14]

2) *The connection* between the Viking home societies in Norway and Denmark and the settler communities abroad seems to have been very tight, and on the increase. The ship-traffic criss-crossing the waters seems to have included all classes of the population; – men and women, thralls, merchants, and kings and chiefs with their crews and soldiers.

3) Very little written information exists about *the society in Norway* before the beginning of the 10th century, and certainly not about foreign influence on this society. The above mentioned archaeological findings in Rogaland do, however, render some evidence that an influx of foreign impulses, brought in either by Norwegians who had been abroad for some time, or by foreigners brought home by them, has made itself felt at least along the coasts already at this early stage.

The Wessex kingdom and its particular strategy

The broad network of connecting lines as we have tried to depict it here continued and increased also during the course of the 10th century. Nevertheless, within this general picture one particular channel for Christian influence on Norway now comes into sight. And the point of departure for this channel is not to be found in any of the Viking ruled settler communities, but in the kingdom of Wessex with its subjugated and associated areas, at this time the only political unit in Britain that had maintained to withstand Viking rule. The fact that one of the Norwegian kings, and one whose reign also was rather long, was fostered and trained at the court of one of the Wessex kings, appears as a unique event in Norwegian history. It is not possible here to go into detail on the different theories put forward on relevant dates in connection with the life and reign of king Håkon the Good.[15] The exact dating is also not necessary for

---

[14] Snorre Sturluson, *Norges kongesagaer*, Vol. 1, Oslo 1979 p. 63.
[15] O. Einarsdóttir, "Studier i Kronologisk Metode i Tidlig Islandsk Historieskrivning", *Bibliotheca Historia Lundensis* XIII, Lund 1964, "Datering av Harald Hårfagres Død", *HT* 47(1968).

the purpose of this study. But the basic facts are important, and these say that Håkon, the youngest son of Harald Fairhair, was brought to the court of king Athelstan for a 10 year period from the age of 10 to 20, and that this period lasted from approximately the year 925 to 935. After that he returned to Norway, became king and ruled for a period of 26-27 years, i.e. from 935 – 961/962. King Håkon's close contact with the Wessex kingdom and his reign in Norway are important as a platform for a particular mission initiative from Wessex to Norway which developed into what seems to have been a planned enterprise that should last for more than 130 years. For the understanding of Håkon's operations in Norway some characteristics of the society and culture in Athelstan's kingdom should be noted.

Some traits of the Wessex kingdom at the time of king Athelstan

1) At the time of king Athelstan the kingdom of Wessex with its royal court represented an important diplomatic centre with connections in many directions, towards the continent and also with king Harald Fairhair, the first king of a united Norway. The diplomatic relations were taken care of through agreements with other rulers and kings, exchange of gifts, by the marrying off of the king's daughters and sisters, and by inviting allied princes to send their sons to be brought up at the king's court. The Norwegian Håkon is known to have been fostered at Athelstan's court within a group of young princes including Ludwig, son of Charles the Simple, Alan, count of Brittany, and two of Athelstan's own younger brothers.[16]

2) Another important trait of Athelstan's reign was his initiatives for a better organisation of the administrative structure of the country, especially with regard to the so-called witenagemot i.e. special councils in which the chiefs of the kingdom participated together with the bishops. It is of interest to note that some of Athelstan's chiefs were carrying Norse names.

3) A third point to note is Athelstan's ambulant court. This by no means was specific for him, but in our context this ambulant court gives

---

[16] T. Jørgensen, *Fra Wessex til Vestlandet : Om kristningen av Norge i tidlig middelalder*, Stavanger 1990 p. 9.

ground to assume that Håkon and the other foster-princes must have been brought about to different parts of the kingdom, and in this way also most likely must have visited the old and famous monastery at Glastonbury.

4) At Athelstan's court some of the clergymen that would come to play central roles in the development of the church later in the century were present. The famous Dunstan, abbot at Glastonbury 939 – 956, and archbishop of Canterbury 956 – 988, came to the court in 926. Also Ethelwold, a central person in the 10th century revival movement, was connected to the court. It is hardly possible to imagine that the young Norwegian prince did not make the acquaintance of these persons.[17]

5) King Athelstan was also a brave and clever warrior fighting many battles. Fridtjov Birkeli, who in a meritorious way has focused on the significance of Athelstan's influence on Håkon for the Christianisation process in Norway[18], has a tendency to draw a picture both of the Wessex king and his foster-son as being too pious and peaceful. Håkon, when he came back to Norway, also entered into battles, not only in order to fend off rivals to the throne, but also to enrich himself by raiding the Gothaland coast.

6) The sixth and last point to be noted is the strong expansive power of the tradition of Anglo-Saxon Christianity. At Athelstan's time the tradition of sending missionaries to other parts of Europe had been going on for many years, counting names like Willibrord, Boniface, Lull, Willihad, Alcuin and others. The emergence of a mission initiative towards Norway, thus, forms a natural continuation of this tradition.

Håkon's missionary bishop

Church-historians have for long been aware of William of Malmesbury's list of 10 Glastonbury monks ending up as bishops, and living at the time of king Edgar's reign (958 – 975).[19] D. Whitelock and F. Birkeli have demonstrated the probablility that only the first five names belong to the original list.[20] Number four on this list is called *Sigefridus norwegensis*

---

[17] P. Ashdown, *Dunstan: a millenial handbook*, Baltonsborough 1987.

[18] F. Birkeli, *Norge møter kristendommen : Fra vikingtiden til ca. 1050*, Oslo 1979.

[19] William of Malmesbury, "De Antiquitate Glastoniensis Ecclesiae", *Gesta Pontificum*, Ed. N.E.S.A. London 1870.

[20] D. Whitelock, *The Beginnings of English Society*, London 1952, F. Birkeli, *Norge møter kristendommen...*Oslo 1979, and *Tolv vintre hadde kristendommen vært i Norge: Historiske perspektiver på kristningsprosessen*, Oslo 1995.

episcopus, of the other four two became bishops in Wells, one in Crediton and one in Winchester. Since all the five bishops came from Glastonbury, they must in all likelihood have been monks in the monastery when Dunstan was abbot there.

There should be every reason to take it that Sigefridus norwegensis episcopus on William of Malmesbury's list is identical with the bishop whom Håkon the Good, after some time as king in Norway, sent for in England. This piece of information is given both by Snorre and by Ágrip, Snorre by stating that Håkon *"sent for a bishop and some other clergymen from England, and when they came to Norway he declared that he would order Christianity in all his kingdom"* and Ágrip by writing that *"he built some churches in Norway and appointed learned men to them"*.[21]

In addition to these mutually independent English and Norwegian sources, also Adam of Bremen testifies the same by mentioning that Norway already before the reign of Olav Tryggvasson had received a bishop and missionaries from England.[22]

By taking Håkon's growth and upbringing into account, his presence in the group of foster-princes at the very time when Dunstan served at the king's court, and his probable acquaintance and perhaps also friendship with him, it must have been very natural for him to send his messenger to his old friend who had now become abbot at Glastonbury, for a monk who could assist him in his enterprise of bringing Christianity to the Norwegians, and of establishing a Christian church in one of the Viking home countries.

Håkon's reign as testified in the saga literature

However, how can this picture of king Håkon the Good as a mission king be balanced against the picture of him that appears in the saga literature?

The saga description of Håkon the Good as king of Norway, and especially of his role in religious matters, is one full of contrasts. All seem to agree on his Christian upbringing in England, on the fact that he was a good ruler, loved by his people, and that he improved the naval defense –

---

[21] Snorre Sturluson, Vol 1, 1979 p. 87, *Ágrip or Noregs kongesoger*, Transl. by G. Indrebø, Norrøne bokverk 32, Oslo 1973 p. 25.
[22] *Adam av Bremen : Beretningen om Hamburg stift, erkebiskopenes bedrifter og øyrikene i Norden*, Transl. by B.T. Danielsen and A.K. Frihagen, Oslo 1993 pp. 89, 102, 106, 213.

the leidang – and the judicial system. But they differ considerably in the way they describe his religious aims and acts. Although the saga literature as a whole is a late source, put down some 200 – 300 years after Håkon's reign, and as such very questionable when it comes to historical credibility, it should be expedient in this context briefly to recount what the different sagas in the main say about him.

It is natural then to start with the only written source that dates back to Håkon's time, viz. the poem (kvad) – *Håkonarmål*.[23] The poem was produced by Håkon's own scald, Øyvind Finnson Skaldaspille, right after the battle of Fitjar, in which Håkon was fatally wounded and died a few days after. The poem only gives an account of the battle, it renders no depiction of Håkon's life. About Håkon's end the scald says that Håkon went to the heathen (heiðin) gods, i.e. the scald declares to the world that the beloved and honoured king ended where all honoured kings according to traditional Norse faith should end, in Valhalla. However, it is of interest to note that the scald also states that Odin was angry with Håkon, but he took it as a mitigating fact that Håkon had protected the pagan temples (hovene). It would have been of great interest for us to know why Odin was angry with Håkon. Could it have something to do with his activity in favour of Christianity? And why does the scald find it necessary to state that Håkon protected the pagan temples, which would simply have been a matter of course if he was an ordinary heathen king? The question is therefore, do we here in Skaldaspille's poem see an indirect indication that Håkon was not an ordinary heathen Norse king? The fact that Skaldaspille also uses the word heiðin, should indicate that the wordpair Christian – heathen was already well known and in use among his Norwegian contemporaries, i.e. in the mid 10th century.

The *Flateyarbook* and the saga of *Theodoricus monachus* only deal very succinctly with Håkon. Flateyarbook simply states in a very categorical man-ner that Håkon was a Christian (kristinn). Theodoricus gives no information at all about Håkon's religious faith and doings.[24]

Historia Norvegiae describes Håkon in crass and critical terms, saying that *"He, who had been fostered in such an appropriate way by the Christian king of England, turned into such a delusion that he chose the perishable kingdom before the eternal one and became an apostate, and*

---

[23] Snorre Sturluson, Vol. 1 1979 pp. 101-104.
[24] Tjodrek munk, *Soga um dei gamle norske kongane*, Transl. by E. Skard, Norrøne bokverk 29, Oslo 1932 pp. 14f.

turned into idolatry by serving gods and not God".[25] Also Historia Norvegiae does, however, admit that Håkon better than his predecessors protected the law and the decisions from the things, and that this made him popular both with the chiefs and the common people.

The saga of *Ágrip* renders a more detailed and shaded account of Håkon the Good.[26] First he states that *"Håkon himself was Christian, but he had a heathen wife. For her sake and in order to please the people he deviated from Christianity"*. On this point his version is in line with that of Historia Norvegiae, and perhaps also with Håkonarmål. But having said this, Ágrip goes on by listing up a number of elements indicating the opposite, i.e. that he did stick to his Christian faith also after he became king of Norway. Among other things he observed Sundays and fasted on Fridays, further he removed the celebration of the Norse mid-winter festival, the jul, to the time of the Christian Christmas, and as already mentioned, he sent for clergymen from England. Ágrip also adds that many people converted to Christianity during Håkon's reign for the reason that he was so well-liked. When he after the battle of Fitjar realised that he would come to die, his friends offered to take his body to England and bury him at a church. This he refused by saying: *"I would not be worthy of that. Like heathen men I lived in many ways. Therefore you shall bury me like heathen men. After that I hope for more mercy from God himself than I deserve."*

It is, of course, difficult to place too much confidence in a late source like Ágrip. But it is of interest to note that it seems to go well with Håkonarmål's version. If there is some historical ground behind the friends' offer to the dying king, this is a noteworthy indication of their knowing where the king after all felt that he belonged. And if it is true that Håkon observed Sundays and fasted on Fridays, this must have been noted as a very conspicuous and provocative challenge of customary behaviour and cult. Whether this was a risk for the young king in a situation when he had to fight for regal power, depends on how far the ground for such a step may have already been prepared among his new subjects in Norway.

If we turn to *Snorre*,[27] he in broad outline follows Ágrip. But Snorre adds that Håkon when coming to Norway related to his Christian faith in a

---

[25] "Noregs historie", *Den eldste Noregs-historia*, Transl. by H. Koht, Norrøne bokverk 19, Oslo 1950 pp. 37f.
[26] *Ágrip* 1973 pp. 23-29.
[27] Snorre Sturluson, Vol. 1, 1979 pp. 79-104.

secret (lønnlig) way. How this took place in practice is well illustrated in Snorre's accounts of Håkon's encounter with the chiefs of Trøndelag, in which he only pretended that he took part in the traditional sacrifice (blot). This make-believe performance was staged by his earl Sigurd of Lade as some sort of a compromise by which neither the Christian faith of the king nor the pagan cult of the people of Trøndelag were intolerably challenged.

Snorre also reports that the people in Trøndelag (mid-Norway) burnt down three of the churches that Håkon had built there, and they put three of his priests to death. On the whole Snorre gives the impression that all the dramatic events as far as religious affairs were concerned during Håkon's reign took place in Trøndelag. On the coasts further south it seems as if his religious innovations have been tolerated. Does this imply that the real frontline along the coasts of Norway between Christianity and paganism at Håkon's time was to be found somewhere in the Møre-area on the north-western coast?

If we combine these pieces of information with what we have already pointed out about the traffic across the North Sea and the assimilation between the British and the Viking settlers already in the 9th and 10th centuries, there should be fair reason to suggest that the ground along the Norwegian coasts to some extent was already prepared for religious change at the time when Håkon the Good became king. His own reign also probably contributed to accelerate this process. We have already mentioned that it must have been very natural for Håkon to send for clergymen in England with his old acquaintance Dunstan, abbot at Glastonbury, and with king Eadred, one of his own foster mates in Wessex. But this must also have been a most convenient opportunity for them to obtain some of their goals, for Eadred to reduce the threat from raiding Norwegian Vikings, and for Dunstan to include them into the sphere of Christendom.

The continuation of the line – Jon Sigurd and Grimkell

Also Håkon's successors continued to maintain contacts with Britain, but during the reign of the Eirik-sons and the earl Håkon of Lade these relations seem more to have been directed towards the Norse settlement communities and Denmark than towards Wessex. Some of the priests coming to Norway together with bishop Sigefridus might, however, well have continued their work in Norway some years after Håkon's death.

But towards the end of the century the direct line to the milieu in Wessex was renewed. Four persons distinguish themselves as the salient links in the chain of continued contact; viz. the two Olav-kings, *Olav Tryggvasson and Olav Haraldsson*, and their respective bishops, *Jon Sigurd and Grimkell*. There is no room in this paper to go into details on the life-courses and the acts and doings of the four in more general terms. What is of relevance to note here are: 1) their vital roles in the continuation of the Christianisation process, and 2) their relations with the Wessex kingdom.

There is ample evidence in both Norwegian and British sources telling that *Olav Tryggvasson* had converted to Christianity before his installation as king of Norway in 995, and that his contacts with Wessex were of importance in this regard. Norwegian sources concentrate on Olav's contact with a wise man on the Scilly Islands, whereas British sources tell that he stayed in London, Canterbury and Winchester for some time during which he received ecclesiastical confirmation, even with king Æthelred standing sponsor, and also that he received some religious instruction.[28] The Norwegian sources are rather unanimous in their stating that Olav brought a bishop and priests with him from England at his return to Norway in 995. In the sources the bishop is alternately called *Jon* and *Sigurd*, Adam of Bremen refers to him as *Johannes*.

Like Olav Tryggvasson also Olav Haraldsson had a background as Viking chief in Normandy and England. Among other activities he took part in the conquest of Canterbury in 1012, as one of the Danish chief, Torkel the Tall's, men. On this event he probably witnessed the murder of Ælfheah the archbishop. After that some of the Vikings must have joined forces with the English, and both Torkel and Olav are known to have supported Æthelred against the invading army of king Swein in 1013.[29] According to the Old Norwegian Book of Homilii, Olav "started to believe in God in England, and in the city called Rouen he was christened".[30] When returning to Norway to take over the throne, he is known

---

[28] *The Anglo-Saxon Chronicle*, Transl. by G.N. Garmonsway London 1953/1986 pp. 126-129, *Theodoricus monachus,* 1932 p. 18, *Ágrip,* 1973 pp. 40f, Snorre Sturluson, Vol 1 1979 pp. 143-146, Odd munk Snorresson, *Soga om Olav Tryggvason*, Transl. by M. Rindal, Norrøne bokverk 46, Oslo 1977 pp. 46f.

[29] N. Ashdown, *English and Norse Documents*, London 1930 pp. 293f.

[30] *Gammelnorsk homiliebok*, transl. by A. Salvesen, Oslo 1971 p. 141. The question where Olav was baptised is discussed also by *Theodoricus monachus*, 1932 p. 25.

to have brought as much as four bishops with him from England together with priests and lay assistants.[31] The names of the bishops were: Grimkell, Bernard, Rodolv, and Sigfrid. According to Theodoricus monachus Grimkell was *"the brotherson of bishop Sigurd whom Olav Tryggvasson had brought with him from England"*.[32]

What appears from these observations is that the leading ecclesiastical groups in Wessex as soon as the opportunity arose were more than willing to take up the effort from the days of Håkon the Good by sending missionaries to Norway. Neither of the two Olavs were staying very long in Wessex. Nevertheless, they both came to be well supplied with bishops and priests from this kingdom when they returned to Norway to become kings. There is still a lack of sources explicitly referring to any planned strategy on this point with the Wessex authorities and clergy. But the fact that the number of bishops mentioned seemed to have been ready to enter on such an enterprise on such short notice, can be interpreted as an indication that some sort of an explicit aim of pursuing mission work among the Norwegians must have existed in these groups of Wessex society. As far as the family-connection between Sigurd and Grimkell is concerned, we can mention that in turn, Grimkell's nephew, Asgaut, became bishop in Oslo by the mid 11th century.

The significance of Sigurd's and Grimkell's efforts for the further progress of the Christianisation process and the consolidation of a church organisation in Norway, is undisputable. Sigurd accompanied his king during the five intensive years of his reign on his journeys to the different parts of his vast kingdom, supporting him actively in his achievements. Grimkell did the same during the reign of Olav Haraldsson. Among other things he played a most active role at the so-called Mostra-thing of 1024, where the foundations were laid for the Christian legislation (kristenretten) to be decided at the regional things. But above all Grimkell's important role in Norwegian church history is connected to his activities after Olav Haraldsson's death at Stiklestad in 1030. According to Snorre, the rumours of miracles happening at Olav's grave seem to have come up very spontaneously, but Grimkell took an active and leading part in leading the strong reactions these events called forth among broad layers of the people into an organised worship of Olav as a saint.

---

[31] *Adam av Bremen*, 1993, p. 102.
[32] *Theodoricus monachus*, 1932 p. 42.

Concluding remarks

Looking at the impulses from Christianity making themselves felt in Norway during the 9th and 10th centuries, we have made an effort here to put together information from different sources[33] indicating that such impulses were brought to the country by different groups of people at different levels of society, and that these impulses must have created a prepared ground for the more organised missionary efforts that took place in the 10th and early 11th centuries. We have also tried to substantiate that among the organised efforts to christianise Norway the leading clergy of the Wessex kingdom played a decisive part. In fact the vast majority of bishops operating in Norway up to the reign of Olav Haraldsson inclusive, were recruited from Wessex. One can hardly escape the conclusion that some sort of a planned missionary effort for the christianisation of Norway must have existed among the leading clergy in this South-English kingdom.

In my presentation here I have by no means managed to collect all the pieces of skin contained in the source material to cover the body of my elephant. But I do hope that my observations and conclusions do carry some similarity to a living being.

---

[33] For a selection of the texts referred to, see T. Jørgensen, *Gjør døren høy; Kirken i Norge 1000 år,*...and I. Montgomery, J. Schumacher, Oslo 1995.

The Acceptance of Christianity in Iceland: An attempt at a new interpretation

Hjalti Hugason

Introduction

In public writing and discussion about the acceptance of Christianity in Iceland in the year 999/1000 there is a general consent that it happened suddenly and without much preparation or prelude. Scholars have also agreed that the acceptance of Christianity was relatively extensive and successful and there never came to a pagan reaction. In addition to this writers have emphasized their opinion that the conversion process in Iceland was unique and differed in most ways from the conversion process in other countries.

A similar view of the acceptance of Christianity is still evident in scholarly research. The reason is that the acceptance of Christianity happens in prehistorical times, before writing is introduced in Iceland. Indirect evidence of the acceptance of Christianity is scant. It is mentioned briefly in Adam's of Bremen, Gesta Hammaburgensis ecclesiae pontificium from 1070. The oldest detailed account of the event was however not written until 120 - 130 years after it occurred. This account is in *Íslendingabók* (The Book of Icelanders) written by the first Icelandic saga writer, *Ari Þorgilsson*(see appendix). The basic elements of Ari's account had been preserved as an oral tale for three generations in the family that most eagerly advocated the acceptance of Christianity and was instrumental in the establishing of the Church in Iceland. We have to assume that this tale underwent some changes because of the passing of time and because of the interests of this family and the Skálholt-diocese. In fact the two first bishops in Skálholt belonged to this family. It is also likely that the social situation at the time of writing and the motives of the writer have affected the account. At the time of writing the country was on the brink of a civil war. By his book *Ari* was trying to bring about unity and peace among his people. This motive is clearly visible in his account of the acceptance of Christianity.

In the following I will introduce some basic factors in my research of the acceptance of Christianity in Iceland and call for discussion about them.

Model of interpretation

It was a turning point in Icelandic history when Icelanders left behind their old Nordic beliefs and became Christians. Because of the situation in the 10th century this was more than a change of religion. At this time in history religious beliefs were important factors in people's lives, both as individuals and groups. Every aspect of human experience was affected by these beliefs directly or indirectly. Religion was an important basis for the value system of society. Religion was connected to public life, its holydays and ceremonies, in different ways and it provided milestones for the individual from birth to burial. These changes in beliefs that took place in Iceland around the turn of the tenth century do therefore mark one of the most complex watersheds in Icelandic cultural history.

On the other hand we should bear in mind that this was not a sudden change. The Icelandic people did not change their religion overnight without preparation. On the contrary we have to consider that the events of Alþingi 999/1000 had a long prehistory which is partly known and partly not. It was not clear right away what had really happened when Icelanders changed their religion. The acceptance of Christianity was mainly a reversal in a long term development which was already started but now became more vigorous and evident. This development went on after the acceptance of Christianity and has in fact been continous since then. The driving force of this development is the interaction between Christianity and Icelandic folk culture. After the acceptance of Christianity Icelanders were increasingly moulded by the ethical and religious message of the Christian faith. They were also under more influence from the European culture of the middle ages which had developed for centuries on the basis of Christianity. In return Icelanders did make their special mark on Christianity and European culture. Their historical heritage, their religious and cultural background, their social and psychological premises were different with the effect that they understood and accepted Christianity in their own special way. Local adjustment like this occurs everywhere when an international religion becomes rooted in a new ground.

A development as complex as this one can not be successfully described in any simple way and there is no one term or concept that envelopes all its elements or stages. Nevertheless the simple way has been chosen in the past. This complicated development has usually been called *kristnitakan* (the acceptance of Christianity). In the sagas *kristnitakan* was however sometimes referred to as *siðaskipti* (siða: customs, skipti: conversion). These concepts have in common that they are easy to understand and use. The meaning of *kristnitaka* is the event when people accepted Christianity. In Old Icelandic the meaning of *siður* was broader than today. Then the word could among other things mean beliefs or religion. Then *siðaskipti*means simply the process or development that consists in the conversion from one religion to another in general.

The term *kristnitakan* has a narrow meaning. In general usage it only refers to the events that took place on Alþingi in the summer of 999/1000. That is why it is too narrow or limited to be used for the complicated long term development that was going on before and after these events. The concept *siðaskipti* would however be perfect for that purpose. But there is one catch. This term and related terms have been used for the events in Icelandic Church history around the middle of the 16th century when the Evangelical-Lutheran doctrine replaced the Catholic doctrine as the official doctrine of the Church. The older and broader meaning of the word is now mostly forgotten.

In reaction to this problem and to draw a more complex and analytical picture of the development I will choose to make a distinction between *kristnitakan* (*the acceptance of Christianity*) on the one hand and *trúarbragðaskipti* (*conversion of religion*) on the other. The term *conversion of religion* will be used for the complex longterm development which led Icelanders to turn their backs on old pagan beliefs and become Christian. This kind of change cannot occur without an interactive development on many levels. Partly this development has been of an informal kind, consisting of unorganized, dispersed and incidental influence of Christianity, which prepared the ground for a larger change. On the other hand a much more formal development was taking place. An organized mission was followed by a legal decision that in the future Christianity was the common and official belief of Icelanders. Hereafter this part of the development will be called the acceptance of Christianity (*kristnitakan*). Finally the institution of the Church was established all over the country with everything that comes with it. That part of the development will be called the *institutional development*.

The conversion of religion did not only take place on a formal and an informal level because in this context it is also possible to make a distinction between the individual level and the collective level. The term *conversion of religion* will be used for the process when a group of people, especially a whole society, converts from one religion to another. However, when we speak of the conversion of individuals the term *conversion of faith* is used.

On the basis of the model of interpretation that I have introduced I have attempted in my research to see the conversion from a broader perspective than scholars before me. Therefore I deal with the entire conversion to Christianity in my research. In the following I will explain the neccessity of applying various methods and perspectives when one is interpreting a development of this kind.

The Book of Icelanders by *Ari þorgilsson* and other old literature which discusses the conversion in Iceland almost invariably deals only with the legal procedure, that is the events on Alþingi in the year 999/1000 and the events leading right to it. However the Conversion is more than just a legal procedure. It meant a thorough cultural watershed in Icelandic history. Icelanders turned their backs on their old Nordic heritage and headed in a new direction, towards the Christian culture of Europe. Such change will not take place without a complex long term development. The authors of the old literature do either simplify their account of the conversion or see their subject from a narrow perspective. There is no reason to assume that these characteristics of the accounts of the literature from the middle ages are caused by deliberate partiality or falsity on behalf of the writers. It is more likely that normal forgetfulness is the cause of most of this because the accounts were not written down until a long time had passed. Another important thing is the perception of reality and the historical consciousness of the writers. It was completely different from the perception and historical consciousness of historians today.

Because of this it will never be possible to understand and explain the Conversion on the basis of documented accounts from the middle ages only. Critical and historical research of the old texts will only answer a limited number of questions they pose. The result of such criticism is probably only going to be that *Ari fróð* did not only try to give an account of the events but also made an attempt to bring an important message to his contemporaries. This he did for example by building up a dramatic suspense in his account of the acceptance of Christianity. For that purpose he mentions þorgeirs stay under the cloak, his speech, the reaction of the members of Alþingi and þorgeirs proclamation of the new law whose content he dictated alone. By historical criticism it is even possible to arrive at the conclusion that the prelude to these important events at Alflingi in the summer 999/1000 was more likely to be some complicated negotiations between pagans and Christians that resulted in an agreement to stand united in accepting the new religion but keep the law otherwise mostly intact. Icelandic historians have for example often interpreted the prelude to the acceptance of Christianity in this manner. However this does not explain the conversion of religion. For example it does not explain what were the grounds for negotiation and why the Christians had such a good bargaining position in a pagan society.

It is necessary to apply diverse methods from different disciplines to explain the complicated process which the conversion of the entire society is . I will not attempt to give account of all the explanations that have been put forward, but instead I will try to look at the development from so many angles that the audience will realize how complicated this development was and how it was influenced by various forces.

The conversion of religion and the nature of beliefs

Religion is always complex by nature. It is said that most of them cover intellectual, emotional, ideological, ethical and social elements as well as the ritual concerning their cultus. It is however dangerous to define the limits of the various spheres that religion covers too exactly because the spheres are related and interactive in various ways. The content of these spheres and the relationship between them is also dependent on the religion in question and the historical circumstances.

Nordic beliefs are often seen as having no real theology. Because of this it is probable that at the time of the acceptance of Christianity many people did not have clear ideas about religion and the public did not stick to any developed religious doctrine. Under such circumstances we have a reason to think that the intellectual and ideological elements of the beliefs did not play a large role but the emotional and psychological elements were all the more important. That is why people's trust in the protecting powers of certain gods or supernatural beings had a conclusive influence on their religious beliefs, but not developed ideas about the qualities of the supernatural beings they believed in. When discussing the belief in the

Nordic gods and other branches of Nordic beliefs it is therefore natural to put intellectual, ideological and emotional elements in one category and see the beliefs as consisting of three spheres, one wich could include faith and religious ideas, one which includes ritual and cultus, and the third includes ethics or morality.

The analysis of the conversion of Icelanders and other Nordic people has sometimes been based on such threefold division of their beliefs. Then it has been emphasized that conversion of religion is a complex development which takes place in all the main spheres of religion. It has especially to do with a change in faith, religious ideas or religious feeling which we might call *actual conversion of faith*; changes in the sphere of cultus or *conversion of ritual* and changes in the sphere of morals which here are termed *conversion of morality*. Scholars that have interpreted conversions of religion in this manner have explained the relationship between various factors in different ways.

The Norwegian Fredrik Paasche thought that in Norway the conversion of religion happened in such a way that the conversion of ritual came first. This happened relatively quickly and without any compromise. What came next was the conversion of morality with the effect that people's conduct was influenced by the ethics of the Church to the same degree as was common in Christian countries at the time. Finally the conversion of morality was replaced by the actual conversion of faith. Paasche thinks that this last stage took longest time to pass and it did not lead to a complete conversion because remnants of former beliefs survived. According to this interpretation the conversion of Nordic people was mainly the turning of worship to a new god. In the wake of this change was supposed to come a long term development in the spheres of ethics and religious ideas. Interpretations of this kind have had some following.

The Swede Helge Ljungberg used similar analysis of different spheres of Nordic beliefs. He thought that in general the actual conversion of faith came first and conversion of ritual second and last came the conversion of morality. He bases his assessment on the idea that Nordic belief like polytheism in general was liberal in the sphere of religious ideas and doctrine. Consequently it was easy to adopt the belief in a new god, if he showed himself to be worthy of the same trust as the old gods. Because of this he thinks that the first stage of the conversion passed quickly, at least until people realised the Christian demand, that they should turn their backs on all other gods and deities. This demand is caused by the fact that in these matters Christianity is unconditional and exclusive like other monotheisms. On the other hand Ljungberg thinks that old Nordic beliefs were exclusive in the sphere of ritual, because the ritual sacrifices and worship of the gods was intended to support the gods in their eternal struggle for peace and prosperity. If people gave up this ritual worship and indroduced Christian worship it was probable that the world would go haywire or the old gods would revenge the people for neglecting their religious duties. That is why he thinks that the conversion of ritual was not possible until the actual conversion of faith was well under way. Christianity was in contrast relatively open in the sphere of ritual which made it possible to adopt religious customs or rituals of foreign religions and give them a new Christian meaning. This quality may have made the conversion of ritual easier. In the ethical sphere old Nordic beliefs were rather obscure and made vague demands on people's way of life. In this sphere Christianity was much more demanding. The ethical norms of these two religions were also complete opposites. The core of pagan ethics was its strong awareness of the honour of individuals and families and which should be preserved by all possible means, including revenge. These ethics were in direct opposition to the Christian demand for conciliation, forgiveness, moderation and humility. Because of this Ljungberg thinks that the conversion of ethics came last and took the longest time.

Pagan attitudes in Nordic countries towards worship and their gods were coloured by utilitarianism. It is probable that this had effects on the actual conversion of faith and ritual. There was hardly a place for personal religious experience in Nordic beliefs. People were always ready to accept a message that there were other gods that could increase the prosperity of groups or individuals. It has been pointed out that an example of this attitude is the willingness of so called godless men to accept Christianity and the reason is thought to be their open pursuit of prosperity.

The interpretations that I have mentioned here shed light on the conversion of religion from the perspective of the history of religion. On the other hand it is advisable to avoid too much distinction between various stages in its development. We have to view this primarily as an integrated process where it is impossible to fully separate the actual conversion of faith, the conversion of ritual and the conversion of morality, from each other.

From polytheism to monotheism

Here above I attempted to analyse the conversion of religion as a whole from a historical-religious perspective. Let us now look at the acceptance of Christianity in particular and try to realize its importance in the history of religion. We will especially try to answer the question; what situation did it put an end to and what real effect did it have on the position of Christians among the Icelanders.

When we discuss the acceptance of Christianity in this manner it is necessary to realize the different position of religions in society. This position we can use to make a distinction between religions and classify them as common, uniting or *official beliefs*, *unofficial beliefs*, *permitted beliefs* and *forbidden beliefs*. This classification is partly based on the legal position of religions but does also take into account elements of social nature.

By *official beliefs* one is refering to religion which large groups of people, for example inhabitants of one country, have in common and in former times this was one of the strongest binding elements of society. Therefore we could also call this class *uniting beliefs* when we view it with its social role in mind rather than its legal position. Often it is pronounced directly or indirectly in laws what is the official belief, how it is privileged compared to other beliefs, and what should be the relationship between belief and society. This is done for example in the constitution of the Republic of Iceland were the Evangelical-Lutheran Church is proclaimed the state Church of Iceland. Official beliefs are under such circumstances an important part of the defined and declared ideological basis of society. Sometimes its role is not as evident and its position is best seen in the connection between religious practice and various public and legal ceremonies. Example of this are religious ceremonies in connection with the assembly of parliaments. At last we may mention that society often develops religous institutions on the basis of official beliefs and erects a common official system for religious worship as was the case with the national Church of Iceland and the Icelandic clergy.

The class *unofficial beliefs* is on the other hand defined according to sociological norms. This is a belief which is independent of the official belief but develops parallel to it. In fact we can say that this is a collective class wich consists of all religion and religious ideas that exist in society but do not have the status of official belief. Ususally the various forms and kinds of unofficial beliefs are practised by large and small groups but not the public in general. And they do not have a legal and official role as a uniting factor in society.

Laws can either be silent about unofficial beliefs or they can define its status and its followers in society. Because of this it is possible to divide these beliefs into *permitted beliefs* and *forbidden beliefs*. These classes are of legal or judicial nature and are defined according to the different legal position of the beliefs. Forbidden beliefs are religions whose practice is illegal. What is then left of the unofficial beliefs is classified as permitted beliefs. Usually the law is not exhaustive regarding the definition of the status of all unofficial beliefs. Therefore we have to assume that there is a variety of beliefs in the unofficial sphere apart from the religious ideas that are forbidden in a formal legal way.

When we analyse religious circumstances in Iceland before the Conversion according to this classification system it is clear that the belief in Nordic gods had a special status compared to other beliefs in the country. It was in various ways connected to the public sphere in Iceland. This is apparent in the fact that Icelandic chiefs occupied both leading religious and secular posts at the same time. The laws have on the other hand hardly defined the status of the belief in Nordic gods in society and there was no offical system of worship because there was no clergy and no common official places of worship like churches in Christian society. Because of this the belief in Nordic gods was formally rather the uniting belief than the official belief of society. Its social function was however the same as the function of official beliefs later on. The unique status of this belief should be seen as a product of the social structure which was charachterized by limited separation and specialization of institutions from individuals and consequently the laws concerning the official sphere were simple. Other branches of the old Nordic beliefs like belief in various supernatural beings and different kinds of folk beliefs had lesser and more obscure connection with the official sphere and did not have the same function as a uniting factor. On the other hand the role of these beliefs was probably much more important in the sphere of personal religious practice. Therefore this should be viewed as an unofficial belief. The same was probably true for Christianity which we have to assume was present in the country from the beginning of settlement even if it was practised with secrecy before the acceptance of Christianity. We have no evidence that any beliefs or religious ideas were forbidden by law. That is in agreement with the fact that belief in Nordic gods was polytheism and its practitioners had no problem tolerating people's beliefs in other gods.

The believers in Nordic gods had themselves for long time combined this belief with other branches of Nordic beliefs like the belief in supernatural beings. In pagan times it seems that all unofficial beliefs were permitted beliefs. That is even true for the end of the mission period when laws had been made to protect pagan beliefs. If accounts of old literature are to be trusted these laws were made to stop the attacks of Christians on pagan worship but were not directed against Christianity as such.

The acceptance of Christianity brought many changes about. The primitive Christian law code wich was approved in Alþing 999/1000 was made of one main provision and three exemption clauses. The main provision was that Icelanders should become Christian and be baptized if they were not baptized already (In this fashion Icelandic society had an official belief in a legal and formal sense.) One of the exemption clauses did however reflect the realistic view that it was not possible to eliminate pagan beliefs altogether by lawmaking. Because of this the law provided some immunity for those people who kept the old faith but did not practise it in a provocative way. The former official and uniting belief, the belief in Nordic gods, became consequently only forbidden in the official sphere of society. The exemption clause shows however that the belief in Nordic gods was tolerated in the unofficial and personal sphere if practiced in private. Nobody was forced to a more personal or direct renunciation of the old beliefs than beeing baptized. It was also provided that all possible means should not be applied to uproot hidden remnants of pagan beliefs. Because of this it is impossible to assume that the belief in Nordic gods became a forbidden belief as soon as it was owerthrown as the official belief. The same is certainly true for other branches of the Nordic beliefs.

The law that accepted Christianity signified an important compromise when we take into account that Christian religion is absolutely monotheism and therefore naturely exclusive regarding the worship of other gods. Most of the old law was still valid and it was proclaimed that in two important matters old customs should be kept even if this was in opposition to Christianity. These customs were the eating of horse meat and the exposure of infants. The old common value system was therefore mostly reaffirmed when Christianity was accepted. From the perspective of theology and religious history it seems that the acceptance of Christianity brought about an intermediate stage between the old situation and what we might call a Christian society where only Christianity was the defined ideological foundation of society. This interpretation of the acceptance of Christianity as a compromise is in fact apparent in *Ólafs saga Tryggvasonar hin mesta* from the late 14th century.

The reasons for this compromise are many. Even if the Christians had such a strong position that they could get a formal acceptance of Christianity from the pagans, their position was not strong enough to force the development further. The Church as an institution was nonexistent in the country and spiritual leaders of the Christians were few and their influence little. The knowledge of Christianity was also limited among Icelandic Christians and they were not fully aware of the demands of the new religion on its followers. People did not have the preconditions to take more than one step towards Christianity in this first attempt.

It is highly questionable to analyse the stage of Christianity, which became the official belief when Christianity was accepted, with the help of concepts or classification systems which are not directly derived from the historical situation at the time. However I will try to clarify the development with the help of general historical-religious analysis.

The law accepting Christianity provided that the whole population of the country should be baptized in the name of God, the Father, the Son and the Holy Ghost. According to canon law and theology these people were rightly accepted as members of the Christian Church. Because of this we can claim that the accepting of Christianity did in fact mean that Christianity was established by law. On the other hand we know that the knowledge of Christian doctrine was limited among most Icelanders, the understanding of the new religion was coloured by their old belief and their religious ideas would hardly deserve to be called a syncretism by modern standards. Finally we should bear in mind that Christian religion and worship are legally proclaimed in the official sphere but pagan worship at least tolerated in the unofficial sphere and its practitioners secured some immunity. If we take full account of this fact it may be said that when Icelanders accepted Christianity they established Christian monolatri by law as the official and uniting form of belief. Monolatri does not mean that the existence of other gods but the one which is worshiped is renounced. Consequently it is not as exclusive and absolute as monotheism. On the basis of monolatri it is easier to ignore the worship of other gods than on the basis of monotheism like Christianity in its pure form.

When we look at things from the perspective mentioned above it is clear that the conversion of religion in Iceland was a slow and steady development in a few stages. This development did not cause a sudden break or an extermination of the old beliefs. This explains why the Conversion was so peaceful. This peaceful development could partly explain the fact that there is no pagan reaction in Iceland after the accepting of Christianity, even if Ólafur Tryggvason, the main supporter of Christianity according to accounts, died and the position of Christianity in Norway became precarious. It has however been claimed that the old uniting belief of Icelanders, the believe in Nordic gods, had primarly a political and social role but did not rest on personal faith or conviction. Therefore it was mainly a part of the official and public life but was foreign to people's everday life, its sorrows and joys. If the conversion of religion developed in the way described here it is probable that Icelanders that had no personal knowledge of Christianity or Christians accepted Christianity generally as a foreign superstructure on top of the many religious ideas that Icelanders sought comfort in personally both before and after the acceptance of Christianity. This position explains why pagans did not make any attempt to restore their old belief in Iceland.

The interpretation of the acceptance of Christianity that is presented here is consistent with the above-mentioned ideas of Fr. Paasche about the nature of conversions. According to these ideas it is assumed that the conversion was in the beginning mostly in the sphere of worship or ritual. This interpretation also gives a good explanation of why certain parts of the old beliefs survived the acceptance of Christianity. The beliefs were allowed to develop on their own terms in the sphere of unofficial beliefs. It is possible that before the acceptance of Christianity the Nordic gods were worshipped and brought sacrifices in public by large groups of people but supernatural beings and other lower ranking deities were worshipped in the privacy of homes. The change that the acceptance of Christianity brought about was only directed against the belief in Nordic gods. Belief in various supernatural beings and other branches of the old Nordic beliefs and popular religion were not affected by these changes and possibly became stronger after the acceptance of Christianity. After the acceptance of Christianity people could practise their everyday-worship in the same manner as before even if the major public holidays gave way to new ones and these days were few and maybe they did not matter very much to the general public.

The next stage in the historical process after the acceptance of Christianity was the elimination of pagan worship in the unofficial sphere. This includes the elimination of secret worship and other obvious and apparent remnants of pagan times in law and public life of society. A part of the old Nordic beliefs, mainly the belief in Nordic gods, did hereafter have the status of forbidden beliefs. Similar changes have occured in the sphere of morality and religious ideas. It is common to assume that these changes took place during the reign of king Ólafur Haraldsson (1015-1030). It is probable that the missionary bishops that he sent to Iceland facilitated this development. It is however most likely that this was a slow process that lasted all the 11th century. Maybe the concecration of the first bishop in Iceland made a difference in this matter. Included in this development was the rooting of Christianity and an ecclesiastical development.

Concluding remarks

If the acceptance of Christianity occurred in stages, as I assume in my hypothesis, it can explain why the acceptance was so peaceful. On the other hand it also shows what a slow and complex development the conversion was. If there had been a possibility and a precondition to force the development further at the acceptance of Christianity and if this force had been applied it is probable that pagan opposition had asserted itself and the further development of the conversion had been less peaceful and more complicated.

(This paper is part of a large work. Full text can be ordered from the author at University of Iceland, Sudurgata, 101 Reykjavik.)

The Vikings' relationship with Christianity reconsidered

Dawn M. Hadley

Long after the Vikings had ceased raiding the English coast chroniclers still wrote with horror about the atrocities that they had committed against ecclesiastical targets. Although admitting that there may have been some later embellishments, modern scholars have, on the whole, accepted the picture painted by chroniclers of an English Church brought to near ruin by a vicious band of heathens. Stenton was in no doubt that "the Danish invasions of the ninth century shattered the organisation of the English church",[1] and few have sought to disagree with this sentiment, in particular where northern and eastern England are concerned. The distribution of wealthy and important churches in Domesday Book, and the nature of ecclesiastical provision in the Danelaw have come to be used as a barometer of the disruption caused by the Viking invaders, and it is on this premise, in particular, that this paper will focus.

***

Admittedly narrative sources present a dire picture of the Viking invaders, in which they inflicted terrible, sometimes irreparable, damage on the Anglo-Saxon Church.[2] Later chroniclers make the greatest accusations against the invaders, and their ability to render a fanciful story from a terse entry in the *Anglo-Saxon Chronicle* is well-known,[3] but it is clear that contemporaries did fear for the safety of the Church. However, although it is undeniable that the Vikings posed a real threat to the Church, their behaviour was not unique. The ninthcentury witnessed a struggle among kings, bishops and lay lords for control over monasteries and their possessions, and well before the Viking invasions not only had gifts to the Church declined, but in some cases had actually been

---

[1] F. M. Stenton, *Anglo-Saxon England* (3rd edn., 1971), p. 433.
[2] See, for example, Alcuin's description of the fate of the church of St.Cuthbert, Lindisfarne; *English Historical Documents, c.500-1042*, I, ed.D. Whitelock (2nd. edn., 1979), (hereafter *EHD*) no.193.
[3] R. I. Page, "A Most Vile People": *Early English Historians on the Vikings* (1987).

diminished by royal seizure of ecclesiastical land and revenue.[4] This may provide a context for those ecclesiastical sites which archaeological evidence reveals were either abandoned in the eighth and ninth centuries[5] or else experienced lay encroachment.[6] A contemporary consciousness that there had been a decline in Christian standards explains the emphasis placed by chroniclers on the heathenism of the Vikings; they were a form of divine retribution.[7] The Vikings did not so much originate the decline as exacerbate the condition of an already weakened Church; a Church apparently undermined by royal depredations and by the apathy of potential recruits.[8] In sum, there was a general decline in the fortunes of the Church in advance of the Viking invasions.

Despite these considerations, however, the traditional view that the Viking invasions were inimical to the fortunes of the Anglo-Saxon Church does seem to be corroborated by Domesday Book. It reveals that monastic houses and secular minsters were more densely distributed in the south and west of England than in the north and east,[9] and that the amount of land held by the Church was much greater in the south (around a fifth to a third) than in the north and east Midlands (less than a tenth), with the exception of the fenlands where tenthcentury monastic reformers had heavily endowed their foundations.[10] This has been taken to indicate that the Church in the Danelaw suffered particularly badly from the Viking invasions and settlement, which resulted in a much weakened ecclesiastical structure in that region.[11] However, issue can be taken with this conclusion. So little is known about the Church in the north and east of England in the ninthcentury that, given the state of virtual civil war in

---

[4] See, for example, *The Anglo-Saxons*, ed.J.Campbell (1982), pp. 135, 139; N. P. Brooks, *The Early History of the Church of Canterbury* (1984) pp. 184-6.

[5] For example, R. D. Carr, A. Tester & P. Murphy, "The Middle Saxon Settlement at Staunch Meadow, Brandon", *Antiquity*, 62 (1988), pp. 371-7; V. Fenwick, "Insula de Burgh: Excavations at Burrow Hill, Butley, Suffolk, 1978-81", *Anglo-Saxon Studies in History and Archaeology*, 3, ed. D. Brown *et al.* (1984), pp.35-54.

[6] I owe this point to Dr.John Blair. See R. Cramp, "Monastic Sites", *The Archaeology of Anglo-Saxon England*, ed. D. M. Wilson (1976), pp. 223-41.

[7] Alcuin believed, for example, that the raid on Lindisfarne was not entirely unexpected;*EHD*, I, no.193.

[8] *Alfred the Great*, eds. S. Keynes & M. Lapidge (1983) p. 103.

[9] J. Blair, "Secular Minster Churches in Domesday Book", *Domesday Book: a reassessment*, ed.P. H. Sawyer, (1985), pp. 104-42

[10] R. Fleming, "Monastic Lands and England's Defence in the Viking Age", *English Historical Review*, Vol.CCCXCV (1985), pp. 247-265, at 249.

[11] A. Rogers, "The Origins of Newark: the evidence of local boundaries", *Trans. of theThoroton Soc.*, Vol.LXXVII (1974), pp. 13-26, at 15; Morris, "Churches in York and its Hinterland", *Minsters and Parish Churches*, ed.J.Blair (1988) pp. 191-9.

Northumbria, it is not entirely safe to conclude that major churches were especially well-endowed or well-staffed on the eve of the Viking invasions and settlement. Indeed, there are indications that the troubled fortunes of successive kings of Northumbria encouraged them to make good their losses at the expense of the Church.[12]

Furthermore, the sparsity of documentary evidence also renders us ill-informed about how the West Saxon kings treated the Church as they took control of the Danelaw. It is apparent that they encouraged their nobles to buy up land from the Vikings in the early years of the tenth century[13]; and this was followed by substantial grants of land to leading Englishmen who were, given the tenuous grasp of the house of Wessex on the region, probably left to bring the land under control themselves.[14] Such policies affected the Church, and Robin Fleming has argued that the West Saxon kings used the ecclesiastical land which came into their hands from the 880s as currency for rewarding royal officials and supporters.[15] She suggested that this ecclesiastical land was acquired following Viking devastation, but it is suspicious that it is in strategically important places (on coasts, major rivers, and along the Danelaw boundary) that the West Saxons acquired a number of monasteries and their estates. The implication is that the West Saxon monarchy did not simply absorb abandoned or devastated monasteries, but that they were more deliberate than that. Of course, successive West Saxon kings both endowed existing churches and founded new ones, often in association with their administrative changes and the construction of new *burhs*.[16] But it is clear that those churches which received substantial royal patronage in the early to mid-tenth century were those which were of most importance to the West Saxon kings in their efforts to secure control over, successively, Mercia and the Danelaw. Finally, it should be remembered that the Church did not only lose land to the Vikings or during the early stages of the West Saxon conquest; churches in the Danelaw often struggled to hold on to their endowments in the late tenth and early eleventh centuries.[17]

In sum, to attribute the regional difference in ecclesiastical organisation and resources solely to the Vikings underplays the role of the

---

[12] *The Anglo-Saxons*, ed. Campbell, p. 135.
[13] F. M. Stenton, *Types of Manorial Structure in the Northern Danelaw* (1910), p. 74.
[14] P. H. Sawyer, "The Charters of Burton Abbey and the Unification of England", *Northern History*, X (1979), pp. 28-39.
[15] Fleming, "Monastic Lands", p. 252.
[16] J. Blair, "Secular Minster Churches", pp. 118-9.
[17] J. Blair, "Introduction", *Minsters and Parish Churches*, pp. 1-19, at 3-5.

house of Wessex, and of any earlier regional differences. Furthermore, the distribution of wealthy and well-endowed ecclesiastical communities in Domesday Book may not be an especially relevant criterion for assessing the fate of the Church in the Danelaw during the late ninth and early tenth centuries.

***

Surprisingly, given the reputation of the Vikings, it is possible to make a case for elements of continuity in ecclesiastical organisation through the period of Viking settlement. In some parts of the Danelaw there is a striking correlation between the sites of middle-Saxon monasteries and the locations of later mother churches serving large parishes. Examples include Repton, Wirksworth, Derby, Bakewell (Derbs.), Southwell (Notts.), Gilling, Ripon, Howden, Otley and Beverley (Yorks.). A significant characteristic of many of the major churches in the region is that they commonly coincide with the great estate centres of Domesday Book. A number of these estates can be demonstrated from charter evidence to have existed over a century earlier, and the parishes of these churches commonly coincide with the secular estates on which they sat. For example, the estates of Howden, Sherburn and Southwell described in charters of the mid-tenth century are mirrored by the parishes of their respective churches.[18] The parishes of other churches incorporate much secular estate fragmentation, and since there is charter evidence to show that the separate manors which comprised the parish existed as separate estates by the mid-tenth century it suggests that the parishes had been framed by that date. For example, Newton (Derbs.) was granted to AEthelgeard in 956 and was a separate manor in Domesday Book, yet belonged to the parish of Repton.[19] Many of the major churches and estate centres of the region have origins in the pre-Viking period, and this creates an appearance of a degree of continuity through the Viking invasions. Admittedly, constituent members of these estates may have been lost and gained, but is it inconceivable that the Domesday estate of, for example, Ripon was broadly descended from the seventh century

---

[18]For these, and other, examples see D. M. Hadley, "Danelaw Society and Institutions: East Midlands' Phenomena?" (Unpubld. Univ. of B'ham, PhD thesis, 1992), ch.5; R.K.Morris, *Churches in the Landscape* (1989), pp. 133-9.

[19]For this and other examples see Hadley, "Danelaw Society", pp. 232-263.

estate granted to Bishop Wilfrid?[20] Or that the estate of Repton was the remnant of the 31 *manentes* "called *Hrepingas*" granted to the abbot of Breedon-on-the-Hill in the late seventh century?[21] The absence of Scandinavian place-names among the members of Sherburn's estate – which is in an area with an otherwise dense distribution of such names – has prompted Sawyer to postulate that it reflects the fact that the estate remained intact and in English, probably archiepiscopal, control through the Viking invasions.[22] Continuity cannot easily be substantiated, but cumulatively the evidence cited provides a starting point from which to consider the question of continuity.

If it is that these estates survived relatively intact from the pre-Viking period, the question arises of whether the parishes which were framed around them similarly pre-date the Viking invasions. The answer to this question is problematic, not least because the nature and functions of parishes developed in significant respects through the Anglo-Saxon period, and early pastoral care may have been rather different from that exercised in later medieval parishes. To speak of a clearly defined parochial system at the time when the earliest missionary churches were founded in the seventh and eighth centuries would almost certainly be anachronistic.[23] Nonetheless, it is not unreasonable to suggest that by the ninth century such a system may have been crystallising, and on large estates of great antiquity pastoral care is likely to have long been dominated by the church at the estate centre. We must consider, however, whether this apparent continuity is anything more than illusory, after all there is little unambiguous evidence for the continuous occupation of churches. It is not difficult to imagine that, for example, church-founders of the tenth century might choose to build a church on the site of a former church, to lend their foundation a historical context and tradition; this could create for us an appearance of continuity. On the other hand, important tenth and eleventh century churches so commonly occupy the sites of pre-Viking communities that it would be unconvincing to explain this coincidence by reference to refoundation following a period of abandonment in all cases. The large corpus of tenth century sculpture in the

---

[20] *The Life of Bishop Wilfrid by Eddius Stephanus*, ed. B. Colgrave (1927), p. 16.
[21] A. Rumble, "*Hreopingas* reconsidered", *Mercian Studies*, ed. A. Dornier (1977), pp. 169-72.
[22] P. H. Sawyer, *Kings and Vikings* (1985), p. 86.
[23] See, for example, Morris, *Churches in the Landscape*, p. 138; C. R. E. Cubitt, "Pastoral care and concilliar canons: the provisions of the 747 Council of *Clofesho*", *Pastoral Care Before the Parish*, ed. J. Blair & R. Sharpe (1993) pp. 193-211.

Danelaw suggests that many churches were in constant use in the period before the Danelaw was fully conquered by the West Saxons. Moreover, the survival of pre-Viking buildings to their full height at places such as Wearmouth and Jarrow would appear to militate against decades of abandonment.[24]

There is also a small body of evidence pointing more explicitly to continuity in religious observance and organisation. A passage in the early twelfthcentury *Libellus AEthelwoldi* concerning the church of Horningsea (Cambs.) is important in this context. Even when

> "the pagan army was ravaging in the area, the priest Coenwald exercised sacerdotal office there. Later the people of the place who had joined together from paganism in the grace of baptism gave this minster five hides at Horningsea and two at Eye. When Coenwald died he was succeeded by the priest Herewulf".[25]

Coenwald's successor is alleged to have been a follower of Athelstan, which suggests that Coenwald remained in post for a substantial number of years. Apparently, even in the vicinity of Viking activity a church continued to exercise its pastoral role, and even succeeded in converting some of the pagan invaders to Christianity. That Christianity was thriving in the Danelaw is also suggested by the careers of Theodred, bishop of London (926x57) and Oda, archbishop of Canterbury (941x58), who were both from the Danelaw; Oda indeed was of Danish descent, and possibly educated in the Danelaw.[26]

However, a case for widespread continuity in ecclesiastical organisation in the Danelaw requires a great deal of justification, because it contradicts traditional images of the Vikings. Yet there are grounds for arguing that, on religious grounds, the Vikings were not openly hostile to Christianity. Some Vikings (such as those who fought against Alfred at Edington[27]) converted at an early date, and collaboration between natives and Vikings was clearly a feature of the late ninth and early tenth centuries (as is witnessed by the flight of Alfred's nephew AEthelwold to

---

[24]Cramp, "Monastic Sites", pp. 229-241.
[25]From the *Libellus AEthelwoldi*, ch. 42, ed. E. O. Blake, *Liber Eliensis*, Camden Third Series, XCII (1962), pp. 105-6
[26]A. F. Wareham, "St.Oswald's family and kin", *Oswald of Worcester*, eds., N. P. Brooks and C. R. E. Cubitt (forthcoming).
[27]*Alfred the Great*, ed. Keynes & Lapidge, p. 85.

the Northumbrian Vikings who accepted him as king).[28] Political reasons for conversion and collaboration were obviously important, and the northern Church made a point of reaching an understanding with Viking rulers. Given the accusations levelled at Osbert and AElle concerning their plundering of ecclesiastical lands it is perhaps not surprising that the community of St.Cuthbert should have been prepared to engage with the Viking Guthfrith, whose succession it ensured, and who was more disposed to endow the community than had been recent Northumbrian kings.[29] However, other evidence suggests that the Vikings adopted Christianity with more vigour. Monumental stone sculpture was an almost exclusively Christian preserve, virtually unknown in contemporary Scandinavia; the huge corpus of Anglo-Scandinavian sculpture in northern England denotes a fusion of native Christian practice with the artistic influence of the invaders. Furthermore, there appears to have been a massive increase in sculpture production and in the number of sites at which it was produced; as Richard Bailey puts it "stone carving did not just continue into the Viking period but was *enthusiastically* taken up' both at existing sites and at places where it had not previously been known.[30] Admittedly, Scandinavian iconography does not prove Scandinavian patronage in all cases, but if native lords patronised such sculpture it suggests that the Scandinavian influence in the region was manifest and acceptable to them. Moreover, if Scandinavian rulers were not considered reasonable overlords of the Church then the adoption of Scandinavian motifs would have been wholly inappropriate.

Many examples of this sculpture can be characterised as funerary monuments suggesting that they mark sites where burial was undertaken. Given that some of this sculpture is found at sites with pre-Viking funerary monuments it perhaps denotes that the Scandinavians used pre-existing Christian burial grounds. This is supported by a few examples of burials accompanied by Scandinavian-style items in Christian churchyards. However, the occurence of such burials is problematic, not least because it is unclear whether accompanied burials should be interpreted as being pagan. They may indicate that although the Vikings were burying their dead in the pre-existing burial grounds of local

---

[28]*EHD*, I, no.1, s.a. 900; see also *ibid.*, s.a.943; *Alfred the Great*, ed. Keynes & Lapidge, p. 83.
[29]*EHD*, I, no.6; *Church Historians of England*, ed. J. Stevenson, Vol.3, pt. 2 (1885), p. 664.
[30]R. Bailey, *Viking Age Sculpture* (1980), p. 81.

communities, they had yet to accept Christianity, and its burial practices.[31] Conversely, it could be argued that the Vikings had accepted Christianity but had yet to abandon all of their traditional practices; most obviously, burial with grave-goods. In this respect, the problem of Viking age burial reminds us of the debate about Anglo-Saxon burial in the post-Conversion period, which is no less imperfectly understood.[32] The burial evidence is ambiguous; it is not impossible that many more accompanied burials have been lost due to subsequent burials in the graveyard, but caution should be exercised when attributing religious belief on the grounds of the absence or presence of grave-goods, even if their absence makes a persuasive argument for rapid conversion.

Arguments for the integration of natives and Scandinavians based on the corpus of Anglo-Scandinavian sculpture and the nature of Viking-age burial practice are speculative, but they do find some support from other evidence. The coinage of the Danelaw bearing the name of St.Edmund, whom Vikings had murdered and which appeared perhaps as early as the mid-890s, and the names of St.Martin and St.Peter, which were minted at Lincoln and York respectively, indicates that local Scandinavian rulers were at the very least tolerant of Christian ideology, if they were not actively promoting it.[33] Guthfrith's patronage of the community of St.Cuthbert's fits into this context.

Given that we know that the Scandinavian control of half of England was not destined to last, it is easy to overlook the fact that the Vikings did indeed settle and establish political control. This was achieved, in part, through co-operation with leading ecclesiastics who continued to play an important role in political life through the period of Viking settlement. Guthfrith, Olaf Guthfrisson and Eric Bloodaxe all benefited from ecclesiastical support.[34] The unification of England could barely have been foreseen in the early tenth century, and we should not make the mistake of believing that the indigenous population of the Danelaw was awaiting salvation in the shape of the West Saxons. It is hardly surprising that the Church should have come to terms with the invaders; indeed, Archbishop Wulfhere of York seems to have had as much to fear from

---

[31] J. Graham-Campbell, "Pagans and Christians", *History Today* (Oct. 1986), pp. 24-8, at 25.
[32] D.M.Hadley, "The Early Inhumation Cemetery at Bromfield, Shrops", *Trans. of the Shrops.Arch. and Hist.Soc.*, Vol.LXX (1995), pp. 45-54.
[33] *Medieval European Coinage, I, The Early Middle Ages, 5th-10th Centuries* (1986), ed. P. Grierson & M. Blackburn, pp. 319-23.
[34] *EHD*, I, no.1, s.a. 943, 947-8.

native English rulers as he did from Viking leaders.[35] Tales of ecclesiastics fleeing their churches in Kent has done little for the reputation of the Vikings, but perhaps, as Janet Nelson has said, "they fled too soon", since the outcome of this was to enable Alfred to plunder church lands.[36] By contrast, in the Danelaw some of the leading churchmen received patronage from Scandinavian rulers and served as political advisers.

We may have overlooked the extent to which the Scandinavian settlers invested in the region. In many respects the Danelaw appears to have experienced expansion in the late ninth and early tenth centuries. Urban and market centres mushroomed at York, Lincoln, Stamford and Ipswich,[37] and it has been suggested that the Vikings imported continental moneyers and potters into the Danelaw to introduce new techniques and to help accelerate economic growth.[38] Settlement nucleation, the creation of open-field systems and the origins of the hundred system have also been attributed to this period.[39] With the benefit of hindsight it is easy to categorise the period of Scandinavian rule in the Danelaw as transitory, but there is reason to believe that the Scandinavians expected to remain and there is evidence to suggest that they invested heavily in the Danelaw. In this context, much of the corpus of Anglo-Scandinavian sculpture can perhaps be interpreted as yet another example of this investment. The production of the huge body of stone sculpture, as much as the promotion of the cult of St.Edmund[40] and the production of coinage bearing the names of Christian saints, may have been an attempt by Scandinavians both to assimilate to the culture of the region in which they had settled

---

[35]Symeon of Durham, "Letter concerning the Archbishops of York", *Church Historians of England*, Vol.3, pt.2, p. 773.
[36]J. N. Nelson, "A King across the sea" : Alfred in continental perspective", *TRHS*, 5th ser., 36 (1986), pp. 45-68, at 63.
[37]R. Hall, *The Viking Dig* (1984), ch.5;*idem*, "The Five Boroughs of the Danelaw: a review of present knowledge", *Anglo-Saxon England*, 19 (1989), pp. 149-206, at 176-187, 196-200; K.Wade, "Ipswich", *The Rebirth of Towns in the West AD 700-1050*, ed. R. Hodges & B. Hobley, CBA Res. Rep., 68 (1988), pp. 93-101, at 97.
[38]R. Hodges, *The Anglo-Saxon Achievement* (1989), pp. 160-2.
[39]J. G. Hurst, "The Wharram research project: results to 1983", *Medieval Archaeology*, 28 (1984), pp. 77-111; P. Hayes, "Relating Fen Edge sediments, stratigraphy and archaeology near Billingborough, south Lincolnshire", *Palaeoenvironmental Investigations*, ed., N. R. J. Feiller (1985), pp. 245-69; M. Harvey, "Planned field systems in eastern Yorkshire: some thoughts on their origins", *Agricultural History Review*, 31 (1983), pp. 91-103; D. Roffe, "The Lincolnshire Hundred", *Landscape History*, 3 (1981), pp. 27-36; Hodges, *Anglo-Saxon Achievement*, pp. 154-162, 166-77.
[40]S. Ridyard, *The Royal Saints of Anglo-Saxon England* (1988) pp. 211-26.

both to assimilate to the culture of the region in which they had settled and to redress the balance for the atrocities committed by their pagan ancestors.

Given the evidence for Scandinavian patronage of the Church, Julia Barrow has commented that it is surprising that the Danelaw should have been deprived of bishops for so long.[41] She has suggested that the West Saxon kings may have been responsible for depriving the northern regions of bishops; that it was political opportunism which saw the bishop of London given temporary control of East Anglia, the moving of the see of Leicester to Dorchester, and the disappearance of the see of Lindsey. Depriving the Danes of access to the Archbishop of Canterbury who would be required to consecrate new bishops to the north and east of England, Barrow suggests, was a political move by the West Saxons to prevent the Danes from further strengthening their position, and it may have had the double motive of undermining Mercian separatism. Certainly in the tenth century the West Saxon kings appear to have attempted to manipulate the see of York by ensuring that it was held in plurality with a southern see, as a block to the Archbishop indulging in the politics of Northumbrian separatism.[42]

***

Despite the case made above, it is nonetheless commonly recognised that the nature of ecclesiastical organisation in the Danelaw was different from that in regions to the south and west, and this is consistently attributed to the Vikings. The recent development of the so-called "minster model" as a framework for the evolution of the Anglo-Saxon Church has increased this sense of contrast. It emphasises the systematic foundation in the seventh and eighth centuries of churches which, although the composition of their communities may have varied, typically had pastoral responsibilities which they met through defined territories or *parochiae*, which were often of substantial size. This network, it is argued, can be reconstructed using largely late medieval evidence.[43] Existing studies of

---

[41]J. Barrow, "English Cathedral Communities and Reform in the Late Tenth and the Eleventh Centuries", *Anglo-Norman Durham*, ed. D.Rollason *et al.* (1994), pp. 25-39, at 26-39, at 26-29.

[42]Whitelock, "The Dealings of the Kings of England with Northumbria", pp. 73-6.

[43]Blair, "Introduction", pp. 1-2; S.R.Bassett, "In Search of the Origins of Anglo-Saxon Kingdoms", *The Origins of Anglo-Saxon Kingdoms*, ed. *idem* (1989), pp. 3-27, at 18-21.

the post-Conquest period, but whether this results from "genuine regional variation or derives from differing evidence and the pre-conceptions of local studies" is a question that has been asked, but scarcely answered.[44] Parts of the Danelaw do appear to conform to the "minster model"; as has been seen, a number of pre-Viking foundations emerge later as mother-churches serving large parishes. However, where ecclesiastical organisation differs from this pattern of mother-churches and large parishes, it is not helpful to assume that a similar pattern once existed but had been broken up before the earliest documentary sources detailing ecclesiastical organisation become available. Here is not the place to review the "minster model", but there are grounds for suggesting that it is not an appropriate model for analysing the development of ecclesiastical organisation in the Danelaw.

First, evidence from Yorkshire reveals a much more complicated picture of early ecclesiastical organisation, in which churches were founded in the period before the Viking invasions in a number of contexts. Royal and monastic or ecclesiastical foundations at estate centres can be found alongside churches founded on outlying parts of estates; in some parts of Yorkshire early foundations were widely scattered, in others they were densely clustered.[45] Some may have been the dependencies of minsters, of the type that we know existed on the estate of Whitby, for example. Others seem likely to have been aristocratic foundations; there is evidence for the consecration of churches on the estates of thegns, and others may have been of the type that Bede bemoaned.[46] It seems clear that early church foundation and the extent of pastoral care must have depended on the initiative of the local aristocracy, as well as on royal and episcopal support. If middle Saxon foundations provided pastoral care within defined territories – a proposition open to some debate – aristocratic foundations are likely to have served only the founder's estate. It is not surprising, then, that many churches with pre-Viking origins served, at a later date, relatively small parishes. In such cases it would be wholly inappropriate to postulate a model for the loss of "minster" characteristics, including large parishes. Some of the contrasts in the distribution of churches and the nature of ecclesiastical organisation in the period after the Viking invasions derive, in other words, from the distribution of churches of varying origins in the pre-Viking period. As

---

[44]Blair, "Introduction", p. 2.
[45]Morris, *Churches in the Landscape*, pp. 110-139.
[46]*HE*, V, iv-v.

Richard Morris has said, "the idea that all religious communities, royal or comital churches were intended as bases for systematic evangelical action, or that their *parochiae* should give uninterrupted coverage across an entire kingdom, is a modern assumption".[47]

Secondly, although some of the most important mother-churches of the Danelaw were royal or episcopal foundations of great antiquity, and their area of pastoral responsibility may have been framed well before the tenth century around the estate on which the church sat, are we to assume that all superior churches of the post-Conquest period have similar origins? It is clear that the parishes of the region were influenced by the estate structure, and since there is evidence to suggest that some of the territorial sokes described by Domesday Book were relatively recent creations we might consider whether changes to the estate structure similarly caused alterations to ecclesiastical organisation. Furthermore, there is evidence from the southern Danelaw that some churches which display mother-church attributes were founded only in the tenth century, often as part of the West Saxon conquest.[48] Such churches were commonly well-endowed with land and tithes, and we might question whether churches in receipt of tithes from a large area really were particularly ancient, or whether the area from which they received it had long been associated with that church. The manipulation of estates and tithes in the post-Viking period (alongside the foundation of new royal and aristocratic churches) may have significantly altered ecclesiastical organisation. It is suspicious that Grantham (Lincs.) was said to receive the tithes from the wapentakes of Threo and Winnibriggs "in respect of all the sokes and inlands which the king has there", and that Conisbrough and Wragby (Lincs.) received tithe from far-flung places which show no other signs of belonging to their parishes. As a diagnostic feature of important early churches, then, the receipt of tithe is not necessarily a reliable guide to either the antiquity and status of the church concerned or to the extent and antiquity of its parish.

There are a number of churches in Yorkshire and Lincolnshire which in the later Middle Ages display superior characteristics, but for which there is no good evidence for early origins (Osmotherly, Upper Poppleton, Topcliffe, Silkstone, Barnburgh, Hundleby and Withcall, for example). Some of these churches had communities of clergy in the post-

---

[47]Morris, *Churches in the Landscape*, p. 138.
[48]Blair, "Secular Minster Churches", pp. 118-9.

Conquest period and they may be examples of a stratum of secular collegiate churches founded in the late Saxon period. They may, perhaps, have been associated with lords of medium sized estates (since the parishes of such churches commonly extend to five or six townships).[49]

Much of Lincolnshire also fails to correspond to the "minster model", and there are grounds for suggesting that ecclesiastical organisation was dictated by the patterns of secular landholding which developed there in the later Anglo-Saxon period. Numerous early churches are known in Lincolnshire from documentary, sculptural or archaeological evidence,[50] but unlike in other parts of the Danelaw few of these churches display significant mother-church attributes in the post-Conquest period. This dichotomy has traditionally been explained as the result of the destruction of earlier monastic communities during the Viking invasions, after which their pastoral work and nascent parishes were usurped by later foundations.[51] Another interpretation is possible, however, which starts from the premise that pastoral provision and the distribution of churches in Lincolnshire developed differently from that in other parts of the Danelaw because the estate structure of much of Lincolnshire was different. Large estates in Lincolnshire commonly comprise only portions of vills and regularly overlap with other estates; this contrasts with other parts of the northern Danelaw where estates comprising whole vills are more common. The implications of this for ecclesiastical provision are manifold. Vills which belonged *in toto* to a larger estate are unlikely to have had a church beyond the level of a chapel of the church at the estate centre, since there would have been no opportunity for another lord to found an estate church. However, on estates which comprised only parts of vills lords may not have thought it necessary to provide churches other than at the estate centre when they only had an interest in a few of the inhabitants of outlying vills. Moreover the opportunity for other lords to found churches in those vills was much greater, and it is notable that in a number of cases a church is recorded in Domesday Book not on the sokeland in a vill which pertained to a distant

---

[49]Morris, *Churches in the Landscape*, p. 135.
[50]D. Stocker, "The Early Church in Lincolnshire", *Pre-Viking Lindsey*, ed. A. Vince (1993), pp. 101-22; B. Whitwell, "Flixborough", *Current Archaeology*, 126 (1991), pp. 244-7.
[51]D. M. Owen, "Medieval Chapels in Lincolnshire", *Lincolnshire History and Archaeology*, 10 (1975), pp. 15-22; idem, *Church and Society in Medieval Lincolnshire* (1971), p. 1.

manor, but on a separate manor within that vill.⁵² The absence of significant royal patronage of ecclesiastical communities in Lincolnshire contributed to their declining fortunes; doubtless it prevented many from preserving or developing large parishes and it left them prey to neighbouring East Anglian houses which were not averse to stealing relics from them. Clearly, then, the Viking invasions were but one of many factors that shaped ecclesiastical organisation in the Danelaw.

Furthermore, the resources of the Church were not diminished solely by the Scandinavian invaders. For example, St.Cuthbert's community lost some of its land when one of its tenants fell in battle against the Viking Ragnaeld who took his lands.⁵³ We can only surmise the extent to which the difficult circumstances which the Viking invasions undoubtedly created enabled tenants to usurp the land which they held from the Church. The Scandinavian settlement did not instigate a one-way flow of land away from the Church. The best documented ecclesiastical community in the Danelaw, that of St.Cuthbert's, was rewarded with land in return for suggesting Guthfrith as king of the local Vikings, and it regained the land taken by the Viking Onlafbal following the battles of Corbridge (914 and 918) when he died. The strategic interests of successive West Saxon kings as they sought to extend their control over the region were also instrumental in defining the fortunes of the Church in the Danelaw. Undoubtedly, the strategic value of the community of St.Cuthbert's at Chester-le-Street will not have been lost on Athelstan when he endowed the community in 934; it proved a useful ally in the succeeding battle with the Scots. Meanwhile, the value of having an Archbishop of York who would remain loyal to West Saxon overlords in the face of Scandinavian rulers in York and in defiance of the Northumbrian desire for independence was presumably a factor which persuaded Athelstan to make a large grant of land in Amounderness (which he had acquired with his own money) to Archbishop Wulfstan of York.⁵⁴ On the whole, however, the patronage of the Church by tenthcentury English kings was much less generous in the north than in southern, western and eastern England. Part of the explanation is clearly political; royal resources and patronage were generally more densely

---

⁵²Examples include the churches of Searby, Bigby, Grasby and Hackthorn.
⁵³*EHD*, I, no.4; see also, C. D. Morris, "Northumbria and the Viking Settlement: the evidence for landholding", *Archaeologia Aeliana*, ser. V, 4 (1977), pp. 81-103.
⁵⁴Whitelock, "The Dealings of the Kings of England with Northumbria",pp. 70-2.

distributed in southern England in the tenth and eleventh centuries.[55] It is suspicious that successive Archbishops of York appointed by the southern English kings were commonly of a monastic background (and included one of the greatest of reformers, Oswald) yet were apparently singularly unsuccessful at reviving monasticism in the north of England. Whatever the commitment of the house of Wessex and their aristocracy to the monastic lobby, they did not refrain from endowing secular communities. Could it be that one reason why monasticism was not revitalised in the north was that it was not sufficiently close to the hub of court politics in the late tenth century? Without this factor there was little need for the king, his bishops or the aristocracy to over-exert themselves in the monastic interest in the northern Danelaw.

We should also not forget that some religious houses suffered depredations at the hands of the West Saxon kings of England and other, better patronised, houses; the loss of relics to houses in Wessex, western Mercia and East Anglia appears to be symptomatic of the fate of many houses in the Danelaw (including Bardney, Repton and Ripon). Hanbury (Staffs.), which is on the edge of the Danelaw, provides an interesting example of the fate of a religious house at the hands of the Vikings and, subsequently, the West Saxons. A chronicle which appears to have been written at Hanbury after the Vikings had been raiding in the area (perhaps written after 873-4 when a Viking army wintered at neighbouring Repton) suggests that the community survived the experience and retained the relics of St.Werburgh; the loss of the relics can be attributed more obviously to Æthelflaed, who seems to have transferred them to Chester, which may help to explain the demise of the community at Hanbury.[56]

Although large and wealthy communities were rare in the Danelaw in the tenth and eleventh centuries, and the Church appears to have held comparatively little land, it does not necessarily follow that the Church in that region was moribund. This is belied by the proliferation of local churches in the later tenth and eleventh centuries,[57] and ordinary (manorial or village) churches are much more common, as a rule, the

---

[55]The density of towns and mints, for example, mirror the distribution of wealthy and well-endowed churches. See, for example, Hodges, *The Anglo-Saxon Achievement*, pp. 155-166; M. Dolley & M. Metcalf, "The Reform of the English coinage under Edgar", *Anglo-Saxon Coins*, ed. R. H. M. Dolley (1961), pp. 136-68.
[56] D. W. Rollason, *The Mildrith Legend: A Study in Early Medieval Hagiography* (1981), pp. 26-8.
[57] P. Stafford, *The East Midlands in the Early Middle Ages* (1984) pp. 184-7.

further eastwards and northwards we move in Domesday Book.[58] The fragmentation of tenure within many vills in Lincolnshire, as in East Anglia, appears to have encouraged church founding and many vills have more than one church, each attached to a separate manor in the vill. Competitive church-building may have been a result of the region's social structure. As Williamson has suggested questions of status may have been very acute in a region in which there was a complex gradation between "lords" and "peasants", and church-building may have been an expression of status.[59] We should not assume that only lords built churches; in one case there is explicit evidence in Domesday Book for the foundation of a church by a group of free neighbours.[60] Such activity, combined with the absence of royal patronage of major houses, must have served to prevent many churches from protecting and consolidating sizeable parishes. This pattern is suggestive of significant lay patronage of the Church, but not at the level of the minster church so much as at the township or village level, or even at the manorial level in the cases where multiple churches are found in single villages. Equally, it is in the Danelaw that the greatest numbers of urban churches are to be found in the later Middle Ages; by 1100 Lincoln possessed perhaps as many as thirty-seven churches and Norwich some forty-six churches and chapels.[61] Most of these churches had their own parishes and full rights to perform pastoral functions for their parishioners. This contrasts with the west Midlands where there were generally fewer urban churches and where it was not uncommon for towns to be dominated by a single mother-church which might restrict burial to itself.[62] This contrast suggests that the laity may have played a more active role in church foundation in the towns of the Danelaw. That is not to say that the ecclesiastical hierarchy entirely approved of this religious enthusiasm. In the *Northumbrian Priests' Laws* and the *Canons Enacted under King Edgar* criticism was made of the integration of the clergy into secular society.[63] Yet this was a region in which lay enthusiasm for the Church was unrivalled.

---

[58] Blair, "Secular minsters", pp. 112-3.
[59] T. Williamson, *The Origins of Norfolk* (1993) p. 158.
[60] P. Warner, "Shared churchyards, freemen church-builders and the development of parishes in eleventh-century East Anglia", *Landscape History*, 8 (1986), pp. 39-52, at 42; F.Barlow, *The English Church, 1000-1066* (1963), p. 193.
[61] Morris, *Churches in the Landscape*, pp. 169-173.
[62] C. N. L. Brooke, "The missionary at home: the church in the towns 1000-1256", *Studies in Church History*, IV (1970), pp. 59-83.
[63] *EHD*, I, no.128; *Wulfstan's Canons of Edgar*, ed. R. Fowler, Early English Text Society, 266 (1972).

***

Ecclesiastical organisation in the Danelaw was shaped by a number of factors, including the nature of pre-Viking ecclesiastical organisation, the Viking invasions and the West Saxon conquest, the estate structure and the peculiar social structure of the region. Apparent examples of continuity in ecclesiastical organisation can be found, but there also appears to have been a significant period of change and development in the tenth century only part of which can be directly associated with the Vikings. The lack of wealthy churches with large communities in Domesday Book in the northern Danelaw presents a distorted picture of the vitality of the Church. Although few of the post-Conquest churches of the northern Danelaw had substantial communities or possessions, it was nonetheless the case that many of them had wide-ranging parochial functions. The role of mother-churches was, and long remained, instrumental in dictating the development of pastoral care in many parts of the northern Danelaw. That the territories for which they provided pastoral care survived in some instances from the before the Viking invasions – even if the precise nature of pastoral care did not remain constant – is made plausible by the fact that the churches concerned have pre-Viking origins and their later medieval parishes reflect secular territorial organisation which can be traced in some cases back to the early tenth century. It is also clear, however, that this pattern is not characteristic of all parts of the Danelaw. In parts of Yorkshire, Lincolnshire and East Anglia the special circumstances of the estate structure and of the social structure, combined with an absence of patronage of major houses in the tenth century resulted in the proliferation of local churches. The failure of the Danelaw to meet the criteria established by the "minster model" does not, I would suggest, add support to the argument that the Vikings destroyed the fabric of ecclesiastical organisation in the Danelaw. Indeed, there is evidence to suggest that as a diagnostic model it is wholly inappropriate to the Danelaw; and its applicability to other regions must remain an open question.

Clearly the economic position of the Church in the Danelaw was threatened by the events of the late ninth to eleventh centuries. Although it may seem paradoxical our evidence suggests that the Church continued to function institutionally even though it was impoverished, seemingly through local lay patronage and piety. This paper does not seek to absolve the Vikings of all blame It would be foolish to deny that the Viking invasions posed a real as well as an imagined threat to the Anglo-Saxon Church. However, it is clear that this is not the whole story, and that the traditional image of the Vikings requires qualification. In particular, this image cannot be supported by the fact that ecclesiastical organisation in the Danelaw was different from that in midland and southern England.

Runic Inscriptions, Liturgy and Eschatology

Per Beskow

Inscriptions made with runes are the oldest Christian monuments in Scandinavia. They have often been made on standing stones but also appear on wood and on various objects. The majority of the rune-stones are evidently of Christian origin, which is evident from the big decorative crosses. Many of the inscriptions on the rune-stones include Christian prayers for the souls of the deceased, with phrases like: "May God (or Christ, or the Mother of God or Michael) help his/her soul." In this lecture I want to analyse these prayer formulas and investigate which beliefs they express.

Prayers for the soul

There is a consensus among modern historians that the Christian rune-stones were erected along the roads, and that one of their functions was to remind the by-passers of the deceased persons and request them for their intercessions. Praying for the dead was not part of pre-Christian Norse beliefs; it was a custom brought to Scandinavia by the Christian missionaries, and the runic inscriptions clearly demonstrate how fast it took root among the population.

It has sometimes been suggested that the prayer formulas would express an indigenous, Nordic interpretation of Christianity, or that they might have been influenced by Byzantine Christianity, carried to Scandinavia along the trade routes over the Baltic and along the Russian rivers. But the truth seems to be far more simple. The formulas seem most likely to have been derived from the Christian vocabulary brought to Scandinavia by missionaries from Northern England and/or Hamburg-Bremen.

The greater part of the earliest Christian vocabulary in Scandinavia consists of loan-words from Anglo-Saxon, continental Saxon and Frisian, which is clearly shown in the runic inscriptions. This also applies to the prayers for the souls of the deceased, which contain obvious references to the Latin liturgy, especially to the Mass for the dead. These short and simple prayers have probably been formulated on the Continent or in England and have been carried to Scandinavia by the missionaries. The decoration of the runestones continues the old Viking tradition – although sometimes with Christian motives – but the content of the prayers themselves has certainly been imported from abroad.[1]

Helpers of the soul

Usually the soul or spirit of the deceased (*saul, sal, sol, sel, sil* etc., *ant, at, ot* etc. respectively) are mentioned in the prayers. These two words seem to be used synonymously without any metaphysical distinction between spirit and soul. This concept of the soul/spirit is obviously of Christian origin and has no counter-part – philologically or ideologically – in pre-Christian Scandinavia. The prayers are said for the soul of the deceased, not for the person as a whole, which makes it clear that the soul is considered to have left the body in death and is treated as a separate entity. On the other hand, the resurrection on the day of judgment is never mentioned in the runic inscriptions. These two features – the separation of soul and body, and the lack of references to the final resurrection – entirely correspond to the formulas of the Masses for the dead: they contain a great number of prayers for the salvation of the soul (*anima*) of the deceased, while there are no references to the resurrection of the dead. This has been the custom until our time; it was only the Roman Missal of 1969 that began to emphasize the resurrection of the dead in the requiem Masses.

As the runic inscriptions indicate, the souls of the dead are believed to be in need of helpers. A common formula is: "May God and the Mother of God help his/her soul", a phrase unknown elsewhere. That Mary is referred to as "the Mother of God" is only to be expected. This expression is no proof of a Byzantine influence, which has sometimes been suggested. "Mother of God" is a well-known name for the Virgin Mary in the West Germanic languages, as in Old English (*Se halige Godes modor*), and in Middle Dutch (*Gods moeder*). Both correspond to Latin *Dei Genetrix*, "God-bearer" (which is has in turn been derived from the Greek

---

[1] Per Beskow, Runor och liturgi, *Nordens kristnande i europeiskt perspektiv, Tre uppsatser av Per Beskow och Reinhart Staats* (= Occasional Papers on Mediæval Topics 7), Skara 1994, pp. 16-35. I am preparing a more extensive essay on this subject.

Theotokos), an expression common in Latin liturgical language during the centuries preceding the conversion of the North.

The Virgin Mary has no prominent position in the Masses for the dead, but she was no doubt a central figure in the Christian faith as preached by the missionaries. In Old Swedish she is often referred to as a "helper" (corresponding to Latin *adiutrix*), and she was also invoked in the hour of death, as in *The Book of Nunnaminster,* a Latin prayerbook from *circa* 800:

> Sancta Maria gloriosa Dei genetrix et semper virgo... esto mihi pia dominatrix, et cordis mei inluminatrix, et adiutrix apud Deum Patrem omnipotentem, ut ueniam delictorum meorum accipere, et inferni tenebras euadere, et ad uitam æternam peruenire merear.[2]
>
> "Holy Mary, glorious Mother of God and ever virgin... be to me a kind patroness and enlightener of my heart and helper before God, the Father Almighty, so that I may receive forgiveness for my offences and escape the darkness of hell and attain to eternal life."

More unfamiliar to us is the common expression "God and the Mother of God". When God is mentioned in a Christian context without any further specification, the word generally refers to the Father, not to Christ, who is obviously referred to in these phrases. There was however a common tendency in the age of the Scandinavian mission, which may be named *christomonism*. For the missionaries it was necessary to emphasize the unity of God in contrast to the beliefs of Norse polytheism. Preaching about God and his Son as two distinct entities would immediately lead to serious misunderstandings. Therefore it became a trend in Christian language to identify them both completely. "You shall believe that Christ is the Creator of heaven and earth and of all men", said Saint Olav to Arnljot, according to Snorri Sturlason. Or, as it is expressed by one of the ancient Swedish laws (*Söder-mannalagen*) in a sentence, which is of course theologically absurd:

---

[2]Mary Clayton, *The Cult of the Virgin Mary in Anglo-Saxon England* (=Cambridge Studies in Anglo-Saxon England 2), Cambridge 1990, p. 98.

> "Every Christian man who wants to bear the name of Christ, shall believe in Christ alone, that he is sovereign in divinity and threefold in name, Father, Son and Holy Spirit."

The common word for the Lord in the runic inscriptions is *Drotten* (corresponding to Anglo-Saxon *dryhtin*), which here refers to God as well as to Christ. The name of the Church of St. Drotten in Lund probably corresponded to "Christ Church" in other places (such as Canterbury), but when it was later named *Sanctæ Trinitatis,* there was probably no feeling that the *patrocinium* of the church had been changed.

But let us return to the supernatural helpers of the soul. The belief that the soul is led to heaven by angels has its origin in the parable of the rich man and Lazarus (Luke 22), where it is said that the poor man died and was carried by angels to Abraham's bosom. In early Christian literature, the idea of angels as leaders of the soul are very common. Michael often functions as a *psychopomp,* corresponding to the role of Hermes in pre-Christian Antiquity. This very ancient concept appears sometimes in the runic inscriptions, as in the formula *Mihel kati at hans,* "May Michael take care of his spirit". This expression has a close parallel in a formula belonging to the Mass for the dead. The Offertory of the Requiem Mass, *Domine Jesu Christe* (used until the liturgy reform of 1969) runs as following:

> Domine Jesu Christe, Rex gloriæ, libera animas omnium fidelium defunctorum de pænis inferni, et de profundo lacu; libera eas de ore leonis, ne absorbeat eas tartarus, ne cadant in obscurum; sed signifer sanctus Michaël repræsentet eas in lucem sanctam; quam olim Abrahæ promisisti et semini ejus.
> "O Lord Jesus Christ, deliver the souls of all the faithful departed from the pains of hell and from the deep pit; deliver them from the lion's mouth, that hell may not swallow them up, and may they not fall into darkness; but may the holy standard-bearer, Michael, lead them into the holy light, which you promised to Abraham and to his seed of old."

An Icelandic prayer from the 14th century shows how the belief in Michael as a leader of souls prevailed also in the late Middle Ages:

> I pray to you in love, holy Archangel Michael, you who have the power to receive the souls, that you may receive my soul when it is carried away from my body. Guard it against the power of the enemy, so that it may pass the gates of hell and the streets of darkness, so that it is not hindered by the lion or the dragon which carries the spirit to hell or leads it to eternal suffering. I pray to you, o Lord, my God Almighty, to send me your holy Angel for my rescue.[3]

The holy light appears in the expression "light and paradise" in several inscriptions such as:

> [Kr]istr lati kumo ot tumo i lus yk baratisi yk i þon em besta kristnum.
> "May Christ let Tumo's spirit come into light and paradise and into the best world for Christians."

It seems evident that these two words refer to the beginning and the end of the Latin liturgy of the dead respectively. The Mass for the dead began with the Introit *Requiem æternam:*

> Requiem æternam dona eis, Domine, et lux perpetua luceat eis.
> "Eternal rest give them, o Lord, and let perpetual light shine upon them."

This prayer has been inspired by the Vulgate text of 4 Ezra 2:34f: *requiem æternitatis dabit vos,* "He will give you the rest of eternity" and *lux perpetua lucebit vobis,* "eternal light will shine upon you". The two first chapters of 4 Ezra are only known in a Latin version; in the Eastern Churches they are unknown, as is also the liturgical formula *Requiem æternam.* This formula occurs in North African epitaphs from the 6th century and was soon to be commonly used in the liturgy of the dead, as in the texts gathered by Dom Claude Gay.[4] *Requiem æternam* is most

---

[3]Quoted from Fredrik Paasche, *Møtet mellom hedendom og kristendom i Norden,* ed. by Dag Strömbäck, Oslo 1958, p. 31f.
[4]Dom Claude Gay, O.S.B., Formulaires anciens pour la messe des défunts, *Études grégoriennes* 2 (1957) s. 83-129 Important for the study of the Mass for the dead and the burial liturgy in the Middle Ages is Damien Sicard, *La liturgie de la mort dans l'église latine des origines à la réforme carolingienne* (=Liturgiewissenschaftliche Quellen und

commonly used as Introit but also appears as a Gradual. *Lux æterna luceat eis,* Domine ("May light eternal shine upon them, o Lord") is a frequent Communion verse in the Mass for the dead. The phrase *Locus refrigerii, lucis et pacis,* "a place of happiness, light and peace" appears in the prayer for the departed (*Memento etiam*) in the Canon of the Roman Mass. In the liturgy, light is thus a well established metaphor for eternal life, and is often put into contrast with the darkness of hell.

The word *paradise* (the gender of which is not evident in the runic in-scriptions but which is a neuter in later Old Swedish) has probably come to Scandinavia from continental Germanic languages, and not from Anglo-Saxon, where it is a masculine. It occurs only twice in the New Testament referring to the heavenly world: in Jesus' word to the good thief on the cross (Luke 23:43): "Today you shall be with me in paradise" and in St. Paul's statement (2 Cor. 12:4) that he was "taken up to paradise". In later Christian tradition the word "paradise" in this sense is far more frequent.

In the Latin liturgy of the dead, paradise was a recurring word. When the deceased person was taken to his grave after the Mass, the antiphon was sung: *In paradisum deducant te angeli,* "May the angels lead you into paradise." This liturgical formula is one of the oldest parts of the Roman burial liturgy, and the loan-word "paradise" in the runic inscriptions has certainly been derived from this phrase. The first example of paradise in Old Swedish is found in an ancient law, called *Västgötalagen* (IV:16), in the sentence: *Än hälhir änglär tokowið sial hans oc förðþo hanä til paradis,* "that rather angels took his soul and lead it into paradise", which is a direct allusion to the antiphon mentioned. The two words "light" and "paradise" are thus a summing-up of the prayers for the deceased at his/her funeral. This gives us a clear picture of the process in which the liturgy functioned as a transmitter of Christian beliefs.

The Journey of the Soul

In the Christian inscriptions on rune-stones there is nothing which might indicate the survival of pre-Christian ideas about the life after death or the other world. It is an entirely Christian universe that we encounter in these inscriptions. But this universe cannot be simply described as "mediaeval",

---

Forschungen, Veröffentlichen des Abt-Herwegen-Instituts der Abtei Maria Laach), Münster 1978.

as the eschatological ideas were in a state of change during the whole of this period.

First of all, the prayers in the runic inscriptions cannot be connected with the belief in purgatory, because this belief did not yet exist at this time. As the French historian Jacques Le Goff has shown, the belief in purgatory was not fully developed until about 1170, and it would probably last a considerable time until it was generally accepted in Scandinavia.[5] Purgatory in Le Goffs's sense presupposes three elements, which occur in earlier literature but seldom together: the spacial concept of a place where the souls dwell for some time; its purpose of cleansing the souls before their entrance into heaven; and the idea of the cleansing as a fire. Expressed in this explicit way, purgatory does not appear until the 12th century. Le Goff's account, however, has some serious flaws. He leaves out the 11th century, which is of special interest for us here, and, most important, he does not give us a clear concept of the beliefs about life after death which were common in the period before the belief Purgatory took roots, although such beliefs often appear in his own material.

From the 7th century onwards, there was a common belief in what we may call "the journey of the soul".[6] The soul of the dead person was believed to take on a dangerous journey to the other world. This belief has a long history with roots in the religions of Antiquity and is often mentioned in early Christian literature. The *Dialogues* of St. Gregory the Great, however, gave this belief a new life in the Western Church. An entire literature was created with stories describing experiences of such journeys. Some of these narratives have a strange similarity to reports on near-death-experiences in our own time. During a severe illness, the narrator has found that his soul has left the body and is on its way to the other world. It is conducted by angels or saints, it sees the pains of hell and gets a glimpse of the eternal happiness of the righteous, and finally it is drawn back into his body again. In the *History* of St. Bede the Venerable there are two such accounts (told by Fursey and Drycthelm

---

[5]Jacques Le Goff, *La naissance du purgatoire,* Éd. Gallimard 1981; English translation by Arthur Goldhammer, *The Birth of Purgatory,* Chicago 1984, Paperback ed. 1986.
[6]On the journey of the soul in general, see Alfons Rosenberg, *Die Seelenreise,* Olten und Freiburg i. Br. 1952. On accounts of such journeys, see Carol Zaleski, *Otherworld Journeys: Accounts of Near-Death Experiences in Medieval and Modern Times,* Oxford 1987. On visionary literature in Scandinavia, see Dag Strömbäck, Resan till den andra världen: Kring medeltidsvisionerna och Draumkvædet, *Saga och sed* 1976, pp. 15-29; *idem*, Visionsdiktning, *Kulturhistoriskt lexikon för nordisk medeltid,* vol. 20, Malmö 1976, coll. 171-186.

respectively.). St. Boniface mentions a similar story in a letter, written about 717. In his *Vita Anskarii* (written after 865), Rimbert tells us that St. Ansgar had a similar experience in his youth.

During the 12th century new stories were added to this literature: the vision of Alberic from Monte Cassino, the English vision of Tundalus and the vision of Owein with its account of St. Patrick's purgatory. More popular versions (from the end of the 12th century and the beginning of the 13th) are the North German vision of Godschalk and the English vision of Thurkill. Some of this literature was soon translated to Nordic languages and influenced the beliefs in Scandinavia.

A bridge for the soul

In this literature, the road to heaven is described as long and weary. The soul has to pass through thorns or flames of fire, and over a turbulent river, sometimes on a bridge, which is broad for the righteous but narrow and slippery for the sinners. The bridge is a puzzling element in these stories. The belief in such a bridge to heaven is part of ancient Iranian religion (the Çinvat bridge), but it is unknown in the early Church and in the Christian East. Is it perhaps an Old Germanic belief of early Indo-European origin, which has survived in Christian England during the centuries preceding the Christianization of the North. In the pre-Christian religion of Scandinavia there was a belief in the *Gjallar* bridge, which the dead had to pass, but it cannot be excluded that this belief has been influenced by Christian ideas. The bridge of the soul appears in the *History of the Franks* by Gregory of Tours (IV.33) and in the *Dialogues* of St. Gregory the Great (IV.37). The name of the *Gjallar* bridge still appears in the Norse *Draumkvæde* (which is probably late mediaeval), and it is still referred to by a Swedish Lutheran writer of the 17th century as an example of Catholic superstition.

In the late Middle Ages, the motif of the bridge could be combined with that of purgatory, as in the *Lyke-Wake Dirge* from Yorkshire:

> From Whinny-Moor that thou mayst pass
> Every night and awle,
> To Brig o' Dread thou comest at last,
> And Christ receive thy sawle.

> From Brig o' Dread, na brader than a thread,
> Every night and awle,
> To purgatory fire thou com'st at last,
> And Christ receive thy sawle.

In about a hundred runic inscriptions from Sweden it is mentioned that the deceased person has built a bridge, an act which must have been considered to be an especially good deed at a time when the Church was being established and the roads were becoming important means of communication. From the 11th century onwards, such a work were reckoned as an act of mercy and "a redemption of the soul". In Swedish texts they are sometimes referred to as *salubot* (cf. lat. *salus animæ*, "redemption of the soul"). In many cases it is said that someone has built a bridge for his soul or for the (spirit and) soul of a departed relative. (*fyriR hans salu, fyriR and ok salu þæira*). These inscriptions are thus related to the prayers for the soul, such as:

> Lifstæinn let gærva ser til sialubotaR ok sinni kunu Ingirun ok sinum sunum Iarun[d]r ok Nikulas ok Luþinn broan.
> Lifstein had these bridges built as a redemption of the soul for himself and for his wife Ingerun and his sons Jorund and Nikulas and Luthinn.

This is certainly to be understood in a very concrete way. To construct a bridge with the intention for your own soul or for a the soul of a relative was a guarantee that the soul would be able to pass the bridge to paradise.[7]

One could imagine that such an ideal could be found in ecclesiastical literature from this time, but the evidence is scarce. There is, however, a homily attributed to Archbishop Wulfstan of York (d. 1023), where this motif appears, though not in connection with the journey of the soul but with its fate on the day of judgment (*domes dæg*).

> wa ðæs mannes sawle, e betynð his duru ongean godes þearfan
> for ðam þingon, þæt hine lærð se deofol; swa him bið betyned

---

[7] On the otherworld bridge and bridge-building, see Peter Dinzelbacher, *Die Jenseitsbrücke im Mittelalter* (Dissertationen der Universität Wien 104) Vienna 1973. Peter Dizelbacher & Harald Kleinschmidt, Seelenbrücke und Brückenbau im mittelalterlichen England, *Numen* 31 (1984), pp. 242-287. On these concepts in Scandinavia, cf. Aslak Liestøl, Innskrifta på Eiksteinen, *Stavangers Museums Årbok* 1972, pp. 67-76.

heofona rices duru ongean on domes dæge. ac beon we æfre cumliðe; ure sawel bið Cristes cuma on þam forhtigendan domes dæge. utan lufjan ure cyrican, forðam heo bið, ure friðjend an werigend wið þæt micele fyr on domes dæg. and wyrcan we simle brycge an þa betan. ðeah se man nime ænne stan and lecge on fûl sloh, þæt se ælmesman mæge mid þam oðrum fet steppan on ða clænan healfe, þæt him bið micel ælmesse and micel med for gode. eac beðearf seo sawel on domes dæg rihtes weges and clænes and staðolfæstre brycge ofer þone glideran weg hellewites brogan.

"Woe to that soul which closes his door to his duty against God because of those things which the devil has taught him. In the same way will the door of the kingdom of heaven be closed to him on the day of judgement. And let us always be hospitable. Our soul will be the guest of Christ on the terrible day of judgment. Let us love our Church, for it will be our protector and defender against the great fire on the day of judgment. And let us always build bridges and maintain them. You should therefore take a stone and put it on the foul mud, so that the almsman may walk with his other foot on the clean half (of the road), so that he may receive many alms and much reward from God. Also the soul will need a straight road on the day of judgment and a clean and steady bridge over the slippery road of hell."

Similar thoughts are expressed in a penitential rule from the same time, preserved in one single manuscript (Corpus Christi, Cambridge, 201). Different forms of penitence here mentioned are building a church and, if possible, donating a piece of land as a building site, but also facilitating for people to travel on bridges over deep waters and muddy roads (*godiges folces fær med bricgum ofer deôpe wæteru and ofer fûle wegas*) and being willing to give *Godes þances* (to do it in order to be rewarded by God in the future). Good deeds can be made on behalf of one's own soul or of somebody else's soul.

Both these Anglo-Saxon texts conform to the runic inscriptions insofar as they refer to works for the benefit of everyone, including the building of bridges. Peter Dinzelbacher and Harald Kleinschmidt cautiously suggest that this idea was brought to England from Denmark during the period of Danish rule. Their main argument is the fact the building of bridges as good deeds was far more prevalent in Scandinavia than in England.

There are, however, reasons for taking an opposite view, that this idea originated in England and was brought to Scandinavia by the missionaries. The political and social situation in these areas was quite different. In England, the building of bridges was a duty prescribed by the King (*brycgbôt*), before as well as after the Norman conquest. It was a heavy burden, which the Church opposed, and there was little opportunity for private initiatives. In Scandinavia, however, there were no such official duties, and it was possible to understand the building of bridges as a penitential act or as a voluntary good deed. If Wulfstan is the author of the homily, he may have had Scandinavians in mind, as he was himself involved in the Nordic mission.

Building a bridge for somebody's soul implies that the soul is believed to be an entity, separable from the body, and that it has to pass a bridge, as in St. Gregory's *Dialogues* and in other accounts of otherworld journeys. These concepts have been carried to Scandinavia by the Christian mission, and quite possibly from England. *Godes þances*, the expression we have seen in the Corpus Christi manuscript, also appears in a Norwegian runic inscription from Eik (in the form *kouspaka*) and is certainly a loan from Anglo-Saxon. This confirms that the idea of a reward for good deeds is not an indigenous idea but has been brought to Scandinavia by the missionaries.

Conclusions

When two culture meet and finally merge, it is to be expected that both parts make their proper contribution to the new synthesis. The expansion of Christianity and the conversion of various peoples has always resulted in the formation of new patterns of thoughts. This is certainly valid also in the conversion of Scandinavia, but which are the specifically Nordic contributions?

In Scandinavia, the Western Latin Church was the dominant partner, which greatly influenced both culture and society. Denmark, which was first to accept Christianity, has a rich source-material, indicating how fast this kingdom was incorporated into Christian Europe. In Sweden, the sources are more scarce, but the success of the mission is evident. Between the destruction of the pagan temple in Uppsala (*circa* 1080) and the formation of the archbishopric (*circa* 1164) there was less than a century, and there may have been some who had the chance of experiencing both these events. The Church had a greatest impact on the ruling class and in the more densely populated areas. The many parish churches from the early 12th century an onwards are a clear indicator of this success. But also from the 11th century, there is a plenty of archeological evidence, remains of wooden churches and of Christian tombs, showing that the Church was well established in some areas already in the period of the rune-stones.

Christian beliefs soon replaced the old Norse religion. Before Baptism, the old beliefs had to be renounced and the new faith confessed. The Christian believer did not only belong to his family or his people but also to the Catholic Church, and had to share its faith. The liturgy was an important means of instruction, probably far more common than expositions of the Bible.

Specifically Nordic features are obvious in the social structure of mediæval Scandinavia, such as the role of the king or of the thing, as well as in the ideas of law and justice (such as ownership and inheritance). But theologically the Church soon took control. The knowledge of writing – also the use of runes – became largely a business of the clergy, which also decided what was to be written down. Pre-Christian beliefs survived in oral tradition but seldom in written material. This was also the situation in Norway and Iceland, where the memories of Viking culture has been better preserved than in Denmark and Sweden. The poems of the scalds and the Edda-works of Snorri Sturlason contain many references to pre-Christian culture but belong themselves to a mediæval Christian universe.

The Scandinavian languages were (and are) part of the Germanic group and shared in the vocabulary of the Anglo-Saxons and of the continental Germanic peoples long before the Christianization of the North. These languages were more close to one another in those days, and it was fairly easy to communicate with words. As we have seen, a great deal of Christian vocabulary in Scandinavia has been taken over from West Germanic languages, and its most important transmitters were the men of the Church, not tradesmen or vikings. Some of the Nordic features in mediæval Christianity seem to be results of a conscious pastoral strategy.

The fate of man after death was obviously an important question for the first generations of Christians, reflected also in the change of burial customs. With the Christian faith came the hope for eternal life, which was one of the attractive features of the new faith. But the promise of eternal life was not unconditional. Good deeds, masses and prayers for the departed were a condition for the happy journey of the soul to heaven. St. Gregory's *Dialogues* inspired to an imagery of the beyond, which developed into a rich popular literature. The prayers in the runic inscriptions show us how the important these concepts have been in the first Christian generations of the North.

Part II

The Reformation

Late Medieval England:
Road to Reformation, or Road to Deformation?

Robert N. Swanson

At the heart of recent controversy on England's Reformation lies a simple question: Reformation from above, or from below?[1] If from above, as "revisionists" argue, the religious changes under Henry VIII, Edward VI, and Elizabeth I were a Deformation, the emergence of a revised catholicism under Mary I the "real" Reformation. If from below, late medieval catholicism was a religion of externals, its participants mere automata who conformed while desiring something different. This paper lacks the ambition – or recklessness – to try to resolve the issues. It simply looks at the evolution of religious practices in late medieval England, and tries to suggest how that evolution might have continued.

***

Undeniably, the Reformation happened. At issue, however, is whether it was the logical culmination of widespread spiritual developments. The Reformation's occurrence imposes a perspective consciously or unconsciously driven by hindsight, which affects all attitudes to and interpretations of the period and imposes a sense of obligation to justify its happening. A different approach is applied here: if the dramatic events of the Henrician Reformation were not absolutely inevitable and predestined, how was English religion evolving before 1530? When Parliament assembled in 1529, was the Protestant rejection of catholic stances on so many issues bound to take hold; or was it more likely that England would remain catholic (whatever that might actually mean)?

Alongside that question of evolution – towards reformation or deformation – the type of reform to be implemented also demands attention. The emphasis on religious evolution means that structural changes need little consideration. Whilst undoubtedly important, from a late medieval perspective many aspects of the Reformation changes are

---

[1] But cf. A.G. Dickens, *Late monasticism and the Reformation* (London and Rio Grande, 1994), p. 129.

irrelevant, because they need not be theologically partisan. Some were, like the elimination of chantries, monasticism, and papal headship; but selective dissolutions of chantries and religious houses, and even extensive opposition to interventionist papal jurisdiction, were traditional features of ecclesiastical evolution.[2] The structural changes proposed and almost implemented by Thomas Wolsey were just as radical as the essentially catholic Parliamentary reform programme advocated by Christopher St German in 1531.[3] Fifteenth-century English bishops seemingly had notions of collegiality and independence of Rome which recalled ideas of earlier centuries;[4] yet they did not feel compelled to quit the papal church.

The difference between reformation and deformation would lie in the latent theological and spiritual evolutions. "Reformation" would let the ecclesiological and theological guidelines remain, but change the emphases (exactly how is of no immediate concern); "deformation" would bring a radical rejection of the received formats and formulations and a novelly different religion. This may raise questions of possible differentiations and distinctions between "élite/clerical" and "popular/lay" religions; but those cannot be addressed here.[5]

***

A major problem with late medieval catholicism (not confined to analyses of English religion) is a general, tacit assumption that it can actually be pinned down. The idea that the whole of the period's religious experience should be seen as "traditional" religion has much to recommend it, by

---

[2]M.D. Knowles, *The religious orders in England*, 3 vols (Cambridge, 1948-61), ii, pp. 163-5, iii, pp. 157-8, 161-3; B. Thompson, "Monasteries and their patrons at foundation and dissolution", *Transactions of the royal historical society*, 6th ser., 4 (1994), pp. 113-16; M. Harvey, "Unity and diversity: perceptions of the papacy in the later middle ages", *Studies in church history*, 32 (1996), pp. 145-53, 168-9.
[3]For Wolsey's changes, P. Gwynn, *The King's Cardinal: the rise and fall of Thomas Wolsey* (London, 1990), pp. 267-70, 273-4, 316-17, 321-3, 464-70, 477-80. For St German, *The complete works of St Thomas More, vol. 10*, ed. J. Guy, R. Keen, C.H. Miller, and R. McGugan (New Haven and London, 1987), pp. xxxvi-xliv.
[4]M. Harvey, *England, Rome, and the papacy, 1417-1464: the study of a relationship* (Manchester, 1993), pp. 214-15, 234, 248.
[5]On such issues, J. Delumeau, *Catholicism between Luther and Voltaire: a new view of the Counter-Reformation* (London and Philadelphia, 1977), pp. 159-61; J. Wirth, "Against the acculturation thesis", in *Religion and society in early modern Europe, 1500-1800*, ed. K. von Greyerz (London, 1984), pp. 66-78; G. Langmuir, *History, religion, and antisemitism* (Berkeley, Los Angeles, and Oxford, 1990), pp. 236-7; E. Duffy, *The stripping of the altars: traditional religion in England, 1400-1580* (New Haven and London, 1992), pp. 2-3, 283, 292, 298.

recognising its vitality and wide ranging concerns.[6] Yet that very word, "traditional", can conjure up false connotations, of something relatively static, perhaps monolithic.[7] The religion of this tradition, this handing-on, was constantly in flux, variegated by regional identities and manifestations. To talk of "English" religion may, indeed, be a misnomer.[8] Regionalism was vital, and to ignore such religious localism in England overlooks a key feature of the late medieval church. While regionalism is recognised in comments on the responses to the Reformation,[9] equivalent awareness for late medieval England is lacking. Despite regional studies of the church, distinctly regional spiritualities receive little attention. It may be sheer chance, but much recent discussion of English spirituality actually deals with a regional spirituality, of East Anglia.[10] Signs of distinct spiritualities do appear elsewhere, for example in Devon and Cornwall, and perhaps Yorkshire. As yet, however, the full scale and importance of regionalism in pre-Reformation English religion lacks proper assessment.

Despite such localism, in England as a whole the evolution was towards greater integration and cohesion. Critical here was the process of liturgical change, linked with printing. The liturgical imperialism of the Use of Sarum is a feature of the early sixteenth century: only it and the Uses of York and Hereford managed to achieve print.[11] Indeed, the Edwardine reformers stressed that their liturgical changes would remove the confusion and regionalism of the distinct Uses.[12]

If assertions of an "English" dimension in pre-Reformation religion paint too broadly, so do assertions that English catholicism was simply an undifferentiated segment of continental catholicism. There were, indeed, overlaps; but if an "English" spirituality is imaginary, so is an all-

---

[6]Duffy, *Stripping of the altars*, p. 3.
[7]But note Duffy's disclaimer: *Stripping of the altars*, p. 3.
[8]R.N. Swanson, ed., *Catholic England: religion, faith, and observance before the Reformation* (Manchester, 1993), p. 7.
[9]D. MacCulloch, "England", in *The early Reformation in Europe*, ed. A. Pettegree (Cambridge, 1992), pp. 176-86, esp. 176-80; Dickens, *Late monasticism*, pp. 111-28, 130.
[10]Notably A.E. Nichols, *Seeable signs: the iconography of the seven sacraments, 1350-1544* (Woodbridge, 1994); G. McM. Gibson, *The theater of devotion: East Anglian drama and society in the late middle ages* (Chicago and London, 1989).
[11]A.A. King, *Liturgies of the past* (London, 1959), pp. 276-8, 331; W.G. Henderson, *Missale ad usum precelebris ecclesiae Herefordensis* (Leeds, 1874), p. v; R.W. Pfaff, *New liturgical feasts in later medieval England* (Oxford, 1970), p. 8.
[12]E. Duffy, "Continuity and divergence in Tudor religion", *Studies in church history*, 32 (1996), p. 176; King, *Liturgies*, p. 276. See also Pfaff, *New liturgical feasts*, pp. 5-8.

encompassing catholicism. The pre-Reformation western church is perhaps best imagined as a composite church, a collection of distinct entities with some common characteristics but retaining significantly different identities, a union with subsidiarity.

The constant transformation in religion was perhaps coming to a head in early-sixteenth-century England. Monasticism, for instance, perhaps seemed decreasingly relevant to contemporary spiritual concerns, producing a widespread desire to switch its resources to other (equally pious) uses.[13] Arguably, continental spiritual influences were also being keenly felt at this point. The printing revolution made new forms of spirituality widely available: Thomas à Kempis's *Imitation of Christ* was one of many continental texts to gain a widespread English audience only after 1500.[14] New feasts were still being imported and fitted into English liturgies.[15] Novel manifestations of spirituality included several ecstatic women laying claim to spiritual leadership on models earlier encountered on the continent, and their followings were all important in showing the vitality of catholicism.[16] The first attempts to establish a Bleeding Host cult appear under Henry VIII.[17] Even so, England's insularity and regionalism must be stressed. Rites, devotions, attitudes, all had local manifestations and interpretations which distanced them – no matter how slightly – from continental developments.

In the midst of all this change, precisely what constitutes evidence of "catholicism" requires clarification. Arguably, for instance, adherence to the papacy is optional: the papacy's role was apparently seen as primarily disciplinary, rather than as a necessary component of spiritual existence.[18] The revival of episcopal collegiality in fifteenth-century England made the diocese the primary focus of ecclesiastical structures, the local bishop the prime administrator and father in God.[19] This collegiate attitude may well have reduced the bishops' dependence on Rome, especially in the

---

[13]Thompson, "Monasteries and their patrons", pp. 107-23.
[14]R. Lovat, "The *Imitation of Christ* in late medieval England", *Transactions of the royal historical society*, 5th ser., 18 (1968), pp. 99-100.
[15]Pfaff, *New liturgical feasts*, esp. pp. 4-5, 38-9, 80-1, 90-5, 101-3, 115, 123-4, 127-8, 131; K.L. Wood-Legh, *Kentish visitations of Archbishop William Warham and his deputies, 1511-1512*, Kent records, 24 (1984), pp. xix (and refs), 100, 110-11, 118, 220.
[16]R. Rex, *Henry VIII and the English Reformation* (London, 1993), pp. 85-6 and refs.
[17]Rex, *Henry VIII*, p. 94.
[18]Harvey, *England*, pp. 247-9; but cf. Harvey, "Unity and diversity", pp. 167-8.
[19]Harvey, *England and Rome*, pp. 215, 248.

shadow of the crown.[20] Paradoxically, the supreme manifestation of such localism in pre-Reformation England, Wolsey's legatine rule, was predicated on acceptance of papal jurisdictional and disciplinary claims. That legation created for the first time a truly nation-wide ecclesiastical structure, united under a single clerical head who was actually resident within the country.[21] In turn the administrative and jurisdictional papacy perhaps became less relevant to the English; although with little sign of formal resentment of its spiritual and doctrinal powers. The general stance was probably one of indifference, as it was again under Mary.[22]

***

While transformation was inherent in late medieval catholicism, it remained a "traditional" religion, handed down across the generations. Catholicism was a fundamental feature, a building block, of contemporary culture and society, transmitted as part of that culture. At every turn some aspect of catholicism was affirmed or reaffirmed, by family-based instruction; priestly sermons and pulpit-led instruction; and a massive amount of devotional and instructional reading. Devotional mimicry was built into children's games; literacy was acquired through prayer.[23] Churches, processions, plays, household rules, traditional invocations, and over all a concern for the salvation of the soul after death, all interdependently made catholicism both a cultural and spiritual phenomenon. There is no sign that this situation was seriously threatened before 1530. Rather, the available evidence seems to demonstrate catholicism's continued vitality in the pre-Reformation period. The laity were developing and increasing their investment in clerical personnel, intercessory institutions, and parochial worship, through the parishes and

---

[20] J.I. Catto, "Religious change under Henry V" in *Henry V: the practice of kingship*, ed. G.L. Harriss (Oxford, 1985), p. 115.

[21] R.N. Swanson, *Church and society in late medieval England* (2nd ed., Oxford, 1993), pp. 15-16, 317, 348-9.

[22] D.M. Loades, "The piety of the Catholic restoration in England, 1553-1558", in *Humanism and reform: the church in Europe, England, and Scotland, 1440-1643. Essays in honour of James K. Cameron*, ed. J. Kirk, Studies in church history: subsidia, 8 (Oxford, 1991), pp. 293-4.

[23] N. Orme, "Children and the church in medieval England", *Journal of ecclesiastical history*, 44 (1993), p. 570; M. Denley, "Elementary teaching techniques and Middle English religious didactic writing", in *Langland, the mystics, and the medieval English religious tradition: essays in honour of S.S. Hussey*, ed. H. Phillips (Woodbridge, 1990), pp. 223-41; J.A.H. Moran, *The growth of English schooling, 1340-1548: learning, literacy, and laicization in pre-Reformation York diocese* (Princeton, NJ, 1985), pp. 39-49.

private donations.[24] Recruits in unprecedented numbers were becoming clerics, which presumably reflects at least an appreciation of employment possibilities (although the market was possibly saturated by the mid-1520s).[25] Guilds and fraternities were vital components of lay religion; pilgrimages and shrines attracted considerable offerings, and were multiplying; indulgences and confraternity documents sold by the thousand; devotional and liturgical works were the bedrock of the printing industry.[26] The clergy were apparently doing their jobs effectively, and perhaps being more insistent about the obligations of Christianity through use of *pastoralia* literature.[27] While the counterblast of "Lollardy" did exist, Lollardy was a minority movement, if a movement at all.[28]

While many of these developments involved a "laicisation" of catholicism, with the laity taking increasing responsibility for their devotional and liturgical arrangements,[29] other trends were equally significant. The fifteenth century suggests a critically important and fundamental shift in attitudes: an increasing emphasis on sacerdotalism. This is highlighted in reformist tracts of Henry VIII's early years, notably William Melton's sermon for ordinands, and John Colet's Convocation oration 1512.[30] More widely, eucharistic devotion, mystical appreciations of the mass, an emphasis on penance, and concern for a good death (mediated by a priest) suggest a greater sense of lay dependence on priests. Religion also became more sacramental, perhaps stressing the

---

[24] B. Kümin, "Parish finance and the early Tudor clergy", in *The reformation of the parishes: the ministry and the Reformation in town and country*, ed. A. Pettegree (Manchester and New York, 1993), pp. 43-62; C. Burgess and B. Kümin, "Penitential bequests and parish regimes in late medieval England", *Journal of ecclesiastical history*, 44 (1993), pp. 610-30; J.A. Ford, "Art and identity in the parish community of later medieval Kent", *Studies in church history*, 28 (1992), pp. 225-37.

[25] Swanson, *Church and society*, pp. 35-6.

[26] Swanson, *Catholic England, passim*; Rex, *Henry VIII*, pp. 78-84; C. Haigh, *English Reformations: religion, politics, and society under the Tudors* (Oxford, 1993), ch. 1.

[27] P. Marshall, *The Catholic priesthood and the English Reformation* (Oxford, 1994), *passim*; H.L. Spencer, *English preaching in the late middle ages* (Oxford, 1993), pp. 196-201, 207-27.

[28] Below, n. 44.

[29] Kümin, "Parish finance", p. 56; C. Cross, *Church and people, 1450-1660: the triumph of the laity in the English church* (London, 1976), ch. 1-2.

[30] William de Melton, *Sermo exhortatorius cancellarii Eboracensis hiis qui ad sacros ordines petunt promoveri* (London, c.1510); P. Heath, *The English parish clergy on the eve of the Reformation* (London and Toronto, 1969), pp. 70-2; C.H. Williams, *English historical documents, 1485-1558* (London, 1963), pp. 652-60; C. Harper-Bill, "Dean Colet's convocation sermon and the pre-Reformation church in England", *History*, 73 (1988), pp. 192-3.

priest's role as mediator of those sacraments.[31] The depiction of the sacraments on fonts which were prominent in the lay area of the church is significant evidence here, for clerics were always accorded a prominent role. This applies even to baptism and marriage, sacraments which in theory needed no priestly involvement. If priests were making themselves increasingly indispensible in church-centred spirituality, this would be another significant change.[32]

Its precise significance, however, is elusive. As the artistic material generally reflects lay investment, it must reflect lay acceptance of the new view. The emphasis on priest-mediated sacraments perhaps also responded to tensions which arose from assertions of lay control and devotional autonomy. While an interpretation which sees the sacramental emphasis as a riposte to Lollardy is doubtless valid,[33] the stress on priestly power might more directly respond to general lay spirituality which otherwise limited priestly participation. Such priestly assertiveness, if emphasising the rigid distinction between clergy and laity,[34] could bring major new tensions into the personal relationships on which catholicism was founded.

The shift to sacerdotalism is important, and was seemingly widespread. Its occurrence raises another spectre, of anticlericalism. However, for pre-Reformation England, claims that anticlericalism was widespread seem to be a red herring.[35] Some priests did arouse personal hostility; but extensive opposition to priesthood as a status or sacramental function has yet to be proved. What was sought was better priests, not no priests; and priests who would not disrupt lay life with their claims to jurisdictional and fiscal privilege.[36] That ambition was shared by catholic reformers – probably also (in different terms) with Protestants: the latter's call for change could therefore piggy-back on a general desire which need not have shared the same aspirations. Indeed, with the link of

---

[31] Marshall, *Catholic priesthood*; Nichols, *Seeable signs*, ch.3.
[32] Nichols, *Seeable signs*, esp. pp. 170, 202-4, 275, 281.
[33] Nichols, *Seeable signs*, ch. 2, esp. pp. 91, 128.
[34] Marshall, *Catholic priesthood*, pp. 45-6, 105, 108-9, 117-19, 125-7.
[35] On this debate, Dickens, *Late monasticism*, pp. vii, 151-75; C. Haigh, "Anticlericalism and the English Reformation", in *The English Reformation revised*, ed. C. Haigh (Cambridge, 1987), pp. 56-74; R.N. Swanson, "Problems of the priesthood in pre-Reformation England", *English historical review*, 105 (1990), pp. 846, 868; Marshall, *Catholic priesthood*, pp. 83, 195-211, 235. Also R.A. Cosgrove, "English anticlericalism: a programmatic assessment", in *Anticlericalism in late medieval and early modern Europe*, ed. P.A. Dykema and H.A. Oberman, Studies in medieval and reformation thought, 51 (Leiden, New York, and Köln, 1993), pp. 569-81.
[36] Cf. E. Cameron, *The European Reformation* (Oxford, 1991), p. 61; Swanson, "Problems of the priesthood", p. 868.

sacraments and sacerdotalism in pre-Reformation England,[37] the aspirations were clearly very different.

Nevertheless, "anticlericalism' may have been important in one particular area: the association between attitudes to priests and gender relations. Whatever its other effects, Protestantism reinforced patriarchy[38] – but the patriarchalism of the catholic continental Reformation rebuts any claim that the changes led inexorably to Protestantism.[39] The early 1500s seem to witness a climacteric in the balance of relationships between women, priests, and lay males. The balance was triangular, between what were arguably three (rather than two) genders. But there could only be two sexes; and associations between women and priests, in excessive confession, and ultimately in sexual relations, obviously challenged the self-esteem of lay males.[40] Moreover, gender differences in spirituality, where women were seemingly the more devout sex, and accordingly evolved religious activities which met their desires and aspirations while men did not, increased the tensions.[41] The English Reformation has been seen as men taking on women's religion, and winning;[42] how far that is true – and whether the battle necessarily brought a victory for Protestantism – must still be properly assessed. It does appear that most late-medieval heretics and opponents of the church were men; and even though women's role within Lollardy has been emphasised, they were still a minority.[43]

---

[37] Below, n. 45.
[38] P. Crawford, *Women and religion in England, 1500-1720* (London and New York, 1993), pp. 41-3, 47, 49, 51-2.
[39] J. Delumeau, *La peur en occident, XIVe-XVIIIe siècles: une cité assiegée* (Paris, 1978), pp. 324-5.
[40] Marshall, *Catholic priesthood*, pp. 23-6, 148-50; cf. L. Roper, *The holy household: women and morals in Reformation Augsburg* (Oxford, 1989), pp. 17-18, 104-6; also cf. Delumeau, *La peur*, pp. 319-20.
[41] Marshall, *Catholic priesthood*, p. 76; C. Richmond, "The English gentry and religion, c.1500', in *Religious belief and ecclesiastical careers in late medieval England*, ed. C. Harper-Bill, Studies in the history of medieval religion, 3 (Woodbridge, 1991), pp. 140-2.
[42] Richmond, "English gentry and religion", p. 142.
[43] On Lollardy see A. Hudson, *The premature Reformation: Wycliffite texts and Lollard history* (Oxford, 1988); R.G. Davies, "Lollardy and locality", *Transactions of the royal historical society*, 6th ser., 1 (1991), pp. 191-212. On women, C. Cross, "Great reasoners in scripture': the activities of women lollards, 1380-1530", in *Medieval women*, ed. D. Baker, Studies in church history: subsidia, 1 (Oxford, 1978), pp. 359-80; M. Aston, *Lollards and reformers: images and literacy in late medieval England* (London, 1984), pp. 49-70; S. McSheffrey, "Women and Lollardy: a reassessment", *Canadian journal of history*, 26 (1991), pp. 199-223.

Increased sacerdotalism brought other tensions, especially by elevating the claims of priests as channels to divinity.[44] Concurrently, that elevation made it more difficult to accept the priest's humanity, and the likelihood of failure. Lay people demanded paragons; they got sinners. The demands regarding character and quality being made of priests were perhaps becoming too restrictive by the early 1500s, putting clerics in an impossible situation where their status, and lay acceptance of it, became increasingly strained and fragile.[45] Perhaps the intolerability of those demands explains why so many challenges to pre-Reformation catholicism actually came from clerics.[46]

***

English perceptions of catholicism may have been entering a critical phase after 1500. The increasing sacramental emphasis, and the heightened status theoretically accorded to priesthood, contrasted markedly with the realities of priestly lives (and, sometimes, characters), and the growing view of clerics as mere employees. Lay acceptance of the rhetoric of priestly status increased demands that clerics match the model. Growing awareness of the gap between divine requirement and human reality may explain the complaints against the clergy in the early sixteenth century, and a view that if clerics could not reform themselves, the laity should do it for them. If that lay-directed reformation failed, priesthood itself would have to be amended.

Lay appreciations of catholicism were perhaps reaching a critical point for other reasons. The massive investment in the church affected local economic balances, and perhaps made the church seem more oppressively fiscal.[47] The cumulative impact of generations of demands and obligations imposed on heirs and successors was approaching breaking point, with people willing to pray for souls, but not to pay for

---

[44] Marshall, *Catholic priesthood*, pp. 40, 44, 69-72; Swanson, "Problems of the priesthood", pp. 855-60.

[45] Marshall, *Catholic priesthood, passim* (esp. p. 235).

[46] Knowles, *Religious orders*, iii, pp. 55-60.

[47] On incumbents' finances, R.N. Swanson, "Standards of livings: parochial revenues in pre-Reformation England", in *Religious beliefs and ecclesiastical careers in pre-Reformation England*, ed. C. Harper-Bill (Woodbridge, 1991), pp. 152-61; M.L. Zell, "Economic problems of the parochial clergy in the sixteenth century", in *Princes and paupers in the English church, 1500-1800*, ed. R. O'Day and F. Heal (Leicester, 1981), pp. 35-40; cf. Haigh, "Anticlericalism", p. 69.

them.[48] Institutional – but not spiritual or theological – resentment offered fertile ground for those advocating changes which might be immediately perceived as institutional, rather than spiritual or theological.

***

As the Reformation advanced and the old order retreated, spiritual opportunities and practices changed. This is the crux for the debate over popular reactions to the English Reformation. The adoption of changes with little sign of effective resistance, especially when key aspects of old-style catholicism disappeared, becomes evidence for lack of real adherence to catholicism. Failure to oppose the new order is taken to indicate acceptance of it. But could practices be eliminated only because they lacked support? That may misread catholicism's cultural significance in pre-Reformation society.

Vital in assessing popular responses to the Reformation is the relative weakness of the preceding structures. It is much easier to destroy than to create; the argument that Marian religion appears unvital precisely because of the economics, that flamboyant catholicism could not be entertained when the basic arrangements had first to be reconstructed, has much to recommend it.[49] The contrast between aspirations and abilities is important: a hankering for the past may have been widely shared; but actually reinstating the old arrangements might be too costly, or too insecure a process.

Here there is a risk of overstating the case. Despite the waves of destruction, the retention of catholic artefacts and practices in the parishes is often remarkable.[50] There may be a basic division between the implementation of religious changes within the churches, and the many non-parochial celebrations. Admittedly, there was iconoclasm – as there had been earlier; but its popularity is unclear.[51] To destroy was easy;

---

[48]C. Burgess, "'By quick and by dead': wills and pious provision in late medieval Bristol", *English historical review*, 102 (1987), p. 857.
[49]Duffy, *Stripping of the altars*, pp. 545-58, 563.
[50]A. Walsham, *Church papists: catholicism, conformity, and confessional polemic in early modern England*, Royal historical society studies in history, 68 (Woodbridge, 1993), pp. 14-18; R. Hutton, "The local impact of the Tudor Reformations", in *The English Reformation revised*, ed. Haigh, pp. 134-7; D.M. Palliser, "Popular reactions to the Reformation during the years of uncertainty, 1530-1570", *ibid.*, p. 103.
[51]J. Phillips, *The reformation of images: destruction of art in England, 1535-1660* (Berkeley, Los Angeles, and London, 1973), pp. 41-100; M. Aston, *England's iconoclasts, i: laws against images* (Oxford, 1988), pp. 210-77.

reconstruction required much more effort and expense. Before the Reformation, such burdens could be, and were, spread via indulgences.[52] If the machinery for such distribution disappeared, reconstruction would become more difficult. Possibly the collapse of their similar collecting machinery had similar ramifications for the great fraternities. Fraternity numbers and memberships did decline with the assault on Purgatory and saints, until the nationwide dissolution of 1547, arguably indicating declining commitment.[53] It would be foolish to deny such a decline; but for the supra-parochial associations the collapse of the collecting machinery was perhaps just as important. If the drop in fraternity membership does reflect lack of commitment to them, presumably the same applies to attitudes towards cathedrals. Their fabric funds were maintained by identical arrangements (often, indeed, called fraternities) with diocese-wide collections. That machinery also disappeared, and cathedral fabric funds took a corresponding knock.[54] The abolition of the touring collectors for guilds, hospitals, churches, and cathedrals may not have been immediately noticed. Yet the willingness to give to good causes may not have died. In 1542 collections (without indulgences) to defend Christendom against the Turks raised nearly £2000, which compares well with the £2300 obtained (with indulgences) towards rebuilding St Peter's in 1517-20.[55]

The Reformation eliminations, and the resultant undermining of catholic practices, were fundamental changes. Particularly important in their enactment was the complicity of authorities and victims in the processes. The elimination of monasticism, for instance, was not a fell swoop. Henrician Caesaro-papalism and monasticism were not incompatible, as is shown by the existence of "Anglican" monasteries up to 1540.[56] Equally important, the dissolution of the monasteries did not eradicate all the prayers for souls offered by chantries established within them. Following

---

[52]M. Aston, *Faith and fire: popular and unpopular religion, 1350-1600* (London and Rio Grande, 1993), pp. 232-5.
[53]R. Whiting, *The blind devotion of the people: popular religion and the English Reformation* (Cambridge, 1989), pp. 108-12; J.J. Scarisbrick, *The Reformation and the English people* (Oxford, 1984), pp. 34-5.
[54]E.g. L.S. Colchester, *Wells cathedral fabric accounts, 1390-1600* (Wells, 1983), pp. 6, 10, 17, 22-3, 29, 36, 44-5, 50, 57.
[55]C. Kitching, "Broken angels: the response of English parishes to the Turkish threat to Christendom, 1543-4", *Studies in church history*, 24 (1987), pp. 215-17; W.E. Lunt, *Financial relations of the papacy with England, 1327-1534*, Mediaeval Academy of America publications, 74 (Cambridge, Mass., 1962), pp. 611, 620.
[56]Knowles, *Religious orders*, iii, pp. 336-49; Thompson, "Monasteries and their patrons", pp. 117-18, 122.

fifteenth-century precedents, some chantries continued, albeit as pensionary institutions which made their later termination much easier to implement.[57]

Other religious changes did involve force. The destruction of shrines and seizure of treasures violently attacked catholic practices; but it remains unclear how completely the shrines (taken to include all the wayside crosses and statues, as well as sites with physical remains) were actually destroyed, and how popular that destruction was.[58]

Continuity, where and when feasible, remained strong; and those denouncing the old ways often tacitly acknowledged their appeal. Overall, the ferocity of the attacks on shrines, sacraments, and images conveys the desperation of their would-be eliminators.[59] The continuity (and ambiguity) of devotional practice is also striking.[60] Emphatically catholic books still circulated, even if with Protestant marginalia and commentary.[61] Here the labelling of the combined changes as "The English Reformation" may be simplistic: in comparison with the continent, the English changes began late, and were completed only slowly. Slow erosion rather than sudden disappearance was the norm, perhaps especially at the parochial level under Henry VIII.[62] Paradoxes abound, like the retention of chantries after the attack on Purgatory in Henry VIII's later years. Especially significant in this regard was the practice of people combining to hire a priest, at parochial or chapelry level, to supplement normal priestly provision. This was often specifically identified with chantry concerns.[63] Such chantries, funded "out of devotion", were much less securely based than full benefices. Despite that, many of these chantries

---

[57] E.g. E.A. Fry, "Dorset chantries", *Proceedings of the Dorset natural history and antiquarian field clubs*, 27 (1906), pp. 230-1; 28 (1907), pp. 17-18, 24; see also A. Kreider, *English chantries: the road to dissolution*, Harvard historical studies, 97 (Cambridge, Mass., and London, 1979), pp. 128-9.

[58] The intense campaign against wayside crosses may have been delayed until 1548: R. Hutton, *The rise and fall of merry England: the ritual year, 1400-1700* (Oxford and New York, 1994), p. 85 (but see Aston, *England's iconoclasts*, p. 212).

[59] Nichols, *Seeable signs*, p. 84.

[60] Duffy, "Continuity and divergence", pp. 188-203.

[61] See M.W. Driver, "Pictures in print: late fifteenth- and early sixteenth-century English religious books for lay readers", in *De cella in seculum: religious and secular life and devotion in late medieval England*, ed. M.G. Sargent (Woodbridge, 1989), pp. 231-2.

[62] Hutton, "Local impact", pp. 116-19. Cf. Marshall, *Catholic priesthood*, pp. 191-2; Nichols, *Seeable signs*, pp. 83, 349.

[63] W. Page, *The certificates of the commissioners appointed to survey the chantries, guilds, hospitals, etc. in the county of York*, 2 vols., Surtees society, 91, 2 (1894-5) e.g. ii, p. 279.

survived until 1547; as did those funded by pensions from suppressed religious houses.

The history of chantries encapsulates the complexity of responses to the Reformation. Although reformers insisted that individual souls could not benefit from the celebration of masses, the utility of masses to aid souls in Purgatory was widely accepted in Henry VIII's later years (not least by Henry himself). The ambiguous doctrinal stance on Purgatory meant that prayers were still said, and sought.[64] The ingrained habit of praying for souls may have been extremely difficult to root out: the retention of "*orate pro anima*" inscriptions under Elizabeth suggests that even then people reacted to the traditional cues.[65]

***

The key to the complexity of the English Reformation may be provided by the changes within the clergy. One reason for the relative success of Elizabeth's Reformation lies in the complete transformation of the priesthood, both in status and numbers. The years after 1530 saw a crisis in clerical careers, the drop in ordinations creating a generational gap which allowed a new type of cleric to emerge, lacking the burdens of his pre-Reformation archetype.[66] But the break was not total: ordinations were still held in Henry VIII's later years, and some of the ordinands had presumably intended to become priests under the old order. Equally significant may be evidence of delays until catholicism returned, perhaps particularly notable with expelled monks.[67]

Yet the cesura in clerical careers at the Reformation (despite instances of longevity) is significant. A critical unknown for the Henrician clergy (especially the unbeneficed) is where they all were, and where they all went in the 1530s and 40s. The booming clerical recruitment before 1530 presumably reflects a perception that employment prospects were

---

[64] Marshall, *Catholic priesthood*, pp. 52, 55, 95; Kreider, *English chantries*, pp. 135-8, 175-6 (cf. p. 156); M. Knight, *Piety and devotion among the Warwickshire gentry, 1485-1547*, Dugdale society occasional papers, 32 (Hertford, 1989), pp. 27-8. See also the comments by Marshall, *Catholic priesthood*, p. 57.

[65] For continued extra-ecclesial prayers for souls, Hutton, *Rise and fall*, pp. 106-7; Palliser, "Popular reactions", pp. 103-4.

[66] R. O'Day, *The debate on the English Reformation* (London and New York, 1986), pp. 184-90; S. Doran and C. Durston, *Princes, pastors, and people: the church and religion in England, 1529-1689* (London and New York, 1991), pp. 145-53; for reaction to the new model, Haigh, "Anticlericalism", pp. 73-4.

[67] Marshall, *Catholic priesthood*, p. 230.

good. What happened to these priests after ordination? A tax return for Lichfield diocese in 1533 listed 1625 parochial clerics – beneficed and unbeneficed.[68] Between June 1530 and June 1531, the last twelve-month period offering full records, 117 priests were ordained.[69] On these figures, the diocese's parochial clergy could be completely replaced within fourteen years. Clerical post-ordination life expectancy was longer than this: where did all the surplus priests go? Most, as Thomas More complained, presumably sought posts as household chaplains.[70] As the religious houses disgorged their inmates, as the chantries, colleges, and other intercessory institutions disappeared, their clerics also flooded the market. No wonder that fewer men sought ordination.

But all these ex-monks, ex-friars, ex-cantarists entered a smaller and more competitive job market. What happened to them? Some acquired benefices, or stayed as assistant priests supported from parish funds or their state pensions. The rest, if they did not retire or unobtrusively revert to lay status, presumably found another existence compatible with their priestly status – their *catholic* priestly status.[71] Here ignorance is important: while they lived, these clerics could constitute an alternative church, possibly beyond the disciplinary control of the new establishment. While attention has recently focussed on tracing the Reformation through churchwardens' accounts,[72] the most significant area which remains unstudied – possibly because it is unstudyable – is household religion.[73] Private chapels, private clerics, may have provided a catholic continuity which official sources could not oversee. Under Mary, then, were domestic chaplains being promoted to benefices? Had catholicism continued as a domestic religion while Protestantism apparently prevailed?[74] If so, the

---

[68]London, British Library, MS Harley 594, ff. 116r-154v.

[69]Lichfield, Joint Record Office, B/A/1/14ii, ff. 208r-18r (previous twelve-month periods had occasionally almost doubled this figure).

[70]*The complete works of St Thomas More, vol. 6/i*, ed. T.M.C. Lawler, G. Marc'hadour, and R.C. Marius (New Haven and London, 1981), pp. 301-3; compare *The complete works of St Thomas More, vol. 9*, ed. J.B. Trapp (New Haven and London, 1979), pp. 187-8.

[71]Kümin, "Parish finance", pp. 53-5; C. Haigh, *Reformation and resistance in Tudor Lancashire* (Cambridge, 1975), pp. 150-1. On numbers, ibid., pp. 154-6 (but cf. p. 157).

[72]Hutton, "Local impact", pp. 114-38; also in Hutton, *Rise and fall*, ch. 3, with comment on the material's limitations at pp. 69-70.

[73]K. Mertes, *The English noble household, 1250-1600: good governance and politic rule* (Oxford, 1988), does not discuss the Reformation's impact on household religion.

[74]The flurry of dispensations for private chapels issued before Cardinal Pole's arrival in England seems relevant here: Loades, "Catholic restoration", p. 304. For one chapel, Haigh, *Reformation and resistance*, p. 65. The preservation of "discarded" ecclesiastical

Edwardine interlude rather than catholicism's restoration became the anomaly which had to be excused. Yet Marian catholicism retained all the old weaknesses; indeed, the Marian authorities perhaps prevented full restoration in order to introduce a different type of catholicism.[75] Noticeably not restored were indulgences and some of the chantries.[76]

The church which came in from the cold under Mary did not last. Questions raised by post-Marian catholicism closely mirror those raised by pre-Reformation Lollardy, with assessment further complicated by the addition of confessional polemic to the available sources. Formal recusants were not the only catholics in late Elizabethan England; but with the deaths of Marian priests who had been a fifth-column within the newly settled church, catholicism again became an extra-ecclesial religion. As such it faced critical difficulties in ensuring continuity. The erosion may have taken a long time but gradually, perhaps inexorably, "church papists" became Anglicans.[77] The Church of England, arguably, won by default.

***

The last few paragraphs go beyond this paper's stated theme. Yet they are relevant; for the mechanisms which permit an evolution necessarily affect that evolution. In sum, it can reasonably be argued that England's religious history before 1530 indicated that a reformed catholicism was being developed. While Lollards and Lutherans reveal antipathy to catholicism, Lollardy was small scale, and Lutheranism was effectively countered in the 1520s.[78] Humanists and reformers promoted a newer catholicism. Its precise format is nebulous, but because it retained the old frameworks, it would, by definition, be catholic.

---

impedimenta under Edward VI (Scarisbrick, *Reformation and the English people*, pp. 99-103) also offers intriguing possibilities.

[75]On Marian catholicism, Loades, "Catholic restoration", p. 303; Duffy, *Stripping of the altars*, pp. 525-7, 564. Cf Hutton, "Local impact", pp. 131-3.

[76]On new primers, which did not restore indulgences, Duffy, *Stripping of the altars*, pp. 539-40. For deliberate non-restoration of chantries, L.C. Colchester, *Wells cathedral, communars' accounts, 1327-1600* (Wells, 1984), pp. 223, 226, 236, 241, 245, 252, 257, 260.

[77]Walsham, *Church papists*, esp. ch. 2, 4; P. McGrath and J. Rowe, "The Marian priests under Elizabeth I", *Recusant history*, 17 (1984-5), pp. 103-20.

[78]R. Rex, "The English campaign against Luther in the 1520s", *Transactions of the royal historical society*, 5th ser., 39 (1989), pp. 85-106. (Lutheranism revived later: B. Hall, "The early rise and gradual decline of Lutheranism in England (1520-1600)", in *Reform and reformation: England and the continent, c.1500-c.1750*, ed. D. Baker, Studies in church history: subsidia, 2 (Oxford, 1979), pp. 103-31.)

That evolution would be driven from above rather than below. How the mass of catholics would have responded, and how readily they would have adopted the new model, remain open issues. For them, Duffy's traditional religion would still have operated, and still have evolved. There would have been considerable inertia; but inertia could be overcome, or might itself overcome. Institutional change, perhaps accommodating features of the 1529-32 legislation, even monastic dissolutions, would have aided the process; so would the liturgical uniformity imposed by a printed Use of Sarum (possibly alongside a retained Use of York). How the imbalance of the chantry arrangements would have been resolved is unclear; but perhaps prayers would have gradually gained more support than masses.

The 1530s dramatically changed the position. When change occurred at the top, under Tudor after Tudor, latent lines of evolution disappeared. Deformation was imposed; Reformation prevented.

The contradiction between evangelical faith and the political aims of the Danish exiled King Christian II with reference to his relations to King Henry VIII (1523-1559)

Martin Schwarz Lausten

During his 10 years reign (1513-1523) over Denmark-Norway-Sweden, naturally Christian II ruled officially as Catholic king, but from around 1520 he clearly demonstrated that he intended to break the economic and political influence of the aristocracy and the bishops, and that he was to introduce radical changes in commercial life, legal life and in educational matters; in short he was going to create a modern European empire governed by himself, of which biblical humanism and Reform catholicism were to constitute the spiritual foundation.[1] However, as from the end of 1522, nobility and bishops revolted against the king, who, in April 1523 was driven away from Denmark. Accompanied by his Queen Elisabeth (sister of Charles V), three under aged children, and a group of loyal collaborators/associates, he arrived in the Netherlands on May 1st, where he expected to gain economic and political support from the queen's imperial family. This exile, which caused the king numerous disappointments and defeats, came to last 8 years, until finally he was able to persuade the emperor to assist him in an attempted reconquest in October 1531. The re-

---

[1] This paper is based upon the research, which will be published in my book "Christian d.2. mellem paven og Luther. Studier i forholdet mellem tro og politik omkring Christian d.2. i eksilet og i fangenskabsårene 1523-1559." (Christian 2nd between the pope and Luther. Studies of the relation between faith and politics by Christian 2nd in his exile and in his imprisonment, 1523-1559), Akademisk forlag, Copenhagen, approx. 540 p. Appears about July 1995. Written in Danish, but supplied with a summary in English.

The sources are the archives of Christian 2nd. Most of them are published in "Diplomatarium Norvegicum", ed. C. Unger et al., Vol. 8-18, Christiania 1874-1919, but some unedited sources are still to be found in Rigsarkivet, Copenhagen, and in the archives in Vienna, Dresden, Weimar and in den Haag, the Netherlands.

The latest works in English about the Danish reformation are collected in The Scandinavian Reformation. From evangelical movement to institutionalisation of reform, ed. O. P. Grell, Cambridge University Press 1995. The contributors are Ole Peter Grell, Jens C. V. Johansen, E. I. Kouri, Martin Schwarz Lausten, Thorkild Lyby, Ingun Montgomery. Other relevant treatises in English are E. Doernberg: Henry VIII and Luther, Stanford 1961, G. R. Elton: Reform and Reformation. England 1509-1558 (The New History of England Vo. 2), London 1977, Jens Chr. Beyer: King in exile: Christian II and the Netherlands 1523-1531, in: Scandinavian Journal of History Vol. 11, 1986, 205-228.

conquest failed and Christian II was arrested by the new King of Denmark (Frederik I) and held imprisoned for 27 years, until death liberated him.

One of the most significant reasons as to why Emperor Charles V and his co-reigning members of the family in Europe did not wish to help Christian II, was the fact that shortly after the beginning of the exile, the king of Denmark and his queen expressed a strong fellow feeling towards the evangelical movement, strong enough for them to be described as Lutherans. Taking the king's first direct meeting with Martin Luther in October 1523 as a starting point, it is possible to establish how firmly convinced of the truth in the evangelical perception of Christianity the king and queen came to be.

During the king's several months' stay in Wittenberg shortly after, this firm belief was strengthened just as it was during the following years through continuous contact with Luther, George Spalatin and the Danish theologian, Poul Kempe, in Wittenberg. In his numerous and lengthy letters to the king, especially the latter expressed his view about the king's expulsion from his kingdom from a religious, evangelical standpoint, developing for the king his theology of "cross and suffering" which served both to explain to him that God had bestowed a unique vocation on him, and comfort him in his adversity and admonish to undaunted perpetual adducing of a Lutheran religion. The king's Lutheran attitude was additionally reinforced by the fact that a great majority of the men who had joined him in his exile also became evangelical. Through correspondence and personal contacts with the king and with each other, they consolidated the new faith.

The king and queen converted to the Lutheran perception of Christianity no more than two years after Luther and his brothers-in-faith were condemned at the Diet of Worms and a ban on evangelical literature had been instituted, thus at a time where the difference between Catholics and evangelicals absorbed princes, politicians, counsellors, theologians and jurists, and this religious issue was combined with the social and political conditions in the individual territories. The first direct consequence was the king's initiative to translate the New Testament into Danish, which was completed and published in short time. This was a typical feature of the Reformation, but characteristically used for the political purposes of the king also: to keep the common man in Denmark-Norway in the faith of the exiled king. In the translation of the Pauline letters a preface was inserted, written by the king's most trusted man in his exile, *Hans Mikkelsen*, former merchant and mayor in Malmø. During the last period of Christian II's reign in Denmark, he had played a significant part as counsellor to the king and co-author of his sensational reform laws, and he had participated in the translation of the New Testament. In this preface, he brought a serious accusation against the leaders of the Roman Catholic Church in Denmark for their participation in religious and political crimes: they had corrupted the true meaning of the Scripture to the common man, and on several occasions they had issued anti-Christian papal bulls and advanced clerical rights, and thus had deceived the common people and kept them in "Babylonian Captivity". He emphasized that now he and the king had discovered the truth in the evangelical perception of Christianity and realized that salvation was possible for the Danish population because their natural King Christian II had become evangelical, and the preface concluded in an appeal manifesting obedience to this king. Here, Hans Mikkelsen referred to the well-known texts (Rom. 13 and 1. Pet.), and sinister eschatological tones were set in the conclusion of the preface. Thus, the religious and political message was united in this prominent place, in the middle of the New Danish Testament (1524).

Yet another consequence of the king and queen's Lutheran faith was on a *personal* level, since they immediately incurred anger, indignation and hostility from the queen's devoted Catholic imperial family, – on whom they were dependent both economically and politically at this time. Both Emperor Karl 5th, regent Margrethe, and Archduke Ferdinand expressed these feelings in several ways, and the disparity between the king and queen together with their closest associates, and regent Margrethe and her associates, culminated at first at Queen Elisabeth's deathbed. In a letter to Luther, the king gave an account of the queen's last hours, emphasizing that she passed away in the evangelical faith, just as he was intensely polemical against Catholicism throughout the letter: however, a detailed report was composed by the Catholic counterpart, a report which was put in the coffin of the deceased. The Catholic priest Thomas Blanckaert, who was present at the queen's deathbed, wrote this report which maintained that she passed away in the Roman Catholic faith and under observation by Catholic ceremonies (masses, Extreme Unction etc.), just as the grand funeral (in the town of Gent) naturally took place as a Catholic ceremony.

The death of the only 26-year-old queen, caused the greatest sympathy amongst the population – dirges were composed about her wretched fate and the three small children who were left behind – and amongst the European princes. The queen's brother, Emperor Charles V, was deeply affected, and the death was a terrible blow to Christian II. He and the queen had become very attached to each other during their years in exile. The incompatible statements in the sources makes it difficult to determine whether she died in a Catholic or an evangelical manner, however it may be revealing that the Catholic regent Margrethe and her staff found it necessary to place the discussed report in the coffin. The issue of the upbringing of the motherless children turned out equally controversial: the Imperial family insisted upon a Catholic upbringing and education. Christian II's attempt to let confirmed evangelical men assume this job was rejected, and his subsequent attempts to "get" his children back were denied. The only persons allowed to stay at the children's Court were men whom regent Margrethe and her staff assumed to be Catholic.

A third consequence of the king and queen's new faith was the fact that they were in direct communication with evangelical circles in Antwerpen, Mecheln, Lier and probably other places in the Netherlands as well. This took place exactly during the years and months where the evangelicals were persecuted on a large scale, and where executions or other means of punishment of these Lutheran heretics were carried out nearly every month. Both the king and the queen interceded for prisoners, and the king was known to have had meetings with the evangelicals.

A fourth consequence was that the king attempted to appoint evangelicals at his Court in Mecheln, and when the Lutheran faith gradually became politically dangerous for the government, arrests of the king's people were instituted. One of them, Wilhelm von Zwolle, Master of the Royal Household, was burned at the stake as a Lutheran heretic. This incident which has never been investigated before, indicates that apparently he was connected with others of the king's close evangelical circle, perhaps even the king himself, while he was imprisoned and frequently put through examinations in order to account for his faith.

The king's new visits to Wittenberg (1526 and 1527), where we again have knowledge of Luther's sermons, which were attended by the king, only improved his evangelical attitude, and his "need" to confess united with his dynastic motives, reached its peak when he planned and put into effect that his sister Elisabeth, who had also become a convinced Lutheran, fled from her Catholic sworn husband in Berlin, Elector Joachim of Brandenburg (1528). On the basis of a series of unexploited documents, it has become apparent that it was Christian II himself who handled the entire matter, and that the confessional motive was undoubtedly the most influential when it comes to both the king and his sister. The flight was a political scandal of huge dimensions, and absorbed princes of both confessions and their counsellors for years, but the king and his sister were both immovable from their Lutheran confession. It is important to stress, however, that there were other motives to Elisabeth's flight as well, among other things her fierce disapproval of her husband's adultery, and his preoccupation with "the black art".

In spite of the many Lutheran actions, the king never lost sight of his *political* aim: the reconquest of the Kingdom of Denmark-Norway, and during all those years, he allowed ministers to display a frantic diplomatic activity, which first and foremost centered about achieving the support of Emperor Charles V and his dynasty, but he also tried to persuade other kings and princes to help him. In this case, as in previous incidents, the confessional attitude of the king was to play a fatal role. One time after another, his political possibilities were destroyed, because either directly or indirectly, he never stopped confessing a Lutheran faith, and the rumour of his heresy was well known all over Europe. Already during the national assembly in Nürnberg (March 1524), the queen's Lutheran confession had caused indignation and anger with her Catholic family as well as with the ministers of the Pope and the Catholic politicians. This reoccurred during the *Hamburg meetings* later the same year. The princes whom Christian II tried to influence in particular, were, besides regent Margrethe in the Netherlands (the aunt of the Emperor and Queen Elisabeth), Emperor Charles V and his brother Archduke (later King) Ferdinand – Queen Elisabeth's brothers – the devoted Catholic Elector Joachim of Brandenburg (Christian II's sister's husband), Duke Albrecht of Mecklenburg, but also several evangelical princes such as Elector Frederik of Sachsen and his successor Johann Friedrich, Philip of Hessen, the evangelical city-state of Bremen and others.

During the first stage of his exile, Christian II staked much on help from *King Henry VIII of England*. No more than a few weeks after the expulsion from Denmark and the arrival at the Netherlands (the 1st of May 1523), Christian 2nd and Queen Elisabeth travelled to England accompanied by 80 people, where the king negotiated with Henry VIII and Cardinal Wolsey in Greenwich and London; however, the relationship between the two kings was not good because of previous disagreements regarding commercial policy, and because, rightly, Henry VIII felt that Christian II was favourably disposed towards John of Albay in Scotland, one of Henry VIII best-hated men. Christian II and Wolsey engaged themselves in a lengthy discussion about the rebellion against Christian II in Denmark, where the king explained to him the conditions concerning constitutional law, the elective kingdom and the "paragraph of revolution" of the coronation charter, and Cardinal Wolsey did not fail to express his astonishment that Christian II thus had given up and let himself be driven away from his kingdom. To Christian II,s surprise, King Henry VIII and Wolsey suggested that the King of Denmark should return to Denmark and thus fight for his right. King Henry VIII, who was appalled to learn that subjects were able to rise against their chosen king like this, also wrote to Emperor Charles V, asking him to summon a conciliation conference between Christian II and the new sovereigns of Denmark. Together with the Emperor, Henry VIII would offer his services as mediator, and as a first gesture, he promised to send ministers to a such conciliation conference. Moreover, he promised to address the pope, who was to write to bishops and subjects in Denmark and Holstein. Henry VIII suggested to the emperor that it was possible to threaten Christian II's enemies with a discontinuation of their commercial privileges and military operations, in case the negotiations of conciliation did not have a positive outcome.

In addition to the personal meeting between the King of England and the Danish exiled King, four other contacts between them were established during these years, and in all of them the confessional issue played a significant part.

(1) Henry VIII sent two ministers, Bishop Henry of Assaph and Knight John Baker to the *Hamburg meetings* (April 1524), to where Christian II's delegates and his opponents in Denmark, Holstein and Lübeck were sent in order to negotiate for his potential recovery of Denmark, and during the negotiations, the confessional issue became a central concern, but the whole matter was immensely complicated. Formally, Christian II was supported by Emperor Charles V 's ministers and the emperor had also convinced the pope to send a minister. The emperor 's motive for his support was predominantly dynastic political, and this Catholic group of people were additionally supported by the English Catholic ministers. However, at this time Christian II had become a devoted Lutheran, and his delegation as well as the ministers of the emperor and the pope had to face reproaches from the counterpart because they supported a Lutheran heretic! During the meetings Bishop Henry of Assaph became doubtful towards Christian II 's orthodoxy, as he realized that the king had inspired the recent Danish translation of the New Testament, but the English ministers formally supported Christian II dur-

ing the meetings, and John Baker also participated in the subsequent, equally unsuccessful negotiations in Copenhagen.

(2) Henry VIII's declaration of providing support to Christian II, however, was hardly meant seriously. At least he did not intend to help him in other areas than the conciliation negotiations, because immediately after the meetings in Hamburg, Christian II sent his minister *Claus Pedersen* to England, where his goal was trying to procure a loan of 100.000 guilders from Henry 8th, or trying to sell Christian II's famous ship "Maria" to the King of England. The king had ordered him to give the island of Iceland as security for the loan! Claus Pedersen obtained an audience with Henry VIII in Greenwich (May 1524), but the king had repeated that he would not install a direct intervention against Christian II's opponents, instead he would try to mediate if the emperor would do the same. Naturally, he also warned the King of Denmark against the Scottish regents, and initially Claus Pedersen got a positive impression of the attitude of the King of England: "From the king's (Henry VIII) words, I gathered that from all of his heart, he truly means well for Your Majesty, and that he will support You until you recover Your kingdom". However, during the following negotiations with Cardinal Wolsey he accomplished nothing. On the contrary. He was immensely shocked at the arrogant and condescending attitude Wolsey had assumed towards him. From Hampton Court, Claus Pedersen wrote to Christian II that he had had several meetings with Cardinal Wolsey without receiving his final reply, and that he had said both "kind" but also "strange" words to the minister. Later in the month his patience wore out. In an indignant letter addressed to Cardinal Wolsey, he accused him of stalling time, rejecting personal meetings and using one excuse after another in order to avoid giving a direct answer. "As God be my witness", the Danish minister wrote to Wolsey, "I do not recall my ever being so unfortunate on a diplomatic journey of this sort, although I have previously negotiated with the pope and famous cardinals in Rome, with the emperor, with the Archduke of Austria and with nearly all the princes in Germany..." And from England, the minister told Christian II: "This "chief of priests", which he called Wolsey mockingly – "treats me, and especially You, Your Majesty, in a cruel manner. He will not give me his answer, he puts me off with promises day after day, and I cannot understand what his intentions are. Never in my life have I had to deal with such an arrogant man. It inflicts great anger to deal with an "adventurer of this sort". The minister

encouraged the king to drop Henry VIII and only stake on the emperor and the pope in the future.

(3) There is one more incident between the exiled King Christian II and King Henry VIII, which ought to be mentioned. As is generally known, the *works of Luther* had started spreading in England as early as in 1520/21, and a small group in Cambridge ("Little Germany") under the leadership of Robert Barnes were greatly absorbed by the evangelical perception of Christianity: however, as soon as in March 1521, Cardinal Wolsey initiated a public burning of Luther 's writings, and the next month King Henry VIII had read Luther 's "Of the Babylonian Captivity of the Church". The king himself wrote a powerful book, rejecting Luther 's theology, a book which was revised by Thomas More. It was published in Latin and shortly after in German editions. Luther responded in an equally stern polemical tone (Contra Henricum Regem Angliae, 1522).

In the beginning of the year 1525, however, Luther realized that King Henry VIII was turning evangelical, and Luther was persuaded to write a letter in which he apologized to the English King for having driven him all the way to the evangelical wing. It may have been Christian II who via Spalatin told Luther about this new attitude of the English King. This, however, is hardly likely. Another possibility is Hans von Minckwitz. Either way, Luther did write the letter in question, and sent it to Spalatin for examination and possible revision, since both he and Spalatin realized that a letter of this character had to be authorized by Luther 's temporal authority, the Electoral Prince of Sachsen. The letter proved to be a fatal misunderstanding. The English King was definitely not approaching an evangelical attitude, and he took advantage of the situation: in a writing he published Luther 's humble letter of apology and added a fierce denunciation of Luther himself and his theology. In Germany the Catholic Duke of Sachsen quickly initiated the confession of Luther and made sure that it was propagated. Other Catholic writings against Luther followed in succession.

It is difficult to determine the role of Christian II. It has been commonly held, that he thus deliberately attempted to involve Luther, in order for himself to gain personal political advantages with the King of England, – but this does not seem likely. Spalatin 's letters to the king in 1525, do not elicit the presemption that it was Christian II who took the initiative, quite the contrary: late in June 1525, he responded to his letters of 13/5 and 1/6 (which are now lost), in which he among other things had asked Spalatin to send him "the books of the King of England". Spalatin replied that neither he nor Luther had any idea what he was thinking of. Apart from the fact that Christian II may have wanted a copy of Henry VIII's book from 1521, it would have been natural, on this occasion, for Spalatin to mention Christian II's request to Luther to write the letter of apology, since in fact Luther sent this letter to Spalatin in May. At least Christian II became involved, when Spalatin sent Luther's completed letter to Christian II in September and solicited him for the further dispatch of the letter to King Henry VIII. In this letter, he also enclosed a letter from Luther to Christian II (now lost, 22/9 1525). At the same time, Spalatin had sent a German translation of Luther's letter to the Electoral Prince Johann of Sachsen in England. In this stern writing, the King of England had apparently no knowledge of the fact that Christian II was to have affected Luther in writing the letter. As soon as Henry VIII's mentioned writing was received, Spalatin sent a writing to Christian II, in which he related of the insulting manner in which he had mentioned Luther; Spalatin had even instituted a German translation of some parts of the letter, while others were related in short extracts in order for Christian II to read for himself about "the great blindness and callousness of the world and implore God's mercy, enlightenment and help". The translated extracts gave a strong impression of the accusations of the King of England against Luther for him being an arch heretic, causing the peasants' war, mocking the Cross of Christ and so forth, like equally he called Luther's wife a whore. Spalatin did not in one word mention the allegation of Christian II's involvement in Luther's writing.

Luther's response and the subsequent contacts between him and the King of England are not to be dealt with here. The incident does not appear to have been mentioned in Christian II's correspondence, but he, Spalatin and Luther have no doubt discussed the matter when Christian arrived in Wittenberg shortly after the publication of the English writing.

(4) Finally, it ought to be mentioned that Christian II and Henry VIII also were in touch soon after *Queen Elisabeth's death*. In the correspondence dealing with the death, the king, the members of the family, the princes and counsellors, this double aspect is reflected. Only one of the letters sent by the king seems to be reciprocated (in concept), but it is fair to presume that it has been typical of the style used when writing to Catholic princes, from whom he anticipated political support in the future. This is the case about the letter to *King Henry VIII of England*, in which Christian II informs him that Queen Elisabeth died in the Catholic faith: *She passed away as a firm believer in the faith and the soul received all the*

gifts included in the Sacraments of the Christian religion. In his letter of condolence Henry VIII expressed his grief and compassion, but the king's wishes of political support in the recovery was answered in quite noncommittal locutions. Moreover, in his desperate situation, Christian II tried to get help from Scotland later on, but also here the confessional attitude of the king presented a problem. From the legation journey to Scotland Christian II's delegate was able to report to his king: "In Scotland it is rumoured that Your Majesty is deeply involved in the poisoneus Lutheran and heretical dogma, into which Your Majesty has been seduced by one of Your appointed men, so that Your mind is solely concentrated in this and in the recovery of the kingdom".

One problem which presented itself in the investigation of the relationship between the confession and politics of the exiled King Christian II is the influence on the King's contemplations and actions, which was exercised by the *Royal Counsellors* and by the more or less attached employees coming and going at the exile Court, who were instrumental in bringing about news of reliable or doubtful reputation. There were always men from "the old days", that is from the reign in Denmark, and they were of Catholic conviction (among others the chosen Archbishop of Lund Johan Weze, Gotskalk Eriksen Rosenkrantz, Melchior de Germania and during the last years the Swedish exiled Archbishop Gustav Trolle). Furthermore, there was a series of the king's men who had equally converted to the Lutheran faith (among others Hans Mikkelsen, Jens Mikkelsen, Poul Kempe, and Hans Hansen). The king was dependent on both groups. He used the Catholic-minded for delegation journeys to the Imperialists, and found use of the Lutherans and other evangelicals in Wittenberg. The question is open as to how much the king himself worked out analyses and plans of action, but in several cases it can be demonstrated in what way his personally written comments, notes or instructions elucidate his evangelical attitude. In addition, it becomes clear that his ministers who were sent to the emperor, his brother Ferdinand or the Regent often faced difficulties, precisely because the Lutheran confession of Christian II was in opposition to the political and religious aims of the Catholic Imperial dynasty. It is safe to maintain that time and again, the king ruined the political ambitions he had concerning the recovery of Denmark-Norway for himself.

Yet, in the late 1520s, several circumstances made the king realize that he would have to assume a more friendly attitude towards the emperor, if he was to hope for efficient support from his side: His increasingly desperate state of economy, the failure of the meetings where German princes were to make the final decision about helping him in the recovery (Naumburg 1528), the division of the Protestant princes and theologians, the fact that after the Cambray peace (1529) Emperor Charles V had the most influential political power, the pressure of both Catholic and Lutheran counsellors, and the pressure of the emperor, King Ferdinand and regent Margrethe.

The 8th of February, in a written declaration to regent Margrethe, he promised that he would dissociate himself from the Lutheran faith and return to Catholicism, and he repeated this personally to Emperor Charles V in Augsburg (May 1530), immediately before the famous national assembly in Augsburg. At the same time he confessed to Johann Fabri, King Ferdinand's confessor who was appointed for this task by the papal legate Lorenzo Campeggio. However, in a corner on the back of a still preserved note where the king has written down the demands which were expected of him here, he wrote *Primo querens regnum dei et iust.* (seek first the Kingdom and Justice of God (then everything else shall be given you in addition, Math. 6,33). In what way do they give an impression of his compunctions? Do they reflect a fierce debate between Christian II and his counsellors, or is it a word of comfort from the Scripture, which the king gave himself? At the same time as the king announced his return to Catholicism, both he and his associates continued to order Lutheran books, just as he engages in other Lutheran-minded actions. Incidentially, the counterpart also seems to have questioned the earnestness of the king's statement.

Even though the Catholic party appeared to have "triumphed", as Christian II renounced this Lutheran faith, the exact opposite was the case. Regent Margrethe made yet another attempt to remove the Lutheran associates of the king, however, it is beyond a question of a doubt that these men, as well as the king himself, were deeply rooted in the Lutheran tradition, but with the ingenuity of "realpolitik", the king now used the question of confession to his own advantage, which he continued during the attempt to recover Norway in the winter of 1531/32, where initially Norwegian Catholic bishops gave him their support. However, during the 8 months stay in recovered Norway it became more and more obvious, that the king and the convinced Lutheran men he had brought with him from the Netherlands, naturally promoted the Lutheran views, for instance regarding the appointment of offices. This line culminated in Christian II's correspondence with the new King of Denmark, Frederik I.

In this correspondence, Christian II called for a reconciliation in referring to their common Lutheran faith.

There is no doubt that after the subsequent personal meetings with Luther in October 1523, Christian II had become confirmed evangelical. But he was aware of the fact that he was dependent on the Catholic political forces in Europe, if he was to expect the fulfillment of his political aim: the reconquest of the lost kingdom. Disregarding personal ambitions, the king was of the firm conviction that God had chosen him for the royal post. He had been chosen, anointed and crowned, and with his background in the Lutheran perception of authority, he frequently cited this calling. His closest Lutheran counsellors and associates supported him studiously in this aspect. First and foremost, this is true of Martin Luther himself, who in the famed writing "Ob Kriegsleute auch in seligem Stande sein können" (1526) mentions by name the king's expulsion from Denmark as a horrifying example of the way in which subjects were able to revolt against their king who was chosen by God. In Christian II's Danish New Testament and in the proclamations which were sent to Denmark from time to time from his exile, this idea is submitted. To these thoughts of calling was added the personal evangelical faith of the king. He had a lot to answer for from the period of his reign. The responsibility for a, at times, both ruthless and brutal rule, which reached its zenith in "the Masacre of Stockholm" (1520), in which nearly 80 people were executed in the name of the king, lay heavily on his shoulders, however, notes and actions indicate that the king had repented. This was also Martin Luther's professed impression.

Only reluctantly had Emperor Charles V given his support to his quite troublesome brother-in-law in the attempt at recovery in 1531. In reality, he and the other Catholic princes had washed their hands of him long ago. Instead they staked on the king's son, still minor Prince Hans, in whose name they were to claim the Danish throne. He was to be king and a regency appointed by the emperor was to rule for the present time. Christian II was well aware of these plans. Perhaps they were in his thoughts as the prison gate slammed behind him, after he had been outwitted by King Frederik I in the summer of 1532, – the very prison in which he spent the following 27 years, until death liberated him.

However, three days after Christian II had been imprisoned, his twelve-year-old son Prince Hans passed away. In the crypt underneath the cathedral in Odense (Funen), three stone plates lie in the floor. Underneath rest the bones of King Christian II, Queen Elisabeth and Prince

Hans. The coffins of the two latter were brought home to Denmark from the Netherlands in 1883.

The early Reformation in Sweden

Simo Heininen

At the end of the Middle Ages three Nordic kingdoms belonged to the Union of Calmar, a personal union created in 1397. By the beginning of the 16th century it was close to collapse – there were tensions between the leading Denmark and Sweden, which was governed by Regents of the house of Sture. Gustav Vasa laid the foundations of the modern Sweden on the ruins of the medieval Union, and had to fight against the legacy of the Union. This included the medieval church, as well.

The coronation of the last king of the union took place in Stockholm in November 1520. At the end of the banquet, Christian II, with the help of the Swedish archbishop Gustav Trolle, arranged a massacre, the "blood-bath" of Stockholm. Two bishops, some noblemen and a great number of the leading anti-Union burghers of Stockholm were slaughtered.[1] Gustav Vasa, a young nobleman, whose father was one of the victims, rose in rebellion, and expelled the king and his army from Sweden. With the help of the mighty Hanseatic city of Lübeck the Danish fleet was defeated, too. Gustav Vasa was elected king in 1523.

His path to power had not been easy, neither was the establishing of his rule. Christian II was still the legitimate king. Exiled from Denmark, too, he waited for his opportunity to return and had supporters in both countries. Lübeck had not given her support for nothing, and wanted the money back that she had lent.

Gustav Vasa was a political genius, a born agitator and not too scrupulous when it came to selecting his means. The late medieval Swedish Regents had already tried to diminish the power of the church; for example they borrowed money from the the church and were very reluctant in repaying it. The new king went further and tried to cancel the power of the church and confiscate her tax revenues and property. This seemed to be the only means to pay the debts of the Swedish crown – and

---

[1] Danish and Swedish scholars have written several book concerning this blood-bath. They have not been able to agree who was the villain: King or Archbishop. Unfortunately, the people in Stockholm that autumn had not yet read these books and took both for murderers.

the opponents could not provide any alternative, either. The church owned one-fifth of the landed property.[2]

Five of the seven episcopal sees were vacant; the archbishop had fled the country, two bishops had been executed in the "blood-bath" and two had died during the war. So Hans Brask of Linköping, the last of the great medieval prelates, felt like a *passer solitarius* in his effort to defend *libertas ecclesiae*.[3] He was in his sixties, a learned canonist and capable administrator who had visited Rome and was well versed in international church politics. He was loyal to the king, although he tried to defend his church against the claims of the crown and against the new Lutheran heresy.[4] But the game was not fair. Brask wrote in 1524 to Gustav Vasa's sister and expressed his doubt, "that somebody at the court of our Gracious King is always reversing our words and deeds". [5]

His suspicions were not unfounded. The man pulling the strings in the royal church policy was Laurentius Andreae, Archdeacon of Strängnäs, the key figure of the Swedish Reformation. He was born in the 1470's, studied in Germany and spent some years at the Papal Court. He was from 1498 a member of the chapter of Strängnäs, and from 1518 its leading prelate. At that time the Swedish Reformer, Olavus Petri, returned from Wittenberg and was appointed secretary to the bishop of Strängnäs. He soon won the Archdeacon over to the new faith.[6]

Laurentius Andreae acted as Secretary and Master of Ceremonies at the election of the king, and was thereafter made Royal Chancellor. He soon gave his master extensive information as to that how Dr. Martin Luther had revolted agaist the Pope, cardinals and great bishops. Luther had also shown that there was nothing in the Bible on which to build their great authority. That was the evangelium the king listened to with pleasure, and the king did not wait long to draw his conclusions.[7]

The new Chancellor had to normalize Swedish relations with Rome. The vacant sees were filled with men loyal to the king. The Swedish-born

---

[2] *E. I. Kouri* The early Reformation in Sweden and Finland, in *O. P. Grell* The Scandinavian Reformation, Cambridge 1995.

[3] Brask to Pope Hadrian VI 18.7.1523. *Hedda Roll* (ed.) Hns Brask, latinsk korrespondens 1523. Studia latina Stockholmiensia 19. Stockholm 1973, No. 46.

[4] *Herman Schück* Ecclesia Lincopensis. Stockholm Studies in History 5. Stockholm 1959, 151.

[5] *Knut B. Westman* Reformationens genombrottsår i Sverige. Stockholm 1918, 189.

[6] *Sven Kjöllerström* Laurentius Andreae, in Svenskt biografiskt lexikon 22. Stockholm 1979, 358-363.

[7] *Westman* 1918, 158-159.

Papal legate, Johannes Magnus, was elected Archbishop. Gustav Vasa asked the Pope in September 1523 to depose Gustav Trolle and confirm the elected bishops.[8] But Rome had already found a different way. Hadrian VI had appointed to the See of Skara an Italian curialist, who had not the slightest intention of leaving for Sweden. The Pope further told the king that he should let the legitimate Archbishop Gustav Trolle return or be excommunicated. To hold on to "the blood-stained traitor" was one of the mistakes that Rome commonly made in her Scandinavian policy.[9] It became the last one. The king wrote another letter to the Holy Father, and the tone of the letter drafted by Master Laurentius was arrogant. Should the Holy Father support Trolle, runs the letter, the King would *"per liberam et regiam nostram auctoritatem ita de ecclesiis et Christiana religione in terris nostris disponere, secundum quod Deo et omnibus Christianis principibus credamus"*.[10] And should the Pope refuse to confirm the elected bishops, *"cogitabimus desolatas et viduatas ecclesias alio modo restituere, earumque electos a solo et summo pontificio Christo potius confirmari faciemus, quam ob sedis apostolicae negligentiam ecclesias illas et religionem ipsam corruere patiamur"*.[11] This meant de facto a break with Rome.

Conditions for the Swedish *Fürstenreformation* were present towards the end of 1523. The crown was poor and the church was rich, the curial policy incompetent. The Lutheran Reformation presented the theological arguments for crushing the political power of the church. Gustav Vasa and his Chancellor did not hesitate to seize the opportunity.

We hear of evangelical preaching for the first time in 1522. Some German merchants are said to have brought this abominable heresy to Stockholm. At the same time some of the mercenaries sent by Lübeck to help Gustav Vasa had spread Lutheranism in Söderköping. The same year Hans Brask says that he had in his diocese forbidden the selling, buying and reading of heretical pamphlets.[12]

The following year we see more and louder complaints by the *episcopus Lincopensis*, and these already provide a clearer picture of the heresy. According to Brask, the Lutherans attacked various religious or-

---

[8] Gustav Vasa to Hadrian VI 10., 12. and 14.9.1523. Konung Gustaf den Förstes registratur (GR) I. Utg. af Victor Granlund. Stockholm 1861, 129-140.
[9] *Westman* 1918, 177-180.
[10] Gustav Vasa to Hadrian VI 1.10.1523. GR I, 145.
[11] Gustav Vasa to Hadrian VI 2.11.1523. GR I, 173-174.
[12] *Westman* 1918, 148, 226.

ders,[13] encouraging lay people to judge priests[14] and to restore the apostolic poverty of the church[15]. He assumes that the heresy had its origin in Russia, whereas, according to Johannes Magnus, the Hussites had been reborn.[16]

Brask was soon informed that the heresy was propagated especially by Master Olavus, the schoolmaster of Strängnäs. This Swedish Reformer was born in 1493 in Örebro, where his father worked as a blacksmith. After studying at the University of Uppsala he matriculated in the summer term of 1516 at Leipzig, but soon moved to Wittenberg and was promoted in February 1518. At home he became secretary to Master Matthias, the bishop of Strängnäs. He escorted his bishop to the coronation of Christian II and had to witness his bishop's execution.[17]

Brask tried to persuade the leading prelate in Strängnäs to suppress the heresy, but he soon discovered that Laurentius Andreae was supporting it.[18] On the other hand, the Dean of the Chapter, Nicolaus Benedicti, a learned Thomist, – in an act perhaps inspired by Brask – drew up a catalogue of the errors of Olavus Petri and refuted them.[19] Brask had the catalogue in his hands in July 1523 and sent copies to his friends. It is the first presentation – albeit critical – of the preaching of Olavus Petri and bears the title *Isti sunt errores magistri Olavi discipuli Martini Luther, quos, ut asseritur, dixerat successive in sermonibus suis de ambone*. It contains eight points, refuted one by one by the Dean:

1. In scriptura autentica non reperitur quod sancta

2. Sanctus Ioseph, qui fuit sponsus beatae Virginis, non fuit senex sed iuvenis.

3. Item nullus predicaverit hic veritatem nisi ego.

4. Item nullus religiosus mendicare debet, quia habetur Deuteronomii xv in principio: Et omnino indigens et mendicus non erit inter vos.

---

[13] Brask to the abbot of Nydala 23.5.1523. *Roll* no. 32.
[14] Brask to the bishop of Skara 12.6.1523. *Roll* no. 42.
[15] Brask to Johannes Magnus 5.3.1523. *Roll* no. 10.
[16] Brask to the convewnt of Vadstena 20.7.1523. *Roll* no. 45.
[17] *Robert Murray* Olavus Petri. Strockholm 1952, 7-22.
[18] Brask to Ericus Svenonis, electus of Turku. *Roll* no. 45.
[19] *Roll* no. 38.

5. Item nullus debet ponere fiduciam in homine, utin beata Virgine vel aliquo alio sancto, sed in solo Deo, iuxta illud Iheremiae 17: Maledictus homo qui confidit in homine.

6. Item officium praedicationis in ecclesia Dei est praecipuum et maius quam celebrationis.

7. Item confraternitates psalterii beatae Virginis et aliorum sanctorum non sunt admittendae sed frivolae, quia ex nullo loco sacrae scripturae trahunt originem.

8. Item confitendum est mentaliter soli Deo et non sacerdoti.

The old doctor was evidently irritated by the self-confidence of the young Master (3). The picture this catalogue gives of the new doctrine, although polemical, already reveals some central themes in Olavus Petri's preaching familiar in his later works: the authority of the Bible (1, 2, 4, 5, 7), attacks on mendicant orders (4), on the cult of saints (5, 7) and on the mass (6).[20] The last point in the catalogue is too superficial to reveal what Master Olavus had against the confession; in his works he fails to reject it, although he denies that it is necessary for salvation.[21]

Brask tried by every means possible to extinguish the new heresy. He encouraged his friends by telling them of the set-backs the heresy had encountered abroad. In his letter to the Pope in July 1523 he depicts the situation in Sweden in dark colours; the heresy is even blamed for the murder of the bishops in the "blood-bath".[22] As a result, the Pope sent the learned humanist Johannes Magnus to Sweden in order to expunge Lutheranism.[23] Next, Brask tried to persuade the legate to set up an inquisition tribunal to investigate the preaching of Olavus Petri, but the king refused to give his consent. According to the legate, the king had, with tears in his eyes, deplored the fact that he had to take subsidies from the church. He had also promised to remove the heresy by royal authority,

---

[20] *Westman* 1918, 166; *Sven Ingebrand* Olavus Petris reformatoriska åskådning. Studia Doctrinae Christianae Upsaliensia 1. Lund 1964, 54-64.
[21] *Westman* 1918, 167; *Ingebrand* 1964, 336-339.
[22] Brask to Hadrian VI 18.7.1523. *Roll* no. 46.
[23] Hadrian VI to Brask 11.3.1523. *Roll* no. 38; *Kurt Johannesson* Gotisk renässans, Johannes och Olaus Magnus som politiker och historiker. Stockholm 1982, 26-30.

but it had to be done *magis industria et modestia quam tumultu*.[24] So although the legate drew up a draft for a Royal mandate suppressing the new doctrine, but it was never published.[25] The legate succeeded, however, in bringing peace to the Chapter of Strängnäs: Olavus Petri and Nicolaus Benedicti promised to refrain from any public debate.

The Chapter of Uppsala, surely because of a proposal by the king, elected Johannes Magnus Archbishop in August 1523. Because Rome was still holding onto Gustav Trolle, the new archielectus became a pawn in the political game of Gustav Vasa, and could not do very much against Lutheranism.[26] Thus the attempt to obtain the support of the worldly authority for the suppression of Lutheranism failed. This was not a good omen, and little by little Brask and the other men of the old faith noticed that the king did not wish to fight the new doctrine, in fact because he supported it himself.

Brask did not, however, give up. His printing house published Swedish devotional books, tracts and songs against Lutheranism.[27] He provided polemic literature from abroad for his clergy and for the monasteries in his diocese. They include:

1. The papal brief *Postquam ad aures* (23.8.1518) to Cardinal Cajetan, instructing the legate to take Luther into custody.[28]

2. The condemnations of Luther pronounced by the universities of Louvain and Cologne (printed 1520).[29]

3. *Assertio septem sacramentorum adversus Martinum Lutherum* by Henry VIII (1521).[30]

4. Anonymous *tractaculus de erroribus Ruthenorum*.[31]

5. *Assertionis lutheranae confutatio* by John Fisher (1523).[32]

---

[24] Johannes Magnus to Brask 1.8.1523. *Roll* no. 48.
[25] GR I, 116; *Roll* no. 48.
[26] *Johannesson* 1982, 31-33.
[27] *Isak Collijn* Sveriges bibliografi intill år 1600 I. Uppsala 1938, 279-284.
[28] *Roll* no. 20; WA 2, 23-25.
[29] *Roll* no. 41; WA 6, 171-180.
[30] *Roll* no. 45.
[31] *Roll* no. 45.

6. Imperial edict issued against Luther, presented in Antwerp 21. 2. 1525.[33]

7. Duke Georg of Saxony's letter to Luther (28. 12. 1525).[34]

8. *Enchiridion* by Johann Eck.[35]

In addition, Brask asked his friends in Rome and Poland for books by Johannes Cochlaeus, Johannes Fabri and other opponents to Luther.[36] Brask and Nicolaus Benedicti declared themselves against the new doctrine using as support various kinds of arguments. The Dean attacked the first and fourth error of Olavus Petri as follows:

1. Contra hoc videatur Catholicon super verbo Iohannis et collecta communis de sancta Anna, quae sic incipit: Deus qui beatae Annae tantam etc.

4. Hoc interpretetur de Iudaeis secundum Liram. Sed quod religiosi maxime de ordine praedicatorum et minorum mendicari possint, ad hoc videatur sanctus Thomas 2:a 2:dae q: 187 arti: 4 et 5.

Other arguments used by the Dean were of the same kind. He called a huge cloud of witnesses against the new faith. He cited the Bible, the Legends of the Saints, liturgical texts, Canon Law and the following authors: Ambrose, Boethius (*De consolatione philosophiae*), Thomas ab Aquino (*Summa theologiae*), Johannes Balbus (*Catholicon*), Nicolaus de Tudeschis alias Panormitanus, Nicolaus de Lyra and Antonius Florentinus (*Summa moralis*). The defense of the old faith was, however, not very convincing.

The first confrontation between the Reformers and defenders of the traditional faith in Sweden followed the same path as did religious disputes on the European continent. The Reformers did not accept the old rules and authorities, and so any discussion was in vain. The combatants

---

[32] *Westman* 1918, 257.
[33] *Westman* 1918, 288-300; *Collijn* 1938, 283.
[34] *Westman* 1918, 300; WA BW 3, no. 956.
[35] *Westman* 1918, 313.
[36] *Westman* 1918, 256-257.

did not speak to each other. Neither the Dean of Strängnäs nor any other defender of the traditional position could agree with Olavus Petri, who insisted that the Bible should be accepted as the only norm and authority.

The Genesis of the Reformed Danish Ordination Ritual of 1537

Marianne Jensen-Broby de Perez

The Danish National Church, which is an evangelical-Lutheran church, has an ordination ritual that appears to contradict the theology on which it is founded. Why is that so?

In 1535 a liturgy for ordination of evangelical ministers, composed by Luther, was put into use in Wittenberg – for reasons that were apparently *not* of a theological kind. Therefore, the practice in the evangelical communities *before* 1535 is of particular interest.

This study involves the first two decades of the Reformation in Germany as the background of the early evangelical-Lutheran ordination practice in Germany and Denmark. It is based on writings by the three principle characters behind the Reformation in these two countries, Martin Luther, Philip Melanchthon and Johann Bugenhagen.

It is not possible to reconstruct an apostolic ritual for ordination to priesthood or ministry. The only text in the New Testament mentioning ordination by the 12 apostles is Acts 6,6. But the objects of this ordination are deacons, not priests or bishops. And the passages about gifts of grace in connection with prophesy and laying on of hands can be found in only two texts, namely 1. Timothy 4, 14 and 2. Timothy 1,6. The genesis of the Pastoral Letters, however, is not easy to determine. They may express an early, but not necessarily an aboriginal, and not necessarily a generally practised tradition. An "apostolic ritual" for ordination to priesthood cannot be read out of the New Testament.

As far as a ritual from the time of the early Reformation is concerned, the picture is also not so clear. Documentation can be found of various forms of the act of introduction of a minister in a parish, but there are a few invariable elements:

> 1. No one was made a minister without an actual congregation to serve.
> 2. The act of introduction would always be preceded by vocation by the local congregation or representatives of it.

3. The act would be repeated in every new place of service,
4. and it would take place in the parish church.

The priesthood of all believers

The understanding Luther has of justification by faith alone, SOLA FIDE, is of conclusive importance to his view of ministry. No acts or deeds can help anything at all to promote one's salvation.

Equally important is his other guideline concerning the understanding of Christianity, the principle of SOLA SCRIPTURA, only the Scripture. Luther will base his views on the Word only, i.e. the Bible read in a christological way.

On these two grounds, mainly, he has to reject the Roman Catholic idea of ministry, because it ignores the fact that priesthood belongs to all believers. Priesthood in the sense of "sacerdotium" makes no sense, as the redeeming act of Christ happened once and for all. The distinction between clergy and lay people is false, says Luther, it is "pure invention".[1] All Christians truly belong to the clergy, and the only consecration or ordination that happens in the life of a Christian is baptism. When we are baptized in the name of the Father, the Son and the Holy Spirit we all receive the blessing of and the duty for the Word of God. All believers share the responsibility of making the pure and undefiled Gospel known to all people. "The pope or bishop anoints, shaves heads,[2] ordains, consecrates, and dresses differently. That can make a hypocrite, but never a Christian or a clergyman". With reference to the New Testament he quotes 1. Peter 2,9: "You are a royal priesthood and a priestly realm", and Rev. 5,9f: "Thou hast made us to be priests and kings by thy blood".

The assumption of an indelible character over and above the one which is rendered in the holy baptism is contrived talk and human regulation.[3]

---

[1]Martin Luther: An den christlichen Adel deutscher Nation von des christlichen Standes Besserung, in: Horst Beintker (ed.): Martin Luther. Die reformatorischen Grundschriften, Band 2: Reform von Theologie, Kirche und Gesellschaft, München 1983, p. 70 ff.
[2]Monks' tonsure.
[3]Horst Beintker, 71 ff.

The office of ministry

According to the Augsburg Confession[4] the purpose of ministry is to convey faith. Ministry is defined by its function, which is to preach the Gospel and administer the sacraments, as these are the channels, the only channels, whereby the Holy Spirit brings about and strengthens faith. And Luther explains: "Whoever comes out of the water of baptism can boast that he is already a consecrated priest, bishop, and pope, although it is not seemly for everybody to exercise such office. Because, as we are all priests of equal standing, no one may push himself forward and take it upon himself to do that for which we all have equal authority. For no one should take upon himself what is common to all without the consent and authority of the community".[5] "Consequently, when a bishop consecrates", he says, it is to be understood as "nothing other than in the place and stead of the whole community, all of whom are like in power, he takes a person and charges him to exercise this power on behalf of the others".

In principle there are no services in the church that cannot be performed by any baptized Christian, like preaching, baptizing, administering the communion, giving absolution. But we cannot all exercise that office. It is like St. Paul has it in the letter to the Romans 12,5 and the 1. Corinthians 12,17ff: We are one body, but different members with different tasks. If all the members were eyes, how could we hear? – and if all were ears, the body could neither smell nor taste. This is a parallel to the different tasks in the community. There cannot be only mayors or only bakers or only priests. The office of ministry is like any other office with the exception that the public office of the Word[6] can be assumed only as a consequence of vocation from the community.

Vocation itself is the true ordination. "Vera ordinatio est vocatio ad pastoralem curam".[7] The vocation is sacramental,[8] because it is performed by the Holy Spirit: "non vocant eum, sed spiritus sanctus, sed confirmant vo-

---

[4]Philipp Melanchthon: Confessio Augustana, 1530, (CA), Art. 5, in: Den danske Folkekirkes Bekendelsesskrifter, by Leif Grane, København 1981, p. 49.
[5]Horst Beintker, 71 ff.
[6]When Luther talks about the Word it includes the sacraments, communion and baptism, as they become sacraments only through the Word and without it does not exist at all.
[7]Horst Beintker, 71 ff.
[8]Martin Luther: Werke. Kritische Gesamtausgabe, Weimar (WA), Bd. 38, 401; 238: "Verum sacramentum ordinis est vocatio".

cationem hanc".[9] The election carried out by the community is the confirmation of a divine call.

Reformation practice – Luther

There is plenty but scattered information about Luther's theology of ministry. Known examples of how he applied it in practice are more scarce. We know that the form under which ministers came into office varied. There is even an example of an ordination which was done with retrospective effect, so to speak. A pastor Sutel from Göttingen wrote to Luther for advice. He was not sure of his own authority to administer the sacrament of Communion, as he had not received an ordination. Luther advised him then to gather the other ministers of the city in the church of his parish and make them confirm his authority before his congregation by laying on of hands and prayer in front of the altar. This was very typical for Luther. The form is variable. Important is to make sure that nothing stands in the way of the Gospel. What counts is the faith and the intention behind, namely to be of service in such a way that faith in God is strengthened through the Word of Christ.[10] The way it is done is not important as long as it is not considered a necessity. Any practice that comes to be understood as necessary, however, should be changed or done away with. Luther illustrates this with examples from the New Testament[11]: Paul had Timothy circumcised, *not* because it was necessary, but only in order not to confuse those (Jews) whose faith was weak.[12] Conversely, he would not allow that Titus be circumcised, because this was being forced on him as a necessity for his salvation.[13]

Necessary rituals do not exist. Piety comes only from faith, never from rituals or acts. Rituals and ceremonies cannot bring anybody closer to salvation; their function can merely be as a tool to help others find and keep faith. Whereas rituals that contribute to doubt or infidelity or misconceptions are condemnable.

A humorous but serious example illustrates this attitude: The rural dean of Berlin, George Buchholzer, wrote to Luther in 1539 because he was

---

[9]WA 38, 402.
[10]WA 38, 402 f; 406.
[11]Luther's Skrifter i Udvalg, Institut for dansk Kirkehistorie, København 1962, Bind I, 312.
[12]Acts 16,3.
[13]Paul's letter to the Galatians 2,3.

bothered by some regulations imposed by the Elector, stating that he had to wear a certain garb for the purpose of walking around the church in procession on Sundays, singing and carrying a cross. Luther's advice goes: "If your master the margrave and Elector will let you preach the Holy Gospel of Jesus Christ plain and pure without human additions, and let you administer the sacraments of Baptism and Communion according to the Lord's own institution, and if he will refrain from invocation of Saints, from processions with the sacrament, and from the daily celebrations of Mass, vigils and requiems for the dead, and stop the consecration of water, salt and herbs, – if he agrees to that, then do in the name of God join the processions, do carry a golden or silver cross, and do wear a garb of velvet or silk or whatever; and if your Prince is not satisfied with one, do wear two or three on top of each other. And does your Prince not find satisfaction in one procession around the church yard, with singing and jingling, then walk seven rounds. Such things can neither encourage nor impede the Gospel at all, providing there is no abuse, and providing it is not regarded as something necessary for salvation, and providing they do not fetter the consciences". And then he adds that if he could only get that far with the Pope and the papists, he would thank God and be happy.

In other words, there is no need to change or abolish the old ceremonies, but they must be optional things that can be kept, where that seems appropriate, and changed where it becomes necessary for the sake of the Gospel.[14] The criterion must always be to serve the pure an undefiled Word of God. Luther performed and recommended what the situation called for in each particular case and place also in regard to the practice of installing a new pastor in his office. But he did put down in writing what the content of the procedure should be, the essence of which can be summed up in 4 points[15]:

1. Serious and thorough contemplations about the person's abilities and dignity for the office.
2. Vocation.
3. A ceremony in the church whereby the elect, who has been appointed by the municipality, is confirmed and recommended to the congregation.
4. Intercessory prayer and laying on of hands.

---

[14]Regin Prenter: Reformatoren Martin Luther, 2. udg., Aarhus 1980, 41.
[15]Letter to the municipal corporation of Prague 1523, in: WA, Bd. 12, 160 ff.

So, when Luther talks about ordination, he does not mean a ceremony only; he means the entire procedure that brings a person to serve a parish as its minister.

Reformation statutes. – Johann Bugenhagen

The main organizer of the many new evangelical churches was Luther's close colleague among the reformers, Johann Bugenhagen (1485-1558). He was the architect behind the ecclesiastical statutes, the earliest of which were those in Braunschweig (1528), Hamburg (1529), and Lübeck (1531), followed by Pomerania (1534/35) and Denmark (1537).

Bugenhagen stated in writing his theological views and reasoning behind the statutes. In the statutes of Lübeck he initiates the regulations for ordination like this: "We need priests, ministers or pastors. What their office is, is clear. They must all be upright, honest, honourable priests, preachers of the pure and undefiled gospel of Christ, the like of which the New Testament Scriptures call bishops, priests, pastors, teachers, prophets, evangelists[16] – who are capable of teaching the Holy Scripture powerfully to the learned and the unlearned and refer them to Christ".

Bugenhagen calls the act "introduction into the church of the servants of the Word", and he says: "Such elected servants of the Word, anointed or not anointed, receive in the church on Sunday in front of the congregation the ecclesiastical duty. From then on they can be said to be ordained to ministry, – "non literae gamäss", he adds with a quotation from 2. Cor. 3, dissociating the Reformation understanding of ordination from the Roman Catholic. From this passage we can tell that

1. a Roman Catholic ordination was neither qualifying nor disqualifying, and
2. an ordination was *not* required ahead of this act of introduction, and therefore not constituent for serving as a minister, even if there might have existed an evangelical one.

The Augsburg Confession confirms this. Confessio Augustana does not mention ordination at all.

---

[16]Paul's letter to the Ephesians 4,11. Wolf-Dieter Hauschild (ed.): Lübecker Kirchenordnung 1531, Lübeck 1981, 89.

The act initiating ministry took place in the local church to which the ordinand had been called, and in which he was going to serve. Also Melanchthon attaches importance to this principle: ministry is "immer Amt an einem bestimmten Ort, an einer bestimmten Gemeinde", always in a particular location for a particular congregation.[17]

As for the indelible character Bugenhagen says like Luther: "it has been invented. Anointment and shaving do not help in this service, only the gifts from God, the gift that God has made you an honest and decent man, who is able to teach the Word of God and be a defence against enemies". As a biblical reference Bugenhagen quotes 1. Tim. 3,1-4 that talks about all the qualities a servant of the Word should have.

Since the laying on of hands in connection with initiation of ministry is an apostolic tradition (which is not instituted by Jesus), Bugenhagen reluctantly includes it in the ritual. But he draws the attention to the fact that laying on of hands is just an external sign and it may lead to all kinds of fanaticism.[18] His warning was well placed. Already in Hamburg's revised statutes of 1539/56 a remark is added, saying that those who have been ordained before, should not be installed with laying on of hands for the second time. So this external indication, the laying on of hands, *had* come to be understood as having an importance in itself. The non-repeatability, however, was at this time not yet applied to the whole act, which was still repeated with every change of parish.[19]

Why did this new rule occur about the laying on of hands? – Why may it not be repeated? The only other act of the church that can never be repeated, is baptism. What is this other than a rehabilitation of the invented indelible character.

Bugenhagen's ritual for initiation of ministry

According to Bugenhagen's original statutes, here quoted from those of Hamburg 1529 and of Lübeck 1531, the authorization of a new pastor has the following procedure:

---

[17]Helmut Lieberg: Amt und Ordination bei Luther und Melanchthon, Göttingen 1962, 341.
[18]P.G. Lindhardt: De danske ordinationsritualer, in: Kirkehistoriske Samlinger 1977, 8.
[19]Frieder Schulz: Die Ordination als Gemeindegottesdienst. Neue Untersuchungen zur evangelischen Ordination, in: Jahrbuch für Liturgik und Hymnologie, 23. Band 1979, 12.

Prayer of thanksgiving

"First of all, in order to stop the betrayal of the old and the new seducers, and in order to get real evangelical preachers, we must keenly thank the Father of all mercy from the bottom of our hearts for the Gospel of our Lord Jesus Christ, which he reveals to us so abundantly these days, and by means of which we can realize our sin, error, and hypocrisy, and through faith in Christ also can receive forgiveness for our sins, be God's children and blessed, and realize, what good deeds really are, and that bearing ones cross with patience is pleasing to God – like Paul with his own example teaches us to thank God, Col. 1."

Intercessory prayer

"Subsequently, we must pray to the Lord of the harvest that he will send us good workers for his harvest, like Christ teaches according to Matt. 9; it means that he will provide us with good preachers. . . . He prayed the whole night before selecting his 12 apostles according to Luke 6. We should pray likewise. These prayers should be said publicly from the pulpit as well as prayed in silence".

Vocation

The selection of a suited person is carried out by all the "fathers of the church" together, with advice and help from the superintendent and the other pastors. Then he should be appointed by the councellors in his parish and the people's assembly, the superattendant, and the other pastors.

This vocation obviously happens before the ceremony in the church takes place, so – with Luther's words about VOCATIO in mind[20] – the person concerned *has* already the status of priest when the laying on of hands is done in the church.

"The same people who elect and appoint somebody are also the ones to dismiss him if necessary". This paragraph, too, is in agreement with Luther, who says that the position of a priest should not be anything other than that of a prefect. As long as he holds office and does not abuse of the trust he has been shown, he is a priest. If for some reason he has to be deprived of his

---

[20]Luther on vocation, see above p. 134.

office, he is again a peasant or townsman like everybody else.[21] He is certainly not a priest when he is no longer in office. The talk about an indelible character is invented and twaddle. The only difference between priests and everybody else is their task and the purpose of their function. Like Luther, Bugenhagen refers to the letter to the Romans 12 and 1. Cor. 12 about the different members of the one body, and says: "Christ does not have two bodies or two kinds of body, a secular one and a clerical one. He is one head, and he has one body.

The ritual.

The act of introduction forms part of a usual Sunday service. After the reading of the Epistle a preacher or chaplain goes to the pulpit to talk about the initial praying, the election that has been made, and the qualities that are required of some one in the office of ministry:

> "Dear friends in Christ, you know that we have prayed in public that God for the sake of Christ, his dear son and our Lord, will send us good superattendants, pastors and ministers, chaplains and preachers. Those of us to whom it has been assigned have used their diligence and they have elected NN whom we consider – as far as this is possible for human judgement and reason – honest, capable and uncorrupted, not avaricious and without offence, he as well as his people who are with him, – and whom we also regard as able to teach our consciences and silence the contradictors with the words of the Lord, like Paul has it in the letters to Timothy and Titus, and like Christ teaches us about the conscientious steward according to the Gospel of Matthew Chapter 24".

And then he admonishes:

> "Pray, therefore, that God will give him grace through Jesus Christ our Lord, and that his service may lead us to salvation. Be aware of the example that Christ himself has given us in Luke 6: alone on the mountain he prayed the whole night before selecting and calling the 12 apostles to the task of preaching. Therefore, we should likewise

---

[21] Horst Beintker, 71.

entrust God with this matter through our prayers. In this way it cannot go wrong, even if unknowingly in spite of all earthly diligence we happen to have elected a Judas".

The preacher continues:

"So this NN is now to be presented before you in front of the altar with singing and praying and laying on of hands, so that we in this way commend him for the grace of God to this our ministry, and so that this congregation knows that this person has been entrusted with such an office with us.

I admonish the honourable council, the church fathers, and the public, young as well as old, to pray while the children sing the Halleluja".

Prayer.

During the singing of Halleluja and the psalm "Veni sancte spiritu" everybody is praying in silence.
All the preachers stand up and lay their hands on the ordinand including the ordinator, who reads the following prayer as he faces the congregation:

"Let us pray. Almighty, eternal Father. You have taught us through our only Master, Jesus Christ: "The harvest is rich, but the labourers are few, so ask the Lord of the harvest to send labourers to his harvest.

These words admonish us to pray sincerely for good labourers, that means preachers of your grace. We beg your groundless mercy that you may look to this servant of yours, our chosen preacher, with your grace and have mercy on him, so that he will industriously preach your Word Jesus Christ as our only salvation, teach the souls and comfort, punish, threaten, admonish with all the patience and love, so that the Holy Gospel can always stay pure with us, without addition of human doctrine, and bear fruit to eternal salvation for all of us through Jesus Christ our Lord".

Everybody responds with AMEN.

Now follows a psalm about the Holy Spirit sung by the congregation during which the priests kneel, committing the matter to God through Christ. And while the singing continues they quietly, "with dignity", leave the church to go back to their own pulpits to pray for this ordinand with their congregations.

The service continues in the usual manner with sermon and communion. Bugenhagen's final remark is: "We do not use any special attire or splendour for this occation". He emphasizes that this way of installing a servant of the Word is in accordance with the apostolic practice, short and Christian, and he concludes: "This ordination is valid before God and before the people for salvation".

The Wittenberg ordination of 1535

While the number of Lutheran communities was growing fast, Luther had to defend what he considered the apostolic view of ministry against two opposite parties, on the one hand the "papistic abuse", and on the other hand those extremists who found no need for the office of ministry at all. Confusion prevailed even among some of the ministers. Provoked not least by the persistent accusations from the Roman Catholic church, a manifestation came to be felt as a need, of the legitimacy of evangelical ministers' authority which would be acceptable to themselves as well as to the outside world.

In 1535 the Elector of Saxony complied with this demand by imposing an evangelical ordination ceremony. He ordered Luther to frame an ordination liturgy, which Luther reluctantly did.[22] The examination and ordination of the candidates were delegated to the University of Wittenberg, which meant in practice: to Luther and Bugenhagen. From then on, Lutheran ministers could be ordained in Wittenberg with a ceremony that was *not* to be repeated. Luther points out that this is "in accordance with the wish and denomination of the congregation, and our consent and choise".[23]

Apart from the non-repeatability, there are three new elements of importance in the new ordination ritual compared to the earlier practice. They are important because they lead the way to misinterpretations. Firstly, the ordinand is asked to give his vow to the ordinator. Secondly, the ordinator

---

[22]De biskoppelige handlinger. Præste- og bispevielse, provsteindsættelse og kirkeindvielse. Betænkning afgivet af Kirkeministeriets liturgiske kommission, nr. 848, København 1978, 8.
[23]WA 6, 408.

delegates to the ordinand the ministry of the Word, and thirdly, he gives the ordinand his benediction.

There are several versions of Luther's ordination ritual,[24] but the basic content is the same in all of them. The main element is still the same as in Bugenhagen's ritual: prayers of thanksgiving and intercessary prayer, and the ordination is still part of a usual service, but the ordination part has been expanded by incorporation of elements from the Roman Catholic ceremony, though emphasizing the difference from it, for instance in the interpretation of the readings from 1. Timothy 3 and Acts 20 that talk about bishops and superintendants. It says: "bishops are preachers and pastors", they are different words signifying the same task, namely that of "feeding God's herd with the Word and protect it against the secterial religions of papists, muslims and other hordes" in order to "preserve them in the old apostolic faith".

As a rule Luther used the traditional rituals in his liturgical directions, as long as they did not call for abuse or misconceptions. But in his ordination prayer the tradition cannot be traced. The choise of text material as well as the composition is original, and it is generally referred to as "Luther's Prayer". It is built over a coordination of the harvest motive from Matthew 9 and the first three articles of the Lord's Prayer, "may your name be held holy, your kingdom come, your will be done". Luther chose to use the Lord's Prayer for this purpose, as these are "your own words, because you know them by heart. You cannot pray in a better or more powerful way than this".

Although this procedure is "in accordance with the wish and denomination of the congregation, and our consent and choise", as Luther put it,[25] and although it is prescribed that the reading and the prayers must sound "loud and clear in front of the congregation" and not in Latin but in their native language for them to participate fully in the ceremony, this new practice differs destinctly from that of Bugenhagen. It indicates a delegation of power for the office of ministry, and it appears as a clerical confirmation of the vocation, which was of course the whole purpose of introducing a centralized ordination act. The practical circumstances seem to have been overwhelming enough to overpower considerations of the theological consequences.

---

[24]WA 38, 427 ff.
[25]WA 6, 408.

The earliest directions for a Danish ordination

The evangelical-Lutheran Reformation came through in the Danish Church in August 1536. In January 1537 a draft of the new statutes for church affairs was worked out.[26] The chapter on "How the servants of the church should be introduced"[27] has directions very similar to those in Bugenhagen's previous statutes.[28] It is initiated like this:

> "As ordination for priesthood is nothing other than a custom of the church whereby somebody is called to serve in the word of God and the sacraments, no one dare intrude into a parish and assume this service on his own without being lawfully called to do so.
>
> When a servant of the church is needed, there will be prayed hard before any one is selected. When those in need of such a person together with the rural dean ask the superattendant for a certain person, he is not to be introduced by the dean to serve in the church until he has been thoroughly examined and found sufficiently suitable for receiving the spiritual order to preach the Gospel to the congregation and to – not make the sacraments but distribute them, 1. Cor. 4".

After that, the dean installs him in his parish church during a Sunday service with psalms, prayer, laying on of hands and reading of the Holy Scripture from Titus.[29]

This first version of the Church Ordinance follows the directions we have seen in Bugenhagen's early ordinances, with one exception: Before the laying on of hands the ordinand promises to live up to the admonition that has just been read aloud. This element is found in Luther's ritual.

This ceremony is ordination and installation in one to be repeated every time a parish gets a new priest, in accordance with Bugenhagen's other church ordinances. There is no other ordination ceremony mentioned in this "original" church ordinance.

"This act of installation is completed by committing the matter to God with the words from Paul (1. Tim. 4,4-5) saying that the creature is made holy by the word of God and prayer."

---

[26] Martin Schwarz Lausten (ed.): Kirkeordinansen 1537/39, København 1989 (KO).
[27] KO 64 ff.
[28] See above p. 137.
[29] Titus 1,5-9. KO 65; 191.

The chapter is closed with the following comment: "These two both belong to assuming the service in the church: prophecy, that is scholarship and understanding of the Scripture, and a rightful calling, and whoever is missing one or both of these, cannot stay in office in any parish".

The Danish Church Ordinance of 1537/39

Later in the same year, 1537, a Latin version of the Church Ordinance is given and printed. Bugenhagen was called in to add the final touches. The new version presents several changes as far as the ordination is concerned. It is not known why or by whom the changes were carried through, but it is obvious that the Wittenberg ordination that was established two years before has played a role. The final result is a mixture of evangelical theology, as expressed in the German ordinances up to 1535 and in the first version of the Danish ordinance, – and Luther's Wittenberg ritual of 1535.

From now on two ceremonies are required instead of one. The first one is done by the superattendant, and is not to be repeated. It renders a clerical authorization. This is preceeded by an oath sworn to the king.

In the second ceremony which takes place the following Sunday, the rural dean introduces the already ordained person in his parish church, recommending him to the congregation in his sermon and reading aloud to them a letter of recommendation from the superattendant stating that he has the rightful calling, has been thoroughly examined and ordained etc.

It is interesting to note that the paragraph is retained which says that parish priests who have been ordained to the spiritual service in the church can be regarded as such as long as they stay true to the right learning of the Gospel in their preaching and in their mode of life. If they do not and a reprimand does not help, they are to be considered and called *un-ordained* like everybody else.

This paragraph is important because it shows that the idea of an indelible character has not found a revival in the Danish Church Ordinance of 1537/39, although the ordination procedure and ritual could seem to indicate it. But the practice which developed later on in the Danish Church certainly shows that derailment.

Conclusion

"It is against the Scripture to found traditions and pretend that observance of these can make us deserve justification. This is an insult to the justification brought to us by Christ".[30]

There is, however, no need to abolish traditions and old ceremonies, as long as it is understood that they are neither necessities nor in any way helpful for attaining salvation.

The crux of the matter in regard to ordination is when laying on of hands comes to be understood as a divine necessity, instead of what it is meant to be: a gesture to show that this Christian has been chosen by a congregation of Christians and found suited for the office of ministry by the person who represents knowledge of the undefiled apostolic faith, the superattendant or bishop.[31]

It is crucial, because it misleads into a falsified perception of ministry, a perception that elevates man, fails to recognize what belongs to God, and disregards the absoluteness of the redemption through Christ.

It is crucial when the ritual phrase "receive the office of ministry" is misunderstood as a clerical delegation of some degree of divine power, instead of what it is meant to be: a ceremonial repetition of VOCATIO with a sign, laying on of hands, indicating that this person is now to take up the duty of the Word, and our prayers concern his success with that.

Ministry is defined by nothing other than its function,[32] which is to preach the Gospel and administer the sacraments, and thereby be instrumental for the Holy Spirit to reach man, inspire faith and lead to salvation.

The church has to preserve the apostolic faith, but in principle there is no need for an ordination ceremony to do this. The apostolicity is ensured by observing what Luther and Bugenhagen pointed out: serious contemplation and thorough examination of the knowledge, faith and qualities of the candidate, a rightful vocation and prayers to God.

During the first two decades of the Reformation in Germany there was no ordination for Lutheran preachers, and the first version of the Danish Church Ordinance does not indicate ordination. There was an act of prayer

---

[30]CA 28, Grane p. 92.
[31]Superattendant and bishop are synonymous. The title of bishop was avoided the first years after the Reformation, because it was such a tainted title. After a few years, however, the traditional title of bishop was again in common use.
[32]CA 5, Grane p. 49.

in the parish church for the person who had been called, tried and appointed, before he assumed office.

In Luther's own words, rites that mislead and "fetter the consciences" are condemnable. Ironically enough, Luther's own ordination practice in Wittenberg after 1535, indeed forced by circumstances, seems to have been the very cause of the fact that evangelical churches lapsed back into exactly the misconception that the reformers fought so persistently against: the invented indelible character.

The paragraph that talks about the loss of clerical status when a "servant of the church ceases to be what he was" is found with perseverance in the writings of Bugenhagen and Luther as well as in the Danish Church Ordinance, but that particular instruction has to the best of my knowledge never been executed. Once ordained in the Church of Denmark you keep your clerical status for as long as you live, regardless how much you change from what you were or believed at the time of your ordination.

A Reformation without Reformer
The Realisation of the Reformation in Norway

Ingun Montgomery

In Norway the Reformation never attained the same great importance as in the neighbouring countries, Sweden and Denmark. Because of many reasons it became a rather dull and silent process.

The Norwegian historians never have had much to tell about the Reformation in Norway. It has never been regarded as important for the people or the country. It did not bring freedom either individually or politically. It is frequently seen just as a consequence of what happened in Denmark. In the royal charter of Christian III in 1536 it was stated that Norway should no more exist as an independent country but become a province of Denmark "since the realm of Norway is now so reduced, as well in power as in wealth".[1] The Norwegian council of the realm had dissolved when the Catholic bishops disappeared. The aristocracy in Norway was not strong enough to keep alive a council of state of their own. Therefore the Danish councillors became responsible also for the circumstances in Norway, for the royal legislation and administration of justice as well as of all major resolutions. Thus the king and the nobility were to share power during the period from the inauguration of the Reformation until absolutism was established in the year 1660.

The importance and influence of the church was largely reduced by this new power structure but that of the king was increasing and he got an extended responsibility for the church as well as the spiritual well-being of his subjects.

In the years around 1530 Norway was of small economic and political importance. Therefore the land had difficulties in adapting to the new ideals and life style which were arising in Central Europe. One of these new phenomena was the nation-state. But the most obvious reason perhaps was that the country did not have a responsible and unifying royal dynasty.

---

[1]Christian IIIs Haandfæstning af 30. October 1536. Printed in Samling av Danske Kongers Haand-fæstninger. Kbhvn. 1856/58, 1974.

Norway still had its financial centre in the Western part of the country with Bergen as its biggest city and centre of commerce. Therefore the Reformation started in Bergen, where it was first preached. And the first superintendent of Norway was appointed there when Geble Pederssøn was installed in his office at almost the same time as the first seven Danish superintendents, August 26 1537, by Luther's emissary Johan Bugenhagen.[2] But as soon as Norway was made a part of Denmark in 1536 the importance of Bergen declined as Oslo gradually became the centre of the administration, finances and defence of Norway, maybe the most important reason was that it was closer to Copenhagen.

At this time Norway was a rather poor country and scarcely populated. It had not yet recovered from the damage inflicted on it by the Black Death in the 1350s. About 1530 the three biggest cities of the country were Bergen with about 6-7 000 inhabitants, Trondheim with about 2 000 and at last Oslo which had almost 1 000 inhabitants.[3]

It looks as if the introduction of the Reformation in Norway simply was an administrative act. Questions of theology and belief seem to have played a minor role. Norway never got a native reformer who could personalise, internalise and propagate the message of the Reformation as for example Hans Tausen did in Denmark and Olaus Petri in Sweden.

This administrative aspect of the introduction of the Reformation in Norway is clearly seen in a letter from the king, Christian III, to the county governor, Eske Bille, of Bergen in the summer 1537.[4] In this the king ordered that no changes should be made in the religion until he had found a "better solution" how to lead the people with adequacy to "the right understanding of the Word of God". Thus it is obvious that the Reformation was carried out in Norway simply by accepting the Church Order because it was proclaimed the official confession of Denmark in 1537. And the Danish church order would be valid for the next 68 years in Norway until it in 1607 became its own Church Order.

Regarding Norway it seems that the introduction of the Reformation was set forth just simply by the clergy's accepting the new church order. We do not hear much about the feelings of ordinary people, neither of their acceptance nor opposition. Perhaps because in the beginning neither

---

[2]A. Chr. Bang, Kirkehistoriske Smaastykker. Chr. 1890. P. 226ff.
[3]A. B. Fossen, Bergen bys historie. Vol. 2. 1979. P. 3
[4]Christian IIIs Befaling til Befalingsmanden paa Bergenshuus angaaende Kirkevæsenet i Bergens Stift. 17de Juni 1537. Printed in Gjør døren høy. Kirken i Norge 1000 år. Drammen 1995. Pp. 289f.

rituals nor the content of the dogma were changed. The central administration in Copenhagen regarded just the acceptance of the Reformation and the new church order as its main interest, a task which was handed over to the secular authorities. The clergy retained the responsibility for interpreting the Scripture and applying it to every day life and morality. But in the first period of the Reformation period a spiritual authority was missing which could actively propagate and set the new doctrine through.

The king kept to his "go slow-tactic" and waited until 1541 to appoint superintendents in Stavanger and Oslo. Trondheim did not follow until in 1546. But on the other hand there was nobody, still in duty, who actively propagated the old Catholic religion. Therefore, more or less, nothing happened in Norway besides the formal adaptation to the new evangelical belief.

Setting through the Reformation

By this means the Reformation at first did not bring very many positive innovations. The new Church Order prescribed delegated responsibility according to which the parish members together with the dean should select the local vicar, and the local county governor together with the superintendent should co-operate in financial and legal matters. A co-operation of this kind demanded a new way of thinking which was not yet established and therefore in the beginning these innovations did not have any effect. But the negative effect of the Reformation, the collapse of the old school system, became very soon obvious.

In the beginning a lot of vicarages could not be filled with evangelical preachers so the clergy of the Catholic times stayed undisturbed in their ministry. In addition to that, the reformed clergy first had to find their places and define their position in relation both to the secular authorities and to their parishioners.

In the following we will refer to three of the main ways which were used to spread the new evangelical practice to the people.

Direct influence and information from Denmark

The main document of the Reformation was the Church Order of 1537/39. A part of the old Norwegian church law was confirmed in a royal letter in 1548.[5] These two documents did not include all questions to which the reformed church had to give responses in terms of rules so they had continuously to be supplemented by royal decrees.

The collection of standards, which thus arose, became very important. It was the duty of the Superintendents to be well acquainted with it, and to inform their clergy about it. Therefore it was copied and continuously systematised in order to be promulgated at synods as well as in circular letters to the clergy.

In 1550 the first complete Bible translation into Danish was published. Peder Palladius published in 1556 his service book, and in 1569 the first authorised hymn book was published by Hans Thomesen. Before publication it had been vetted by the professors of Theology at the university of Copenhagen and then approved by the king. To that must be added the unceasing demands of the authorities in Copenhagen for uniformity in liturgy and organisation of the church. All the Norwegian superintendents tried to comply with the required standardisation. It was attained mainly through visitations and synods of which the visitations turned out to be a problem because of long distances and bad roads, but also because the local vicars remained so passive.

Visitations

Franz Berg of the diocese of Oslo and Hamar was the one of the Norwegian Superintendents, who most systematically tried to carry out visitations. In 1555 he thus complained that he had "heavy work and great trouble with frequent visitations over mountains and valleys" and that the parishioners did not attend his visitations.[6] His successor Jens Nilssøn maintained practising visitations, while in office.[7] It was emphatically laid down in the new church order, that visitations had to be maintained by the

---

[5]Aabent brev om Frederik den Andens Hyldning av 1548. In H. Paus, Kongl. Forordn. II. Kbhvn 1751/52. p. 307
[6]Norske Riksreg. I. p. 124. H. Paus, Kongl. Forordn. II. Kbhvn 1751/52. p. 315f.
[7]Biskop Jens Nilssøns Visitatsbøger og reiseoptegnelser 1574-1597. Ed. Dr. Y. Nielsen. 1885

superintendent as an office duty. Visitations by the deans had also been provided there: "and once a year they should visit their diocese".

Peder Palladius had written down these regulations in his book *Formula visitationis provincialis*, which was published in 1555. It was to be of great importance for the Church of Norway, but not at once. A different kind of visitation was performed in the diocese of Trondheim. On December 24th 1586 the county governor, Christian Friis, on behalf of a royal letter, asked the Superintendent Hans Mogenssøn, and Hans Sigvardssøn, dean of the cathedral, and Jens Anderssøn, lecturer in the Latin school, to visitate the diocese together with him.[8] This visitation journey, which lasted for two years, was summed up in a report, which is called "Den Throndheimske reformats av 1589".[9] Since the county governor and the Superintendent, as it had been stated in the Church Order, made this visitation together, it was possible to accomplish many necessary alterations. But such an enterprise proved to be too comprehensive to become regular.

Synods

Diocesan synods are mentioned in the Danish draft of the Church Order. Its intention was that the Superintendent twice a year should call in his vicars and test them on doctrinal questions. But when the Church Order finally was published in a printed version, this passage was missing. Gradually, anyhow, it grew into a habit in the reformed church that the vicars met to discuss common problems and doctrinal questions. In Denmark the custom of summoning the clergy to synods gained a large importance in establishing the reformation.

Maybe the habit of this kind of meetings was left over from catholic times which helped it to become a natural part of the administration of the church even after the Reformation. In Denmark there existed three different kinds of Synods: The National synod where all the Superintendents and sometimes also the professors of Theology gathered together. The Diocesan synods (in Danish, *landemoder*) where each Superintendent assembled all his deans and sometimes also some of the

---

[8]Norske Riksreg. II. P. 688f.
[9]A. M. Hamre, Trondhjems Reformats 1589. (Norske Kyrkjelege Jordebøker II) Oslo 1983

vicars of his diocese. And at last the assemblies of the rural deanery where the deans reported to the vicars about what they had heard at the synod (in Danish *kalenter*).

Regarding Norway only the last two kinds of assemblies came into question. In his comprehensive work of consolidating the evangelical church, Bishop Peder Palladius systematically built up the synods into institutions of the ecclesiastical administration. Also his brother, Niels Palladius who was Bishop of Lund, adopted the system of diocesan synods. Like most of the reformers he emphasised the importance of teaching as a reason for calling synod meetings. In preaching the true doctrine all evil could be surmounted and the true church re-established. In order to preserve the true doctrine, which is the foundation of the church, the Superintendent and his deans must get together once or twice a year.[10] Their aim shall be *concordia et uniformitas doctrinae*.

Whether it was possible to apply these instructions to the church in Norway, we may ask. It took a long time before the synods became a permanent institution in Norway. During the time which we here are researching, i. e., the last decades of the 16th century, it seems that there had not been any synod at all in the dioceses of Oslo and Hamar. On the contrary, we get the impression that the Superintendent Franz Berg and his successor Jens Nilssøn spent all their time and efforts in carrying out their visitations.

Jens Nilssøn did indeed deliberate the possibility of holding synods. When he stayed in Denmark in 1580 in connection with his appointment as a Superintendent, he, in the form of questions, formulated the greatest difficulties faced by the church in his diocese, which he posed to the Superintendent of Seeland, Povel Madssøn. Among these, question number 15 read: "If it was allowed to have *synodum provincialem* once a year comprising both his dioceses, like the vicars in Denmark are used to have, and like it somewhere has been done and sometimes still is done in this area". He got a very clear and positive answer: "*Vtile esset si primo generalis, deinde provincialis synodus institueretur, semel in anno, circa festum Johannis. Sed abusus diligenter est cavendus, quem potissimum parit nimius luxus, celebretur igitur synodus provincialis a pulledio. P.M. praescriptam*".

---

[10]Niels Palladius, *Oratio de vera et catholica Ecclesia*. 1556. M. Schwarz Lausten, Biskop Niels Palladius. 1968. P. 45f.

The only evidence of synods during this time, anyhow, is to be found in the two dioceses Stavanger and Bergen in West Norway. In Stavanger synods were held in 1573, 1593 and in 1594. In the records of the synod of 1573 its aim is stated as being the implementation of the Church Order.[11] It was the main purpose of the other two synods too. Also from Bergen we have got the records of three synods. The first one was in 1569, when Jens Skielderup was Superintendent,[12] and the other two took place in 1584 and 1589 at the time of Anders Foss.[13] At these synods questions regarding all areas of church life were discussed. They were concerned about the vicars, their discharge of official duties and their private life as well as morals and ethics in the parish, worship orders, churchly ethics and legal matters, which fell under the church law. It may be of interest to notice, that the county governors usually took a negative stand against the synods and in some cases even tried to sabotage them, which was against the church order.

A short biographical background of Anders Foss

To show the contents and the proceedings of synods in general, the synods in Bergen in 1584 and 1589 are chosen as examples. On 12th June 1583 the King appointed Doctor Anders Foss as Superintendent of the diocese of Bergen.[14] Already during the autumn of this year he took up his duty in Bergen. He held his ministry until 1607, when he died at the age of 63 years. Like all the other Norwegian Superintendents of this time he was a Dane. Anders Foss was a well educated man for his time. He had studied not only in Copenhagen but also in Rostock, Leiden, Holland and France.

When he got back from his studies abroad he became headmaster of the convent school at Antvorskov in 1565. In July the following year he passed his master-of-arts degree in Copenhagen and soon thereafter he became a clergyman in Stege on the island of Moen and finally in 1583 he was, on the proposal of the Superintendent of Seeland, Povel Madssøn, appointed Superintendent of Bergen.

---

[11] Printed in Theologisk Tidskrift for den evangelisk-lutherske kirke i Norge. Vol. II. 1859. P. 245-259
[12] Norske Rigsreg. I. P. 228. Abs. Pederssøns Dagbok. Ed. R. Iversen. 1968. P. 149
[13] Norske Magasin II. P. 92-98. Edv. Edvardsens Bergen beskrivelse II. Ed. O. Brattegaard (Bergen hist. Foren. Skr. Nr. 57/58). 1951/52. P. 181-220
[14] H. Rørdam, Hist. Kildeskr. II. 1875. P. 544

It seems that Foss, as Superintendent of Bergen, tried to push through the idea of having annual synods, which at least one of the governors, Peder Thott, heavily opposed. On October 9th 1590 a report from the Administrator of Bergen to the government in Copenhagen speaks about the "incompatibility and hate" between the Superintendent and the governor.[15] In an attempt to settle the quarrel, the governor persuaded Foss to withdraw his "articles", which seemed to have referred to the articles of the synod of 1589.

There are detailed statutes preserved from the synods of 1584 and 1589. There are indications that a synod has been held also in 1585. But there is no evidence allowing us to draw the conclusion, that Foss succeeded in having annual synods, in spite of his coming from a diocese where this had been a well established custom. It looks like the synod of 1589 was to become his last one, just because of the governor's vehement opposition. These contradictions between governor and superintendent did not only concern official matters. Almost at the same time, the governor supported an accusation against the wife of Anders Foss, stating that she was a witch. Not until after two visits to the King in Copenhagen did Anders Foss manage to repel the accusation and thus free his wife, as well as himself indirectly, from the suspicion which at this time was a quite dangerous one. When the governor Peder Thott finally left Bergen in 1596, circumstances calmed down. In 1604 Foss became a member of the committee, which was at last commissioned to prepare a special Norwegian Church Order.[16]

The Synod of 1584

In the report of the proceedings of this synod interesting evidence of the attempt to consolidate the reformed church in a peripheral province of the Danish kingdom and of Reformation Europe is given. At this first synod, which was convoked soon after the arrival of Foss he had to handle a bundle of questions which without any doubt seemed elementary to him, who came from Denmark. He based his remarks mainly on the instructions given in the Church Order, the decisions of the two synods in Copenhagen of 1540 and 1542, at Ribe in 1542 and at Antvorskov in

---

[15]Norske Rigsreg. III. P. 150. Printed in H. Rørdam, Hist. Kildeskr. II. P. 550f.
[16]Norske Rigsreg. IV. P. 40f.

1546. All these documents were at least forty years old and still not well known in Norway.

The minutes of 1584 open with some more general remarks concerning the church. Then the Synod documents follow in 37 points, which will be briefly named here in order to show the kind of matters a Superintendent in Norway had to concern himself with: The questions are arranged in the following way: 1 - 3 deal with the office of the deans, 4 - 9 with those of the parish clergy, 10 - 14 are about general duties of the vicars in their parishes, 15 -16 and 37 are about financial duties. The main part of the issues, 17 - 36 is about liturgy and the practising of church order.

Themes of this kind are quite normal and supposed to be discussed at synods. But the most surprising fact is that they are dealt with so late in Norway. It is about forty years later than in Denmark.

In 1585 the minutes of the synods in Copenhagen in 1540 and at Antvorskov in 1546 were added in full to these statutes. Whether this was done by a new synod or was added as a supplementary clause, we can not say for sure. But in spite of their importance it is obvious that the decisions of Copenhagen and Antvorskov were so little known in Norway that they had to be published *in extenso.*

The synod of 1589

The minutes of this synod are opened with a preface, to which so far nobody has given any attention. Anyhow it gives a lot of information. The Superintendent seems to have started his inauguration speech by complaining about the fact that four years had passed since the last synod. If we take it for granted that Foss did not count wrong and that the synods usually were held in July or August, as in Denmark, we could draw the conclusion that a synod really had taken place in 1585. Then he is blaming his deans and vicars for forgetting what had been agreed in the last synod. To avoid this happening in the future he supports the idea that synods ought to be held every year. After briefly naming the questions which had been discussed in the previous synods, which concerned the way of life among the clergy, he gave a reminder of important ordinances and regulations which had newly been promulgated, and a short summary of the Church Order since its decrees were still not followed by all the clergy. Moreover the clergy were blamed for being lazy and indolent.

Therefore, the Superintendent tells them, that he intended at this convocation to repeat once more what he had said on the previous one, as well as promulgating new decrees. The deans should come together once each year in a synod. They should furthermore observe *De visitatione provinciali praepositorum* (1555) by Peder Palladius. The annual synods should be held according to the model formed by Palladius in 1540. At last the closing words of the statutes of Antvorskov are quoted word by word as an example of the annual synods as they were arranged in the diocese of Seeland. For eleven years Foss himself had been partaking in these meetings in Roskilde together with the governor, the Superintendent and 24 deans of the diocese, from which he had learned a lot.

When he starts speaking about the profit and pleasure which he had experienced at these synods, his way of speaking drops into a style which could be called a "synod sermon". He ended his sermon with an exhortation to the participants of 1589 to write down exactly what they were going to hear and discuss about. Then the statutes follow which are to be debated. Through this preface we can get at least a vague impression of what such a synod looked like.

If we go back to the synod of Roskilde in 1564 which is seen as a model by Foss, we can find some further details about the proceedings, because in the minutes of this meeting is reported: "At the beginning of the meeting the hymn *Veni sancte Spiritus etc.* had been sung and the Collecta Prayer had been said by the Superintendent.[17] Then he made an exegesis of the words of Paul in 1 Tim. 4.12 'set an example for the believers in speech, in life, in love, in faith and in purity.' He ended the sermon with a prayer for the preservation of the Gospel and of everything else that was necessary. Then he inquired thoroughly if all the deans were present and admonished them that everything that would be agreed in the statutes of the synod had to be carried out. After that the following articles were laid down..." In this passage we clearly can discern the tradition to which Foss had got used during his eleven years in Stege and it seems natural to think that he tried to establish something similar in Bergen.

Let us go back to the synod in Bergen in 1589 and we will find that many of the questions which were debated here were of almost the same nature as at other synods. But those which were new should be mentioned, among them are the behaviour and way of dressing of the clergy. Thus

---

[17]Kirkehistoriske Samlinger, 2R. P. 479ff.

the clergy was admonished to behave in a more friendly way to each other and to dress in a proper manner.

In this synod, for the first time the deans are asked to change the old altar pieces to the new pieces with texts from the catechism painted on them. Such text altar pieces are quite typical for the Reformation in Norway and they are more widely spread here than in any other Scandinavian country.

Conclusion

The aim of Anders Foss was to create a unified, reformed church in Norway following the same order as in Denmark. To reach this goal he applies for annual synods and convocations. As we have seen in both of his synods he tries to inculcate the stipulations from the Church Order and Ribe articles. He also quotes many of the minutes from the other Danish synods as well as the pastoral writings by Peder Palladius.

He also tries to make the church more independent from the governor and the civil authorities in stressing that they do not have the competence to determine inner ecclesiastical questions.

The Making of a Protestant Nation: "Success" and "Failure" in England's Long Reformation, c. 1530 – c. 1830

Jeremy Gregory

This paper has arisen from teaching a number of courses in religious history, from the late medieval to the late modern periods, during which I have become increasingly struck by what appears to me to be underlying common methodological and conceptual concerns faced by historians working on religious themes from the sixteenth to the nineteenth centuries, but who, nevertheless, are not always aware of work in periods deemed to be different from their own. The matter was crystalised when, in two review articles published recently, I learned on the one hand from Diarmaid MacCulloch that the Reformation had been a "howling success" by the early seventeenth century in its aim of making England into a Protestant nation (noting that when Civil War broke out in 1642, it was fought overwhelmingly between Protestants),[1] and on the other hand I was informed by Simon Green that the Victorians saw their own time as the beginnings of the Christianisation of the British people (of which Protestantisation was a part).[2] What is going on here? Do these two historians mean different things by terms such as "Christian" and "Protestant", do they (and/or their sources) differ in their ways of measuring religious commitment?, or are we talking about change over time (in this case a real decline in religious sensibility)?

One possible solution, which might appeal both to historians of the seventeenth and nineteenth centuries, though it would probably find less favour with historians of the eighteenth century[3], is that during the sixteenth and early seventeenth centuries England had indeed been Protestantised, but, because of the secularising tendencies of the century

---

[1] D MacCulloch, "The Impact of the English Reformation", *The Historical Journal*, 38 (1995), p. 152.
[2] SJD Green, "Unestablished Versions: Voluntary Religion in the Victorian North", *Northern History*, XXX (1994), p. 193.
[3] See, for example, JCD Clark, *English Society, 1688-1832. Ideology, Social Structure and Political Practice during the Ancien Regime* (Cambridge, 1985), and the contributions to *The Church of England, c. 1688- c. 1833. From Toleration to Tractarianism*, ed J Walsh, C Haydon and S Taylor (1993).

and a half after 1660, there was a need to start the whole process off again, allowing historians to talk of a "religious revival"[4] in the Victorian period. Another possible answer is that the remarkable upsurge in the number of Catholics after 1830, for whom a re-converted nation appeared a real possibility, made the need to protestantise seem more urgent.[5] A third, and perhaps rather more plausible explanation, is that many of those who might well have called themselves Protestant were not, or at least not in the eyes of the clergy and those members of the laity who considered themselves part of the religious elite. The problems which I had in reconciling these two review articles opens up the inter-related conceptual and methodological concerns of this paper: when was England made into a Protestant nation, and how have historians attempted to measure the success of that endeavour.

The question of time-scale is clearly important. Alongside the perennially fascinating, and certainly unresolved question of why the English Reformation happened, historians have become increasingly pre-occupied with the question of how it happened. Over a decade ago Christopher Haigh formulated a useful (and influential) schema whereby he suggested that the answers given to this second question could be broadly classifed under four heads: it was either a "rapid" Reformation imposed from "above"; or a "rapid" Reformation from "below"; a "slow" Reformation from "above"; or a "slow" Reformation from "below".[6] Whilst some historians have expressed doubts about the applicability of the Haighian model, and in particular have worried about the binary opposites implicit in the formula (and adding other variables in accounting for the uneven social and geographical spread of the Protestant message, such as north/ south; centre/ peripheries; town/ country; youth/ old-age; and gender), it has certainly been a stimulating framework for discussion.[7]

---

[4]For aspects of that "revival" see O Chadwick, *The Victorian Church* 2 vols (1970).

[5]JF Supple-Green, *The Catholic Revival in Yorkshire, 1850-1900* Leeds Philosophical and Literary Society, XXI (1990). It was perhaps such growth in numbers which led to a renewed anti-Catholicism: see, J Wolffe, *The Protestant Crusade in Great Britain, 1829-1860* (Oxford, 1991).

[6]C Haigh, "The recent historiography of the English Reformation", *The Historical Journal*, XXV (1982), pp. 995-1007.

[7]See the comments in D MacCulloch, *The Later Reformation in England, 1547-1603* (1990), pp. 125-143; id, "England", in A Pettegree ed, *The Early Reformation in Europe* (Cambridge, 1992), pp. 166-87 ; S Brigden, "Youth and the Reformation", *Past and Present*, XCV (1992), 37-67; P Crawford, *Women and Religion in England, 1600-1720* (1993). The ways in which regionalism affected the spread of the Reformation can be

But in some ways, the resonances of Haigh's schema have not been fully explored. Historians have paid more attention to the implications of the "above" and "below" aspects of the question, than to the chronological problem within Haigh's model: the question of when the Reformation happened. The confident assertions of AG Dickens, that England was by 1553 so firmly Protestant that Mary's attempt at Counter-Reformation was necessarily bound to fail,[8] and of GR Elton, that England in 1558 was more Protestant than anything else,[9] have been challenged by revisionists who, increasingly it seems, incline to the slow Reformation model.[10] Yet even for those historians who favour the slowest of slow Reformations, England was effectively and to all intents and purposes a Protestant nation by the end of Elizabeth's reign. Not only is this the view of historians sympathetic to the cause of the Reformation, it is an opinion shared by Catholic historians such as Eamon Duffy, who has been the most recent and the most vigorous defender of the strengths of late medieval Catholicism: "by the end of the 1570s", he has remarked, "whatever the instincts and nostalgia of their seniors, a generation was growing up which had known nothing else, which believed the Pope to be AntiChrist, the Mass a mummery, which did not look back to the Catholic past as their own, but another country, another world".[11]

At one level, of course, it must be true that England was Protestant by the late sixteenth century. If we define a Protestant nation as one that was not-Catholic, or one that was indeed anti-Catholic, then there seems no doubt of this. Evidence of all kinds, from historians of national identity, to social and cultural historians, and to estimates of Catholic strength, indicates that the majority of Englishmen and women (save perhaps in Lancashire, some areas in the north-east and the west Midlands, and in the few pockets of parishes in the south which conformed to John Bossy's model of seigneurial Catholicism) clearly identified themselves as anti-Catholic (or perhaps, rather, anti-papist), to such an extent that popular

---

seen in the contrast between P Clark, *English Provincial Society from the Reformation to the Revolution: religion, society and politics in Kent, 1500-1640* (Hassocks, 1977) and C Haigh, *Reformation and Resistance in Tudor Lancashire* (Cambridge, 1976).

[8]AG Dickens, "The early expansion of Protestantism in England, 1520-1558", *Archiv für Reformationsgeschichte*, 78 (1987), p. 220.

[9]GR Elton, *Reform and Reformation: England, 1509-1558* (1977), esp. pp. 382-9.

[10]Especially the contribtions to C Haigh, *The English Reformation Revised* (1987). Note Haigh's own comments in the Conclusion, p. 214: "By the 1580s, however, the Protestants had effectively won the struggle".

[11]E Duffy, *The Stripping of the Altars. Traditional Religion in England, 1400-1580* (New Haven, 1992), p. 593.

celebrations, the lighting of bonfires and the ringing of bells marked Protestant highdays and holidays within the calendar.[12] Indeed Jeremy Black has argued that "anti-Catholicism"[13] was the major ideological determinant for most seventeenth and eighteenth-century English people, marking them off from a foreign "other", and Linda Colley's exploration of national identity in the eighteenth century has amply demonstrated the role of anti-popery in forging a concept of Britishness.[14] Such statements seem to confirm Jan Albers' point that we need to think of religious identity in broadly based social and cultural terms, which could encompass enormous variations in theological understanding, and which removes us from the snare of rating or grading religious commitment on some sort of piety scale.[15] Yet the methodological problem of Albers' position, it seems to me, is that she nearly comes close to saying that if people in the past saw themselves as Protestant, then historians ought to view them as such. But we need to recognise that, even in the period, there were doubts about the real meaning and significance of such anti-popery. As late as 1724, Daniel Defoe, after nearly two centuries of anti-Catholic propaganda, could despair of those "who would spend the last drop of their Blood against Popery...[and] do not know whether it be a Man or a Horse".[16] We clearly shouldn't conflate a virulent anti-Catholicism (which as Colin Haydon has demonstrated penetrated far down the social scale) with a rigorous or even perhaps with a sufficient understanding of Protestantism.[17] How far does evidence of deep-rooted anti-Catholicism mean that the English were a Protestant nation in any meaningful sense? Christopher Haigh (again) has usefully observed that churchgoers in the late sixteenth century were "de-Catholicised but unprotestantised. What they were not is a good deal clearer than what they were".[18] He himself has interpreted the complaints of Puritan writers to

---

[12] D Cressy, *Bonfires and Bells. National Memory and the Protestant Calendar in Elizabethan and Stuart England* (1989).

[13] J Black, "The Catholic Threat and the British Press in the 1720s and 1730s", *Journal of Religious History*, 12 (1983).

[14] L Colley, *Britons!: Forging the Nation, 1707-1837* (New Haven, 1992).

[15] J Albers, "'Papist traitors' and 'Presbyterian rogues': religious identities in eighteenth-century Lancashire", in Walsh, Haydon and Taylor, *Church of England*, esp. pp. 319-20.

[16] Daniel Defoe, *The Great Law of Subordination Conside'd* (1724), p. 20.

[17] C Haydon, *Anti-Catholicism in Eighteenth-Century England. A Political and Social Study* (1993).

[18] C Haigh, *English Reformations. Religion, Politics and Society under the Tudors* (Oxford, 1993), p. 290.

suggest that what was more apparent by the early seventeenth century was the failure rather than the success of the protestantisation process (which, for him, helps account for the acceptance of Laudianism in the parishes).[19] Indeed some historians, echoing the laments of early seventeenth century puritans, have argued that far from creating a truly Protestant nation, the upheavals associated with the first century of the Reformation had created a godless nation, one where large numbers stayed away from church, neglected the sacrament, and indulged in shopping on Sundays. For Robert Whiting, the century witnessed less a transition from Catholicism to Protestantism than a decline from religious commitment into conformism or indifference.[20]

This raises the methodological problem of how one should gauge the extent and the degree to which Protestantism succeeded. In answering this, a number of definitional and conceptual problems spring to mind. What, for example, did a Protestant nation look like? How far need it have been a "confessional" state comparable to those emerging in early modern Germany?[21] In any case, how should an individual's commitment to Protestantism be measured? Attendance at church can be counted, but it is impossible to penetrate the personal commitment of believers, or their sincerity. Furthermore, what demands did Protestants make of individuals before they could be regarded as Protestants? To what extent did parishioners have to be able to read and understand Protestant doctrine before they could accept its arguments. To put in bluntly, do things need to be coherently understood to influence thought and behaviour? Moreover, how far is instruction a way to measure the effectiveness of the Protestant message? (These are of course concerns not only facing modern historians: the problem of establishing the degree of commitment required before being counted a Protestant, and indeed defining what was meant by Protestant provided the very stuff of the religious debates in the three centuries after 1530).

One of the problems in assessing the extent to which the English had been protestantised at any given moment is that the sources are

---

[19]C Haigh, "The Church of England, the Catholics and the People", in *The Reign of Elizabeth I* (1985), ed. Haigh, pp. 169-220.

[20]20.R Whiting, *The Blind Devotion of the People. Popular Religion and the English Reformation* (Cambridge, 1989), p. 268.

[21]See, for example, EW Zeeden, *Die Entstehung der Konfessionem: Grundlagen und Formen der Konfessionsbildung in Zeitalter der Glaubenskampfe* (Munich, 1965) and his *Konfessionsbildung: Studien zu Reformation, Gegenreformation, und Katholischen Reformation* (Stuttgart, 1985).

ambiguous. My title is in part a reference to a debate amongst historians of the European Reformation, inaugurated in 1975 by Gerald Strauss, who controversially argued that, largely because of the methods employed in educating people into the fundamentals of the Protestant faith, the German Reformation was, at least until the late sixteenth century, more a tale of "failure" than a "success" story, creating indifference rather than religious commitment.[22] The most obvious pieces of documentary evidence, such as visitation returns (the sources which Strauss himself exploited to indicate the failure of the German Reformation to disseminate the essentials of Protestant doctrine) are fraught with interpretative problems, dealing as they do with the outward behaviour of parishioners, and being essentially the view of the religious professionals. Some instances at any point in the period from 1530 to 1830, it is true, can be used to subvert Strauss's picture of failure, suggesting that his gloomy analysis needs to be more nuanced: evidence can certainly be found of a religiously well-educated laity who regularly attended divine service and received the sacrament, who sent their children and servants to be catechised, and who, in the view of one early seventeenth-century minister, made England "the only nation, almost, that doth openly and solely profess the true religion of God".[23] But, it cannot be denied that a recurring theme of such replies is a sense of failure and frustration. Clergy frequently complained of the theological ignorance of their parishioners, and often behind their complaints is a sense of nostalgia for a religious world which had been lost, with regular comments on the decay of religious practice, and at times a suggestion that secularisation was occurring.[24] In 1602, even after the efforts of the godly pastors so admired by Professor Collinson, Josias Nichols complained that only 1 in 10 of the inhabitants of a Kentish parish with 400 inhabitants of communicable age knew the basis of Protestant doctrine.[25] A similar point was made in

---

[22]G Strauss, "Success and Failure in the German Reformation", *Past and Present*, 67 (1976), pp. 30-63. See also id., *Luthe's House of Learning: Indoctrination of the Young in the Germann Reformation* (Baltimore, 1978) and id., "The Reformation and its Public in an Age of Orthodoxy", in RP Hsia ed, *The German People and the Reformation* (Ithaca, NY, 1988), pp. 194-214. For the debate see, JM Kittelson, "Successes and failures in the German Reformation: the Report from Strasbourg", *Archiv für Reformationsgeschichte* 73 (1982), pp. 153-75, and G Parker, "Success and Failure during the first century of the Reformation", *Past and Present*, 136 (1992), pp. 43-82.

[23]William Whately, in 1623: quoted in Collinson, *Birthpangs*, p. 8.

[24]For example, the lament of in that the influnce of religion had diminished, was diminishing and ought to be increased.

[25]Quoted in S Doran and C Durston, *Princes, Pastors and People: the Church and*

1680s, by the incumbent of Bougton Malherbe[26], though there is perhaps some excuse here because of the ways in which the Civil war had interrupted the protestantising process (or at least that part of the process approved of by the Church of England).[27] But as late as 1758, the rector of Bapchild informed the archbishop of "the great ignorance of the lower sort of people, and servants, in religious matters, not only indeed in this, but in all other parishes in this country, in which I have ever been concerned. There is hardly one in three, that I have ever met with, that knows who Jesus Christ is, and the need and design of his coming into the world".[28] Similarly, a Norfolk cleric in 1843 remarked that after 13 years of preaching the gospel, he was firmly convinced that his efforts had been an entire failure.[29] The point of these instances is to demonstrate that, according to some definitions, the Reformation was not even assured by the early nineteenth century.[30]

Such complaints by the religiously zealous of the religious habits of the rest of the population are, however, probably a misleading guide to the religious commitment of parishioners, provoking historians to question how far can one take the assumptions of the religious die-hards as evidence of the success or of the failure of the Protestant enterprise. The recurring dismay about the religious commitment of large sections of the parish has encouraged historians to wonder about the true nature of those deemed "ungodly" and of what has been termed "popular religion". One of the most influential ways of talking about "popular religion" has been to oppose it to the "religion of the elite"; a whole tradition in historiography, from Keith Thomas, writing on the sixteenth and early seventeenth centuries, through to Jim Obelkevich, writing on the mid-nineteenth century, has highlighted the "magical" and "superstitious" elements within a popular religious culture, stressing the antagonism between this and the official Protestant religion.[31] Yet, as so often with models which implic-

---

Religion in England, 1529-1689 (1991), p. 82.

[26]26.

[27]But see J Morrill, "The Church in England, 1642-9", in *Reactions to the English Civil War*, ed. Morrill (1982), pp. 105-24, for a suggestion of the survival of the Church even during the Interregnum.

[28]Lambeth Palace Library, MS 1134/1, f.33.

[29]The Diaries of Arthur Upcher (in private hands), vol 2, p. 30.

[30]Cf. D Bebbington, 'Religion and Society in the Nineteenth Century", *The Historical Journal* 32 (1989), 997-1004,

[31]K Thomas, *Religion and the Decline of Magic* (1971) and J Obelkevich, *Religion and Rural Society: South Lindsey, 1825-1875* (1976).

itly oppose "elite" and "popular" habits of mind, we might have underestimated the ways in which the official Protestant message could percolate through society, and we may have exaggerated the gulf between "elite" and "popular" religiosity. Whatever the situation in the sixteenth and seventeenth centuries, Mark Smith, in a provocative study, has demonstrated the far-reaching social purchase of the Anglican Church in the most surprising of periods and in the most surprising of places: Lancashire in the late eighteenth century, which may represent an improvement on the earlier situation.[32] It could be that Eamon Duffy's suggestion that for the pre-Reformation church the term "traditional" religion (so long as we remember that is was lively and not as static as the phrase might imply) should replace the term "popular" religion in discussing a shared, rather than a bifocated, relgious culture,[33] has some applicability for the way in which the Protestant faith was able to relate to popular culture in the centuries after 1530.

What we might also be able to learn from the visitation returns is not necessarily that the Reformation in England was a failure (although some historians might suggest that it was), but to indicate that it should be seen as a continuing and complex process and not as an event with a straightforward beginning and end. Indeed, I would want to offer a rival interpretation to the usually limited chronological focus (often amounting to less than a century) which has ended consideration of the Reformation in 1559, 1603 or 1640, by emphasising the long and drawn-out nature of the English Reformation. Even if the political Reformation had been won by the seventeenth century, there was still much to do in bringing the Protestant faith to the hearts and minds of the English people, and this was a process which took centuries rather than years or decades. Furthermore, we will have an improved understanding of what the Reformation implied, and its broad social consequences, if we track its influence and its ideology well into the eighteenth and early nineteenth centuries, for arguably only then were the effects of the Reformation seen in the parishes (such as a professionalised clergy and a religiously educated laity).

In the process of making England Protestant, it might be suggested that historians are currently talking about three inter-related, but in some ways distinct aspects of the process which we now label under the um-

---

[32]M Smith, *Religion in Industrial Society. Oldham and Saddleworth, 1740-1865* (Oxford, 1994).

[33]E Duffy, *Stripping*, introduction.

brella term of the "English Reformation", and while there was clearly an overlap in aims, they need to be unpicked in order to evaluate "success" and "failure". First, there was the process of de-Catholicisation, the weaning away from the old faith. This entailed the dismantling of some of the traditional forms of worship, and was often accompanied by an intense iconoclasm which aimed to destroy an entire religious system.[34] Second, and this might have gone hand in hand with the first type of Reformation, there was a process of Protestantisation (a process, which in its intial stages entailed making committed Catholics into committed Protestants). It was these first two types of Reformation which represented the areas of greatest success in the sixteenth and early seventeenth centuries, although historians have frequently pointed to the dangers of reading changes of heart onto the evidence of changes of behaviour, and even the process of iconoclasm could be a protracted business. As late as the 1770s, for example, die-hards in Gloucestershire were moved to erase a tombstone inscription which seemed to proclaim a belief in prayers for the dead.[35] And the processes of de-Catholicisation and Protestantisation could be unrelated. Robert Whiting, for example, has argued that the destruction of Catholicism owed less to the rise of Protestant convictions than to the motive power of essentially secular compulsions.[36] Third, there was the far harder task of Christianisation, the attempt to make those who appeared irreligious into committed Christians, let alone into committed Protestants. This third aspect of the Reformation was not, of course, limited to Protestants, and a number of historians have demonstrated the similarity (and indeed the continuity) of the Catholic and the Protestant attempts to transform the religious behaviour and attitudes of those considered to be irreligious and ungodly.[37]

In some ways, of course, the aims of "de-Catholicisation", "Protestantisation" and "Christianisation" were bound up with one another, but noting their different aims and objectives, does help us to observe shifts in priorities at specific periods, in different regions, and even among individual clergy, and to recognise that success or failure in one of these objectives was not necessarily matched by success or failure in other areas. The difference in these objectives has been described by David

---

[34] M Aston, *England's Iconoclasts*, I. *Laws against Images* (Oxford, 1988).
[35] Ibid., p. 3.
[36] Whiting, *Blind Devotion*, p. 266.
[37] For example, John Bossy, *Christianity in the West, 1400-1700* (Oxford, 1985).

Hayton who has recently shown how, in Ireland, late seventeenth and early eighteenth century Protestant clergy saw their main task, not of prosleytising Catholics (de-Catholicisation), but of strengthening the nominally Protestant base.[38] We might useful apply this to the English context, where even when the Catholic threat at home was negligible, in the face of what appeared to be the forward march of Catholicism in Europe in the late seventeenth and early eighteenth centuries, the priority was to repel that advance. Because of the fear that through indifference, ignorance, and moral decline the Protestant interest was losing ground, the major imperative was seen as strengthening the Protestant majority, rather than converting the Catholics.

Seeing the Reformation as three separate strands begs the question not only of when the Reformation ended, but also when it began. Patrick Collinson has suggested that as far as the process of de-Catholicisation is concerned we need to go back to the time when Catholicism in England was first challenged to the time when its politcal hopes were finally extinguished: the three centuries from Wycliffe's first intellectual repudiation of the Church in 1378 to the ovethrow of the Catholic James II in 1688/9[39] (although Jacobite historians would no doubt want to extend this latter date to as late as 1745/6 when the danger of a Franco-Spanish alliance to return a Catholic monarchy seemed real).[40] Some historians would argue that aspects of the protestantisation process (such as the interest in individual and private religious practice, and the concern with literacy), can be found in a "pre-mature" Reformation with its origins in the fifteenth century.[41] And as far as the the conversion of the lives of the ungodly is concerned, it has been argued by Martin Ingram that this needs to be fitted into a process going back perhaps a thousand years or more.[42]

---

[38]D Hayton, "Did Protestantism fail in early eighteenth-century Ireland?: Charity schools and the enterprise of religious and social reformation c.1690- 1730", in *As by law established. The Church of Ireland since the Reformation*, ed. A Ford, J. McGuire and K. Milne (Dublin, 1995), esp. p. 175.
[39]P Collinson, "England", in *The Reformation in National Context*, ed. B. Scribner, R Porter and M Teich (Cambridge, 1994), p. 81.
[40]See for example, E Cruickshanks, *Political Untouchables* (1979).
[41]A Hudson, *The Pre-Mature Reformation. Wycliffite Texts and Lollard History* (Oxford, 1988), but note Christine Carpenter's reservations about how far such developments anticipated a Reformation: "The religion of the gentry of fifteenth-century England", in D. Williams ed, *England in the Fifteenth Century* (Woodbridge, Suffolk, 1987), pp. 53-74.
[42]M Ingram,

Stressing the continuing Reformation (the Reformation as *longue durée*), might encourage us to avoid getting bogged down in discussions over terminology, such as the disputes amongst European historians over the beginnings and endings of the "first", "second" and "third" Reformations,[43] and the confusion amongst historians of England over the precise demarcation between the "early" and the "late" Reformation.[44] Continuity may, of course, refer to the absence of change, but, as Peter Burke has pointed out, the term can also be used to describe a particular kind of change, a change which was more or less even in rate and constant in direction.[45] More fundamentally, stressing the long and drawn-out nature of the Reformation, might help us concentrate on the making, and the constant making of the Reformation. Whilst some historians have characterised the Anglican regime in particular as suffering from inertia and hidebound by tradition, that is not the way it seemed to those involved in the process of handing down the Protestant message. The ways in which Protestant (and perhaps above all Anglican) attitudes were diffused is often described in terms of metaphors like "survival" "inheritance" or "legacy", one needs to make an effort to remember that this inheritance was not automatic, and indeed that it had to be worked for, it did not just happen by some kind of osmosis.

In discussing the making of a Protestant nation, historians have spent a great deal of time in looking at those who can be called the makers of the Reformation. The key group, of course, in England as elsewhere, were the clergy. A major theme in the historiography has been to study the creation of a cadre of officials charged with implementing Protestantism in the parishes, usually under the concept of the professionalisation of the clergy, an umbrella term covering the various attempts to re-fashion the clergy along Protestant lines, replacing the intercessor of the Catholic church with the educative and pastoral roles of the Protestant minister. This development encompassed clerical recruitment, education and training, and ought to be seen as a process lasting several centuries, rather than, as some historians have suggested, being limited to

---

[43]For example HJ Cohn, "The Territorial Princes in Germany's Second Reformation, 1559-1622", in *International Calvinism, 1541-1715*, ed. M Prestwich (Oxford, 1985), pp. 135-63; K von Greyerz, *The Late City Reformation in Germany* (Weisbaden, 1980), pp. 196-203; B. Nischan, "The Second Reformation in Brandenburg", *Sixteenth-Century Journal*, 14 (1983), 173-87.
[44]See for example, the dating of MacCulloch's, *Later Reformation*.
[45]P Burke, "Concepts of continuity and change in History", *New Cambridge Modern History*, XIII Companion volume (1979), p. 3.

a couple of periods of intense activity, such as the late sixteenth century and the mid nineteenth century.[46] And if we are talking about the making of a Protestant nation, then the clergy of the Church of England represented the group most likely to think (and possibly to act) in national terms. Their recruitment, education and contacts made them the national profession *par excellence*, and it was they, possibly more than any other section of society, which furthered the creation of a Protestant national identity.

But we also need to look at the mechanisms by which the Protestant message was disseminated and transmitted throughout society. Here, what needs to be highlighted is the massive educational endeavour which underpinned the spread of the Reformation in England. Many of the religious movements and revivals from the sixteenth to the nineteenth centuries, such as Puritanism, Methodism and Evangelicalism, can be explained as renewed efforts in this direction. For all clergy in the post-Reformation world, the sermon was the principal mode of communication (though there were debates about how and where sermons should be delivered), and some groups emphasised the importance of preaching over other pastoral attributes. We ought to pay particular attention to the role of print culture in establishing religious norms, such as through reading the Bible, the writing and the learning of catechisms, the printing of sermons and devotional literature.[47] We should, of course, recognise that this educational mission was not merely an English, or even merely a Protestant phenomenon. John Bossy, amongst others, has forcefully argued for the common shift towards a print religion in both Catholic and Protestant countries.[48] And, it has been suggested that if England stands out as a regime with a high degree of interest in the printed Bible, it was because of the well-established pre-Reformation tradition of having a Bible in print.[49] Yet it might be worth observing that Protestantism did put special emphasis on literacy and understanding. We might note, for example, in a comparative conference like this, the extraordinarily high

---

[46]For example, R O'Day, *The English Clergy: The Emergence and Consolidation of a Profession, 1558-1642* (Leicester, 1979); B Heeney, *A Different Kind of Gentleman. Parish Clergy as Professional Men in Early and Mid-Victorian England* (Connecticut, 1976); A Haig, *The Victorian Clergy* (1984).
[47]On the significance of print generally see, E Eisenstein, *The Printing Press as Agent of Change: commmunication and cultural transformations in early modern Europe* 2 vols. (Cambridge, 1979).
[48]Bossy, *Christianity in the West*
[49]Porter, Scribner, Teich , *Reformation in National Context*, p. 219.

literacy rates in Scandinavia (in some areas a staggering 90% of the population were deemed literate by 1700) which go a long way to explain how it was that the Reformation was so assured there by the mid seventeenth century.[50]

But if the spread of literacy and the related educational endeavour have been seen as vital factors in accounting for the success of the Reformation in England, it has also been suggested that the same process also accounts for the failure of the Reformation amongst some social groups. It can, for instance, be maintained that the Protestant stress on literacy made the message inaccessible to the illiterate poor, and some studies have argued that this led to a further alienation of the poor from the "official" religious culture, perhaps creating disaffection towards the religious establishment, rather than Christianising those deemed to be ungodly.[51] And there is some evidence which indicates that the desire to give information through the diffusion of literature which told the reader not only of the right way to live their lives, but did so by outlining the heresies which had to be avoided, could have unimagined consequences. Robert Payne told the Society for the Propagation of Christian Knowledge in 1729 that, although he held Bishop Gibson's Pastoral letter against Infidelity, which had mentioned the writings of the free-thinkers Toland, Tindal, Collins and Wollaston, in high esteem, "as the poison to which it is an antidote has not spread amongst the poor, he does not think it advisable to put into their hands",[52] and Charles Bean similarly remarked that though "the clergy in these parts have generally thought it not prudent to put the refutations of infidelity into the hands of their country parishioners, lest it should excite them to the curiosity of trying the strength of a poison to which they are hither absolute strangers and think it more beneficial to give them catechetical, devotional and other practical tracts against the common vices".[53]

We also need to stress, as some recent research has done, the attempts to bridge the gap between the literate and non-literate worlds, either through the commitment to spreading literacy through various educational initiatives, such as grammar schools, charity schools, Sunday schools, and the tracts distributed by the Society for the Propagation of Christian

---

[50]Parker, "Success and Failure", pp. 78-9.
[51]Inter alia, Thomas, *Decline of Magic*.
[52]SPCK, LB 234/7, p. 5.
[53]Ibid., p. 14.

Knowledge, which arguably helped to create a ladder joining the two worlds,[54] or through exploiting forms of communication such as visual images and music which might transcend the written word.[55] In any case, the binary polarity implicit in the distinction between literate/ illiterate and between print/ oral culture may be too schematic. We ought to remember that Protestantism was a religion of the word, not just of the book, and that there were ways in which the word could reach even the illiterate.

In disseminating the Protestant message, we need also to point to the effect of regular attendance at church services, above all through the auspices of the Church of England, where the constant hearing of the Anglican liturgy, most notably via the Book of Common Prayer, inculcated religious knowledge in the hearers. Evidence from the parish of Hernehill in the 1830s has shown how the majority of the poor in the parish - many of whom became followers of the Courtenay rising of 1838 - were regular attenders at the parish church, possessed Bibles and other religious books, and that a significant number were dedicated members of the church choir.[56]

Acknowledging the long-tern nature of the Reformation might also help us to think again about the development of nonconformity and dissent, and the position of groups who to some extent rivalled what might be termed "mainstream Anglicanism". On the one hand, it was precisely the debates about what consisted a real Protestant which fuelled the development of Protestant rivals to the Church of England. The emergence of religious groups in the sixteenth, seventeenth, eighteenth and nineteenth centuries, which, to varying degrees seem to have stood outside main-

---

[54]See, for example, the remarks in I Green, "'For Children in Yeeres and Children in Understanding': The Emergence of the English Catechism under Elizabeth and the Early Stuarts", *Journal of Ecclesiastical History*, 37 (1986), 397-425. Dr Green's forthcoming full-scale study of this subject will illuminate the problem.

[55]On the role of printed images, see T Watt, *Cheap Print and Popular Piety, 1550-1640* (Cambridge, 1991). The role and power of music to convey religious sentiments has been almost totally neglected. But some inklings of the possibilities of the subject can be found in W Webber, *The Rise of Musical Classics in Eighteenth-Century England. A Study in Canon, Ritual and Ideology* (Oxford, 1992); J Gregory, "Anglicanism and the Arts: Religion, Culture and Politics in the Eighteenth Century" in J Black and J Gregory eds, *Culture, Politics and Society in Britain, 1660-1800* (Manchester, 1991), esp pp. 96-100, and V Gammon, "Babylonian Performances: the rise and suppression of Popular Church Music, 1660-1870", in E and S Yeo eds, *Popular Culture and Class Conflict, 1590-1914* (Brighton, 1991), p. 62-84.

[56]B Reay, "The Last Rising of the Agricultural Labourers: the Battle in Bossenden Wood, 1838, *History Workshop Journal*, XXVI (1988), 79-101.

stream Anglicanism, and which have had their own lively historiography, such as the emergence of Puritanism, the rise of Laudianism, the origins of Methodism, the impact of Evangelicalism, and the nature of the Oxford Movement, as well as the existence of more obviously dissenting groups, might usefully be seen as a logical consequence of the English Reformation, not only working out tensions which were inaugurated in the early sixteenth century (especially concerning Church authority and organisation), but perhaps more significantly for our purposes, finding different ways of furthering the Reformation in the parishes. It can also be suggested that these surges of religious activity represented some kind of generational revolt, and it might also be possible to attempt a sociology of revival where, most commonly young men, disatisfied with contemporary religious practice (perhaps we should also call them "alienated intellectuals") joined together to form alternative religious cultures. On the other hand, stressing the common aims behind these seemingly diverse groups helps to suggest that the historiographical tendency to emphasise differences between religious movements and to compartmentalise them into separate historical agendas (partly because of religious propaganda, partly for historiographical convenience, partly becuase of an excessively "denominational" approach to religious movements) has been misleading. Rather, we need to emphasise the similarities and connections, both in ideas and personnel, between religious groups, so that seemingly opposed movements can be shown to have shared not only a common inheritance, but could also indulge in shared alliances, which makes it difficult to talk of definite and distinct groupings. Here I would point to the parallel debates in historiography over the distinctions between "Puritans" and "Anglicans" in the late sixteenth century,[57] "Calvinists" and "Arminians" in the early seventeenth century,[58] between Anglicans and "dissenters" in

---

[57]The debates over the relationship between "Puritans" and "Anglicans" are most obviously followed in the works of Patrick Collinson, especially in his *Godly People. Essays on English Protestantism and Puritanism* (1993) and in id, *The Religion of Protestants. The Church in English Society, 1559-1625* (Oxford, 1982). Also, P Lake, *Moderate Puritans and the Elizabethan Church* (Cambridge, 1982) and id., *Anglicans and Puritans? Presbyterianism and English Conformist Thought from Whitgift to Hooker* (1988).

[58]See N Tyacke, *Anti-Calvinists. The rise of English Arminianism, c. 1590-1640* (Oxford, 1987); K Fincham, *Prelate as Pastor. The Episcopate of James I* (Oxford, 1990); P White, "The Rise of Arminianism Reconsidered", *Past and Present*, 101 (1983), 34-54; J Davies, *The Caroline Captivity of the Church, Charles I and the remoulding of Anglicanism, 1625-1641* (Oxford, 1992).

the late seventeenth century,[59] between Methodists and Anglicans in the eighteenth century,[60] and between Evangelicals and High Churchmen in the early nineteenth century,[61] all of which increasingly seem to have had common pastoral aims, and where the polarities were less sharp than used to be believed. Moreover, from the vital perspective of the parish, these distinctions look increasingly blurred. Puritanism, Laudianism, Methodism, Evangelicalism and Tractarianism, as well as "mainstream Anglicanism" represented an attempt to mould religious sensibilites. Instead of concentrating on the differences between the Church and its rivals, it might be worthwhile to think of different religious movements in terms of cycles of Reformation endeavour. For whatever their differences, the professed aims (and often the methods) of these various groups were often strikingly similar.

In understanding the relationship between these groups and the Church of England, we need to see them not only in terms of reacting against the established Church, but more positively in terms of emerging from and drawing on the Church, often building on Anglican pastoral initiatives. Patrick Collinson has shown that some of the supposed hallmarks of Puritanism, such as lectures and prophesyings were entrenched within contemporary Anglicanism.[62] Similarly, John Walsh has demonstrated how far the Methodist interest in the group meeting drew on Anglican models of religious societies.[63] We might also point to the ways in which certain supposedly "evangelical" initiatives, such as the development of Sunday schools in the late eighteenth century, not only had firm Anglican support, but were often instigated by Anglicans.[64] In any case, the fluidity of relations between the Church and dissent allowed

---

[59] J Spurr, *The Restoration Church of England, 1646-1689* (New Haven and London, 1991); J Ramsbottom, "Presbyterians and Partial Conformity in the Restoration Church of England", *Journal of Ecclesiastical History*, XLIII (1992), 249-70.

[60] On Methodism, see J Walsh, "The Origins of the Evangelical Revival", in *Essays in Modern English Church History*, ed. GV Bennett and JD Walsh (1966), pp. 132-62.

[61] See G Rowell, *The Vision Glorious. Themes and Personalities of the Catholic Revival in Anglicanism* (Oxford, 1983), pp. 5-7.

[62] P Collinson, "Lectures by Combination: structures and characteristics of Church life in seventeenth century England", *Bulletin of the Institute of Historical Research*, (1975), 182-213.

[63] J Walsh, "Religious Societies: Methodist and Evangelical, 1738-1800", in *Voluntary Religion*, Studies in Church History 23 (1986), pp. 279-302.

[64] See, for example the role of George Horne, who, as a firm High Churchman, supported the Sunday schools in Kent. See T Laqueur, *Religion and Respectability: Sunday Schools and Working Class Culture, 1780-1850* (New Haven, 1976), who mistakenly assumes that Horne was an evangelical.

"nonconformist" styles and techniques to be re-absorbed (and de-radicalised) within the Church, demonstrating how religious literature such as that by John Bunyan could transcend its denominational roots.[65] These shared aims and the common inheritance of these religious groups and movements supplied the basis for the large amount of inter-denominational co-operation, which as a number of studies have shown, was a constant feature of the English religious landscape.[66] Denominational histories have frequently used sources which suggest conflict, and have tended to play down the common inheritance of these groups, but we need to go beyond such sources to admit the considerable evidence of tolerance and co-operation which might exist in practice. For instance, Timothy Davies has found evidence of co-operation in the 1660s even between Anglicans and Quakers, usually seen as the group who displayed the greatest antagonism towards the Church establishment.[67]

The fact that Protestant groups in England after 1530 had much in common, especially in their pastoral aims, should not be surprising since recent historians have also suggested that there were even similarities between Catholic and Protestant ways of spreading the Christian message.[68] Mark Byford, for example, in a pioneering study of the impact of Protestantism in Essex, has forcefully argued that a great deal of what clergy before and after the Reformation preached and taught was fundamentally the same, allowing him to call the Protestant Reformation a "religious revival", rather than being a new departure.[69] He points to the wide range of pastoral manuals published during the sixteenth century concerning moral advice which stood outside conventional Reformation controversy. In a similar vein, Brad Gregory has demonstrated the ways

---

[65] On Bunyan's popularity within the Church of England, see Gregory "Anglicanism and the Arts", pp. 90-1. A similar remark could be made of the music of Handel, which by the late eighteenth century was an opportunity for co-operation between the Church of England and dissent: Webber, *Musical Classics*, pp. 140, 245.

[66] See, for example, WJ Gregory, "Archbishop, Cathedral and Parish: the diocese of Canterbury, 1660-1805" (Oxford, DPhil thesis, 1993), pp. 181-241; Smith, *Religion and Industrial Society*.

[67] TA Davies, "The Quakers in Essex, 1655-1725" (Oxford DPhil thesis, 1986), esp pp. 261-312. My interpretation of the relationship between the Church and nonconformity receives support from the collection of essays in M Spufford ed, *The World of Rural Dissenters, 1520-1725* (Cambridge, 1995), and from A Urdank, *Religion and Society in a Cotswold Vale. Nailsworth, Gloucestershire, 1780-1865*.

[68] Bossy, *Christianity*.

[69] MS Byford, "The Price of Protestantism. Assessing the impact of Religious Change on Elizabethan Essex: The Cases of Heydon and Colchester, 1558-94", (Oxford DPhil thesis, 1988), abstract.

in which the Puritan Edmund Bunny literally plagiarised the pastoral writings of the Jesuit Robert Parsons, since their essential concern, to instill what Gregory has called "rigorous religion" into their parishioners was practically identical.[70] And in the seventeenth and eighteenth centuries there was a well-established genre of editing Catholic manuals of devotion for Protestant use.[71] The existence of similarities between seemingly opposite religious standpoints makes the use of religious labels a difficult task. For instance, the terms "puritan" and "godly" could be applied to devout Catholics as well as to devout Protestants.[72] And the Protestant William Sheppard was vilified for calling himself a "Jesyutt", meaning, as he tried to explain that he was a follower of Jesus, and not a Jesuit priest.[73] But the fact of continuity between the Catholic and the Protestant pastoral messages may have helped the early success of the Reformation, easing England's transformation into a recognisably Protestant nation. As Byford argues, the more the values emphasised by Protestantism can be seen to have been already present in English religious culture, the less daunting seems its prospect of successfully spreading.[74]

One reason why historians have ignored the problem of the Long Reformation is because several aspects of that endeavour, such as the regulation of people's behaviour, have been side-tracked into the rather different categories of "moral reform" and the reformation of manners, which are viewed as secular rather than as religious concerns. Although historians have analysed the various "movements" to reform manners, such as those in the late sixteenth and early seventeenth centuries, in the mid-seventeenth century, in the late seventeenth and early eighteenth centuries, and in the late eighteenth century, they have usually discussed such movements in terms of social control, and as separate from the religious reformation.[75] It is true that, until the historiographical divide of 1660,

---

[70]BS Gregory, "The 'True and Zealouse Seruice of God': Robert Parsons, Edmund Bunny, and the First Booke of the Christian Exercise", *Journal of Ecclesiastical History*, 45 (1994), pp. 238-268.
[71]For examples, see Gregory, "Canterbury", p. 249.
[72]Byford, "Protestantism", p. 5.
[73]Ibid., pp. 58-60
[74]Ibid., p. 395.
[75]K Wrightson, "Alehouses, order and reformation in rural England, 1590-1660", in E and S Yeo eds, *Popular Culture*, pp. 1-27; K Wrightson and D Levine, *Poverty and Piety in an English Village: Terling, 1525-1700* (New York, 1979); M Ingram, "Communities and Courts: law and disorder in early seventeenth-century Wiltshire", in JS Cockburn, ed. *Crime in England, 1550-1800* (1977), pp. 110-34; id, "Religion, communities and moral discipline in late sixteenth and early seventeenth-century England: case studies", in

the reformation of religion and the reformation of manners are seen as being inter-related, but, even those such as David Underdown who recognise a congruence between religious and moral reform (often under the category of "godly" reform), argue for the end of godly reformation by the late seventeenth century.[76] In particular, Shelley Burtt, in her recent study of the early eighteenth century movement for moral reform has seen this as the period which witnessed the switch from a religious to a temporal justification for action, leading her to make a distinction between Churchmen and moral reformers.[77] And Joanna Innes, who in her elegant dissection of the campaign for the reformation of manners in the 1780s, distinguishes between religious traditions (which emphasised sin), and secular concerns (which emphasised the social consequences of immorality, idleness, improvidence).[78] But it is possible to suggest that "religious" and "moral" reform were twin-aspects of the concern to create a Christian commonwealth, and that this priority continued to influence moral reform well into the nineteenth century. Indeed historians appear to want to have it both ways. A long-observed criticism of late seventeenth and eighteenth century Anglican sermonising, was precisely that it was too concerned with morality and behaviour. Idleness and drink continued to be condemned for religious reasons.[79]

In conclusion, we may recognise that taking a long term view of the Reformation raises several points which need to be stressed. First, we might challenge the traditional periodisation and the historiographical convention which has made a distinction between the vigour of religious activity before 1660 and the stasis after that date. (We might note, incidentally, a parallel in the historiography of the Catholic church, which has led Hanns Gross to talk of the "post-Tridentine syndrome", an entropy

---

K von Greyerz ed, *Religion and Society in early modern Europe, 1500-1800* (1984), pp. 177-93; S Burtt, *Virtue Transformed. Political Argument in England, 1688-1740* (Cambridge, 1992); T Isaacs, "The Anglican hierarchy and the Reformation of Manners, 1688-1738", *Journal of Ecclesiastical History*, XXXIII (1982), 391-411; M Fissell, "Charity Universal? Institutions and Moral Reform in Eighteenth-Century Bristol", in L Davison *et al* eds, *Stilling the Grumbling Hive: The Response to Social and Economic Problems in England, 1689-1750* (Stroud, 1992), pp. 121-44; J Innes, "Politics and Morals. The Reformation of Manners Movement in later Eighteenth Century England", in *The Transformation of Political Culture. England and Germany in the late Eighteenth Century*, ed. E Hellmuth (Oxford, 1990), pp. 57-118,

[76] D Underdown, *Fire from Heaven: the life of an English Town in the Seventeenth century* (1992).

[77] Burtt, *Virtue*.

[78] Innes, "Politics and Morals".

[79] Gregory, "Canterbury", pp. 272-75.

and lack of spirit displayed in the Catholic Church after the late seventeenth century).[80] But seeing the limitations of the earlier period, the period conventionally labelled as the era of Reformation, might help us to see better the achievements of the second period. Indeed, it might be that the success of the Reformation comes later than we once thought.

Second, we need to appreciate how far the need to spread the Reformation was a common concern for all Protestant groups within English society, and that this common aim should be stressed against the traditional picture of inter-denominational rivalry. Moreover, it was the Church of England (through its national clergy and its pastoral initiatives) which played a continuing (and a leading) role in furthering the Reformation.

Third, in evaluating the question of "success" and "failure", we might recognise that to a large extent a Protestant nation was always something to aim for, a process of becoming, rather than of being. Patrick Collinson has indeed suggested that the attempt to create a truly godly society was bound to fail: for Protestants, whose self-perception was defined by opposing the papist "other", always needed to be fighting against something, so that complete success could never have been achieved.[81]

---

[80]H Gross, *Rome in the Age of Enlightenment: the post-Tridentine syndrome and the ancien regime* (Cambridge, 1990).
[81]Collinson, *Birthpangs*, p. 154.

Part III

Free Churches and Revival Movements

"Building up the Walls of Zion" – The Development of the New Connexion General Baptists in Lincolnshire, 1770 - 1891[1]

R. W. Ambler

The Evangelical Revival and the General Baptists – the Context

In 1729 John Hursthouse, who was then living in Boston, published his *Epistle* to the General Baptist churches in the English county of Lincolnshire contrasting their "former prosperous" condition with their "present declining" state. He saw this as the "consequence of their unhappy divisions" and after offering "something by way of encouragement" gave "some useful and proper directions. . . showing them what is necessary to be done in order to restore primitive Christianity in these parts". Hursthouse looked back to the second half of the seventeenth century when the Gospel had been spread, the people gathered in several places and churches settled. His prescription for a restoration of the fortunes of the Baptist churches included the need for spiritual renewal, including fervent prayer, meditation, reading of God's word and using all possible means to increase the sense of God's love in the hearts of the people. He also warned against excessive interest in worldly affairs, while the framework for recovery lay in a greater concern with church order and ministry.[2]

At the time that Hursthouse wrote there were 17 Baptist churches in Lincolnshire served by 18 ministers. The 55 Baptist conventicles recorded in contemporary episcopal visitation returns reflected the spread of members of these churches into the surrounding area where worship at the homes of church members continued a pattern which had developed before the provision of meeting houses.[3] Some forty years after Hursthouse's

---

[1] The work on the Minutes of the annual assemblies of the New Connexion of General Baptists on which this paper is in part based was made possible by a grant from the British Academy for a study of the dissenting churches of Lincolnshire. This assistance is gratefuly acknowledged.
[2] John Hursthouse, *An Epistle to the Baptized Churches in Lincolnshire, &c.*, Lincoln, 1729, pp. 4-5, 15-17, 19-20.
[3] Dr. Williams's Library, MSS 38.5 and 6, Josiah Thompson's Lists of Dissenting Congregations in England and Wales, 1715-1773; *Speculum Dioceseos Lincolniensis sub Episcopis Gul. Wake et Edm. Gibson, 1705-1723*, p.ix.

Epistle the transformation of the General Baptists of Lincolnshire began with the founding of the New Connexion of the General Baptists in 1770. By 1851, the number of places in the county where Baptists worshipped had increased to 62, half of which belonged to the New Connexion, leaving only three with the old General Baptists, 22 Particular Baptist and 6 whose allegiances were undefined. The New Connexion had 17 churches in 1851 and by 1890, the year it ceased to have an independent existence, the number had increased slightly, to 19. The additional 13 preaching places associated with these churches gave a total of 32 New Connexion places of worship in 1890.[4]

Hursthouse's prescription for recovery had been a revival of old forms and attitudes which linked organisational renewal with increased spiritual fervency. The existing gathered churches were to be regenerated, so that renewal was to be expressed in a community gathered to fulfil the spiritual destiny of its members. Church membership confirmed their position as "saints in covenant both with God and with one another". When recovery did come, in the second half of the eighteenth century, it was as a result of the evangelical revival, which challenged the gathered churches to become instrumental in the salvation of individuals rather than confirming it through membership.[5] The New Connexion of the General Baptists represented a distinctive response to this challenge.

The principal agent of the evangelical revival in England was Methodism, which developed as a connexion with local societies served by itinerant preachers and linked into a single national organisation. There were 22,410 Methodist members in England by 1767 and the total had increased to 93,793 by 1800, but this was also a period of significant change among the older and numerically less significant Protestant Dissenting churches. Influenced by Methodism they also adopted itinerant preaching as a means of promoting revival. It was an approach which challenged the congregational basis of the older dissenting churches and in this context

---

[4]Parliamentary Papers, 1852-53, LXXXIX (1690) Population of Great Britain, 1851, Religious Worship (England and Wales) p. ccxi; *Minutes of the Eighty-Second Annual AAssociation of the New Connexion of General Baptists, held at Mary's Gate Chapel, Derby, June 24th, 25th, 26th and 27th, 1851*, Leicester [1851], pp. 6-8 [Minutes of the Annual Association or Assembly henceforth cited as *Minutes* with place of meeting and year, thus: *Minutes, Nottingham*, 1890, London [1890] pp. 62-74; *The Baptist Handbook for 1890*, London [1890] pp. 12-13.

[5]J.H.Y. Briggs, *The English Baptists of the Nineteenth Century*, Didcot, 1994, pp. 14-15, 18; W. R. Ward, "The Baptists and the Transformation of the Church, 1780-1830", in W.R. Ward, *Faith and Faction*, London, 1993, pp. 209-10.

the response of the New Connexion of General Baptists was particularly significant.6

The development of the New Connexion of General Baptists resolved the potential tension between gathered churches and the imperatives of religious revival by building what was described as a connexional form of organisation on to existing church structures. The distinctive form developed in the New Connexion meant that a shared culture could be channelled among the churches through the structures created by the connexion. It enhanced the lives of the churches without detracting from their essential natures, although the use of the title New Connexion was indicative of the way in which its founders looked to Methodism as a model of institutionalised revival. Despite the Arminian theological position which they shared with the Methodists, the Baptist churches never ultimately developed the stronger connexionalism of the Methodists, while the question of infant baptism remained a fundamental point of difference between them.

The growth of the New Connexion was a varied and sometimes complex process, which in itself contributed to the particular character of the Connexion. It hinged on the links which were developed between the Connexion and individual churches. The nature of these links is an appropriate subject for analysis on a local basis and the county of Lincolnshire provides a suitable area for this. The second largest of England's counties, and situated on the North Sea coast, it is approximately 120 kilometres from north to south and 72 from east to west. Some 2,360 people attended General Baptist worship in the county in the early eighteenth century, which made them its largest nonconformist body in the period before the development of Methodism. It also had the second largest number of General Baptists in any county in the country while there were few Particular Baptists. The General Baptists comprised 1.23 per cent of the total population of Lincolnshire and only Kent and Buckinghamshire had larger proportions with 1.88 and 1.26 per cent respectively.7

Despite their relative importance, the Arminian doctrines of the General Baptists isolated them from most other nonconformists except the

---

[6] Robert Currie, Alan Gilbert and Lee Horsley, *Churches and Churchgoers: patterns of church growth in the British Isles since 1700,* Oxford, 1977, p.139; Deryck W. Lovegrove, *Established Church, Sectarian People. Itinerancy and the Transformation of English Dissent, 1780-1830,* Cambridge, 1988, pp. 14-18, 28-9.

[7] Michael R Watts. *The Dissenters: from the Reformation to the French Revolution,* vol. I, Oxford, 1978, p. 509.

Society of Friends, isolation compounded by the divisions which developed between individual churches in the course of the eighteenth century. These encouraged their perception of themselves, in the imagery of the Old Testament, as enclosed gardens. Preaching became concerned with moral issues which, combined with theological freedom, created further divisions. Scriptural precedents used without much regard for context, setting or contemporary relevance became divisive shibboleths which prevented new ideas taking root. The same concern for what was perceived as precise Scriptural exegesis, when applied in theological discussion, also led to a questioning of traditional beliefs about the person of Christ and the doctrine of the Trinity. While some of the churches and ministers in the Lincolnshire Association of General Baptists continued to adhere to "the principles which had distinguished the English General Baptists, in their best days" into the middle of the eighteenth century, others either denied entirely such central teachings as the Divinity of Christ, the Atonement, Justification by Faith alone and regeneration by the Holy Spirit or discussed them in ways which were considered by the more orthodox to detract from their dignity and essential truth.[8]

Divisions between the General Baptist churches were compounded by changes in patterns of ministry and in particular by the decline in the authority of Messengers: ministers appointed with the consent of the churches in an area who acted as overseers and mediators between and within them.[9] By the time Gilbert Boyce of the Lincolnshire churches at Coningsby and Asterby was ordained to the office of Messenger in 1753 the state of division and decline described earlier by Hursthouse was endemic. The impossibility of achieving doctrinal unity was compounded by a "depression of sentiment" and "laxity of principle". The loose networks which were based on associations of churches and ministers did not provide a sufficiently strong basis for unity. Their minutes emphasised "propriety of character and conduct" as important elements of Baptist profession and ministers were enjoined to "explain and reason" resolutions designed to discourage "vain amusements and sinful compliances with the customs and fashions of the world". Any unity which was fostered among

---

[8] Raymond Brown, *The English Baptists of the Eighteenth Century,* London, 1986, pp. 7, 12, 19, 20-21, 26, 58; Adam Taylor, *The History of the English General Baptists*, part II, *The New Connexion of General Baptists*, London, 1818, p. 133.
[9] Thomas Grantham, *Christianimus Primitivimus*, "First Book", London, 1678, p. 165; Taylor, *History*, I, p. 203.

the churches by these shared attitudes was offset by the sense of exclusiveness which they engendered.[10]

The maintenance of "the strictness of their ancient discipline" confirmed their distinctive identities. It was, however, a distinctiveness associated with decline: "One minister after another dropped into the grave; and few were raised up to supply the vacant places. The congregations, of course, dwindled away; and, in many instances, the churches became extinct." Even the Lincoln meeting house,

> for more than seventy years . . . a kind of metropolitan for the baptized churches of the general faith, in Lincolnshire . . . was lent to the particular baptists; on condition of keeping it in repair, and permitting the general baptists to preach in it when they could find opportunity.[11]

The Lincolnshire General Baptists could not stand aloof from the evangelical revival and particularly the growth of Methodism in the county. Gilbert Boyce had written to John Wesley, asking Wesley to stay with him when he was at Coningsby. The pair "confirmed" their "love towards each other" but at the end of the meeting in 1748 there was a vigorous discussion on "the point of baptism".[12] It was a debate which continued for a long time. Boyce's *Serious Reply to the Rev. Mr. John Welsey*, published in 1770, emphasised the central importance of distinctive Baptist teachings on baptism, but its concern with the form rather than the substance of debate reflected the way in which this type of discussion had turned the General Baptist churches inwards and stood in the way of a wider appreciation of the significance of the evangelical revival.[13]

As early as 1745 the Lincolnshire General Baptist Association were forced into a defensive stance against the Methodists, who were reported to be attracting many members away from the Baptists. The Association declared that Methodist faith and practice was "contrary to the holy scriptures, and to the peace and welfare of the societies". Discipline was to be exercised against Baptist church members who attended Methodist

---

[10]Taylor, *History*, II, pp. 112-13.
[11]Taylor, *History*, II, pp. 112-13.
[12]*The Journal of John Wesley, A. M.*, ed. Nehemiah Curnock, vol. III, London [1909] p. 360; Taylor, *History*, II. p. 111.
[13]A.C Underwood, *A History of the English Baptists*, London, 2nd. impression, 1956, p. 149.

meetings. Despite these measures "the warmth and affection which animated the new professors triumphed, in many instances, over the decrees and threatenings of this feeble synod".[14] While their Arminian doctrines with the offer of salvation to all who believed had not been a strong enough safeguard against division in the early eighteenth century, they provided the basis on which General Baptists could respond to revival. The New Connexion created the framework for the development of a reponse to these spiritual imperatives.

The Establishment of the New Connexion

The quest for a more vigorous style of evangelism which provided the spiritual impetus for Daniel Taylor, a Halifax collier and one of the founding fathers of the General Baptist New Connexion, was similar to, but predated, that of the leaders of such branches of Methodism as the Bible Christians and Primitive Methodists. Like the General Baptist New Connexion these Methodist offshoots also had highly localised origins.[15] Taylor's spiritual origins among the Wesleyan Methodists meant that, although he came under the influence of the Baptist churches in the Hebden Bridge area of West Yorkshire where he had gathered a congregation, and although he became convinced that there was no Scriptural foundation for the practice of infant baptism, his Arminianism meant that none of the ministers of the local Baptist churches would baptise him. In February 1763 he attempted to contact a group of General Baptists at Boston in Lincolnshire who were said to hold similar sentiments to his. Before he reached Boston he came upon a Baptist church at Gamston in Nottinghamshire where the minister was willing to baptise Taylor and his companion in the river, after which they both returned home.[16]

Taylor's desire for baptism had impelled him to move outwards from his own congregation. His instinct for association, coupled with a sense of the need for order in church affairs, meant that he was more than an individualist driven by the imperatives of revival and creating a church in

---

[14]Taylor, *History*, II, pp. 110-11.
[15]Robert Currie, *Methodism Divided: a study of the sociology of ecumenicalism*, London, 1968, p. 55.
[16]Watts, *Dissenters*, I, p. 455; Underwood, *General Baptists*, pp. 150-51; Adam Taylor, *Memoirs of the Rev. Dan Taylor, Late Pastor of the General Baptist Church, Whitechapel, London*, London, 1820, pp. 12-13.

his own image. He renewed his attempts to contact the Lincolnshire General Baptists in the summer following his baptism and attended their Association in May 1763.[17]

The contacts Taylor made had a strong personal as well as institutional significance. The church which he had first sought out at Boston had been in a "low" state and held together by a father and son, Thomas and John Saul. They had maintained links with the Lincolnshire Association of General Baptists and were instrumental in an invitation being given to William Thompson of Hull to be their minister in 1762. In just over a year his diligence had produced a revival and church growth. Taylor met Thompson at the 1763 Association and went back with him to Boston before returning to Yorkshire. This movement between churches, but based on personal contacts, was an important element in the establishment of the General Baptist New Connexion. It was also significant because of its basis in a common spiritual experience which was not imposed from above but came from within the churches.[18]

Thompson visited Taylor's Yorkshire congregation, which he formally constituted as a church, and Taylor travelled to Boston to preach at the opening of the new meeting house there in 1764. Taylor's visit to Lincolnshire for the Association of 1765 was the occasion for a preaching tour which took in the General Baptist churches at Boston, Coningsby, Fleet and Toft. The involvement of the Messenger, Gilbert Boyce, in both the ordination of Taylor in 1763 as well as that of Thompson to the pastoral office at Boston in 1764 was a sign of their continuing links with the Lincolnshire Association, but these links were based on concern to maintain church order rather than on the spiritual experience which motivated Taylor's preaching.[19]

After the opening of the Boston meeting house in 1764 Taylor had undertaken a preaching tour during which he collected for a new meeting house at Birchcliffe in Yorkshire. As a result he came into contact with a group of Arminian Baptists at Barton-in-Fabis in Leicestershire. Despite their isolation and dependence on Biblical precedent rather than church tradition, they had not gone the way of the General Baptist churches of Lincolnshire and remained both theologically orthodox as well as actively evangelistic. Their work had spread into neighbouring towns and villages

---

[17]Taylor, *Memoirs*, p. 14.
[18]Taylor, *Memoirs*, pp. 12-14; Taylor, *History*, II, pp. 128-9; Underwood, *English Baptists*, pp. 151-2.
[19]Taylor, *Memoirs*, pp. 14, 15, 17, 20-21; Taylor, *History*, II, pp. 128-9, 131.

so that they had five separate churches by the time Taylor first came into contact with them, a contact which he maintained through later preaching excursions.[20]

Although Taylor and a number of like-minded individuals were particularly attracted to the Leicestershire churches, they could not induce them to join the Lincolnshire Association because of the heterodox opinions of some of its members. The Leicestershire Baptists emphasised the importance of spiritual unity based on the "genuine doctrines" of Christianity and the necessity of a separate organisation for all who shared them. It was impossible for Gilbert Boyce to exercise his traditional reconciliatory role as a Messenger. Religious revival based on doctrinal agreement, superceding past divisions over teaching and practice had become the basis of union. When the New Connexion was formed this experience led to the rejection of the office of Messenger as one of divine obligation.[21]

The New Connexion of General Baptists was established in 1770 following a meeting at Lincoln the year before at which Daniel Taylor and William Thompson, the Boston minister, had met representatives of the Leicestershire churches. The New Connexion's first Association at London in June 1770 was attended by representatives of fourteen churches. After sending a deputation with a farewell message to the General Baptist Assembly, which was holding its annual meeting at the same time, the New Connexion Association drew up six articles of religion. These were not seen as an inclusive creed but dealt with the main points of dispute between them and the old General Baptists. They covered the fall of man, the nature and obligation of the moral law, the person and work of Christ, salvation by faith, regeneration by the Holy Spirit and baptism, but the positive evangelical impulse which informed the Association was based on the provision that "every minister do . . . give an account of his religious experience" at the Connexion's next Association.[22]

---

[20]Taylor, *Memoirs*, p.17; Taylor, *History*, II, p.76; Watts, *Dissenters*, I, pp. 454-5.
[21]Taylor, *History*, II, pp. 134-5; *Minutes of the General Assembly of the General Baptist Churches in England, with Kindred Records,* ed. W. T. Whiteley, vol. II, 1731-1811, London, 1910, p.160.
[22]Taylor, *History*, II, pp. 135, 138-43, 212-13, 328; *General Assembly Minutes*, II, pp. 139-142.

Patterns of Church Growth

The New Connexion grew from 126 members in 1770 to 1688 in 1890 without losing its basis of gathered churches with settled ministers, but the growth which resulted from revival came in a variety of ways.[23] These can be be broken down into three main types: that which came from the recruitment of churches to the Connexion which had been in existence, often for a long period, before they joined it; allogenous growth from non-church members and autogenous growth from the families of church members. Not all of these types of growth were affected in the same way by revival and while different growth patterns are often associated with various stages in the historical development of a church, this relationship is more complex in the case of the New Connexion.[24]

Whereas the normal expectation would be for a church to grow initially through allogenous growth, the New Connexion was founded from churches which were already established. Their continued accession to it remained a feature of its development in Lincolnshire. They therefore contributed autogenous growth at a relatively early stage in the Connexion's growth. However, when the New Connexion was formed Baptist ministers were admitted whose churches were not in the Connexion and it was not until 1777 that procedures were adopted whereby churches applied for membership by submitting a written statement of their religious sentiments. In 1795 the annual Association of the Connexion became an assembly of delegates from the churches.[25]

Daniel Taylor's preaching tours both before and after the formation of the New Connexion were undertaken within the framework of existing Baptist churches and were concerned to effect revival within existing churches by arousing evangelical zeal in their members. In 1763 he reported that he preached to "a very great crowd of rude people" at Lincoln but a concern to serve the church there lay behind his efforts. Similarly when he made a week's tour in Lincolnshire in March 1797 Taylor visited a group of churches in the south Lincolnshire fenland. His visit strength-

---

[23] James Taylor, *Statistics of the New Connexion of General Baptists, from its Formation in 1770, to 1843*, ed. J. Goadby, Ashby de la Zouche [1844] pp. 11, 12.
[24] Currie, Gilbert and Horsley, *Churches and Churchgoers,* Oxford, 1977, pp.8-9.
[25] Taylor, *History*, II, pp. 135, 138-43, 212-13, 328; *General Assembly Minutes* II, p. 141.

ened the links with those already in the Connexion, but also included other churches which were to join it later, some only after a number of years.[26]

When the 22 members of the General Baptist church at Maltby le Marsh decided to join the New Connexion in 1772, the fourth church to so, they agreed that because of the low state of "vital religion" they would exert themselves in its promotion while maintaining church doctrine and discipline and encouraging ministers who preached "the essential doctrines of the blessed Gospel of Jesus Christ".[27] In 1830 the long-established church at Coningsby joined the Connexion with 99 members and as late as 1870 one of Grimsby's Baptist churches, which had been founded in response to the development of the town, joined with 40 members. This meant that growth cycles within the Connexion and its churches were not necessarily at the same stage. Fully formed churches brought their particular attitudes and assumptions to be grafted on to those of churches which were the result of allogenous growth.[28]

Another type of church growth was represented by the creation of the fenland church at Gedney Hill out of one at Fleet, eleven miles away, although this was not a move into an area which was totally devoid of Baptist influence. There had been preaching at Gedney Hill in the 1790s, but this did not develop into a separate church until 1820. It was created through the enthusiasm of three members of a family who initially went to Fleet and became members there. They began to hold meetings in a house in Gedney Hill at which one of them preached. A minister visited them occasionally and by 1811 the house had become too small for the numbers who met there. A meeting house was built which also became the base for further growth so that the Gedney Hill church had two chapels by 1843. Their congregations did not separate from each other, as Gedney Hill had done from Fleet, until the effects of rural depopulation forced a reorganisation of the churches of the area in 1887.[29]

The church at Long Sutton was created through the "schismatic" leadership of an individual minister. Henry Poole of Fleet was at the first meeting of the New Connexion, but he did not carry his church into it

---

[26]Taylor, *Memoirs*, pp. 73, 215.
[27]Lincolnshire Archives [hereafter LA], 16 BAPT 2, Maltby le Marsh Baptist Church Book, 1773-1791; Taylor, *Statistics*, p. 18.
[28]Currie, Gilbert and Horsley, *Churches and Churchgoers*, pp. 8-9; *Minutes, Birchcliffe*, 1830, Loughborough [1830] p.3; *Minutes, Sheffield*, 1869, Leicester [1869] p.15.
[29]Taylor, *Statistics*, pp. 55-6; *The General Baptist Repository*, vol. IV, n.d., p.41; *Minutes, Loughborough, 1843*, Leicester, [1843], p. 3; *Minutes, Peterborough, 1887*, London [1887], pp. 37, 50.

with him. His style of preaching was considered to be "too methodistical" and he moved a few miles away and formed another church which was admitted into the Connexion in 1773. A meeting house was built, but although membership reached a height of 34 in 1778, and despite efforts to strengthen it by extending its activities into other places, the Long Sutton church became extinct in 1793 when it had only 12 members. Its decline was hastened by a change in Poole's theological position which, in a development reminiscent of the earlier period of General Baptist disunity, led him and a handful of followers out of the New Connexion. A church was re-established from Fleet which itself had joined the New Connexion. A chapel was built at Long Sutton in 1818, but a separate church was not established until 1840.[30]

Lincoln, as has been noted, held an important place in General Baptist history and the way the New Connexion church was built up in the city through the initiative of the Connexion's annual Association was another variant of the way it grew. It was proposed in 1810 that a minister should visit some of the ancient but decayed General Baptist churches in Lincolnshire. The costs of this were met by subscription and it was on this basis that a Connexional Itinerant Fund was established. The Lincoln church was built up in a meeting house which had formerly belonged to the General Baptists, been used by the Particular Baptists and let to the Congregationalists.[31]

Church Memberships

The actual basis of church membership was a further and significant variable affecting the growth and development of the New Connexion. The sixth of the articles on which the foundation of the New Connexion was based asserted the duty of all who repented and believed the gospel to be baptized by immersion in water. By this they were "to be initiated into a church state". No person "ought to be received into the church without submission to that ordinance".[32] Despite moves towards open membership, with baptism being left to the individual conscience of people who

---

[30]Taylor, *History*, II, pp. 197-8, 285-6; Taylor, *Statistics*, p. 68; *Minutes, London, 1840*, Nottingham [1840], p. 4.
[31]Taylor, *History*, II, pp. 457-8; LA, 'The History of the General Baptist Church in Lincoln', by W.S. Linton, unpublished typescript, 1911.
[32]Taylor, *History*, II, pp.141-2.

applied to join the churches, baptism remained the basis of membership among the Lincolnshire churches. As late as 1889 the church at Sutton St James reported in optimistic terms on the activities of some of its adherents and expressed the "earnest prayer" that "the Lord may soon lead them all through the water, when we should have a prosperous cause".[33]

These diverse influences on the growth of the New Connexion contributed to what were often considerable differences between the numbers of those who had been gathered to worship and participate in the lives of its churches and those who became baptised members of them. The annual reports of churches included comments on attendances so that success in this area of church life was identified with, and recognised by, the Connexion. Apparent buoyancy in church life as indicated by attendance was, however, often contrasted with a less optimistic picture of actual church membership. A report from Spalding church for 1817, for example, referred to large congregations and yet a lack of converts for the "too much neglected ordinance of baptism".[34]

There was an attendance of 3,385 people at the morning services of the 31 New Connexion places of worship in Lincolnshire on Sunday 30 March 1851, 1,479 in the afternoon and 3,640 in the evening, although there was no return of attendances from one. The membership of the New Connexion in the county totalled 1,556.[35] On the assumption that the morning and evening congregations were made up of the same people, this meant that between 43 per cent and 46 per cent of worshippers at each service were members. The minister of the chapel in Gosberton noted, however, that its morning congregation, which comprised some 90 worshippers and 53 Sunday scholars, was made up of people who came from a distance and did not attend in the evening. This meant that "the same persons are not identified with both morning and evening congregations". The evening congregation numbered 170 so that, with a church membership of 50 and using the minister's statement to assume that the total number of individual attenders was 260, the percentage of members fell much lower than the average for the Connexion in Lincolnshire as a whole to just over 19 per cent. Moreover, if all the attendants in Lincolnshire are assumed to have worshipped only once, the percentage of members compared with attenders, at just over 18 per cent, would have

---

[33]Underwood, *English Baptists*, pp. 210-11; *Minutes, Walsall, 1889*, London [1889], p.89.
[34]*Minutes, Castle Donington, 1817*, Derby [1817], p. 11.
[35]*Religious Worship (England and Wales)*, pp. 6 - 7.

come very close to that for Gosberton. At Long Sutton, like Gosberton a chapel in the Lincolnshire fenland, the ratio of members to attenders in 1851 was larger at nearly 27 per cent if it is also assumed that people only worshipped once on a Sunday. In the different milieu of the town of Grantham, where more varied patterns of attendance may have been the norm, the percentage of members to attenders based on one attendance by each worshipper on a Sunday, rose to 36 per cent on actual attendances on 30 March but was 23 per cent based on average attendances over the past year.[36]

These ratios of members to attenders in the General Baptist New Connexion churches in 1851 can be compared with those for the Wesleyan Methodists which were over 40 per cent in some parts of north Lincolnshire. On the other hand the Primitive Methodists had ratios as low as 17 per cent in some of the fenland areas where the New Connexion was also relatively well established. Low ratios of members to attenders among the Methodists can be seen as reflecting a "missionary" situation in which a chapel was still in the process of establishing itself in the local community, but this was not the case with all the New Connexion churches in Lincolnshire.[37] Varied patterns of development in the New Connexion brought differing ratios of attenders to members, although the predominantly low ratio of members to attenders is indicative of the distinctive nature of church membership and the way in which the Connexional impulse towards inclusiveness came up against the bedrock of the gathered church.

Boston and Fleet were the first churches in the county to join the Connexion when it was established in 1770 and had 76 and some 50 members respectively. The number of New Connexion churches in the county had grown to 9 by 1811. Their membership ranged from 19 at Maltby le Marsh to 91 in Boston and totalled 416. By 1820 there were 699 members in 12 churches. These included churches based in one place with one minister, one church in two places with one minister, while others had a presence in a number of places. In 1851 the 1,556 members were in 17 churches. By 1870 the number of churches had increased to 18 and that of members to 1963. By 1880, however, membership had begun to decline, although the number of churches had increased to 21, and by 1890, just

---

[36]*Lincolnshire Returns of the Census of Religious Worshis, 1851*, ed. R.W. Ambler, Lincoln Record Society, vol. 72, 1979, pp. 21-22, 32, 79-80; *Minutes, Derby, 1851*, pp. 6, 7.
[37]*Census of Religious Worship*. 1851, pp. lii-liii

before the separate existence of the New Connexion ended, there were 17 churches with a total of 1,668 members.[38]

The average membership in the Lincolnshire churches of the General Baptist New Connexion in 1811 was just over 46 and by 1820 this had risen to just over 58. It had increased to just over 79 by 1840, just over 91 by 1851, 101 by 1861 and 109 by 1870. The decrease in membership in the county in the 1870s was accompanied by a drop in average church membership to between 87 and 88 in 1880, but although the total membership in the county decreased further, to 1688 in 1890, the number of churches also decreased, so that their average size rose to 99.[39]

Conclusion – Gathered Churches and Revival

The reports to the General Baptist New Connexion annual assembly reflected the spirit which animated the lives of the churches. In these the varied patterns of growth and development which had created and which animated the churches meshed with the spiritual imperatives which had created the Connexion: imperatives based ultimately on the quest for renewal and revival. These reports continue to emphasise the importance of "vital religion" in the lives of the Lincolnshire churches, even if only to express concern for its low state. There was some shift in their tone as a growing concern with the methods through which growth was achieved tended to become more dominant. In 1841 prosperity of the church at Boston was signalled by the ordination of a new pastor, the erection of side galleries and other improvements at the chapel, the expansion of preaching into Swineshead, where a Sunday school had been established and the opening of another Sunday school in a "neglected" part of Boston. In the same year additions and improvements were reported at the chapels and meeting houses in Kirton in Lindsey, Louth and Alford. Increased attendance at worship was a measure of success, new and enlarged chapels were needed to accommodate it.[40]

---

[38]Taylor, *Statistics*, pp. 11-12; *Minutes, Melbourne, 1811*, n.p. [1811], pp. 3-4; *Minutes, Spalding, 1820*, Derby [1820], pp. 3, 7, 9. 11: *Minutes. Leicester. 1870*, London [1870], pp. 22-7; *Minutes, Nottingham, 1880*, London [1880], pp.32-7 and *Minutes 1851* and *1890* cited above.
[39]*Minutes, 1811, 1820, 1840, 1851, 1870, 1880* and *1890* cited above, and *Minutes, Leicester, 1861*, Leicester [1861], pp. 10-12.
[40]*Minutes, Derby, 1841*, Derby [1841], pp. 6-29.

The promotion of the spiritual experience represented by the Connexion led to the development of a culture associated with individual churches but articulated through Connexional structures. These structures could gather converts and develop a common means to sustain them, bringing the inclusiveness of the revival impulse to bear on the potential exclusiveness of gathered church membership while encouraging these members to see themselves as part of a wider experience. This meant that a move to provide support to revive the work of individual churches developed into a Connexional Itinerant Fund and, from 1871, a Home Missionary Society.[41] The establishment of an Academy to train ministers; the publication of a connexional magazine, *The General Baptist Repository*; the establishment of central funds to assist aged ministers and of a religious tract society, as well as the introduction of a hymn book, maintained the connexion's identity. The Connexion also played a role in the diffusion of new ideas and practice in areas such as Sunday school work, friendly and benefit societies.[42]

These measures were not in themselves unique to the General Baptist New Connexion and were part of the common culture of nonconformist life. The Connexion was, however, distinctive for the way in which the churches in it retained their "strictly congregational" discipline and responded in a variety of ways to the challenges of revival. When they joined the New Connexion they were sustained and enabled, but not controlled by it. The churches remained "societies of faithful men, voluntarily associated to support the interests of religion and enjoy its privilege, according to their own views of these sacred subjects".[43] Regenerated by revival they accommodated themselves to its imperatives, but were not swept away by it. That they were able to do this was a measure of the continuing importance of the gathered church in a period of revival. As the development of the General Baptist New Connexion in Lincolnshire showed, the variety of responses of the county's General Baptist churches to revival reflected local circumstances and perceived needs. The type of connexionalism adopted by the General Baptists might offer a shared culture to its constituent churches, but its adoption was voluntary. The General Baptist New Connexion could ultimately only lead by example,

---

[41]Taylor, *History*, II, pp. 457-8; *Minutes, Loughborough, 1821*,
[42]Taylor, *History*, II, pp. 327, 464-7.
[43]Taylor, *History*, II, pp. 468-9.

but never compel, no matter how powerful the impulses for revival which sustained it.

Assessing the Awakening: The 1859 Revival in Ulster

Myrtle Hill

The "Great Awakening" in mid-nineteenth Ulster was, by any standards, a remarkable event. Described by Richard Carwardine as "one of the most extraordinary of 19th century revivals",[1] it was welcomed by contemporaries as "a glorious and unprecedented epoch in the religious history of Ulster",[2] and its "miraculous manifestations, marvellous conversions and mysterious prostrations" were still providing inspiration a century later.[3] Even at the time, however, controversy raged around the interpretation of some aspects of the phenomenon, not only in secular circles, but from within the religious community itself, while modern historical investigation, determined by a new set of preoccupations and priorities, encourages fresh perspectives on old material. Since this particular revival "involved larger numbers of people in sustained common activity than any movement in rural Ulster between 1798 and 1913",[4] I would suggest that any assessment of such an event needs to take account of its impact on social and cultural as well as religious life, and on popular as well as insitutionalised religion. This broader focus reflects my particular interest in how the revival relates to the development of a specific brand of Ulster Protestant culture – one which continues to influence the social and political development of the province.

This extraordinary event in Ulster life was thoroughly documented by contemporaries – literally hundreds of pamphlets, based on personal observations, testimonies and sermons were published both during the revival and in its immediate aftermath. The authors were mostly ministers, recording the experiences of their congregation and neigh-bourhood, concerned to influence and persuade, to capture and convey the sense of urgency and drama which characterised events. Thus their works should

---

[1] R. Carwardine, *Transatlantic Revivalism: Popular Evangelicalism in Britain and America, 1790-1865* (Conneticut, 1978), p.172
[2] Johnston's *Impartial History of the Revival Movement* (Belfast, 1859)
[3] I.R.K. Paisley, *The "Fifty-Nine" Revival* (Belfast, 1958)
[4] Peter Gibbon, *The Origins of Ulster Unionism: the formation of popular Protestant politics and ideology in Nineteenth century Ireland* (Manchester, 1975), p.44

be seen as part of the process itself, dedicated to winning converts and promoting the cause. The revival also had its critics, however, and they too went into print – to query, caution or condemn. The best-known contemporary works on the revival are *The Year of Grace*, an account of the blessings of the movement, by William Gibson, Moderator of the General Assembly in 1859, and *The Year of Delusion*, a savage indictment of the revivalists and their methods, by the Reverend Isaac Nelson.[5] Positioned on opposite sides of the debate, these two works formed the basis of much material published thereafter, and reflected the central areas of concern for both contemporary and subsequent commentators. Where pro-revivalists saw an increase in "zeal, inquiry and earnestness", others were appalled by what they believed to be exhibitions of "blasphemy, fanatacism and pride".[6]

Even a brief perusal of a small selection of revivalist literature reveals that the major focus for those on both sides of the debate was what was known as "physical prostrations"; a phenonemon which took on a variety of forms during the summer of 1859, including striking down, trances- sometimes lasting for days, partial paralysis, visions, speaking in tongues, the reading of the scriptures by former illiterates, strange marks appearing on the bodies of the newly converted. One local minister described a man who had been living for years in gross sin:

> "His tongue was protruded, he foamed at the mouth,
> he could not speak, occasionally he uttered a wild roar
> (and) laboured under a sort of unnatural panting".[7]

For the most fervent revivalists, such experiences were seen as clear evidence of the Holy Spirit at work, although a majority of ministers qualified their approval by explaining that the Holy Spirit was *using* rather than producing these dramatic signs. While recognising the important publicity element of the manifestations, many were sensitive to the accusation of "gullible fanaticism" which inevitably accompanied the phenomena – "Conviction! Convulsions! Epilepsy! Insanity!" pro-claimed a plac-

---

[5] W. Gibson, *The Year of Grace: A History of the Ulster Revival of 1859* (Belfast, 1860); I. Nelson, *The Year of Delusion: a Review of the Year of Grace* (Belfast, 1860)
[6] W. McIlwaine, *Revivalism Reviewed* (Belfast (1859); T. MacNeice, *Words of Caution and Counsel on the Present Revival of Religion* (Belfast, 1859); Anon, *A Few Remarks on Revivals by a Lover of True Religion* (Belfast, 1859).
[7] Peter Carr, *The Most Unpretending of Places: A History of Dundonald, County Down* (Belfast, 1987), pp 136-9

ard in Ballymena.⁸ Others, also conscious of the negative aspect of such publicity, claimed they were the works of Satan, designed to turn attention away from the real work of the revival. Among less impressionable sceptics, they were thought to be "only imagination", or due to hysteria, contagion or conditions in the factories, while one explained the marks as due "to the pinching and squeezing of distressed females".⁹ However interpreted, these dramatic incidents undoubtedly provided the drama and power which brought the revival to the forefront of public affairs and kept it there throughout the summer of 1859.

There were excited reports of mills closing down while an army of ministers attempted to counsel the "stricken" workforce, and of classes of schoolchildren "crying out for mercy". In some areas the press claimed that trade "except in Bibles and Testaments, if not suspended, has been partially paralysed – those who conducted it having for the present given it up or become incapable of transacting it". On one occasion the press itself was affected, with the compositors on the *Coleraine Chronicle* rendered incapable of getting the paper out on time.¹⁰ This type of drama brought scores of curious sightseers from all over Britain to witness the phenomenon, and, it has been suggested, led to a cautious response to revivalism in other parts of the British Isles.

Identified with supernatural intervention, and affecting mostly women and children, these dissociative experiences present difficulties of interpretation for historians as well as contemporaries. On a purely practical level there was, no doubt, at least an element of hysteria since very large numbers were packed into church buildings, and crowd psychology must also have played a part in generating emotion. While the susceptibility of children and their powerful propaganda appeal is fairly obvious, recent studies focusing on gender analysis offer a variety of explanations for the greater visibility of women in this outburst of intense religious excitement. These range from a focus on changing marriage and working patterns to detailed interpretations of visions which suggest that female aspirations frustrated in the secular world could be realised through their religious experience.¹¹ A combination of circumstances and

---

⁸ Quoted in Jonathan Bardon, *A History of Ulster* (Belfast, 1992), p.343
⁹A. McCann, *The Strikings Down and the Marks Vindicated* (Belfast, 1859); Rev. E. Hincks, *God's Works and Satan's Counter-Works, as now carried on in the North of Ireland* (Belfast, 1859), Rev. J. Montgomery, *The Holy Spirit: Its Nature and Work* (Belfast, 1859), F. Moore, *The Truth about Ulster* (London, 1914)
¹⁰Bardon, *History of Ulster*, p. 341
¹¹Gibbon, *Origins of Ulster Unionism*, pp 45-65; Janice Holmes, "The World Turned

influences were evidently at work: vulnerability caused by economic or demographic changes may well have been a factor; and the much more flexible and open religious situation undoubtedly provided the space and the opportunity for women both to respond directly and to be paid much more attention than was usual. It is also clear that the language and imagery of the evangelical tradition was particularly pertinent to young female listeners. The importance of women in popular religious movements generally has been well recognised, but the preponderance of young single women affected by this particular phenomenon would reward further investigation.

Similarly, suggestions that the revival itself, with its paranormal accompaniments, was due to stresses and strains in Ulster society in that year, are worthy of consideration, particularly as it is possible to trace a pattern of revivalistic activity leading to physical manifestations in other periods of social or economic dislocation: Irish Presbyterian minister, Andrew Stewart described events in Sixmilewater in County Antrim amongst the Ulster-Scots community during the instability of the early 17th century:

> "I have seen them myself stricken, and swoon with the Word - yea, a dozen in one day carried out of doors as dead, so marvellous was the power of God smiting their hearts for sin, condemning and killing; and some of those were none of the weaker sex or spirit, but indeed some of the boldest spirits.the stubborn, who sinned and gloried in it, because they feared not man, are now patterns of sobriety, fearing to sin because they fear God."[12]

Another example can be taken from a Methodist revival in south Ulster at the turn of the century.

> "She seemed to be possessed by an evil spirit. She screamed in the wildest manner, five men could not

---

Upside Down: Women in the Ulster revival of 1859" in Janice Holmes and Diane Urquhart (eds) *Coming Into the Light: The Work, Politics and Religion of Women in Ulster 1840-1940* (Belfast, 1995) pp 125-53

[12] Marilyn J. Westerkamp, *Triumph of the Laity: Scots-Irish Piety and the Great Awakening 1625-1760* (Oxford, 1988), p. 15

hold her down; and the more the servants of God prayed for her, the more she raged. At length the Lord was entreated on her behalf; and having lain for some moments as if dead, she rose and praised God for his mercy".[13]

While revivalism was very common in Methodism during this period, the social and political turbulence following the failed rebellion of 1798 witnessed the most spectacular success. It is not suggested that cause and effect can be linked with absolute precision, however, rather that social, economic and political tensions were at the very least conducive to religious revivalism.

The nature and content of religious discourse was also significant. Another, perhaps more directly relevant, common factor in these dramatic local revivals was a distinctive brand of enthusiastic and emotional preaching which seemed particularly appropriate to the context of social disruption. James Glendinning, the prime mover in the 17th century revival, was described as "unlearned", but a powerful preacher, who "inspired by the great lewdness and ungodly sinfulness of the people.preached to them nothing but law, wrath, and the terrors of God for sin".[14] Similarly, the preaching of Gideon Ouseley, Methodist missionary and the main force behind late 18th century revivalism, has been described as "unashamedly emotional and often producing disturbing scenes of physical and psychological excesses".[15] Although the 1859 revival did not owe its origins to charasmatic preachers, the language, images and techniques of evangelicalism had by this stage been adopted by all the major denominations, and direct emotional appeals to the public at large certainly generated enthusiasm. Indeed, the intensity of the religious response in each of these areas at these times seems to be directly related to the urgency of the evangelical emphasis on the sinful state of man and the necessity for personal salvation. One revivalist leader in 1859 explained the emotional impact of the conviction of sin:

---

[13]Crookshank, *A History of Methodism in Ireland,* 3 Volumes (London, 1885-8) Vol II p. 201

[14]Westerkamp, *Triumph of the Laity*, p. 24

[15]David Hempton, "Gideon Ouseley: Rural Revivalist, 1791-1839", *Studies in Church History*, 25 (1989), pp 33-48

"The soul is felt to be guilty and lost. Sin is seen to be loathsome and deadly, and it is generally felt to be an intolerable burthen, crushing the body and soul to hell. Horror unutterable overwhelms the heart, especially of those who feel that the devil is persuading or dragging them to perdition. In almost all the unregenerate (this conviction) produces an intense fear, an awful agonising horror of eternal condemnation."[16]

Almost all conversion narratives related in revivalist literature follow this pattern of an agonising period of self-loathing and self-debasement preceding the peace of submission. Revivalist leaders frequently stressed that the penitent's sense of personal responsibility for their sin was more significant than fear, and though they would have had their own reasons for such an emphasis, this did seem to be a common element in the direct confrontations between penitent and saviour. Such intense personal experiences are virtually impossible to quantify for the purposes of analysis, but the psychological and emotional power of religious conviction should not be underestimated.

Both the religious and secular press sought opinions on the physical phenomena from ministers of religion, medical doctors and the many visitors from England, Scotland and America. Historical precedents were noted by supporters, asylum statistics came under scrutiny in attempts to link incidents of insanity to current religious excitement, and events in Ulster were discussed at the School of Theology in Geneva.[17] At least some of the early enthusiasm for dramatic conversion experiences was later modified, when the immediate sense of urgency had dissipated. Indeed, Gibson, in the second edition of *The Year of Grace* altered or omitted about 10% of his original material – mostly around prostrations.[18] In the face of the exposure of several hoaxes, and in a calmer atmosphere, others were also concerned to put the drama into perspective: The Reverend John Edgar, ardent evangelical and "friend of the revival",

---

[16]Rev. S. J. Moore, *The History and Prominent Characteristics of the Present Revival in Ballymena and its Neighbourhood* (Belfast, 1859)

[17]J. Edwin Orr, *The Second Evangelical Awakening in Britain* (Edinburgh, 1949); Gibson, *Year of Grace,* Paisley, *"Fifty-Nine" Revival*; J. T. Carson, *God's River in Spate* (Belfast, 1958); Revd. J. McCosh, *The Ulster Revival and its Physiological Accidents* (Dublin, 1859)

[18]A. R. Scott, "The Ulster Revival of 1859", Unpublished PhD thesis, Queen's University, Belfast, 1987, p. 199

writing in 1860, admitted that the atmosphere of urgency and excitement had prompted some fraudulent and some short-lived conversions. Of the strange phenomena he thought some experiences were genuinely religious, but others

> "effects of excitement, nervous disease, sympathy; some of deception. The most noted cases were the worst - the more extravagance, the less pemanence. The cases most notorious and assuming the miraculous were chiefly poor females. Many of these do not profess or show saving change. Numbers who raised high hopes have fallen.Sad ills have followed midnight meetings, fondling sentimentalism, promiscuous gatherings. Exaggeration magnified the eloquence of converts, described as like inspiration; and strange things, deemed by some miraculous, are easily explained. The change on many was from fear not change of heart.[19]

Edgar felt he could "afford such deductions (about the impact of the revival), for they affect not its reality, but extent. There remains incalculable good, endlessly varied, and never to die". But the arguments around prostrations – the most extreme expression of revivalist ardour – reflect the emotive and controversial atmosphere in which the churches made their response to the movement.

After some initial caution, the Presbyterian General Assembly was generally welcoming, though not all its members were equally enthusiastic.[20] During the summer of '59 the Church's Annual General Meeting was suspended to allow ministers to cope with the extra burden of work, with the advice that they "guard against the introduction from any quarter of error in doctrine or practice, lest Satan should get an advantage over us, and the Spirit of Truth be provoked to withdraw".[21] The Church of Ireland, as befitted the establishment, was much more cautious in its approach, with individual clergy reacting in a range of ways. Amongst opponents were the Dean of Down, who denounced the revival both in a sermon and through the local press, while the Archdeacon of Derry ap-

---

[19]John Edgar, *Temperance and Revival in Ulster* (Belfast, 1861)
[20]See, for example, J.B. Armour to J. Megaw, Ballyboyland, 14 September, 1859, Armour Papers, D1792, Public Record Office of Northern Ireland
[21]*Minutes of the General Assembly, July 6 1859*

proved the good work, but advised his clergy not to participate in United Meetings. The Bishop of Dromore, on the other hand, presided over United Prayer Meetings in Newry. [22] Even for supporters, however, both the interdenominational tendencies and the popular, anti-intellectual nature of the movement indicated the potential dangers to denominational integrity.

Despite the churches' preparation for revival, it had in fact begun as a lay movement, and the highly-charged emotional atmosphere surrounding individual and mass conversions was considerably strengthened by the use of lay preachers, most often converts themselves. Untrained, women or labouring men, the recently "saved" delivered a compelling message, with all the fervour of new conviction. But while their performances were impressive and produced an effect, not everyone was happy with the direct employment of the uneducated and unqualified in the work of God. There are parallels here again with the mid 17th and late 18th century revivals, when churchmen had been extremely critical of the anti-intellectual fervour of popular preachers.[23] The main, recurring concern, especially given the dramatic nature of many of the conversions, was that they were a product of fear and emotion rather than "sound doctrine".

In the end, however, most churches reached the conclusion that, even if the method was unorthodox and the result uncertain, it was their clear duty to pick up the mantle and guide the newly awakened through their own particular denominational maze. Most clergy responded vigorously, putting on extra services and prayer meetings and opening up the churches at all hours of the day and night. Converts were offered counselling and instruction and pastoral visitations were regarded as an urgent necessity. Many went further to capitalise on the opportunities opening up, holding lunchtime meetings in shipyards and mills and presiding over the mass gatherings at Fair Hill in Coleraine, or Botanic Gardens in Belfast, where thousand gathered to pray. By channelling the movement into acceptable institutional forms, their positive response was not only intended to ensure a sound scriptual basis to the movement, but also reflected the more pragmatic concern, that they could not afford to be left behind in this wave of popular religious enthusiasm.

---

[22]Orr, *Second Evangelical Awakening,* pp 184-6; W. D. Emerson, *The Church of Ireland and the 1859 Revival* (Belfast, 1859)
[23]Letter to Dr. Coke, November, 1799 Ouseley Papers, CR6/3, PRONI; Westerkamp, *Triumph of the Laity*, p. 24

The main priority of the churches, however, was to translate this outburst of popular religious enthusiasm into long-term church attendance — to strengthen the religious institutions themselves by providing a new generation of believers. Despite initial encouraging responses, a great deal of optimism, and claims of as many as 100,000 converts in all, success in this area was much less dramatic than the literature suggests. When compiling statistical evidence there was a tendency to suggest that *all* new buildings or additions to congregations were direct results of the revival, whether or not this was the case; much of the building work completed in 1859 and 1860, for example, would have been in the process of planning and construction before the "year of grace". And since much of the reporting was intended to encourage new recruits rather than reflect accuracy, numerical advances were extremely difficult to monitor at the time, or to analyse afterwards.

All Protestant denominations were affected, though the movement was much more potent amongst Presbyterians than Anglicans. The Presbyterian moderator recorded an increase of 10,661 new communicants in 307 congregations, with the impact most notable in counties Antrim and Down. The statistics are very short-term — up until 1st April 1860, and there are various omissions and qualifications.[24] Amongst the smaller Presbyterian offshoots, the Covenanters recorded a growth in membership from 4050 to 4420, the biggest percentage increase for any similar period.[25]. The Remonstrants and Unitarians were much less impressed. While it is difficult to get an overview of Church of Ireland statistics, studies of various localities indicate an increase in the annual numbers of communicants, by 50, 100, or 150, and the Bishop of Down & Connor reported that while he normally had an average of 250 annual confirmations in his Belfast parish, the number had reached 705 in the year of the revival.[26] Amongst Methodists, of course, revivalism was a more traditional means of recruitment, and they too recorded significant membership increases, as did the Congregational churches.[27]

From a long-term perspective, however, it can be seen that the increases were often short-lived, and fitted into the traditional revival pattern of a steady build-up, a spectacular climax and then a dramatic falling-

---

[24]Gibson, *Year of Grace*, p. 112
[25]A. Loughridge, *Covenanters in Ireland*
[26]Gibson, *Year of Grace*; Carr, *The Most Unpretending of Places*
[27]*Minute of the Methodist Conference of Ireland*; Malcolm Coles, *I will build my Church: The Story of the Congregational Union of Ireland 1829-1979* (Lisburn, 1979)

off. The Primitive Wesleyan Methodists, for example, having incurred losses in the previous three years, show a growth rate of between 2 and 9 per cent between 1856 and 1859, making a massive leap to 53.7 per cent in 1860, but went on to record significant losses for more than a decade thereafter.[28] Within Presbyterianism too, the number of congregations shows steady increases from the 1830s, with a significant boost in the decade from 1850 to 1860, followed by a much slower rate of growth thereafter.

Assessment of the make-up of church membership also requires careful interpretation of the literature. For obvious reasons, revivalist leaders tended to highlight the most dramatic type of conversion experiences, those which demonstrated a marked contrast in lifestyle before and after salvation. Thus drunks, prostitutes and criminals figure largely in the pamphlet material, with the excessive burden of guilt prompting particularly spectacular struggles against Satan. Disproportionate attention is also given to converts from poor and squalid urban areas – suspected dens of vice and iniquity. When examining the accounts and testimonies of those affected, however, what is most striking is their close familiarity with the scriptures. Many, it is clear, were already attending church or Sunday School, or were well-known to the minister attending them. They spoke of fresh meaning given to old texts, or new light thrown on the word of God, of a shocked realisation that their previous religious experience was "mere formalism". This is not to take away from either the intenstity of the experience or its significance to individuals, described as a "mighty impulse heavenward". This revitalisation of those within the christian subculture was probably in the longer term of much greater significance to both the churches and the wider religious community they served than the more dramatic but transient cases. There were many reported instances of serving ministers themselves dating their conversion from 1859, with this "fresh baptism" determining a much-changed approach to their vocation, while amongst the young adults vital to the future of the churches, there was a marked increase in candidates for the ministry.[29]

Another significant consequence of this period of revivalism was the growth of those denominations which required a more visible and positive commitment from their adult members. The combination of independent

---

[28]David Hempton and Myrtle Hill: *Evangelical Prostentantism in Ulster Society, 1740-1890* (Routledge, London, 1992) p. 156.
[29]Orr, *Second Evangelical Awakening*, p. 200. Gibson, *Year of Grace*; Loughbridge, *Covenanters in Ireland*, p. 95

organization, zealous preaching and strict piety led some new converts to forsake the older, more established denominations for the congregations of Baptists and Brethren for whom the period of revival proved particularly fruitful. Again, this indicates a shift in direction on the part of the already religious, rather than totally new recruits to christendom. The revival's emphasis on the gospels and the visible evidence of conversion led to a specific interest in baptism, with Matthew 28 verses 19-20 providing stimulus and justification for ardent believers. The English Baptist, Dr Evans, recalled that "everywhere the baptismal question is arising. Hundreds, if not thousands, throughout this province are enquiring about it".[30]

Indeed, accusations of "poaching" were common in this period – especially in Ballymena, Coleraine and Derry, Presbyterian areas where the secession to Baptist congregations provoked an angry response at Synodical meetings. As a result of this upsurge of interest, the Baptist Irish Society reported that 1859 and its aftermath was "a period of intense activity and growth", and invested a good deal of energy and resources in capitalising on the opportunities provided. £500 was raised to meet the expenses of English visitors (including C.H. Spurgeon), but local Baptists also recognised that itinerant evangelism alone offered no long-term programme of development, and they thus also supported the initial financing of new churches. With this help, the number of Baptist churches in Ulster increased from 9 in 1858 to 15 in 1865.[31]

But even the small and enthusiastic sects found it difficult to maintain their membership figures once the initial excitement of the revival had dissipated. In the Baptist church at Tobermore, for example, the membership of 269 in March 1860 was reduced to 223 by March 1865, and views of the "blessings"; of the revival were being significantly revised, with the pastor reporting,

> "Many of whom I had hoped better things - in whose profession of Christ, in fact, I had taken the most intensest interest, I was obliged to renounce their calling and return to the world; while in the church general

---

[30]Joshua Thompson, "Irish Baptists and the 1859 Revival", *Irish Baptist Historical Society Journal*, Vol. 17 (1984/5), p. 8

[31]Joshua Thompson, "Baptists in Ireland 1792-1922: A Dimension of Protestant Dissent", D. Phil, Regent's Park College, Trinity, 1988

there lacked the warmth and earnestness once so marked among the brethren."[32]

Again, however, not all of those deserting the Baptists *were* "returning to the world". Many moved into Brethrenism, whose historian claimed that the 1859 revival marked the beginning of the main growth of this sect in the north of Ireland. Certainly the method and content of much contemporary popular religious activity seemed particularly appropriate to a sect with an open, spirit-led ministry whose piety and conviction marked them out from others in almost every walk of life. That they also practised believer's baptism by immersion made the transition from Baptist to Brethren particularly smooth, and secessions to Brethrenism were reported by Baptist congregations in Londonderry and Ballymena.

Like the Baptists, the local Brethren movement itself was considerably strengthened by the work of many visitors, mainly from Scotland and America, during and immediately after the revival.[33] It has been claimed that "the result of the efforts of these men and of a long line of their successors has been to make Ulster one of the strongest centres of Brethren work." Within the city of Belfast alone, there were eight Brethren meeting places by the end of the century, and the six different types of Brethrenism recorded in the 1901 census suggests the variety of interpretations they embraced.[34] While the statistical growth in Baptist and Brethren membership is impressive, the shift in geographical distribution is also significant. It was reported that "whereas in 1800 any (Baptist) churches that mattered could be found east of a line from Dublin to Cork, by 1848 almost half the churches were to be found in Ulster".[35] A similar pattern can be traced in the development of Methodism between the late 18th and mid-nineteenth century, and of evangelical voluntary religious agencies in the first half of the 19th century.[36] Ulster was gradually becoming the stronghold of the more intense and zealous elements of Protestantism, whose attraction to and for the province was undoubtedly a reflection of wider social and political developments. By the

---

[32] D. P. Kingdon, *Baptist Evangelism in 19th Century Ireland* (Belfast, 1965) p. 27
[33] Coad, *History of the Brethren Movement*, p.172
[34] *Belfast Directory for 1898*
[35] D. P. Kingdon, *Baptist Evangelism,* p. 19
[36] D. Hempton, "Methodism in Irish Society, 1770-1830". *Transactions of the Royal Historical Society*, 5th Series xxxvi, pp117-42 (1986), M. Hill, "Popular Protestantism in Ulster in the Post- Rebellion Period c1790-1810", *Studies in Church History* 25 (1989), pp 191-202

end of the century a proliferation of city missions and travelling evangelists, gospel halls and tent crusades were visible evidence of a religious activism which supplemented the more formal religious traditions.

But in a society which was already divided along religious lines, the energy and fervour of this religious enthusiasm also contributed to more negative trends in community relations. By the middle of the nineteenth century, Belfast, formerly a small Presbyterian market town, had become a bustling industrial port whose Catholic and Protestant population were both segregated and hostile. In this context, evangelical-style fervour, moving outside the confines of church or meeting house, could, and frequently did, mean confrontation. Sectarian conflict in the northeast was a product of long-term demographic, social and political divisions, but evangelical religion supplied a new generation of religio-political orators, an inherently competitive religious ideology and new occasions for conflict, such as open-air preaching. And while the priority of both Catholic and Protestant church leaders was to win souls for God, the mutual suspicion of their respective flocks ensured that their capacity for conflict was frequently realised.

Open-air preaching, for example, had become accepted as an important means of spreading the gospel by both Presbyterians and Anglicans prior to the revival, but there had been early evidence of the discord it could provoke. For open-air sermons were designed to be more spontaneous and emotive than those addressed to pious churchgoers on a Sunday morning, and the congregation was also less easy to control. Those loitering on the streets, glad of a diversion, and finding an immediate resonance in the preacher's message, could respond directly and violently to the anti-Catholicism inherent, and often explicit, in evangelical ideology. Troublemakers on both sides of the religious divide turned such occasions into riotous examples of evangelicalism"s most pernicious influence. The summer of 1857 was particularly noteworthy for this kind of populist quasi-religious acitivty, with popular preachers from both the Presbyterian and established churches at the centre of incidents of bloody sectarian violence.[37] Despite assertions of peaceful intention, the defiant and emotive rhetoric at the heart of evangelical preaching had an ambiguity which was not lost on mobs of labouring men seeking both explanation and justification for a now traditional communal conflict. On such occasions anti-

---

[37] Andrew Boyd, *Holy War in Belfast* (Belfast, 1969)

Catholicism was a major factor in forging relations between churches and community in which more overtly "religious" values played little part.

Such incidents form part of the backdrop to the enthusiastic assertions of Protestant values in 1859. Anti-Catholicism certainly became more notable in denominational records as the 19th century progressed, but this specific aspect of evangelical ideology did not play a significant part in the events of 1859. A few converts were reported – as many as 3 to 400 by Gibson. Though they were given a good deal of publicity, most commentators would have been anxious not to be associated with the popular communal strife which usually accompanied campaigns of religious proselytism in Ireland. Only amongst Methodist missionary correspondence have I come across evidence of actual hostility stemming from revivalist activity, with tales of attacks, beatings and priestly anger.[38] Otherwise, most revivalist leaders were at pains to suggest that increased social harmony was one of the most welcome "fruits of the revival".

Nonetheless, given the wider context, Frank Wright is probably correct to see the revival as yet another landmark in the religious differentiation between Protestant and Catholic which had become more marked over the bitter educational debates and the new exclusivity of the Roman Catholic hierarchy in Ireland.[39] For many Ulster Protestants, particularly in this period of increasing isolation from the rest of Ireland, the industrial expansion and relative prosperity of the northeast were viewed as a direct consequence of its religious and ethnic base. The rise of a more assertive Catholicism threatened that dominant religious ideology and the cultural identity which it embraced. The revival movement, having little or no impact on Catholic areas, could be interpreted as a divine visitation, offering reaffirmation, justification and divine approval to a society which had undergone half a century of social, political and religious upheaval.

The revival's emphasis on moral reformation also reflected the cultural values of respectable Protestantism, with claims that Ulster society had undergone a complete moral transformation as a result of the spread of "Godly religion".[40] The list of beneficial social consequences, including

---

[38] Methodist Missionary Society Archives, correspondence between London Missionary Committee and Irish Missionaries, boxes 74 and 75, School of Oriental and African Studies, London

[39] F. A. Wright, "Developments in Ulster Politics, 1843-86", PhD thesis, Queen's University, Belfast 1989, pp 291-306

[40] Weir, *Ulster Awakening*, pp 48-59; *Buick's Ahoghill* (Antrim, 1987), p. 81; W. Reid, *Authentic Records of Revival* (Belfast, 1860), pp 161-73; Orr, *Second Evangelical*

a decline in drunkenness, prostitution and criminal activity, was impressive, but hotly contested. As with the physical phenomena, this aspect of the revival's influence was regarded as vitally important by those on both sides of the debate, as it could be cited as evidence of the genuine – or false – nature of the movement itself. It would obviously be significant if it could be proved, not only that individuals had changed their lifestyle, but that a divine influence had permeated wider society. Both private and public morality were thus the subject of heated discussion.

The greatest success in religious circles was felt to be in the drive against the "demon drink" – long regarded as "the national curse of Ireland". At least two distilleries were reported to have gone out of business and dozens of pubs closed down; the tradition of drinking at Protestant funerals was believed to have been much reduced, as was the number of charges of drunkenness in local courts. All, it was claimed, as a result of the revival's influence. Temperance had, however, been a priority amongst local evangelicals for at least 30 years, with the first Temperance Society in Europe formed in Belfast in 1829, its membership numbers reaching 15,000 within four years.[41] While many thousands remained totally unmoved by the crusade, reports of a decline in drinking are too numerous to ignore. No doubt the illicit drink trade and the rowdy activities associated with it suffered heavily as a result of the introduction of revenue police and the reduction of duty on whiskey. It is likely too that increasing demands on time and money in the changing economic environment in both urban and rural areas were as significant as the work of evangelicals.[42]

The response of those who did respond to the evangelical appeal can also to a large extent be related to the emergence of "respectability" as a central feature in Protestant culture. The link between sobriety and social progress was one frequently made in the temperance literature of the period, and during the revival too, examples were given of individuals whose rejection of alcohol led to a substantially improved lifestyle. Religion and respectability were thus perceived to be mutually reinforcing, with the temporal advantages of moral elevation self-evident, and the churches playing an important role in offering support for those pursuing

---

Awakening, p. 179; Gibson, *Year of Grace*; Carson, *God's River in Spate*, pp 96-9

[41]P. T. Winskill, *The Temperance Movement and its Workers* (London, 1892); *Annual Reports of the Ulster Temperance Society*

[42]D. Hemton and M. Hill "Godhness and Good Citizenhip: Evanglical Protestantism and Social Control in Ulster, 1790-1850", *SOATHAR*, Journal of The Irish Labour History (1988) pp 68-80.

a orderly and self-respecting way of life. Many aspects of traditional popular culture were increasingly presented as "sinful", rather than irresponsible, and, where possible, religious alternatives were provided. Thus the temperance movement offered its adherents a range of tea-rooms, reading rooms, temperance hotels, and participations in bands, dances and processions, while churches organised Sunday-school processions and outings in an attempt to undermine "bawdy" secular activities.

Of course, the repressive and narrow ideology of such measures probably alienated as many as they attracted, and evangelical innovations never replaced secular cultural activities. The persistence of more traditional aspects of popular culture should not be underestimated. But with evangelical values dominating and determining the nature of public discourse, the effect was a widening of the gulf between the "rough" and "respectable" elements of society. Thus, although the actual numbers of adherents to a committed evangelical lifestyle was always a minority in terms of percentage of population, the impact of the ideology was pervasive. The religious revival of 1859 helped to both consolidate and promote a religious sub-culture which linked evangelical virtues – frugality, temperance, sabbitarianism and a bible-based education – with the province"s prosperity, and placed itself in opposition to Irish catholicism which was associated with ignorance, sloth and economic depression.

Conclusions

The "Great Awakening" of 1859 did not emerge out of the blue, but was indeed, "the result of the confluence of many tributaries", and the wider social and political context was as important as religious influences in giving shape and direction to the movement. Similarly, the revival itself had an impact on wider Protestant culture, convincing many that God was indeed on their side, and reinforcing the developing ethos of godliness and good citizenship which was inextricably bound up with Protestantism and loyalty to the British way of life. By the end of the century, when the Protestants of Ulster were faced with the Home Rule crisis, the articulation of that culture was a central tenet in their campaign of resistance, and a major leadership role was played by the churches which had retained the loyalty and respect – if not always the individual commitment – of a majority of Ulstermen and women.

The way in which the revival was remembered and recorded is itself part of a vibrant Protestant heritage. It has a central place in local and national denominational histories, where it is presented both as an example of God's power and an inspiration for all believers. The main significance of the revival to the churches of Ulster was in the revitalisation of the religious community rather than expansion into uknown territory, and in the prominence given to the promotion of an inherently "religious" code of conduct. Although we can dispute many of the claims of overenthusiastic revivalists, and even if we omit the drama, hysteria and excesses surrounding the events of 1859, what remains is an articulation of values central to the local community.

The Oxford Group and Group Revivalism in Britain and Scandinavia

Anders Jarlert

1. Group Revivalism and the Oxford Group

In this context, "the Oxford Group" refers to a national or international net-work with a strong, informal organization, working in personal fellowship – both inspirationally and functionally – with Dr. Frank N. D. Buchman (1878–1961)[1] or the team around him, willing to live and work in the Oxford Group way, i.e. according to a certain pattern of attitudes in action. "Group revivalism," on the other hand, presents a varying attitude to Buchman and the Oxford Group, both inspirationally and functionally. Significant for independent Group revivalism – in contrast to the Oxford Group – is often a separation between the message and the methods of the Oxford Group, and always a separation between life and work in the Oxford Group way and the personal fellowship with Frank Buchman and his team.[2]

Mostly literary inspiration was brought about by Geoffrey Allen (1902–1982), later Bishop of Derby, who was a Fellow and Chaplain of Lincoln College in Oxford, considered as modernist in theology. His books from the early 1930s were confessional, edifying, and essayistic, but not very theological. However, Allen's personal growth is of great interest in our context. In the preface to *Tell John*, he expressed his gratitude to "a group of friends," and their "indebtedness to Karl Barth, and other present leaders of continental theology."[3] In *He that Cometh*, Allen's gratitude is directed towards the "fellowship with other disciples in the

---

[1] On Buchman and the development of the Oxford Group, see Lean 1985, and, in Swedish, Ekstrand 1993, Ch.II. See further Jarlert 1995.

[2] In some cases, this independent position was given a fundamental importance, i. e. it developed into Group independentism. Hestvold 1987:132 is one of very few authors correctly distinguishing the Oxford Revival from the Oxford Movement. We prefer "Group revivalism" and "the Oxford Group", respectively. Cf. Belden 1976:383 ff., who regards the *Groups* magazine and independent Group revivalism as a British phenomenon, and not as a common pattern of different times and places.

[3] Allen 1932: Preface. Barth is quoted, p. 35, and on p. 111, both Barth and Brunner.

Oxford Group Movement," but even here, Barth is quoted.[4] At the same time, Allen was influenced by both the radical objectivism of Barthian theology, and the radical personalism in the Oxford Group.[5] These influences changed his image of God:

> The fault of the modern Christian world is not that it has too much theology, nor that it has a formal and dead theology, but rather that it has an untrue theology. Modern theology has taken away the reminder of the anger of God, and has pictured God as an amiable figure, who is allowed to rebuke sin and cannot heal it.[6]

The theological result was that Allen "moved far on from Major's Modernism," while he remained in association with the Modern Churchmen's Union, advocating what he termed "a Penitent Liberalism."[7] His books, especially *He that Cometh*, won great influence even among theologians, for example, the Swedish professor and future bishop Arvid Runestam. In *Christ the Victorious* (1935), Allen was not any longer, according to his own words, "completely in harmony with the inner team of the Group."[8] In the same year, Allen left for Canton, and did not return to the fellowship of the Oxford Group.[9]

The combination of literary and personal inspiration is made clear through the example of the Rev. Erik Arbin in Stockholm. In September 1930, he met a lady who – during a study trip to England – had been converted through the Oxford Group. In the summer 1931, while deputizing for the pastor of the Swedish Legation in London, he attended a house-party. Before this visit, he had read Harold Begbie's *Life-changers*. Having returned to Sweden, Arbin told of his experience both privately

---

[4] Allen 1933^2: Preface, 34, 202.

[5] This combination was used in the advertising for the Danish version of *He that Cometh*, which was understood as Allen's way through Barthian theology into the Oxford Group Movement (see back cover of Russell 1933). This combination seems to have been frequent especially in Britain. In a letter to Bishop Bell, 1940, Nov. 12, Bishop Henson of Durham accused him of being "influenced by Karl Barth and Buchman," Jasper 1967:248.

[6] Allen 1933^2:167.

[7] Stephenson 1984:180.

[8] G. Allen to H. O. Lange [1935; wrongly dated 1933 on the manuscript] March 19 (KBK Ny Kgl. Saml. 3736-4°).

[9] See also Lean 1985:436.

and at a parish meeting. During the following two years, he tried to practise in his youth work what he had learnt in England, by giving a more personal touch to Bible hours and discourses. During the winter 1933–1934, he was often asked to give discourses on the Group Movement, and through these speeches, he became convinced of his own need of a new surrender to God. Through sharing and restitution, Arbin experienced a change in his pastoral work resulting in a new and personal soul-care. At a well attended clerical conference, he testified about his earlier temptations to sin against the Sixth Commandment, and of his recent victories. Arbin was later to take an active and leading part in Swedish Group work, especially in the integrated Church Group work in Stockholm. Through his friendship with Aleksi Lehtonen, from 1934 Bishop of Tampere, and through several speeches, Arbin influenced the development in Finland, too. In July 1933, Lehtonen sent him the Norwegian version of Emil Brunner's reflections on the Group Movement – which accorded with Arbin's own. Through the mediation of Lehtonen, Arbin seems to have come in contact with the independent *Groups* magazine as well. Together they went to the Oxford Group campaign in Denmark in the spring 1935.[10]

In 1932, the Swedish Methodist pastor August Strömstedt met some leading Oxford Group men in the U.S.A., and in England, where he attended a couple of house-parties, and spent a week as guest with Sam. Shoemaker in Calvary House in New York. His impressions were published by the publishing company of the Church of Sweden (SKDB) in 1933.[11] *Den nya Oxfordrörelsen* was the first Swedish book on the movement. After a thorough report on the history, the principles, and the methods of the Oxford Group, Strömstedt referred to the modern Cambridge Movement as a Wesleyan parallel to the Oxford Group Movement. His book was built on personal impressions, and referred to the ubiquitous books by Allen, Begbie, and Russell, as well as to six titles by Shoemaker and seven titles in German. Strömstedt stresses the need for a spiritual movement of life along the Wesleyan lines. He was entirely positive to the life and evangelizing work of the Oxford Group, especially

---

[10] Arbin in *Janus* 1934:107 f., Arbin 1939:48 ff., Hassler 1964:69 f.

[11] Strömstedt's first encounter with the Oxford Group was in the U.S.A., as he – while attending the 1932 General Conference of the Methodist Episcopal Church – received an invitation from Frank Buchman to a hotel dinner followed by conversation (see Halls Berättelser 1935 Nr. 4:6).

when implemented as a youth movement, while he did not show any understanding for its structure of an internationally working fellowship.

This attitude towards the Oxford Group continued in the Methodist Church in Scandinavia. The Swedish translation of Weatherhead's *Discipleship* (1938), with its chapters on surrender, sharing, quiet time, guidance, restitution, etc., could easily be read as representative of an original Group revivalism, in contrast to the programme of a moral rearmament. In his preface, Weatherhead recognized his debts to the Oxford Group Movement, at the same time referring to the brilliant renewal in Britain, thanks not only to the Oxford Groups, but to the Cambridge and Methodist Groups as well. The difference between the Oxford Group work and the Group work promoted by Weatherhead's book is obvious from the subjects for discussions printed at the back of the book.[12]

In July 1934, Børge Hjerl-Hansen, in the Danish *Dagens Nyheder*, answered the so-called critics of the Oxford Movement, and stated that

> 1. We do not wish any *"Oxford"*- Movement, but we do wish a *Group* Movement. ---
> 2. We do not wish direct import of a movement, that is "made in U.S.A." ---
> 3. Several of us are personally indebted to the leaders of the movement in England or in America, but we do not wish the sweet traces of Frank Buchman & Co. as a papal seal of our work.
> 4. We deny any relationship to possible morbid imitations or degenerated forms of the Oxford Group Movement, whether abroad or at home ---[13]

Hjerl-Hansen's statements exposed the fear of especially the American mentality of the Oxford Group, but he emphasized the need of a national leadership, independent of the British team as well.

In Britain, Oxford Group methods (listening for the guidance of God, private sharing, restitution, testifying, etc.) were accepted by some priests and adapted to their congregational work. However, neither they nor their parishioners entered the fellowship of the Oxford Group. In

---

[12] Weatherhead 1938[3]:11 f. Discussions were banned in the Oxford Group.
[13] B. Hjerl-Hansen: "Til Oxfordbevægelsens Kritiker" (*Dagens Nyheder* 1934, July 30).

order to avoid a similar development in Scandinavia, the Oxford Group tried to connect their work directly to the bishops and religious leaders of the National churches, and to reach Germany by way of Scandinavia. The result was that while the Norwegian development went from an Oxford Group revival (1934–35), earlier and stronger than in the other Scandinavian countries, to an integrated Church Group revivalism of some political and cultural importance to the post-war situation, the Danish development went from an independent Group revivalism (1933–34) by way of a short Oxford Group revival (1935–36) to a national rearmament on a broader scale than in the other Scandinavian countries, but with strong tensions between Church Group revivalism and Moral Re-Armament. In Sweden, the development went by way of a very short Oxford Group campaign for Moral Re-Armament (1938–39) into a social and personal work for spiritual preparedness, which emphasized the need for preparing oneself for the post-war situation rather than the need for a moral rearmament.

In Sweden, the Oxford Group phase meant a much stronger connection with the international team, mostly through the foreign full-time workers, who were keeeping in touch with each other whether in Scandinavia, in Finland, or in Britain. Differences of opinion sometimes led to conflicts with the Swedes. Other disagreements were caused by the coming and going of the young foreigners at certain personal and editorial offices, with the aim of changing people, but characterized by Harry Blomberg – even publicly – as dangerous. Among the key persons visited were Crown Prince Gustav Adolf, Prime Minister P. A. Hansson, Foreign Minister Rickard Sandler, the ministers P. E. Sköld, K. G. Westman, G. Möller, the businessman Axel Wenner-Gren, "one of the Wallenbergs," etc. The visits with some of the press men, like Börje Brilioth and Zäta Höglund, were more successful.[14] Local separatist plans in Stockholm to

---

[14]Blomberg to J. Hemmer 1939, Apr. 1 (ÅAB). Together with Fr. Ramm, Blomberg on the previous evening warned about a hundred people in Stockholm about the risk. At the same time, Blomberg stated that the English boys were right in being tremendously stubborn, as they had given up so much. But they had to be helped further on, and all secterism had to be avoided. "Confidentiellt !" (EPC) mentions four personal calls to the Prime Minister, as well as sending him press articles, Bunny Austin's book, and Frank Buchman's radio speech. The Prime Minister said in October 1938 that his party (the Social Democrats) always had aimed at an improvement of conditions, including an improvement of human beings, which could be named a kind of moral rearmament. Margit Wohlin and Peggy Blake had met Mrs. Hansson. See also S. Linton's report (1938, Nov. 16) from an interview with the prime minister. The encounters with the other ministers were less successful, Mr. Sandler refusing a suggested second interview, Mr. Sköld being "sceptical about the value of religion, or its effects, but was all the same

change the direction of the work into something Swedish, through breaking up the national office, and removing two of the foreign full-timers from the country, were relinquished.[15] Instead, the Stockholm team, growing in initiative and responsibility, took over the office, which was refounded.

The German occupation of Denmark and Norway changed the plans and Group work in Sweden as well. Howard Blake was called back to the U.S.A. by Frank Buchman personally.[16] David Grimshaw and Edward Goulding were both in Norway when the German troops marched in, but escaped – Grimshaw to Sweden, where he remained, together with Sydney Linton and Pip Lyth. For some time, these three planned to leave, but the direct advice from Frank Buchman was to consider remaining in Sweden.[17]

The day after the invasion of Denmark by German troops on April 9, 1940, one of the British full-time workers, Andrew Strang, was arrested but released, arrested again a month later, interned, and sent to Germany. The Danish team sent him weekly parcels, and communicated through German friends.[18] Through the mediation of Mrs. Märta Wetterlind in the Oxford Group in Sweden, Strang was visited in Germany by her uncle, Dr. Sven Hedin and his sister, Miss Alma Hedin. Through Dr. Hedin's German publisher, Brockhaus, they sent him money regularly until 1943. In September 1944, Andrew Strang was exchanged against other civilian prisoners, returning to Britain by way of Sweden.[19]

---

interested," Dr. Westman "very reserved and cold, showed no signs of being impressed, nor friendly."

[15]Copy of Linton to Strang, E. Goulding, Lyth, and Grimshaw 1940, March 30 (DWC) positively on the Stockholm team "beginning to take over responsibility for the team all over the country"; to Strang, E. Goulding, H. Blake 1940, Apr. 4 (DWC).

[16]Copy of Linton to H. Blake 1940, Apr. 14 (DWC).

[17]On the escape of Goulding and Grimshaw, see copy of Linton to Goulding 1940, May 31; Linton to Lyth 1940, May 8; to P. Blake 1940, May 10; to F. Buchman 1940, June 6 (DWC). Linton, who had been staying in Karlstad since January 1940, and Grimshaw moved to Stockholm two days before the province of Värmland was closed to foreigners. Lyth returned to England at the end of 1942 ("Kära vän!" Stockholm 1943, Jan. 21, dupl., Alnäs).

[18]Thorvald S. Petersen 1940, Aug. 22 (in copy as appendix to S. Linton to F. Buchman 1940, Dec. 13, NLC).

[19]Hedin 1949:168 ff., A. Strang to A. Hedin 1940, Nov. 9, several letters from S. Linton to S. Hedin, especially 1944, Dec. 13, and G. Jansson to S. Hedin 1942, Feb. 4 (RA). Miss Hedin's description of the conditions of imprisonment is included in copy of Linton to P. Blake 1941, Jan. 18 (DWC). Till Andrew Strangs vänner i Sverige. Gothenburg 1944, Sept. 10 (dupl., Alnäs).

During the war, the remaining foreign full-time workers were isolated from the international Oxford Group team. For example, letters from the U.S.A., posted in January 1942, and containing news from Britain in April 1941, did not arrive in Stockholm until August 31, 1942.[20] When Philip Mottu arrived in Stockholm in January, 1945, it was the first personal visit by anyone from the team in England for five years.[21]

2. The Strategy of Moral Re-Armament

In the 1930s, the Oxford Group changed emphasis from revivalistic personalism to social personalism on a national or supranational level, presenting a utopian alternative to National Socialism and Communism, expressed in 1938 as a strategy of moral rearmament. In social personalism the emphasis shifted from personal problems to the national and universal ones, which were still met with a personalistic attitude or method. From 1943 the strategy of moral rearmament was interpreted as a democratic ideology (ideological personalism), developing into a mixed structure of personalistic mentality and democratic ideology.

This shifting of emphasis – not a change of doctrine – is easily observed, for instance, in Frank Buchman's speech at Visby, Sweden, in August, 1938 ("Revival – Revolution – Renaissance"), with its explicit criticisms of those who wanted to remain at the stage of revivalism. The local teams showed various reactions to this shifting, and some groups – thus loosing themselves from the Oxford Group – continued their work during the war, exclusively on the level of personal revival. Unlike what is commonly believed, the use of Moral Re–Armament as a designation for the fellowship, network, or organization around it, is of much later origin than 1938. As late as in 1939, the Oxford Group obtained legal incorporation, and in his "authorized" account of the principles and growth of its work, 1947, Julian Thornton–Duesbery still uses "the Oxford Group" as the summarizing term.[22]

---

[20]Copy of S. Linton to H. Blake 1942, Apr. 27, Aug. 22, Sept. 1. As early as in the autumn 1940, a letter from England arrived two months after the posting (copy of Linton to Blake 1940, Oct. 15, DWC).

[21]See Ph. Mottu to F. Buchman 1945, Feb. 6 (NLC).

[22]A clearyfing example is given in the invitation to the International House–party at Interlaken, Sept. 2–12, 1938, arranged by the Oxford Group on the theme "Moral re–armament of the Nations". Cf. "Oxford Group" (The Oxford Dictionary of the Christian

Throughout the 1920s as well as the 1930s, up to the presentation of the strategy of a moral rearmament, there had been much talk, in both ecclesiastical and political circles in Europe, about the need for a moral and spiritual disarmament. In 1928, Martin Rade spoke at the World Conference for Promoting International Friendship through the Churches, in Prague, on "Moralische Abrüstung eine *erste* Notwendigkeit," and, having raised the issue as early as in 1925, the Danish Foreign Minister, P. Munch, stated – in the League of Nations in 1931 – that "le désarmement moral est nécessaire," repeating it as late as in September 1936.[23] This moral disarmament meant a disarmament of hatred and hostility as well as cooperation based on good will in and among individuals, churches, classes, nations, etc.

In October 1937, Kenneth D. Belden, working in the fellowship of the Oxford Group, launched the programme "Spiritual Rearmament for Britain" in *The Church of England Newspaper*. Two weeks later, Rom Landau expressed a prevailing attitude with regard to the disarmament/rearmament situation when he stated that "To disarm materially without arming ourselves spiritually is folly."[24]

At a party in Hurdals Verk September 15–25, 1939, 200 leaders from Scandinavia met to plan further activities, and to advance their programme of "The North, Reconcilers of the Nations." A telegram was sent to each of the four Prime Ministers simultaneously meeting in Copenhagen, which emphasized the purpose "through Moral Re-Armament to make Scandinavia the reconciler of the nations," and supported the governments in their peace-making efforts. During the meeting, the Danish historian C. P. O. Christiansen gave a lecture on the Greenland question. It led to a joint statement from the Danes and Norwegians present, that "if Scandinavia is to fulfil its task as reconciler of the nations in the world, then every disagreement between the countries of Scandinavia must be cleared out of the way in the spirit of mutual

---

Church 1977[2]:1019), "Moralische Aufrüstung" (Andresen & Denzler 1984[2]:412). One of the very few correct descriptions is given in Molland 1972[3]:86.

[23]Rade 1928:858 ff.; Munch 1931:37 f; further Karup Pedersen 1970:297, 82, 172 f; 218.

[24]Kenneth D. Belden: "Defend Your Homes: Your Homes Defend Britain" (The Church of England Newspaper 1937, Oct. 22); Rom Landau: "III. The Church and World Affairs" (The Church of England Newspaper 1937, Nov.5). Cf. Runeby 1995:505, who quotes a printed interview with Bo Giertz in 1934, where Giertz is said to have spoken about "moralisk upprustning" (moral re-armament). This is a misquotation, as Giertz in the interview spoke only about the need of a moral clean up ("upprensning").

understanding," and an appeal to the two countries to take up the work of solving the Greenland question.25

From a British full-timer in Sweden, the Scandinavian situation in 1944 was reported to Frank Buchman in the following way:

> The Finns came [to the house-party at Lund] with their conviction that their war has been a private war, which they expected all the Northern countries to understand and support fully. The Norwegians consider it anything but a private war, and were under instructions from their lawful government not to appear on the same platform as Finns at any public meetings. The Norwegians feel very strongly about this. The Swedes, who have talked so much about Folkförsoning [Reconciliaton between nations] that they feel everyone ought to be good friends by now, did not know how to handle the situation, the simplest and easiest form of Folkförsoning we shall ever be called upon to deal with – that among changed people.
>
> The Norwegians in this country do not like Sweden. They escape to this country expecting to be welcomed as front-line soldiers and sent at once over to England – a treatment which they would not like us to apply to German soldiers escaping from Finland and wishing to be sent through to Germany. Clever German propaganda in Norway has convinced them that the Swedes have helped the Germans much more than they have (it was the German interest to tell the Norwegians that both Sweden and Denmark were pro-German, so why not?). The result is that the Norwegians in this country keep themselves to themselves a good deal, and do not care to mix more than necessary with Swedes, for whom they have all the feelings that a fighting people usually have for neutrals.
>
> Sweden is still keen on Nordic unity. Norway won't hear of it, they want to hitch on to the Atlantic powers. Finland seems bound to hitch on eastwards. Voices are raised for

---

25Moral Re-Armament in Scandinavia since the outbreak of the war (dupl., Caux Archives). The statement was signed by Johan E. Mellbye and Count Aage Moltke. H. Blomberg to J. Hemmer 1939, Oct. 3 (ÅAB). Hurdals Verk 15–25/9 1939 (dupl., 350, UBO), "Kära Vän!" 1939, Sept. 25 (dupl., EPC).

223

Nordism everywhere, but the tide is flowing the other way at the moment.[26]

The attitudes of the churches towards the practices of the Oxford Group varied. After leaving the fellowship, Sven Stolpe found that, while the Church of England regarded the Oxford Group as a special, somewhat suspect form of Christianity, with cooperation difficulties as a consequence, the Church of Sweden was almost submissive in her generous and thankful receiving attitude, and could thus be forced by the Group into a precarious situation. The Roman Catholic Church, on the other hand, stated that the Group was splendid, must be supported and taken care of, as the Spirit surely was at work in its action – though it was not Christian, but what it said: a moral rearmament![27] We may add that, while the working practice of the Oxford Group could remind of Methodism, its lack of ecclesiastical structure troubled the Anglicans, while Swedish Lutherans often interpreted the Oxford Group as a new revival inside the ecclesiastical structures of the Church of Sweden.

3. The Scandinavian "Oxford" Novel and the Cultural Renaissance of the Nordic North

The Danish Ollerup party at Easter, 1936, worked as an inspiration for the international Oxford Group work as well: "The youth march – the special songs – these are all new in the history of the Oxford Group," and the inspiration from Ollerup would mean "a step toward finding England's national destiny, as Denmark has already begun to find hers."[28] Simultaneously, Danish criticism was spread in other countries. For example, a criticism of the Ollerup party by Regin Prenter was printed in the Netherlands three weeks later.[29]

Of greater importance was the "Oxford" novel, developing into a significant Scandinavian genre. The Scandinavian "Oxford" novel has not been much noted outside the Nordic countries. A remarkable fact not noted in literature is that the great Oxford writers in Scandinavia –

---

[26]S. Linton to F. Buchman 1944, Nov. 25 (NLC).
[27]Stolpe to A. Runestam 1948, Jan. 6 (Okat.saml. Runestam, UUB).
[28]Dorothy Prescott to Halfdan Høgsbro Apr. 16, 1936 (Pa. 6922:B.3, RAK). Especially the Bridge-Builder Song was frequently sung in the following years.
[29]R. Prenter: "Oxford" (Woorden Geest 1936, May 8).

Ronald Fangen, Sven Stolpe, Harry Blomberg, and Bertil Malmberg – had reflected seriously on art and problems of writing long before their changing experiences. Another remarkable fact is that they left the Oxford Group during or after the World War. Their Group period was not merely an episode, albeit an important, but passing stage in their development.

In a letter to the Norwegian author Ronald Fangen, May 1935, Frank Buchman accused Fangen of not having checked the Dutch translation of his book on the Christian World revolution with "our Dutch Group," and threatened him that the Dutch sale of his book would "largely depend upon the attitude of the Dutch Group towards the book." Buchman stated that Fangen turned to the Oxford Group only when he could not get his own publisher to sell "a Group book." In England, however, "our publisher would not take it unless it had our "O.K.", and he knew we would be responsible for its sale." Buchman especially disliked the expression "American-made," which "certainly ought to be deleted in other editions....A phrase like that I would not pass in any book for which the Group was responsible in selling."[30] He did not want to be hard, but he felt that Fangen had "no idea how carefully all the literature for which the Group stands has been checked and examined from every possible angle."[31]

In his reply, Fangen said that the book had been checked "with members of the norwegian team." The alternative had been to leave the book unpublished. The Dutch edition was made on the translator's initiative, and not on Fangen's. He could not stop the book in Scandinavia. "And even when it does not seem to please you that it obviously works effectively for the Group-message, it can't, I hope, hurt you. I think I have written the book under guidance, and I can do nothing more." If Group-discipline was not based upon loyalty or Christian freedom, "but upon a bit tyrannie [sic] and formalistic state of mind, which in me creates uncertainty and unnecessary problems," Fangen thought it best "to go out of it now. I am more sorry for it than I can say, for I loved the fellowship and the strength of the team. But when fellowship gets a touch of tyranny in

---

[30]The word was not "American-made," but "made in America," Fangen 1935:7, used as a description of Fangen's feelings of fear towards the Oxford Group *before* his changing experience at Høsbjør. It did not express any continued feelings of hostility or criticism.

[31]Buchman to Fangen 1935, May 14 (UBO 488a). For example, the Danish *Vort møde med Oxford-Gruppen* was translated in manuscript for Buchman, who approved its publication.

it, it must be payed with cowardice. I can't pay that price. --- All in all: I think you will do better without me."[32] In his answer, Buchman explained: "I treated you as a fellow-revolutionary, and I find this is not the way."[33]

In the autumn of 1938, Sven Stolpe planned to arrive with an Oxford team of writers and others at the French cultural centre of Pontigny, where the best authors of France, England, etc. normally gathered at conferences. Stolpe had been there together with Thure Oskarsson, and the management was open to the possibility of receiving an Oxford team together with the writers du Gard, Gide, Maurois, Mauriac, Romains, Schlumberger, Fernandez, Capek, Huxley, Curtius, Mann, Ortega, Madariaga, Papini, Munk, Sillanpää, Valéry, Duhamel, Undset, Fangen, etc.[34] In December 1938, Stolpe complained of the total lack of programme for a Christian literature, with a split even on the main points of art and guidance, art and fellowship, and art and life-change. To a planned, private party in February or March 1939, authors like Arne Sørensen, Sigrid Undset, Kaj Munk, Elin Wägner, Sally Salminen, and Johannes Jørgensen ought to be invited. Even Thomas Mann and one of the leading French authors might come.[35] These plans were postponed, as was a planned journey to Pontigny. Instead, Stolpe travelled with Frank Buchman and a Scandinavian team to the United States.[36] From over there, he planned an attack at the writer's congress arranged by the PEN club in Stockholm, in September 1939.[37] The change of plans was

---

[32]Copy of Fangen to Buchman 1935, May 16 (UBO 488a). Fangen's book was rapidly spread in Scandinavia, and in Germany, soon being both read and quoted. Fr. Ramm to Fangen 1935, June 4 (UBO 488a) expressed that the book would have been still better if checked with, for example, Garret Stearly. Now it was too much an individual Fangen-book.
[33]Buchman to Fangen 1935, May 20 (UBO 488a).
[34]S. Stolpe to "Vänner och bröder!" 1938, Oct. 3, copy to Kaisu Snellman Dec. 29 (Okat.saml. H. Blomberg, UUB). In his letter to Snellman, Stolpe regards the list of writers simultaneously as fantasies, and as his guidance. According to Hambro 1937:122, Huxley was strongly influenced by the Oxford Group, though Stolpe 1942:438 states that Huxley – through Philip Leon – came into contact with the Group Movement, was strongly impressed, but declined its basis: the personal reality of God.
[35]Stolpe to Blomberg 1938, Dec. 12, 27, to "Kära vänner!" Dec. 20 (Okat.saml. H. Blomberg, UUB).
[36]Stolpe to Blomberg 1939, Jan. 20 (UUB). Stolpe regarded the trips to the U.S.A. and Pontigny as alternatives. To Pontigny, Hans Johansson [Norsbo] and Fredrik Ramm would have accompanied him.
[37]Stolpe to Blomberg 1939, May 19 (UUB).

probably to some extent due to Harry Blomberg's rejection of a "front" along Stolpe's lines.[38]

Stolpe's search for common cultural tasks was a result of the difficulties of the Oxford Group writer or artist to combine the necessary artistic isolation with active work in the fellowship. Instead of dividing their energy on meetings, artists and writers should concentrate on the common solving of a cultural task under guidance.[39] In Finland, a cultural team was established in August 1939, with the participation of Gertrud Alfthan, Laina Kalmari, Fred Runeberg, Kauko Huhta, Ella Grönroos, and Lennart Segerstråle. The aim was a new way of seeing art, based on guidance, expressing a new mentality, and with the focus on God and not on the artist.[40] The plans for a cultural rising were intimately connected with the endeavours for peace, and strenghtening the Nordic culture inwards around the theme "The thought of peace".[41]

Immediately after the Second World War, the ideological training was concentrated to the United States. Subsequently, the new European centre at Caux in Switzerland radically changed the conditions of the work, reduced some of the national influences developed during the war, and retightened the whole movement around Frank Buchman and his team.

Archives

Alnäs	Villa Alnäs arkiv, Stockholm
Caux Archives, Caux sur Montreux	
DWC	David Wiklund Collection (with the Estate of David Wiklund, Stockholm)
EPC	Erik Petrén Collection (with Dr. Erik Petrén, Gävle)
KB	Kungliga Biblioteket, Stockholm
KBK	Det Kongelige Bibliotek, København
NLC	National Library of Congress, Washington D. C.
RA	Riksarkivet, Stockholm

---

[38]Blomberg to J. Hemmer 1939, Apr. 1 (ÅAB). Because of his contacts in Finland and Norway, Blomberg probably had a clearer view of the actual situation.
[39]Stolpe to B. Malmberg 1939, Sept. 3 (L74:6, KB).
[40]Ekstrand 1993:165 f.
[41]L. Segerstråle to M. Björkquist 1939, Oct. 3 (SIB).

RAK Rigsarkivet, København
SIB Sigtunastiftelsens bibliotek, Sigtuna
SKDP Svenska kyrkans diakonistyrelses bokförlag
UBO Universitetsbiblioteket, Oslo
UUB Uppsala Universitetsbibliotek
ÅAB Åbo Akademis bibliotek

Literature

Allen, Geoffrey & McKay, Roy
1932 Tell John. The Message of Jesus and Present Day Religion. London

Allen, Geoffrey
1933[2] He that Cometh. A Sequel to "Tell John", being further essays on the Message of Jesus and Present Day Religion. London.
1935 Christ the Victorious. London

Andresen, Carl & Denzler, Georg
1984[2] dtv-Wörterbuch der Kirchengeschichte. München

Arbin, Erik
1934 Bör Oxfordrörelsen överföras till oss? (Kristen Ungdom)
1939 Två resor. (Upplevelser och vittnesbörd. III)

Ekstrand, Sixten
1993 Oxfordgrupprörelsen och MRA i Finland 1932–1955. Åbo

Fangen, Ronald
1935 En kristen verdensrevolusjon. Mitt møte med Oxfordgruppebevegelsen. Oslo

Hambro, Carl Joachim
1937 Moderne mentalitet. Oslo

Hassler, Arne
1964 Stockholmspräster. Minnesteckningar vid Stockholms stifts prästmöte 1963. Stockholm

Hedin, Sven
1949 Utan uppdrag i Berlin. Stockholm

Hestvold, Ove
1987 Alex Johnson. Et liv i spenningsfelt. Oslo

Jarlert, Anders
1995 The Oxford Group, Group Revivalism, and the Churches in Northern Europe, 1930–1945, With Special Reference to Scandinavia and Germany. Lund

Jasper, Ronald C. D.
1967 George Bell. Bishop of Chichester. London

Karup Pedersen, Ole
1970 Udenrigsminister P.Munchs opfattelse af Danmarks stilling i international politik. København

Lean, Garth
1985 Frank Buchman: A Life. London

Molland, Einar
1972[3] Fra Hans Nielsen Hauge til Eivind Berggrav. Hovedlinjer i Norges kirkehistorie i det 19. og 20. århundre. Oslo

Munch, P.
1931 La politique du Danemark dans la Société des Nations. Genève

Rade, Martin
1928 Rede auf dem Prager Weltkongreß für Freundschaftsarbeit der Kirchen (Die Christliche Welt)

Runeby, Nils
1995 Dygd och vetande. Ur de bildades historia. Stockholm

Russell, A. J.
1933 Kun for syndere. København

Stephenson, Alan M. G.
1984 The Rise and Decline of English Modernism. London

Stolpe, Sven
1942 Mystik och politik. Aldous Huxleys nya bok (Bonniers Litterära Magasin)

Strömstedt, August
1933 Den nya Oxfordrörelsen. Stockholm

The Oxford Dictionary of the Christian Church
1977[2] Oxford

Vort møde med Oxford-Gruppen
1935 Syv personlige vidnesbørd. København

Weatherhead, Leslie D.
1938[3] Kristen på allvar. Livets förnyelse och världens evangelisering. Uppsala

Church between Society and Association: The Case of the Syrian Orthodox Church in Sweden

Samuel Rubenson

In the last few decades the Christian topography of Sweden has changed rapidly. In what has been a very homogenous Lutheran country with a fair amount of Protestant denominations dating back to the late 19th century revival, there are suddenly new Catholic and Orthodox churches and chapels consecrated every year. For modern Swedish Church history, which has mainly dealt either with the revivalist movements or changes in the organization of the established Church of Sweden, a new page is opening up. On the Catholic Church in Sweden there are a growing number of studies in process, but the history of the Orthodox in Sweden remains a virgin field.[1]

Although there have been Orthodox believers celebrating their liturgy in Sweden since the late 17th century, due to our Russian relations, it was not until the great wave of immigrants arriving during and after WWII that Orthodox Christians began to become part of Swedish Christianity. The first Orthodox Church to establish itself in the Swedish countryside was the Serbian Orthodox due to the large number of industrial workers imported from former Yugoslavia. Consequently it was also within the Serbian jurisdiction that the first Swedish speaking Orthodox parishes were established. But the growing immigration of refugees from the Middle East in the 1970's has completely altered the picture and made the Syrian-Orthodox community the most prominent Orthodox group in Sweden. With some 30.000 members, one archbishop and some 30 priests and parishes, this community constitutes a not negligible part of Christianity in Sweden.[2]

---

[1] The only exception is the small but informative book by G. Hallonsten, *Östkyrkor i Sverige*, Artos, Skellefteå 1992, and a series of popular tracts by Erik Lindberg, published by Sveriges Frikyrkoråd/Moderna läsare *De kommer från öst.... Österländska och ortodoxa kyrkor i Sverige* 1982; *Sankt Savas kyrka. Serbisk-ortodoxa kyrkan i Sverige; Sankt Markus' efterföljare.* 1983 *Koptisk-ortodoxa kyrkan i Sverige* 1983; *Av fädernas rot rumänsk-ortodoxa kyrkan i Sverige*, 1984; *Mellan öst och väst ortodoxa kyrkorna kring Östersjön*, 1985.

[2] The best guide to the Orthodox in Sweden, apart from Hallonsten's book is *Guiden till invandrarnas organisationer och trossamfund*, Statens Invandrarverk 1992.

Their presence in Sweden dates back to 1967, when the first so called Assyrians were given refugee status and welcomed by the Swedish government. The bulk of the community came to Sweden in the 70's but there is a continuing growth of the community with new refugees, mostly with some family connection. Although there is a concentration of Syrian Orthodox in and around Södertälje, a city some 80 km to the south of Stockholm, where about one third of the Syrian Orthodox have established themselves, there are communities all over Central Sweden. Although the leadership in the community as well as in the church remains completely in the hands of the first generation, a second generation which has grown up in Sweden is gradually challenging the traditional structure.[3]

Although there are larger numbers of Syrian Orthodox in some other countries in the West, the community in Sweden is for several reasons one of the most important. First there is the cultural. Due to what has been very generous Swedish immigrant policy the Syrian Orthodox have been helped to organize and educate themselves, creating two of the internationally most well known journals of Syrian Christianity, the *Bahro Suryoyo* and the *Hujodo*. Although a conclusion might be premature, I think that one can safely say that the emphasis which the Swedish authorities have laid upon teaching immigrants their own mother-tongue has greatly helped the modern revival of the Syriac language. Secondly there is of course the financial, with the Syrian Orthodox of Sweden being the probably most important source of income for the Patriarchate in Damascus as well as for the Syrian Orthodox families and parishes in Northern Syria and in Lebanon. But the most essential reason, according to my view, are the constant and often violent conflicts that have marked the short history of the Syrian Orthodox in Sweden, conflicts which have their repercussions throughout the international Syrian-Orthodox community and remain a constant headache to the Patriarchate of the Syrian-Orthodox in Damascus.

In the following paper I will try to analyze this conflict in its Swedish setting keeping in mind that there are also international aspects of importance.

---

[3]On the Syrian-Orthodox in Sweden there have been some minor studies, most noteworthy Stefan Andersson, *Assyrierna. En bok om präster och lekmän, om politik och diplomati kring den assyriska invandringen till Sverige,* Tidens förlag, Stockholm 1983 and Ulf Björklund, *Från ofärd till välfärd,* Stockholm 1980.

The Conflict

On the deepest level the conflict deals with the relation between Church and people in a modern secular and pluralistic society, a relation which is problematic not only for the Orthodox Churches in immigration but also for the established Church of Sweden. That this question has generated such a fierce struggle within the Syrian Orthodox Church in Sweden is partly due to historical developments in the Middle East in the last century, and partly to the ways the Swedish authorities have handled immigrant communities and the models for religious organization in Sweden. A Church in the islamic Middle East is not the same as a Church in a secular society in Western Europe and the Arabic understanding of the concept of nation is not the same as the modern European. In the "strong" Swedish society there is a hierachy of identification in which citizenship is the most important, cultural and ethnic identity the social glue and associations, to which the Church is counted, something belonging to the private sphere. In a "weak" society like the one of Tur Abdin the Church is the most important, constituted by its language and cult, while citizenship is usually only a political label designating a more or less repressive governemnt to which you have to pay your taxes. In need you trust your Church, not the authorities.[4]

In the developments leading to the struggles within the Syrian Orthodox Church in Sweden today I think one can see three different levels. The first has to do with the European influence in the Middle East and the limits of modernization, the second with the nationalistic, so called Assyrian movement, and the third with the encounter between the Oriental Christian tradition and imigration and ecclesiastical politics in Sweden. In Sweden these three levels have been woven together, have been aggravated by conflicts between families and finally found their outlet in a conflict about the designation of the Syrian Orthodox: Syrians or Assyrians.

The Middle East and Modernism

For the Christian population of the Middle East the Arabic-Islamic conquest that began in the seventh century implied an entirely new

---

[4]For the distinction between a "strong" and a "weak" society see Jan Hjärpe, "Tredjevärldsislam och euroislam. Samhällsstruktur och religionens funktion", in *Islam i forskningens ljus* (ed. Nils G. Holm, Åbo akademi 1991, pp. 67–182.

situation. The Christians were no longer *citizens* of the community they lived in, they were a *protected people*. Excluded from political influence, beyond the pale of the law of the country, they had no public recourse but their Churches. These were now to constitute the political organization of the Christians, their legislative and judicial authority. The ecclesiastical leaders thus became political leaders as well. The bishops, and primarily their superiors, the Patriarchs, became the princes of the protected people, responsible to their Moslem masters for everything that happened in their flocks, within their jurisdictions. The concepts of Church and Nation became synonymous.[5]

At the same time it was obvious, particularly in Syria, that a nation was not a group of people united by ethnic, linguistic, or geographical bonds. If there was any region in Antiquity that was multi-cultural and pluralistic it was Syria, this country east of the Mediterranean that through the millennia has been a concourse for nations to meet and to mix, and where, in the course of time, Aramaic had become the *lingua franca*. The ecclesiastical schisms during the period 300 to 600 had resulted in no less than four Churches with mainly Aramaic-speaking members, of whom three (the Maronites, the Syrian-Orthodox, and the East-Syrian Church) employed Syriac as their written language, and one used Greek (the Greek Patriarchate of Antiochia). The theological demarcations were here less conditional on ethnic traditions – difficult to find in this stamping-ground of empires – and more on social affinity, political loyalty and spiritual traditions. The East-Syrian Church was the Church of the Persian Empire, the Greek-Orthodox were loyal to the Byzantine Emperor, and the Syrian-Orthodox represented a tradition critical of a hierarchy too closely allied with temporal powers.[6]

The Arabic-Islamic conquest brought about a marginalisation of the Christians. Their tradition was preserved in clearly defined social strata and geographical areas, the most important being the mountain regions, and certain trades and quarters in the cities. For the Syrian-Orthodox Church the outcome was a growing gap between a destitute and less influential group in the mountains of south-eastern Turkey, and a more

---

[5]For a discussion of the concept of *dhimmi*, that is *protected people*, see Bat Ye'Or, *Dhimmi: Jews and Christians under Islam*, London 1985.
[6]For surveys of the history of Syrian Christianity and useful biblioraphies see Caspar Detlef Gustaf Müller, *Geschichte der orientalischen Nationalkirchen* (= Die Kirche in ihrer Geschichte, 1, D2), Göttingen 1981 and Aziz Suryal Atiyah, *A History of Eastern Christianity, Notre Dame 1968*. The literature on early Syrian Christianity is enormous, but for the time after the Muslim conquest it is much more limited.

prosperous group in the cities of Syria and Mesopotamia, more influential in Church and state. In the mountains the Christians lived in a setting that even under the Moslems was predominantly Christian, preserving a deep loyalty among the people and employing the monasteries as schools, and as focal points for matters ecclesiastical. There was a clear border-line between them and their Turkish and Kurdish neighbours. Language and ethnic identification had become totally linked up with religion. No Christians would regard themselves as Turks or Kurds because they had been forced to learn their languages. In the Arabic cities, however, the Christians were inevitably exposed to Islam and deeply involved in economic intercourse with the outer world. In the course of time Arabic ousted Syriac, and an Arab ethnic identification evolved across the religious borders. In these regions a powerful ecclesiastical organization and a new ecclesiastical leadership was to develop. After the First World War the residence of the Patriarch was moved from Tur Abdin finally settling in the most important Arabic city of the region, Damascus.

The gap between the Syrian-Orthodox inhabitants of the Tur Abdin mountains of south-eastern Turkey, and their fellow believers in the cities of Syria, was enhanced and sustained by Western colonialism in the Middle East, and the fall of the Ottoman Empire. During the 19th century there was a strong Western pressure in the Arabic-speaking areas. The foundation was laid for a secular Arab nationalism, and for an Arabic Renaissance and Enlightenment. The Churches, too, were influenced by this modernism, and by the new political and nationalistic ideas that were disseminated. This influence was, however, limited mainly to the cities, and hardly reached the Turkish- and Kurdish-speaking rural districts in the North. While, in the course of time, *Arab* has become the comprehensive term for Christians as well as Moslems, *Turkish* and *Kurdish* remain synonymous with *Moslem*.[7]

Of decisive importance were the national borders drawn up after the First World War between the British and French spheres of interest and modern Turkey, the remnant of the Ottoman Empire. In opposition to its predecessor, and to the emerging Arab states, Turkey was an unmitigated, and *de iure* a secular, nationalist state. Every citizen should be a Turkish-speaking Turk, and attempts were made to expel, liquidate, or Turkize everyone who was not. Like the Armenians, the Syriac-speaking

---

[7] Fo the modern period and the impact of the West see John Jospeh, *Muslim–Christian Relations and Inter-Christian Rivalries in the Middle East,* New York 1983.

Christians were affected by this policy, and reduced to a comparatively isolated remnant with no great chances of education and no economic and political influence, whether in the Church or in the state. In the new Arab states, Iraq, Syria, and Lebanon, the situation was vastly different; the Christians were often members of the westernized ruling élite. Although this development was to some extent pushed back by the Arab revolutions of the 1950s and 1960s the Churches lived on in a considerably more open and culturally thriving environment.

The discrepancy between the Syrian-Orthodox from the rural districts of Turkey and those from the Arab world is no more remarkable than corresponding regional discrepancies in other Churches. Problems arise, however, when these groups must come to terms within an endangered immigrant Church in an entirely different setting – in modern Sweden. The first immigrant Syrian-Orthodox came mainly from Arab countries, but currently the majority are from south-eastern Turkey. It is not surprising that the present bishop, as well as his predecessor, and the great majority of the priests come from the Arab states, particularly Syria, granted that some of them have their roots in the mountains of Turkey. Although other factors are quite as important and although the actual split does not really represent this geographical division there is no doubt that the disputes that have arisen in the Church while in Sweden have a background in differences between the Tur Abdin group and those from Arabic countries.

Assyrianism

Nothing is so inflammatory in the Syrian-Orthodox world as the term *Assyrian*. To some it denotes the identity of the people, its historical roots, and its ethnic self-esteem. Others see in it a destructive political movement, part heathen, part heretic. The explosive power of this word derives from the intertwining of several quite independent meanings: firstly, the name of a pre-Islamic empire, secondly, the name of a late-nineteenth-century nationalist movement, and thirdly, the modern name for the East-Syrian Church. After the fall of the Assyrian Empire in 612 B.C., and the disappearance of the classical Assyrian language, the term Assyrian lived on denoting a region in the borderlands of present-day Iraq, Iran, and Turkey. As often happens it was also used about the inhabitants of this region, most of whom belonged to the East-Syrian

Church, which after the ravagings of Mongols and Turks had found a haven here. It was not, however, until Europeans and Americans began to find interest in the natural resources and archeological remains of the area, and also in its Christian population, that the term came into widespread and official use. In the belief that the Assyrian people had been found among the ruins of the Assyrian Empire, and in the hope that a westernized and Christian national state could be established by these Christians, the seeds were sown for the modern Assyrian nationalism.[8]

The soil was not infertile for this Assyrian nationalism. The mission schools opened the gates towards Europe, including the national and secular ideals of this continent. Moslem domination seemed to be coming to an end, and the time was ripe to liberate the Christians from the confinement of the Islamic *millet* system. The thought was rooted of uniting all Christians – Protestants, Catholics, East Syrians and Syrian Orthodox – under a single roof, like a nation. But what nation would that be? The answer was at hand – the Assyrian, which had perished but was to be revived. The disintegration of the Ottoman Empire and the Allied triumph over the Turks in the First World War encouraged Assyrian nationalism. The Christians allied themselves with the Europeans in battling the Turks, in the hope of being rewarded with a Christian, Assyrian state of their own. Instead they were abandoned, and crushed between Turkish nationalism, European colonial interests, and Arabian nationalism.[9]

Assyrianism now turned into a secular nationalist movement centred among exiled Syrian Christians, mostly East Syrians but also Syrian-Orthodox and Chaldeans (East Syrians in communion with Rome). Syria tolerated a modicum of cultural activity, but in Turkey and Iraq such efforts were more difficult, and politically more dangerous. The movement was most attractive among the young and the educated, people belonging to a modern society who were looking for their roots, and did not find them in the traditions of the Church. In the Churches, particulary the Syrian-Orthodox, Assyrianism was viewed with alarm. Supporting the idea of a Christian nationalist state was tantamount to a revolt against Moslem sovereignty, and an invitation to persecutions of the Christians.

---

[8]B. Knutsson, *Assur eller Aram,* Statens Invandrarverk Rapport 4/82, Norrköping 1982, discusses the question of Assyrian as a designation for the Syriann Christians of today and gives useful bibliographical information and also hints at important source-material.
[9]See R. Strothmann, "Heutiges Orientchristentum und Schicksal der Assyrer", *Zeitschrift für Kirchengeschichte* 55 (1936), p. 17–18.

Besides, it was not every ecclesiastical leader who was happy to see the people exchange their religious identity, confirmed by the Church, for a secular ethnic identity. If the people were Assyrians, what price their Syrian-Orthodox identity? A movement that was political and secular would bring the Church no good.

When the first members of the Syrian-Orthodox Church arrived in Sweden from Lebanon they were known as Assyrians, a designation commonly used by Westerners in the Middle East for Christians from the Syriac-speaking regions in northern Syria, northern Iraq, and south-eastern Turkey. To the Swedes it seemed rational to call them Assyrians, without reference to political activity. They had to be given a nationality, and they were neither Lebanese nor Syrians, neither Iraqis nor Turks, neither Arabs nor Kurds. As Christians – indeed as remnants of a Christian people in the Middle East – they were received with great interest among various Christian groups in Sweden, particularly among the Free Churches. With the support of the Board of Immigration and a number of national associations, particularly the Council of Free Churches, an Assyrian organization was set up. Released from the Church [leaders], and led by young westernized people critical of the Church, the Assyrian movement soon became a secular association, independent of the Church but with ties to the international, politically active Assyrian World Alliance. Their message was that of the nation, and their ideal the ancient Assyrian Empire with its pre-Christian culture. It was not long before various people, particularly among the ecclesiastical leaders, began to react against this development among the people, i.e. in the Church, and its pagan symbolism. Was it really possible to be an Assyrian nationalist, and at the same time a Syrian-Orthodox Christian? Was not Assyrianism a denial of the Church as the representative of the ethnic identity? Was not a secular identity tantamount to apostasy? Was not Assyrianism tantamount to confessing the East-Syrian Church and its Nestorianism? What grounds were there for the assertion that a Christian nation could be descended from the Assyrians, and for calling the language of the Church Assyrian? These rhetorical questions received a strong response as the immigration of Syrian-Orthodox Christians increased, this time in particular from the Tur Abdin, from where entire villages emigrated in a body. An anti-Assyrian attitude grew up, for reasons not only of ideology but also of power politics. Following this new wave of immigration the Syrian-Orthodox Church established itself in Sweden, with a bishop and an increasing number of congregations. Officially the Church repudiates

Assyrianism; the people as well as the Church are Syrian-Orthodox, ethnic and ecclesiastical affiliation are one and the same. The difficulty that presented itself was finding support for this opinion in Sweden, which has a tradition of ethnical-national and secular identity. (In modern Swedish usage a nation is an ethnic group, while religious affiliation is individual with no links to ethnic origin) As an anti-pole to Assyrianism a *Syrian* secular movement was established, to serve as a national movement. An opposition was created between *Assyrian* – the associations of which word with the East-Syrian Church are gleefully made use of – and *Syrian*, an ethnic identity entirely corresponding to the Syrian-Orthodox Church. Aram is produced from the Bible as an anti-pole to ancient Assur, and the Aramaeans regarded as ancestors. The myth that all Syriac-speaking Christians are *in toto* descended from the race of the ancient Assyrian rulers is replaced with the myth that all Syrian-Orthodox Christians, and nobody outside this Church, constitute the Aramaic people. From what was in the Middle East one Christian minority, one ecclesiastical *millet*, two extremely nationalistic movements are created, each with banners of its own and its own glorious past. One Church is divided into two nations.

The Church and the structure of Swedish society

Ever since Justinian I decided to enforce the decretals of the Synod of Chalcedon, against the opposition of the Syrian Christians, the Syrian-Orthodox Church has lived under a constant pressure from worldly authority. With no backing in the society they lived in, the Church members always had to submit to the favour of the secular masters, and support from those members who had reached a position of political or economic influence. In a "weak" society no trust can be reposed in an impartial jurisdiction, only in good relations with the powers that be. As a prince of the people the bishop has limited authority; he must remain in good standing with the state, and with the rich of his congregation. His authority consists in laying down the rules for admission into the Church, and so to the people – the Church being the people. As the Church finds its shape in Sweden this delicate balance between society, hierarchy and people is totally upset. It is all but impossible to combine the traditions, and the ties to the Church in the old country – which still keeps this balance – with being a Church in Sweden.

From the very beginning the Church as an organization is at a disadvantage in Swedish society. A large number of Swedes are organized in associations of a more or less secular character, forming a conglomerate of organizations. If we disregard the unique position of the Church of Sweden, congregation and association are in Sweden basically the same thing. But during the 1970s and 1980s generous grants were been given to immigrant societies and ethnic alliances, while the treatment that congregations and Churches received was niggardly. Thus it is not only individuals who are subjected to the pressures of secularisation – the collective identity, the lives shared, are secularised as well. Freedom of religion is in Sweden a matter for the individual citizen, what applies to the Churches is freedom of association – offering them equal footing with temperance societies and philatelists' clubs. The Church of Sweden is the only one to be granted a position in public law, the only Church in Sweden possessing the right to be a national Church.[10]

Consequently, in Sweden authority over a nation of immigrants is vested in those who have succeeded in forming a strong national organization, in those who can call themselves elected representatives of the people. Of crucial importance are bureaucratic skills, eloquence, and influence among the people, among those asking who best can defend their rights and give them advantages and security in an alien society. Most important is the control of the nationwide organization, over its governing body, the "government" of the nation. In Swedish society it is this body that represents the "nation", is responsible for social and cultural activities, and assists in obtaining the objects of immigrant policy. It is this body that submits opinions on measures proposed, and receives the generous grants that the Immigration Board gives to immigrants' organizations. But while Immigration Board grants to secular organizations are given primarily on this central level the support provided for denominations outside the Church of Sweden is devised so as to be received not by the governing body but by the local congregations. The congregationalism of the Swedish Free Churches thus adds to the problems faced by the

---

[10]For a discussion about the place of the churches of immigration in Swedish society and law see *Stöd till invandrarnas trossamfund. Rapport från arbetsgruppen för översyn om reglerna om statligt stöd till trossamfundenb m.m.,* Civildepartementet, DS C 1986:12 and Hallonsten, *op.cit,* as well as S. Rubenson, "Staten, samfunden och religionsfriheten ur en invandrarkyrkas perspektiv" (forthcoming in *Religionsmöten i Sverige,* to be published by Libris, Örebro 1996). The difference between Sweden and Germany is great, see Christoph Link, "Die Rechtsgrundlage der Ostkirchen nach dem Staatskirchenrecht der Bundesrepublik Deutschland", *Kanon* 4 (1980), pp. 30–44.

[immigrant] Church in attempting to assert itself against the nationwide [secular] organizations as champion of the ethnic identity.[11]

At the arrival of the first Syrian-Orthodox bishop there were already a number of Syrian-Orthodox congregations, and a strong, well organized, and well established Assyrian National Association. The local sections were divided by controversies arising from the name, and when it became obvious that the Church *qua* Church was unable to undertake the struggle against Assyrianism, and provide a nationwide organization for the Syrian-Orthodox, the Syrian National Association was formed as an umbrella organization for all sections and congregations that had not joined the Assyrian movement, especially those from the Tur Abdin. Since the governing body of the Church rejected Assyrianism as a political movement the Syrians were able to incorporate virtually the whole of the Syrian-Orthodox Church into a viable ethnic and secular organization, with an economic basis of a magnitude that the Church could never expect to find. Those people who did not reject the Assyrian identity and embrace the concept of Syrianism were forced out of the ecclesiastical organization. The Church and the supposedly Syrian people were one. The power, however, was exclusively in the hands of the leaders of the secular National Association, and the Church and its bishop became the servants of the "nation", of the governing body of the Association.

It is not only the economic resources of the secular organizations, and the emotional potential they have in secular society in defining the identity of the people and determining its name and language, that have created difficulties for the Church. Problems are created also by the traditional Orthodox Church structure, originating in the Primitive Church. The primary unit in the Church is the bishop and his parish or, in modern parlance, his diocese. Every true parish has a bishop of its own, and is thus autonomous, parishes without a bishop being, if anything, a kind of subordinate annexes. The Church is not an association of component members but a divine institution, the administration of which has been entrusted to the bishops – this is is original sense of the word *episkopos*.

Contrary to this structure is the concept of independent local congregations electing a joint body for certain specified mandates. This

---

[11]The rules that govern the state subsidies for the immigrant churches and the statistical data is provided by *SST:s Årsbok* (The Year-book of SST, the Government Board for subsidies to religious communities), published yearly by Samarbetsnämnden för Statsbidrag till Trossamfunden.

Swedish model of administering associations would prevail in most cases, helped along by the benign assistance of the Council of Free Churches, which had been entrusted with the administration of State support to the immigrant Churches. Thus this Council with its congregationalist background was to a large extent able to shape the organization of Syrian-Orthodox Church. This is evidenced quite clearly in the congregational statutes that are being drawn up, and in the training afforded the congregation leaders in the 1980s and early 1990s. While the diocesan character is to some extent preserved in the early statutes (1981) for a joint body, the statutes ratified in 1983 for the governing body of the Church display all the characteristics of an elected board of representatives for an organization of local sections.[12] The status of the bishop is not mentioned in either of these statutes. This omission is due to a conscious effort to limit episcopal influence and steer State support towards the congregations. After the formation of the central governing body with its extensive powers the authority of the Church is gathered in a body of elected laymen. Since the Church and the Syrian National Association have practically the same membership they enjoy a virtually complete symbiosis; the Church, however, is the impecunious and ineffectual party, the religious arm of the Association.

A Church of the nation or for the nation

The identification of Nation with Church that had originated in the Islamic environment caused problems for the Syrian-Orthodox Church when confronted with the Swedish social structure. This national Church, which is as it were the Church of a nation, essentially presupposes either a practically homogeneous national state with an established Church, or the Islamic *millet* system. What these have in common is the symbiosis

---

[12]See the following documents: 1) *Stadgar för syrisk-ortodoxa kyrkans riksförsamling i Sverige* (Bylaws of the national council of the Syrian Orthodox congregations in Swede), promulgated at a meeting with the Archbishop April 11, 1981 and accepted by the general assembly on June 6, 1981. 2) *Stadgar för syrsik-ortodoxa kyrkans centralstyrelse i Sverige* (Bylaws for the central board of the Syrian Orthodox Church in Sweden), promulgated at a meeting November 26, 1983. 3) *Syrisk-ortodoxa kyrkans centralstyrelses förslag till stadgar för syrsik-ortodoxa församlingar i Sverige & Skandinavien* (The proposals of the central board of the Syrian Orthodox Church in Sweden for bylaws for the Syrian-Orthodox congregations in Sweden & Scandinavia), dated 1990. The last document has with minor revisions been accepted by a minority of the congregations in Sweden.

between the political and the ecclesiastical leadership, a symbiosis made problematic, particularly for Orthodox Christians, by democracy no less than by secularisation. To the Syrian-Orthodox, having no national state, the absence of a *millet* system in the West represents the end of the Church as the Church of the nation, the end of a symbiosis between a secular and a religious government. If the Church is to continue as a national Church a different attitude to the concept of a national Church is necessary, an independence of the national political movements. The national Church can no longer be the Church *of* the nation, it must become a Church *for* the nation. Lacking both a national state and political power the Syrian-Orthodox Church must in exile choose a model that resembles either the supranational Roman Catholic or the Reformed Congregationalist structure.

By distancing himself from the ethnic national associations and completely disregarding Syrian as well as Assyrian identity the new bishop has taken the first steps towards a change of this nature. Since he has thus deprived the Syrian national movement of its foremost weapon, its identification with the Church, he has met with strong resistance. The struggle has concerned the power over the Church – who should represent the Syrian-Orthodox Christians, who should distribute the economic aid, and so control the establishing of new congregations and the stipends of the clergy. Without support from the Church nobody can claim the leadership of the Syrian-Orthodox, yet the traditions from the "powerless" society in the Middle East demand strong leaders. Without a democratic tradition or training the struggle for leadership will be a matter of economic resources, and of an authority based on the social network – bonds of clan and village.

However, what makes it difficult to find an efficient model for the Syrian-Orthodox Church is not just the resistance from strong nationalist groups, and from elected popular leaders opposed to an emancipated Church, but also the contrast between Syrian ecclesiastical law, originating in an Islamic environment, and Swedish ecclesiastical law and religious legislation. At a synod in 1984 a new, consistent system of rules was established for the Church, introducing democratic processes. These rules, however, are by no means fully suited to the European situation; for instance, no difference is made between regional and local level. All Church property is diocesan, and administered by the bishop. A lay council (*majlis al-milli*) chaired by the bishop is required. The bishop is entitled to a sort of veto, and the authority of the council is actually, as it were, delegated by him. This organization differs radically from the structure of the Syrian-Orthodox congregations in Sweden, built on the concept of the Churches as associations, and of their governing body. Since these are registered as independent non-profitmaking associations the bishop has no legal rights over them, and his chances of upholding the unity of the Church are extremely limited. In litigations taken to a Swedish court of law the statutes registered by the congregations easily override Syrian Church law.[13]

A crucial part in connection with the problems concerning the organization and legal status of the Syrian-Orthodox Church, as well as other Orthodox Churches, is played by the authority distributing State support to the religious communities. In this context the Swedish State looks upon these Churches as *religious* associations, and thus has to decide the question of who their rightful representatives are, and what congregations belong to them. This scrutiny is made today in full accordance with the ecclesiastical law and canonical tenets of these Churches. There is consequently a noticeable discrepancy between how the State views the Churches as recipients of support, and how the judicial system views them in legal matters. This problem came to a head in the disputes in Södertälje concerning the authority of the bishop, and Church property and administration. Since the Church of Sweden is the only Church to be recognized as a Church in Swedish public law the Orthodox Churches have one single resort if they are to preserve their own concept of a Church – to form, as the Roman Catholic Church has done, an autonomous establishment, guaranteeing the independence of see and diocese.

Conclusions

The conflicts within the Syrian-Orthodox in Sweden are only an example of what has become visible also among other Orthodox immigrant Churches, *i.a.* the Serbian Orthodox Church. The perennial problem of how to define the legal status of a Church is here aggravated on one hand by the monopoly of the Church of Sweden as the officially recognized

---

[13] An attempt to use the *dustur* (constitution) of the Syrian-Orthodox Church and the bylaws for the dioceses promulgated by the Holy Synod in Damascus in 1984 in Swedish courts have proven unsuccessful. The two documents have been translated into Swedish, but no English translation is yet available, as far as I know. An account of the canon law of the Syrian-Orthodox Church is given in W. Selb, *Orientalisches Kirchenrecht, Band II, Die Geschichte des Kirchenrechts der Westsyrer,* Wien 1989.

Church on the other by cultural differences. The tensions between the Syrian Orthodox from Tur Abdin in Turkey and those from the cities of Iraq, Syria and Lebanon and the political struggle over Assyrian identity are centered upon the Church. While the bishop and the Assyrians want to hold national and religious affiliation apart the Syrian movement wants to preserve the identification. This means that the ambition of the bishop to preserve episcopal authority must be seen as more modernistic and the emphasis on democracy among the Syrian Orthodox as much more conservative.

A study of the history of the Syrian Orthodox in Sweden and its twenty years of conflict raises many questions about Swedish immigrant and ecclesiastical politics. A comparison between the support given to the secular and ethnic immigrant associations and the support for the immigrant Churches shows a deliberate policy of secularization. The monopoly of the established Church on state recognition throws the Orthodox Churches into becoming democratic associations and thus makes the position of their bishops almost impossible. The loyalty of the ethnic group is thus transferred to a secular body at the same time as the Church is divided by quarrels between private associations.

Part IV

Religion and National Identity

Church and Nation in the 19th century the Case of Norway

Dag Thorkildsen

1. Nation and nationalism

Nationalism is an ideology or a principle, according to which the political and the cultural unit should be congruent. The goal is the independent nation state or domestic self-government. The main problem is that the cultural unit called the nation, is hard to define, or more precisely is defined in different ways. The definitions consist of language, history, culture, religion, ethnicity etc. in all kinds of variations. For this reason you will not find two nations which are defined by the same characteristic features, but all the same we divide the world into nations.

In the study of nationalism there is a fundamental disagreement between the constructivists and the essentialists. While the constructivists claim that the idea of the nation for some reason was constructed or invented in the beginning of the 19th century, the essentialists will deny this and claim that the nation came as a development of – or based on – former historical communities. For Elie Kedourie, one of the constructivists, nationalism is an ideological invention by European thinkers at the beginning of the 19th century. Another constructivist, Ernest Gellner, writes that nationalism is not what it seems, and above all not what it seems to itself. The cultures it claims to defend and revive are often its own inventions, or are modified out of all recognition. Anthony Smith sees on the other side the nation as a development of pre modern ethnical communities and rooted in ancient history and in the consciousness of this history. The transformation of these pre modern ethnies into nations started with what he calls the scientific state. This scientific state was characterised by a successful bureaucratisation, and in the case of Norway the Danish-Norwegian monarchy in the 18th century would be such a scientific state. In this monarchy the rule was based on reason, centralisation, standardisation and enlightenment which created some degree of social mobility and a new elite based on merits, not on class.

My own position in the following will be something in between, although closer to the constructivists. The nation is first of all an *imagined community*, to quote Benedict Anderson (*Imagined Communities*, Verso, London 1991), but it is not an *invented community*. It is based on a historical raw material which the intellectual elites in the last century shaped to the concept of the nation. In this process much of the history and culture which did not fit, was forgotten. But it would be hard to explain why the ideology of nationalism became so powerful if the content was totally new. It would furthermore be difficult to explain why some national projects succeeded and others failed, if the content of the ideology was not based on something existing, and for that reason had more or less appeal to the people.

The nation as an imagined community means that it depends on consciousness, the consciousness of belonging to a national community characterised by certain features. These features create national identity which becomes an important part of individual and personal identity. The peculiarity of national identity is the claim to be of a higher range than all other identities. In the study *Personal identity, national identity, and international relations* (Cambridge University Press 1990) William Bloom discusses the relationship between personal and national identity. He starts with a definition of identity as a process of internalisation. In order to achieve psychological security, every individual possesses an inherent drive to internalise – to identify with – the behaviour, mores and attitudes of significant figures in her/his social environment; i.e. people actively seek identity. Moreover every human being has an inherent drive to enhance and to protect the identifications he or she has made; i.e. people actively seek to enhance and protect identity (page 23). Bloom claims that under the same circumstances a group of individuals will do the same sort of identification and that according to the growth and the evolution of the individual there will be an evolution concerning which communities he or she will identify with, from the parents to more symbolic communities (page 50). On this basis he claims that national identity describes that condition in which a mass of people have made the same identification with national symbols – have internalised the symbols of the nation – so that they may act as one psychological group when there is a threat to, or the possibility of enhancement of, these symbols of national identity (page 52).

The strength in Bloom's study is that he shows how individual identity influences communal identity and vice versa, and that identity thus becomes something dynamic. Furthermore he makes the process of socialisation of the individual the keystone in nation building. For this reason the change of the education systems plays an important role in explaining the growth of nationalism in the 19th century. Through these systems the national myth was spread to the mass of the population.

In the study of nationalism it is also discussed if it is possible – or at least if it is adequate – to distinguish between a cultural and a political nationalism. The adherents of such a distinction will not at all agree upon the definition of nationalism given above. They find the roots of cultural nationalism linked to German romanticism with its cultivation of the language, the history and the organic understanding of the people. Political nationalism is linked to the French revolution with the sovereignty of the people, the individual rights granted to everybody within the boundaries of the state and democratic participation in political power.

One of the strongest defenders of the necessity of such a distinction is John Hutchinson, a disciple of Anthony Smith. He begins his most interesting book *The Dynamics of Cultural Nationalism. The Gaelic Revival and the Creation of the Irish Nation State* (London 1987) with the intention "to show... that cultural nationalism is a movement quite independent of political nationalism" (page 9). Furthermore he defines the nation as a moral community and sees cultural nationalism as a response to the crisis of identity and the interior conflicts which the process of modernisation created at the end of the 18th century. The goal of cultural nationalism is a moral and national regeneration on the basis of the national and historical distinctive character. He describes the cultural nationalists as moral innovators who seek by "reviving" an ethnic historicist vision of the nation to redirect traditionalists and modernists away from conflict and instead to unite them in the task of constructing an integrated distinctive and autonomous community, capable of competing in the modern world. . . The true matrix for both traditionalist and modernist is, the cultural nationalist proposes, the nation in whose inner drive for realisation all must find their individual and collective meanings (page 34). In contrast to Herder and Fichte – two of the founders of the conception of cultural nationalism – Hutchinson claims that historical memory, rather than language *as such* serves to define the national community.

The opponents of such a distinction will claim that cultural and political nationalism are two sides of the same coin and can not be held apart, and they will point to a broad range of historical examples. I do agree that it is difficult to distinguish as consistently as Hutchinson. I have, however, found his theses quite fruitful in my own study of the Norwegian nationalism. For this reason I will use the conception of a cultural nationalism to describe a nationalism which creates or tries to find the common national identity and looks upon the nation as a cultural and moral community, and the goal of which is regeneration and unification. On the other side political nationalism is primarily a territorial nationalism, and its goal is the nation state.

The question of why the concept of the nation grew and became such a powerful idea in the 19th century is complicated. Most constructivists and essentialists do agree that this is linked with the process of modernisation of society. While religion gave legitimacy to pre-modern society, and the prince symbolised the state and kept it together through the local authorities which the Christian should obey and be loyal to according to the will of God, modern society needed another and more functional "glue" that could keep it together. Legitimacy did not come from God, but from the people itself, in the same way as the primary obligation of the individual became the nation and the people, not the prince and the will of God.

2. Norway in the 19th century

In Norwegian history the 19th century is the epoch between the Napoleonic wars and the end of the Union with Sweden in 1905. Norway entered the 19th century as a part of the Danish absolute monarchy which was a multinational state and left as an independent and sovereign nation state. The transformation that took place was largely a process of nation building joined with liberalism and the democratisation of political power. The root of this joint venture was created in 1814 when the new Norwegian state was established at the same time as we got the most radical constitution in Europe.

Before 1814 we find some traces of a Norwegian national consciousness in the small academic elite of civil servants who had got their education at the University of Copenhagen. This consciousness was based on knowledge of the ancient Norwegian history in the time of the Vikings and the Middle Ages when Norway was a sovereign state. We find however no traces of a movement which wanted to part Norway from the Danish monarchy. The demands in the last fifty years of the Union with Denmark were limited to the necessity of establishing central institutions in Norway, first of all a university. This demand must be seen on the background of the feeling of inferiority the Norwegian students had during their studies in Copenhagen. They came from an underdeveloped country and did not speak proper Danish. At the same time most of them had a hard time to finance their studies abroad. In spite of this, their identity was formed by the Danish continental culture, and these links lasted long after the break of the Union. Similar links were never established during the Union with Sweden. Even today the cultural bonds are much stronger with Denmark than any other Nordic country. After 1814 the relationship to Denmark was a mixture of love and hate. At the end of the 19th century the Norwegian nationalists talked about the two unions that had to be broken: the cultural union with Denmark and the political Union with Sweden. For the same reason the Pan-Scandinavian movement between 1830 and 1864 never managed to get a stronghold in Norway.[1] The nationalists thought that this was just another attempt from the Danes to regain their supremacy in Scandinavia.

The first decades after 1814 the Norwegian political elite was mostly occupied with the financial problems caused by the war and with the King's attempts to strengthen his own influence by changing the liberal Constitution. Due to these conflicts the Constitution became the very symbol of the new nation. It became a sort of secular divine law which should not be altered. This view of the Constitution still exists, and most of the Norwegian Constitution is kept unchanged since 1814.

The new nation started in the 1830s the search for its own identity and roots. Who were the Norwegians? What did it mean to be a Norwegian? Which historical goals was the Nation meant to fulfil? From this decade and throughout the century a cultural nationalism was created. The historians played an important role in the creation of the national myth. They established the connection between the new nation and the ancient Norway which had existed in the Viking era and the Middles Ages. They described the glorious and heroic history of the nation. They claimed that Norway was the seat of the Norse tribe which had come from the north east and settled in Norway and northern Sweden. Southern Sweden and Denmark, however, had originaly been populated by south

---

[1] The Pan-Scandinavic movement was a sort of nationalism with a cultural and political goal. The cultural goal was a closer cultural exchange and cooperation between Denmark, Sweden and Norway, while the political goal was a union under the same king or a military alliance. Due to the national conflict with Germany upon the dutchies of Slesvig and Holstein, the Danes were most engaged in the political goal.

Germanic tribes. When these areas were conquered by the Norse tribe, the inhabitants became slaves, and you got a class society, a mixed culture and mixed people. Norway, however, had been a society of free men with equal rights, and the Norwegians were the true heirs of the Norse culture with its treasure of literature. Another consequence of this ethnicity was that the Norwegians not only were equal with the Danes and Swedes, they were superior to them.

Other scientists started the search for the remains of the old Norwegian culture which had survived through the 400 years of oppression and exploitation by the Danes. They supposed that the freeholders represented the original Norwegian culture, and they searched for folk legends, fairy tales, folk songs and folk music. They also examined the dialects people spoke in the different regions of the country in order to change the literary language from Danish into a more Norwegian style, or even to construct a New Norwegian literary language on the basis of the dialects in the parts of the countryside that were not polluted by the Danish culture. In this way a cultural nationalism was created. Around the middle of the century everything considered as being national and coming from the Norwegian people and Norwegian nature was a fashion among the academic and political elite.

3. The 1850s and 60s – the turning point

The writers of Norwegian history usually assert that the 1850s and 60s were quiet and peaceful decades, and that the reign of the civil servants came to its peak. In many ways this is correct, but I will maintain that these decades also represent the turning point both in secular history and in church history.

Among the Fathers of the Constitution and the first pioneers who created a Norwegian cultural nationalism we find quite a few theologians and clergymen. To them there was no problem in combining their profession with their interest in national traditions. They were raised in the mildly conservative, biblical theology that characterised the first two teachers of theology at the newly established University of Kristiania (1811), which Oslo was called. The very leading nation builder in Norway, was Henrik Wergeland, our first national poet or scald, who was educated as a theologian, but never served as a clergyman. The reason was that in the age in which he lived, he was a controversial person. But after his death he became our first secular saint, the symbol of the young nation, and through the school books all Norwegians learned about his importance to the country. Even our National day, the 17th of May, when we celebrate the Constitution of 1814, was tied to his person in such a way that most of the Norwegian people still believe that he started the celebration of this day.

Until 1850 we find no traces of an attempt to link nation and religion together in a national religion. The Fathers of the Constitution could express their experience in 1814 in a way that was inspired by Christian conceptions, for example describing the rise of Norway and the new political freedom in terms of Christ's resurrection from the dead. But there was no attempt to see this as an act or the will of God, to describe the Norwegians as the people of God or to interpret the history of the people as guided by divine providence.

In the 1850s there came a change, first of all a change among the teachers at the Faculty of Theology. A German theologian, called Paul Caspari, was appointed teacher of church history although he had an international reputation due to his studies in the Old Testament, and soon after Gisle Johnson, the mightiest person in Norwegian church life in the second part of the last century, was appointed teacher in Systematic Theology. They represented political conservatism and Lutheran confessionalism, which especially Johnson combined with pietism and low church revivalism. First of all they got rid of the colleagues they suspected of having sympathies with the Danish theologian Grundtvig and the movement he had given name to. Then they gave the students with those kinds of sympathies bad grades in their exams. Johnson had been travelling in Germany in the stormy years that led to the revolutions in 1848, and he looked afterwards with suspicious eyes on all popular movements like the followers of Grundtvig. Such movements might be a threat to the established, divine order of society, but first of all he rejected the understanding of Christian belief that Grundtvig represented. While Grundtvig emphasised the objective sides of belief: the words of the Apostolic Creed, the sacraments, the Christian community, and considered culture and human life as something good, Johnson stressed the necessity for individual conversion followed by a new, pious life, and the Bible as the Word of God. He was sceptical of cultural goods because they could lead the Christian astray. Politically he had no sympathy for democracy or the growing nationalism. To the Christian only the people of God in the meaning of the true believers had any interest, not the national people.

Furthermore Johnson emphasised what St. Paul says in the Letter to the Romans chapter 13: The Christian should obey and be loyal to the authorities because "there is no authority except from God". To Johnson that meant first of all loyalty to the Swedish-Norwegian King due to the Union. For this reason cultural nationalism would easily come into conflict with the authorities when it developed into a political nationalism with demands for national self government. This is exactly what happened from the 1860s. During the constitutional battle in the 1870s and 80s when the issue was the parliamentary system, the King engaged himself on the conservative side and made plans for a coup d'état. The conflict ended in 1884 with the government being impeached, a victory for the middle-class countercultural coalition who gathered around the leftist liberal party, and its democratic and national politic.

In the beginning of 1883 when the situation was very tense, Johnson published an appeal to the friends of the Christianity in Norway. This appeal was a long attack on the leftist party and its democratic politic, and it was signed by 450 prominent men in church and society, among them all the bishops. This appeal scandalised the church for decades and made the gap between the church and the political democratic and national movement obvious. For the rest of the century the church withdrew from the political arena.

But let us return to the 1850s where we find another change. The Norwegian followers of Grundtvig had so far been political conservative, aristocratic and high church in their attitude to the laymen, they paid little attention to the Norwegian nationalism, and they represented a Danish influenced culture. In this way they differed from Grundtvig himself. But at beginning of the 1850s a new generation of Norwegian followers took over. They shared Grundtvig's conversion of 1848 to democracy, his interest in questions concerning nationality and his programme for enlightenment. This change took place at the same time as Grundtvig for the first and last time visited Norway as the main attraction at the Pan-Scandinavian student assembly in Kristiania (Oslo) early in the summer 1851.

These young followers of Grundtvig were the first ones to link nation and religion together. They thought that the nationality is an expression of the character of the people, and that Christianity must be national in order to seize the average man and woman. In the same way as

Grundtvig they claimed that the spirit of the Creator manifests itself in the spirit of the people. It is the power which unifies individuals to a people and maintains it in its relationship to its Creator and to its destiny in history. For this reason the creation (nature and culture) is not only a contrast to Christian belief and life, but has its own value. Likewise the national people has a value in itself, not only the people of God.

An expression of the link between nation and religion is found in our national anthem: "Yes, we love this country". It was written by our second national poet or scald, Bjørnstjerne Bjørnson, around 1860, in the period where he was strongly influenced by Grundtvig. While God had not been mentioned at all in our two first anthems, this one claims that God himself has given the Norwegian people its right and freedom and protected it against the gloom.

4. Nation building and education

The new generation of followers of Grundtvig were often educated as theologians, but they served first of all as educationists. They wanted to create a national education for the people, an education that should make responsible citizens. So far the Norwegian primary school, which was founded in the era of pietism and absolute monarchy, had been a church school, ruled by the local vicar. The purpose had been to teach the children of the lower class how to be pious Christians and obedient subjects. For this reason they had to learn to read. They should be able to read the Bible and to learn by heart the explanation of Luther's catechism. This explanation consisted of 759 questions and answers. The exam was a compulsory catechisation which took place before the confirmation. People could not own property, get married, testify in the court or get a salary as a grown up person before they had passed this. To stay away from the teaching and preparation was punished by the law. To many it was a torture, and to fail was a public shame.

The followers of Grundtvig started a public debate about the school and suggested fundamental reforms, and they succeeded when a new law passed the Parliament in 1860. First of all the secular subjects became an important part of the education. The vicar's absolute power came to an end with the new boards, and the purpose of the school should be to a) support the parent's raising of the children, b) give the children a Christian enlightenment, c) give them the knowledge and skill which each member of the society ought to have, d) give them a general cultural education.

To fill this law with a content the dean at the Cathedral of Oslo, P. A. Jensen, was charged with the task of compiling a new reader. He was strongly inspired by Grundtvig's ideas of nation and culture and had sympathy for the Pan-Scandinavian movement. This reader represented the national breakthrough in the elementary school.

The reader made the home the foundation of society and nation. The nation was nothing else than a gathering of homes. For this reason obedience to the fourth commandment was primarily directed to the parents and not to the authorities. At the same time the concept of the nation is ambiguous. On the one side the reader defined the people as the citizens with civic rights who lived in the country, and on the other as a people of relatives.

Nationality was defined through the heroic national history, through the Constitution with its liberal rights, through the praising and description of nature and through the presentation of the folklore. The purpose was to give the children a historical identity, to point out historical and national values as the basis of a moral regeneration and to evoke patriotism.

The presentation of the national history follows the same pattern which Hutchinson has found in his study of the Gaelic revival, and which he claims is the basis of all cultural nationalism:

1) a migration story:	migration to Norway from north east, Norway is the homeland of the Norse tribe
2) a founding myth:	the Viking era and the unification of the country
3) a golden age of splendour:	the Middle Ages with national independence, christianising, justice and peace
4) a period of inner decay:	the Scandinavian Union of Kalmar and the 400 years of Union with Denmark
5) a promise of regeneration:	begins in 1814 with the Constitution

This pattern is a secular salvation history following the same stages as the history of Israel according to the Deutronomistic writers of history. The national people becomes the secular people of God, the nation is a secularised kingdom of God and the Constitution is divine law.

Furthermore moral values were an important part of national identity; values like love of the home, hard work, moderation, modesty, loyalty, cleanliness, sport, patience, fear of God, daily prayer, salubrity and truthfulness. These values were deduced from the national history. All the same, enlightenment was necessary because there was a lot of superstition among the people. This enlightenment should be an enlightenment for life, not a classical education. This is the same concept as we find in Grundtvig, and the purpose is to evoke patriotism and to serve the common good. This purpose is what Hutchinson claims is the main purpose of cultural nationalism. It intends to create an ethnic historicist vision of the nation to redirect traditionalists and modernists away from conflict and instead to unite them in the task of constructing an integrated distinctive and autonomous community, capable of competing in the modern world.

The nationalism we find in the reader of 1863 fits very well with Hutchinson's definition of cultural nationalism, where historical identity, and not the language is the most important indication of nationality. In the same way we find few traces of a political nationalism which points to a Norwegian nation state outside the Union with Sweden. On the other side however, the democratic political system based on the Constitution and its liberal rights plays an important role in the description of national identity.

In addition to the reforms of the public school the followers of Grundtvig in the 1860s started the first Folk High Schools, which were intended to give the youth a "historical-poetical" education, an education according to the people's character and identity. The national history, the mother tongue, the ancient Nordic myths, the knowledge of the country became the main subjects at the same time as all current questions were discussed in public meetings. In this way these schools became a hearth of Norwegian nationalism.

The process of changing the Norwegian public school into a modern primary school came to an end with the new laws of 1889, which established a national and common school according to the ideology of the leftist liberal party. Around 1890 this party got an anti-Union and anti-Swedish profile, and Norwegian nationalism became more aggressive and was combined with radical and republican sympathies. From 1891 the demand for a separate Norwegian consular service became the symbol of the resistance to Swedish hegemony in the Union. In the longer term the goal was a separate Norwegian Foreign Office, an unacceptable claim to the Swedish King and government.

The new laws of 1889 were once again followed by a new reader, written by Nordahl Rolfsen who was an educationist, supporter of the liberal leftist party and a friend of Bjørnson. The laws and the reader were still influenced by Grundtvig's educational ideas, but the influence was weakened compared to the reform in the beginning of the 1860s. At the same time the secularisation of the school had become stronger. The purpose of the primary school should not be to educate pious Christians, but Norwegian citizens, to give the children a national consciousness and identity. While Grundtvig wrote: human first, secondly Christian, Rolfsen says: citizen first, secondly Christian.

The individual is described not as an obedient subject nor as a Christian citizen, but as an autonomous citizen with democratic rights and a duty to take care of the historical, cultural heritage. The society is understood as a community of equals, where everyone must do his duty and give his contribution. The state is the nation state where cultural and political nationalism have fused.

To a certain degree we find a national religion where the main concepts are: God has given us the country and shaped the national character, and God has ruled the history of the people towards freedom and independence. According to these ideas the fourth commandment is interpreted as patriotism and the will to defend the nation. For the same reason St. Paul's command in the Letter to the Romans chapter 13 is totally absent. The explanation is of course the anti-Union ideology which characterises the reader. As mentioned above, this command had been used against the liberal leftist party and the parliamentarian principle during the political battle in the 1870s and the beginning of the 1880s.

The duty of obedience and loyalty is not directed to the King and the authorities, but to the nation, the Constitution and the people. The reasons do not primary come from religion, but from the heroic and glorious history of the nation, from the people you are related to, and from the emotions – i. e. love of the country and nature. The role of Christianity is reduced to that of being a part of the historical and cultural heritage represented by St. Olav and the Cathedral of Trondheim.

Nationality is based upon the national history, the Constitution, nature, the national industries (agriculture, mining, fishery, forestry) and the folklore. In the same way as the former reader the national history is presented according to the pattern Hutchinson has described. This is the one focus in the national ellipse. The other, which is new, is the national literature and the authors of this literature. These authors personify the national characteristics, and first among them comes Henrik Wergeland, who is called the model of the Norwegian. His successor is Bjørnstjerne Bjørnson. The picture of the Norwegian is supplied by Fridtjof Nansen, the Arctic scientist and sportsman, and Svend Foyn, the whaler and innovator. The understanding of the nation is purely ethnical, the people are relatives with a national character which has been shaped through the history and the nature of the country.

This cultural nationalism cannot be held apart from political nationalism, they are joined together. The history of the nation is not fulfilled. What started in 1814, has not been completed. Two goals must first be realised: national independence and sovereignty and national unification. For this reason the reader represents openly an anti-Union ideology and an anti-Swedish attitude. The picture of the outer threat is rather clear. The Swedes are the historical, traditional enemies.

The outermost symbol of the national community becomes the 17th of May with the children's parade. The celebration of this day had been controversial earlier in the century. Until the second half of the century official Norway had celebrated the 4th of November, the Union day. The parade of children carrying Norwegian flags, which today is the main element in the celebration, was a rather new invention by the time the reader was written. In the story telling about this day and the parade the King is the only person who is not a member of the national community, because he is in Stockholm, and not i n Norway.

The reader completed the Norwegian national myth, and it is expressive that it was compiled only a decade before the Union was broken. The national myth should, however, not only create citizens and evoke patriotism, it should also be an ethical education. Certain standards and values and a certain behaviour became a central part of the Norwegian identity. A common moral consciousness with common ideals was important if people who lived far away from each other and under very different circumstances in the long and tiny country which is called Norway, were to get the feeling of this country as their common native country and their nation – and furthermore make them think of each other as one people. This common moral consciousness had roots in the Protestant ethos, but the reasons were not any longer religious. They came from the people itself, from its history and from the conditions which nature gave. This consciousness was expanded to include values such as home, nature and folklore from the romanticism, liberal values such as enlightenment, freedom, equality, democracy, and national values such as patriotism, will to defend, solidarity and independence.

The superior purpose was to create and educate Norwegian citizens. For this reason the reader can be read as an illustration of the process which leads to the establishment of the national identity where the national myth is spread to the average man and woman. Furthermore this is an illustration of Bloom's definition of the national identity:

> National identity describes that condition in which a mass of people have made the same identification with national symbols – have internalised the symbols of the nation – so that they may act as one psychological group when there is a threat to, or the possibility of enhancement of, these symbols of national identity.

5. National religion

The first attempt to link nation and religion came – as mentioned above – from the followers of Grundtvig. They were, however, almost expelled from the main church life. Instead they gave their contribution to nation building as educationists, and they played an important role in the countercultural alliance gathered around the liberal leftist party. Their ideas of nation and religion survived in the circles around the Folk High Schools and were later in the century carried on in the countercultural youth clubs. These youth clubs were characterised by broad-minded and national Christianity, folklore and New Norwegian, and they became an important popular movement.

Another strong and influential popular movement in the second part of the last century was the low church laymen movement with its roots in pietism and revivals. Its members were in strong opposition to the broad-minded youth clubs which they called the synagogue of Satan because they permitted folk dances, and they were generally ambivalent towards the national movement.

The main stream of official theology and church life separated from the national and democratic movement, and after the battle of the parliamentarian system the church had withdrawn from the political arena. Typically the only clergyman that got elected as a member of the Parliament in 1903, came from the new and radical Labour Party, and that caused a lot of worries to the rest of the church.

For these reasons we do not find a strong national religion in Norway like that in Denmark in the 19th century. The national religion here was linked with Grundtvig and his movement. It was specially evoked and strengthened by the national conflicts of Southern Jutland with the wars of 1848-51 and 1864. In Sweden a national religious revivalism arose as a result of the Union conflict. To a certain degree the same happened in Norway in 1905. All of a sudden a national religiousness broke through, and unified the nation to support of the rebellion government and the Parliament.

Since the 1890s the demand for a separate Norwegian consular service had, as mentioned above, been the symbol of the resistance to Swedish hegemony. In 1903 a solution seemed possible, but the negotiations failed at the end of the next year. In May 1905 a law that would establish a separate consular service, passed the Norwegian parliament. The King, however, refused to give sanction to it. For this reason the government resigned, but the King refused to accept the ministers' resignations, and a serious constitutional crisis arose. The 7th of June the ministers once more resigned during a meeting in the Parliament. The Parliament stated that the King was not able to appoint a new government, and for this reason royal power had ceased to function. Due to this the Union under one king had ceased to exist. Furthermore the former government was asked to continue and also to exercise the functions of the royal power. Practically this meant that Norway was a republic. The same day it was decided upon a proclamation to the Norwegian people which the ministers should read from the pulpit the following Sunday, which was Whitsunday. This proclamation presented the Norwegian view of the events, explained the constitutional reasons for the acts of the Parliament and instructed the people to obey and be loyal to the government.

The Swedish reaction was at first surprise, but soon public opinion changed to fury and demanded punishment of the rebellions in Norway. The Swedish Christians accused the Norwegians of having broken their oath, the 4th commandment and St. Paul's command in the Letter to the Romans, and some requested a war.

In this crisis most of the Norwegian clergymen, the whole laymen movement and the youth clubs strongly supported the government and the actions of the Parliament. They interpreted the national history as the history of God, and the break of the Union was according to the will of God, because his purpose with Norway was National independence and sovereignty.

We shall not follow the events in 1905, just state that the negotiations ended with peace. First of all because there was a will to peace on both sides and no dispute upon which areas belonged to Norway. Neither were there a large minority of Swedes in Norway that could cause problems.

The interesting fact is that in all the three Scandinavian countries acute crisis played an important role in spreading the national religion to the mass of the people. It may be interpreted as the answer to an outer threat and the source of mobilisation and unification. The national religion gave an undisputable legitimacy to the national claim because you do not argue with God and his will.

6. Conclusions

The study of Norwegian nationalism in the 19th century supports Hutchinson's thesis that historical consciousness and not the language serves to define the national community. If the language should be the main characteristic of the nation, Norway would still not be a nation since a majority of the people speak and write a Norwegianized Danish. On the other hand the study does not support his thesis that cultural nationalism is a movement quite independent of political nationalism. Norwegian nationalism consists of both political and cultural elements, and it is impossible to keep them totally apart. They fused from the very beginning and became two sides of the same coin. The main reason was the experience of 1814 where the basis was founded. The Constitution came first, secondly the process of nation building, and the Constitution became the very symbol of the new nation. Already in the first modern reader from 1863 liberal rights were an important part of national identity, and they were rooted in the national history. As democracy was further developed and new groups included in the second half of the century, these rights were never subordinated to national interests, but were linked to them. In the 1890s a new stage of political nationalism came with the claims of national sovereignty symbolised by a separate Norwegian Consular Service and the so-called clean Norwegian flag without the union sign. These claims were however joined with the demand for an extension of the suffrage.

Norwegian nationalism corresponds with Hutchinson's definition of the national community as a moral community. This aspect represents a dimension which is often forgotten or disregarded in the studies of nationalism. A common moral consciousness was necessary to give people living far away from each other and under quite different conditions the feeling of being one people, to create the solidarity and loyalty which is required for becoming a nation. This common moral consciousness had in the case of Norway its roots in the Protestant ethos stressing hard work, moderation, modesty, loyalty, patience and truthfulness, but the reasons for this had been secularised. They came from the people itself, from the national history and from the conditions in the country. Furthermore the moral consciousness contained values from romanticism like the home, nature and folklore, liberal values like enlightenment, freedom, equality and democracy and national values like patriotism, the will to defend the nation, solidarity and sovereignty.

The process of nation building in Norway shows the importance the education system. First of all the quality of the education had to be improved to create responsible citizens who could take part in the modernisation of the country. Secondly the children got socialised into a common national culture. Through this school the national myth was spread to the mass of the population. In order to accomplish these goals the church and the school had to be separated, and a common primary school had to be established. In this way all children got the same basic education, which demonstrated the equality in the national community. This is one of the main reasons why the building of the Norwegian nation state became such a success. Another reason was the joint venture of nation building and democratisation of the political system.

The process of changing the education system may fruitfully be followed through the new readers that were compiled. They can be used as sources to study the content of the national myth which partly built on an existing raw material and partly was constructed. The myth contained elements from different parts of the country in order to unify the whole people as a nation. Furthermore it defined the Norwegian national identity on the basis of national history, national literature, folklore, nature and national industries. The Constitution and the 17th of May became the main symbols of the Norwegian identity and community. In this way there was established an ethnic nationality combined with civil rights.

The followers of Grundtvig in Norway contributed to nation building first of all as educationists, and at the same time nation and religion were tied together in a national religion where the nation was seen under the guidance of God. It is however important to stress that they looked upon nationality as a way in to universality and not as a basis for isolation from it. For this reason they saw no conflict between Christianity and nationality, and they supported the Pan-Scandinavian movement and took a great interest in the European cultural heritage. In this way they differed from the type of nationalism which was created by the historians, and which became predominant in the 1890s.

Due to pietism and revivalism the followers of Grundtvig never got a stronghold in Norwegian church life, and national religion did not play an important role although it influenced the Christian youth clubs. Instead the main stream of theology and church life in Norway separated from the national and democratic movement and withdrew from the political arena. Christianity and nationality were seen as competing identities. Due to the Union the Christian duty of obedience and loyalty to the authorities represented first of all by the King, conflicted with the duty to the nation and the people. The former division of pietism between the converts and non-converts got a new dimension, and the gap between church and society was enlarged, especially because the political and cultural leaders of Norwegian nationalism professed evolution, positivism and criticism of the Christian religion.

The exception concerning national religion came with the crisis in 1905 when the break of the Union was followed by a national religious outburst. In this case the national religion served the purpose of unifying the people and legitimating the rebellion government. In this situation the theologians had to reinterpret St. Paul's command and the 4th commandment. A new criterion was introduced concerning the authorities which the Christian should obey and be loyal to, they should be the *national* authorities. This interpretation became important during the next national crisis, the German occupation from 1940 to 1945. During these years the Church of Norway did not accept that "there is no authority except from God". The church claimed that the authorities also should represent justice. If not, the Christian had no obligation to obedience and loyalty. For that reason the church broke with Quisling's government since it again and again violated justice. During these years a new chapter of the relationship between church and nation was written.

Clergy and Nation-building in Iceland 1830-1850

Pétur Pétursson

This article deals with the role of the clergy in the initial period of the Icelandic nation-building process. It aims at clarifying the complicated constitutional issue raised by the abolition of the monopoly of the Danish King in 1848. It deals with some related issues of the position of the Lutheran Church in Iceland being a part of the Danish administration and at the same time an integral part of Icelandic society. This paper is based on my thesis, Church and Social Change; A Study of the Secularization Process in Iceland 1830-1930.[1]

During the first three decades of the 19th century a majority of the higher officials of the Danish state were greatly influenced by the Enlightenment. They supported both ideologically and practically the administration of the Enlightened Monarchy. This applied as well to the Icelandic officials despite the colonial status of Iceland. The higher officials of the Church, the Bishop and the principal of the Bessastaðir School supported the Establishment and had theological leanings towards Rationalism or a mild form thereof.

The leading officials found national values and customs standing in the way of practical administrative changes. This is illustrated in their decisions in matters relating to administration and publication. The ancient political institution of Alþing at þingvellir (founded in 930) was abolished and replaced by a high court in Reykjavík in 1800. At the same time the old Bishoprics were combined to one with its centre in Reykjavík. The leadership of the Church became thus more dependent on the secular administration.

The Enlightenment in Iceland was naturally combined with progressive ideas in the areas of economics and literature but for various reasons, it did not mobilize much support among the common people. At the beginning of the 19th century the Icelandic Society for Enlightenment was powerful. It controlled the only printing press in the country and held a monopoly on publication rights of any kind of books. This position was consciously used to the advantage of the society in propagating its own re-

---

[1] The thesis was first published by Plus Ultra, Helsingborg 1983 and for the second time by University of Iceland in 1990. References are left out in this presentation.

ligious and ecclesiastical ideals. The society's most powerful leader and, in fact, it's absolute administrator was the Chief of the High Court, Magnús Stephensen. The faithful officials of the Royal administration did little to stimulate the participation of the local people in politics or administration, and on the whole they supported the governing system of authoritarian hierarchy. The masses were to be educated to be submissive to the officials of the state. For the first three decades of the century the general attitude of the common people was characterized by complete political and social apathy. The populace did not see the value of organized activities in the furtherment of their interests. All societies and associations were led by high officials and, with the exception of the Icelandic Literary Society, with no or very limited base among the ordinary farming population. At the end of the 1820s the Society for Enlightenment lost much of its initial vitality. At this time the only available regular Icelandic publication was the yearbook of the Copenhagen Department of the Icelandic Literary Society which included literary and political news from the outside world. The nationalist mobilization which started during the 1830s was led by young Icelandic intellectuals and students at the University of Copenhagen. They were inspired by an intellectual milieu other than that which had moulded the mentality of the previous generation of officials in Iceland. In the political, cultural and theological aspects they were influenced by the Romantic world view. From it the Icelandic students received encouragement in their aspirations for Icelandic nationhood and political rights for their people. In this respect, they were also affected by the political events in Europe including the French June Revolution and, even closer, the events in the Duchies of Schleswig and Holstein, where the national movements of the German speaking population were becoming powerful in their opposition to the Danish administration. In the wake of these events, the Icelandic intelligentsia in Copenhagen constituted a group of considerable political and cultural significance while fulfilling a leadership role in the process of political nation building. The group's location in Copenhagen was crucial in this respect since this was the political centre for Icelandic matters with all major decisions being made here. Copenhagen was also the cultural centre of Iceland.

In their publications, printed in Copenhagen, the intelligentsia were critical of Icelandic politics and presented their political and cultural ideas based on the new trends. Their main objective was in broadening the political rights of the Icelandic people and in nationalizing the administration. Of prime importance, at this time, was the foundation of a separate advisory body elected by the people of Iceland to represent the nation before the Absolute Monarchy. In the minds of the Icelandic students in the 1830s, this idea was closely associated with the glory of the ancient political institution Alþingi at Þingvellir.

Initially, the Danish authorities and several officials in Iceland opposed the idea of a separate advisory body. But in 1839, King Christian VIII exhibited a more positive attitude than did his predecessor. His support for the idea of a special consultative body met increasing sympathy in the higher echelons of the administration, and in 1845, Alþing was re-established in Reykjavík as a representative advisory body. This turned out to be the first step in the development of an independent Icelandic political centre situated in Reykjavík.

Further goals of the National Liberal leaders included the development of higher education, improvements in the Latin School and the establishment of a separate seminary within the country for the education of the clergy. These goals were realized in the 1840s with the Latin School at Bessastaðir relocating to Reykjavík and the founding of the Theological Seminary in Reykjavík in 1847.

The fact that the official Establishment, which supported the idea of Enlightened Absolutism and the power of the Danish centre leaned, theologically, towards Rationalism was of significance for the onset of the national mobilization in religious respects. The opposition of the Icelandic students in Copenhagen towards the hegemonous administration in Iceland, and particularly towards Chief Justice Magnús Stephensen and his Society for Enlightenment, was initially, at least partly theologically motivated. During the first half of the 19th century, a large group of Icelandic students in Copenhagen were theological students. Romanticism was associated with a philosophical and religious reaction to the Rationalistic theology of the Church of Denmark leadership. These reactions were inspired either by the New-Orthodoxy or by a variety of Pietism. The Icelandic students and particularly the theological students at the university were influenced by Romantically-oriented theological ideas and by New-Orthodoxy since the 1830s. The Icelandic students translated and published several works, e.g. the collection of sermons of Bishop Mynster who was greatly influenced by Romanticism and opposed to the Rationalism-inspired clergymen of the Church of Denmark. It has been maintained that the last remains of Rationalism in Iceland were erradicated by this book which became popular as a book of sermons for use in family devotions.

Neo-Orthodoxy was much more similar to the religiosity of the people than was the Enlightenment-inspired theology of the officials. The Icelandic intelligentsia in Copenhagen organized the reprinting of older orthodox religious literature. This same material had been prevented from being published in Iceland by the Society for Enlightenment which, in doing so was acting in accordance with its ideals in the education of the populace. In 1828, for instance, a new edition of the *Vídalínspostilla* (a popular book of sermons from the early 18th century) was published despite the protests of Chief Justice Stephensen who claimed exclusive publication rights of the book for his society. The re-publication was apparently widely appreciated by Icelandic readers and a new edition appeared ten years later.

The Nationalistic Elites and the Dissemination of Their Ideas

The Icelandic intelligentsia in Copenhagen published several magazines to aid them in introducing their national and political ideas and strategies into Iceland. And despite the limited quantity of publications, the material had considerable effect on the population and soon became crucial for the political nation building process. This together with the publishings of the Copenhagen Department of the Icelandic Literary Society constituted the main sources of political and social information, given the very few papers and magazines published domestically.

The first of these political magazines was *Ármann á Alþingi*, published from 1829 until 1833. It included articles on various subjects concerning the socio-economical development. Furthermore, it emphasised cultural elements, particularly the preservation of the Icelandic language as significant for general national improvement. Already its name can be associated with the reconstruction of Alþing as the foundation for national development. This publication, as did subsequent ones to some extent, turned itself to the rank and file of the rural population. Its editor and chief writer was the young lawyer, Baldvin Einarsson, who was also the leader of a group of politically active students called "Brotherhood Alþingi". The co-editor was the young theologian Þorgeir Gumðundsson, who was the central figure in the publication activities of Icelandic religious literature in Copenhagen. In opposition to the monopoly of the Society for Enlightenment, he had already established a distribution network throughout Iceland with clergymen acting as agents by selling his books among their parishioners. This network was also used for distributing *Ármann á Alþingi* which had about 500 subscribers.

A subsequent magazine, *Fjölnir*, was founded in 1835 by four intellectuals in Copenhagen and was published until 1847. The last volumes were published by a society of the same name as the magazine itself. One of the four original editors, Tómas Sæmundsson, returned to Iceland to become a pastor. He served as a crucial link between the Copenhagen group and Iceland using his position at the Official Clergy Meetings to distribute and recommend both the magazine and its ideas. Theologically, he was opposed to the Rationalist ideas of the Enlightenment and heavily criticized the Book of Sermons published by the Society for Enlightenment for use in the households. In 1841, another group of Icelandic students in Copenhagen began publishing the *Ný félagsrit*. The leader of the group and editor of the publication was Jón Sigurðsson who became the most influential political leader among the Icelandic intellectuals in Copenhagen in the late 1840s, and in fact the leading figure in the entire political nation building movement until his death in 1879.

In the 1840s, the situation had changed somewhat. The political goals of the pioneers of a separate consultative body for Iceland had been realized along with the founding of the Theological Seminary and improvements of the Latin School. The hegemony of Magnús Stephensen (d. 1833) disappeared with him in the early 1830s without major conflicts with the nation building movement. No one was left to continue the policy of confrontation against the political nation-building process under the mantle of the previous "Rationalistic Establishment". The president of the flnewly established Theological Seminary was a member of the Fjölnir group and was influenced in his theology by Romanticism. This was also true of the other main teacher of the seminary who was a member of the group around *Ný félagsrit*.

The policy of Jón Sigurðsson was less influenced by Romanticism than his predecessor's ideas had been, and he was less motivated to oppose the ideas of Rationalism. In several respects, his political philosophy was a combination of the romantically inspired conceptions of nationhood and the more rationalistic and practical orientations of the Enlightenment. He and his group wanted Alþing situated in Reykjavík whereas the more romantically influenced thought it should be situated at the "sacred" place of þingvellir. The location of Alþing and the Theological Seminary in Reykjavík along with the Latin School was the beginning of the process to establish Reykjavík as the political and cultural centre of Iceland, which was quite in line with the political programme of Jón Sigurðsson. From the very beginning and throughout his political carrier Sigurðsson was in contact with clergymen in all parts of Iceland. As president of the Copenhagen Department of the Icelandic Literary Society his contact network was further expanded, with the clergy playing a large role in this, too.

An examination of the records of the Copenhagen Department of the Literary Society shows that for the years 1855–1856, 40 percent of all correspondence with the society was from clergymen in Iceland, and these years are no exeption in this respect.

In 1844, 1846 and 1856, *Ný félagsrit* published a list of subscribers and agents and the number of copies each received. Those with multiple subscriptions were, in essence, agents for the periodical. Table 1 indicates the occupational or the social position of these agents.

Table 1 Occupation or Social Status of the Agents of Ný félagsrit: 1844, 1846 and 1856

Occupation or social status	1844	1846	1856
Clergyman	12	24	19
Higher civil-official	5	7	
Student	5	14	1
Farmer		2	4
Farm servant		2	
Merchant	1	3	2
Skilled worker		1	1
No information	3	2	1
Total	26	55	28

According to Table 1, the clergymen were as crucial as mediators in the political mobilization during the 1840s and 1850s as they had been for the editors of *Ármann á Alþingi* and *Fjölnir* during the 1830s. Clergymen comprised nearly half of the agents in 1844 and 1846, and two-thirds in 1856.

There were also single subscribers of *Ný félagsrit*, for instance in 1846, 33 clergymen received one copy of the periodical in addition to the 24 counted previously. Thus, about 30 percent of the clergy received the magazine directly from the editor. Most of the clergymen with whom Sigurðsson had permanent contact supported his policy. His policy was also supported by a large majority of the clergymen elected to Alðing. On several occasions Sigurðsson emphasized the importance of the clergy for the political nation building process and for the social upgrading of the people.

The great majority of the educated class were indeed clergymen and up to the foundation of the Theological Seminary in 1847 a Latin School examination was enough for being ordained as a minister of the Church in Iceland; in essence, all intellectuals were conceiveably an extension of the Church of Iceland during the first half of the 19th century. The church leadership and some of the ordinary clergymen had studied at the University of Copenhagen and were, thus, colleagues and acquaintances of the Icelandic nationalistic leaders in Copenhagen. Some of the most prominent political organizers and ardent supporters of the policy of Sigurðsson were clergymen who had studied theology at the university. Furthermore, a majority of the Icelandic intellectuals had been students at the Bessastaðir School, which functioned as an institute for pastoral education in Iceland. These configurations help account for the role of the clergy in the distribution of the political ideas and programmes of the the nationalistic leaders situated in Copenhagen. The rising political awareness of the people in the 1840s and the beginning of the 1850s, as indicated by the numerous petitions from local meetings all over the country for increased national rights demonstrates that the ideas of the Copenhagen elite reached the farming population.

Religious or Nationalistic Revival?

Neither *Ný félagsrit* nor any of the previous publications of the Icelandic intellegentsia in Copenhagen were primarily devoted to theological issues and ecclesiastical questions. Such matters were dealt with casually in connection with other subjects. An exception is the first number of *Ármann á Alþingi*. It presented religion as crucial for moral and national upgrading. Truthful and devoted religious practice according to the official standards both within the context of the household and the parish services were emphasised much in the same manner as in the Royal regulations on education and religious matters introduced in the middle of the 18th century. The paper's emphasis on the moral and practical aspects of religious life was in line with the official Enlightenment-inspired theology; but, in several instances a shift is noted towards a more orthodox standpoint.

Important among the intelligentsia were items related to the economic status of the clergy and the functioning of the clergy on the social level among the local people, especially in primary education. In one way or another the magazines maintained the view that the official Christian religion was the basis of the social order and that the observance of religious duties was the most vital factor in social solidarity and morality. These issues were presented unassumingly and unproblematically, without direct reference to doctrinal disputes or theological controversies. In describing the European revolutions, with which the writers clearly sympathized, reservations were made for the treatment allotted Christianity and the attitudes of the revolutionaries in this respect.

As presented by the nationalistic leaders, belief in God and faithfullness towards the fatherland were among the values of highest significance to all Christian people. In a philosophical essay dealing with the historical origin of the idea of nationhood in the development of Christianity, the author alludes to the significance of Protestantism. Similar ideas, but in a more popularized version, were a recurrent theme in the first numbers of the nationalistic paper *Þjóðólfur*, started in Reykjavík in 1848.

Somewhat unexpectedly, these publications failed to take issue with any of the contemporary theological debates so characteristic of the contemporary academic milieu and intellectual life in Copenhagen. And although the Icelandic students could hardly have escaped them, the subjects such as issues related to religious freedom, church and state relations, the autonomy of the church and discussions of religion and science were totally ignored.

Even if the leadership of the nationalistic mobilization was not primarily theologically or religiously motivated its is important to notice that it acted in cooperation with the clergy in Iceland. Furthermore, its ideology was in harmony with the religious tradition of the people on one hand and with the New Orthodoxy of the younger generation of theologians from the University of Copenhagen on the other. It was this generation of theologians which, at about mid-century, assumed the leadership of the Church of Iceland.

In comparison to the popular revivals of the other Nordic countries in the first half of the 19th century, we see that the Scandinavian revivals were primarily religiously motivated. The latter were characterized by their pietistic reaction to the Rationalistic Establishment and the attempts to eradicate popular religious literature and bring about changes which downplayed the role of orthodox purity among the common people. These religious revivals were organized as meetings outside the framework of the State Church and the private sphere of the household and were condemned by the authorities as in violation of the established social and political order. Similar meetings did not take place in Iceland during the 19th century.

During the first phase of the political nation building process in Iceland, from 1830 to 1850, the Nationalistic revival had certain social and political functions similar to the religious movements in Scandinavia. Both movements were reactions to the Rationalistic Establishment and both movements mobilized a broader strata of people into what might be referred to as the prelude to a democratic nation building process. The Icelandic revival was dominated by nationalistic and political overtones whereas the dominant theme of peoples movements in the other Nordic countries at that time was centered around religious and theological issues.

The Scandinavian movements opposed the Church which represented the religious framework of the Rationalistic Establishment. The official religious system served to legitimate the hierarchical social order based on a vertical structure of social solidarity, which accounts for the revivalists' uneasiness towards the integration of church and state. On the local level the conflict was directed towards the clergy who, in comparison to the Icelandic clergy, enjoyed a much higher economic and social position than did their farmer parishioners. In Iceland, the ordinary clergy were not affected by Rationalism, and as for social and economic matters, they were on a level much closer to the farming population. This placed the clergy in the position of leadership in the popular revival of both political and social character.

The Constitutional Issue and Political Participation of the Clergy

The political events of 1850–1851 constituted a turning point in the centre building process and affected the entire political development throughout the century. This turning point was even crucial for the plausibility structure of the official theological legitimations.

The end of the Absolute Monarchy and the establishment of a constitution and parliament in Denmark in 1848–1849, aroused the expectations of the Icelanders. Jón Sigurðsson wrote an essay on the consequences of these events for Iceland and its relation to the Danish state. This essay, *(Hugvekja til Íslendinga)*, which was published in *Ný félagsrit* (1848), should be regarded as the political programme for the Nationalist movement for decades to come. In the essay he stated that the decision of the Danish King, Fredrick VII, to renounce his Absolute Power meant that the national rights of Iceland should be restored in accordance with the definitions of the Old Treaty between Iceland, as a free country, and the King of Norway in 1264. The fact that Norway and Denmark came under common rule in 1390 did not alter the formal relationship between the Icelandic nation and the King according to Sigurðsson. Therefore Iceland was now to become a sovereign state in union with Denmark. Neither the Danish parliament nor the Danish government could assume legislative or executive power over Iceland because there never existed a treaty between the *Danish nation* and *Iceland* which could legitimatize such an arrangement. It was maintained in conjunction with the King's renounciation of absolute power, that Iceland would negotiate with him concerning the constitution and a separate government.

On 23 September, 1848, a Royal letter was published which included promises that a decision regarding the relationship between Iceland and Denmark would not take place before a National Convention in Iceland had been given the opportunity to express its opinion. The decree was greeted in Iceland with enthusiasm. Already during the summer of 1848 a free national meeting had been organized at fiingvellir, the first of several fiingvellir Conventions to be held in order to unite the people and express the will of the majority on the constitutional issue.

A new paper, *þjóðólfur*, , was founded in Reykjavík in 1848 for the purpose of supporting the fundamentalist national policy and soon became an influential organ of the political movement. Its first editor was the Rev. Sveinbjörn Hallgrímsson, one of the most active national liberals during these years. The chief organizer of the first fiingvellir Convention was the dean Hannes Stephensen, also a member of Alþing (Jón Sigurðsson resided in Copenhagen). Hannes Stephensen was the leading political organizer of the most intransigent nationalists in the country until his death in 1856.

Elections to the National Convention in Reykjavík were held in 1850, but the convention which was to have taken place that summer was postponed until the following year. By then, the attitude of the Danish authorities toward Icelandic national rights had changed markedly, mostly due to the problems they had had with the Duchies of Schleswig and Holstein. Furthermore, the conservatives throughout Europe were gaining strength, and liberal and constitutional governments were removed from power in several countries.

At the National Convention held in Reykjavík in 1851, the representative of the Danish authorities (the Governor General) introduced a bill suggesting, among other things, that the Danish constitution become legally binding in Iceland. This measure implied that Iceland, as a special region (amt) within the Danish state, would have its own local government and limited authority in certain matters, e.g. financial. In other words, Iceland would have, in practice, little more than colonial status.

The suggestion caused a split among the Icelandic delegates to the convention with the higher officials, appointed by the King (in practice by the Danish Government), proposing a compromising amendment in an effort to avoid confrontation with the government. The majority was in favour of rejecting the government proposition completely and writing a new one based on the premises of the fundamentalist nationalist policy laid down by Jón Sigurðsson who led the group at the convention. However, before the convention could vote on the issue the meeting was adjourned by the Governor General. This resulted in an appeal to the King written by a majority of the convention delegates in conjunction with one of the King's own elect (Rev. Halldór Jónsson) protesting the procedure and requesting a new convention. Of the 37 elected delegates 13 were clergymen; 3 of the 6 Royally appointed delegates were also clergymen.

The official National Convention left the constitutional issue and the legal status of Iceland unsolved, but the Danish Government remained the highest authority for all Icelandic matters and one of its ministers became the Minister of Iceland. The Governor General was subordinate to him but neither was he responsible to Alþing nor to any other authority in Iceland. The relation of Iceland to Denmark was not legally defined until in 1871 with the unilateral passing of legislation by the Danish Parliament against the majority will of Alþing. On the basis of these laws a constitution was introduced in Iceland in 1874, "given", as it were, to the Icelandic nation by the King, in which Alþing was granted legislative and financial authority in such matters as were determined "internal" for Iceland by the Danish authorities.

The Theological Legitimation of Church and State

The late 1840s and early 1850s saw the consolidation of the conservative Danish church policy called the Mynster/Martensen policy, named after J. P. Mynster, Bishop of Seeland, and Professor H. L. Martensen who succeeded Mynster as Bishop of Seeland in 1854. Later, the policy was referred to as the Third Church Policy Programme in Denmark; the other two being Grundtvigianism and the Inner-Mission.

It was particularly Martensen's task to formulate the theology of the Third Church Policy Programme. The primary object of this orthodox theology was to defend the religious homogenity of the country and the unaltered relations between the state and church. The Programme endevoured to maintain many aspects of the previous church of Absolutism. The theology as codified by Martensen represented an extraordinary capacity to integrate the orthodox theological dogmas of the Church and intellectual reflections into a harmonious system. Martensen was highly influenced by German idealism and Hegelian philosophy. His basic principle, taken from Hegelian dialectics, assumed the final unity of all things as determined by the eternal will of God. In this theory there was no contradiction between Christian faith and science; both were expressions of the will of the Almighty. Philosophy was seen as the intellectual expression and interpretation of the essence of religion. Needless to say, the Evangelical Lutheran doctrine was the only true basis on which to build one's world view.

The doctrine of the unity of church, nation and state assumed even an eschatological dimension; the synthesis becomes the basis on which to realize the Kingdom of God, the Christian state. The church was the educator of the nation, and church matters were thus highly relevant for the state authorities. The state could only be a moral order if based on Christian principles. The Evangelical Lutheran faith was the state religion and the unifying symbol was the Crown. In times of uprisings and revolutions as during the years 1848 and 1849, the Crown was, according to Martensen, to safeguard the bonds and the common basis of the church and state (H. Lundsteen 1960: 286).

Thus, theology made universal claims for intellectual legitimations and for social order as well. As an ideology it had no understanding of conflicts or clashes between the clergy and civil officials or between religion and science.

In Denmark the Grundtvigians and the Inner-Mission in the beginning constituted, in many respects, the opposition to church leadership and its theology, and because of popular support, soon gained considerable influence over religious and church life. In the 1850s the Danish Church had to face the critique of Kierkegaard, and in the 1860s, the intellectual debate, which dealt with the issue of the irreconcilability of religion and science, faith and knowledge, resolved that the Martensen synthesis was no longer satisfactory for the intellectual milieu.

The Third Church Policy Programme in Denmark was actually the only church policy in Iceland during the second-half of the 19th century. It was Pjetur Pjetursson, the first president of the Theological Seminary in Reykjavík, who introduced Martensenian theology into Iceland. He was the most influential figure of the Icelandic Church in the latter half of the 19th century, being ordained Bishop of Iceland by Martensen in 1866 and serving until 1889. Thus, he was the teacher and supervisor of several generations of clergymen in Iceland.

The role of the King as a unifying symbol and as head of the State Church is crucial in explaining why the conservative Third Church Policy Programme was the only programme in Iceland. The political reason for this was the emphasis that the fundamental Nationalists injected into the authority of the King as the Absolute Ruler of Iceland. Thus, even though based on different reasons, the Martensenian theologians and the fundamental Icelandic Nationalists supported the supremacy of the King and religious homogeneity as the basis of social order. According to the definition of the nationalistic leaders, the opponent of the Icelandic nation-state building was not the King but the Danish Government and the Danish administration.

The Nationalists thus maintained they could be faithful to the King and oppose the government at the same time. Since 1851, the authority of the King was one of the fundamental pillars of their policy for nation-state building. Thus, it was not in their interest to fight the official model of the state religion whose unifying symbol was the Crown. The nationalistic mobilization of the period 1851–1874 was therefore carried out within the hegemony of the state-church religion and, as indicated earlier, it would have been fatal for this political movement to introduce theological disputes leading to a split between the Icelandic clergy and the political elite in Copenhagen. This accounts for the fact that new ideas on issues concerning religious freedom, religion and science, church-state, etc. in Copenhagen did not appear in the publications of the Icelandic intellectuals. Thus, it seems to have been beneficial for the Icelandic nation-building process to maintain the official religious model of the Danish state as defined by the conservative theology of Martensen.

One item which reveals that the "Church policy" of the fundamental Nationalists and Martensen had important contact points was the vigorous opposition in the Nationalist paper *Þjóðólfur* in the early 1850s against the idea of some Church men of establishing a separate Church Assembly in Iceland. It was argued that it was not in the interests of the Icelandic people to have an assembly with legislative authority in church matters along side Alþing, and therewith, differentiate Church matters from other issues. This issue was not seriously raised again until the last decade of the 19th century.

Conclusions

In general one might characterize the 19th century social mobilization in Iceland as not having perpetrated any significant social differentiation or cleavages between social groups in the country. It did not result in increased separation or differentiation of church and society. On the contrary, in many respects it appears that the already strong bonds between the two were actively reinforced during the first phase of the social mobilization process, i.e. up to 1880, and in some areas, until the turn of the century.

In this context it is important to observe that in the beginning of the political mobilization (1830–1850), the Nationalists favoured theological and religious ideas which were close to the religious understanding of the common people and the majority of the clergy. The clergy served as an intermediary link between the political elite in Copenhagen and the farming population of Iceland. They were in a position to function as leaders of the social mobilization of the broad spectrum of society and to lead the initial construction of an independent and indigenous institutional structure on which the Icelandic centre building process took place. One reason for this was that their education was "Icelandic" i.e. based on the internal clerical education with its basis in the middle ages. Another was their comparatively independent position in the administration as compared to civil officials, due mainly to their source of income not coming from the state.

The clergy represented the interests of the majority of the people in their leadership functions in both political and social issues. The object and purpose of the various local societies were, on the whole, unquestioned by all social groups in Iceland. In their broad role, the clergy represented a homogeneous population on both the local and national levels; therefore, their social and political activities did not interfere with their role as religious and spiritual figures because of the absence of antagonistic economic classes. Many clergymen could combine their functions as parish leaders and political leaders in such a manner that it afforded them an undisputed position as community leaders in almost every respect.

Even though the majority of the politically active clergy were more independent than were the civil officials vis-a-vis the Danish authorities, they were not in a position to alienate themselves from the official Establishment to which they belonged as servants of the State Church. In this respect the political position of the clergy served as a consolidating factor in the political and social mobilization, ensuring this process of a relatively harmonious development, free from disruptions which would have retarded its progression in time.

Religion and National Identity in Scotland since the Union of 1707[1]

Callum G. Brown

I

In the shaping of modern Scotland, religion has played an important part. The question historians have been asking increasingly in recent years is whether the putative emergence or re-emergence of a "national identity" for Scots has been assisted by religion. Since the late 1980s the literature has developed a stridency and a reductive quality that has allowed propagandists for Scottish nationalism to make increasingly sweeping assertions in this field. Historians, sociologists and intellectuals in Scotland, especially those fired by a nationalist zeal, are trying to link a modern *secular* national identity with an earlier *religious* identity.

This paper takes issue with such a tendency. It urges greater caution, more alertness to the realities of Scottish religious history "from the bottom up", and more realism regarding the role of religion in the popular culture of late modern Scotland. Whatever the merits might be of identifying today the existence of a vigorous "national identity" that justifies constitutional self-determination, the argument here is that religion cannot be regarded as a "bridge" between the independent Scottish state before 1707 and Scottish nationalism within the British state in the late twentieth century. Ultimately, it is suggested, religion has not provided any single "national" identity, but rather it has provided a series of sectarian identities which together, in the 1990s, constitute a major block to a victorious nationalist movement.

II

One of the major problems that Scottish nationalists have with Scottish history since the Union of 1707 with England is that there have been

---

[1] An earlier version of this paper was presented to the Conference of the Economic and Social History Society of Scotland at New College, Edinburgh, in November 1993.

relatively few incidents of nationalist revolt. This is important for any nationalist movement, for a distinctive heritage of cultural, ethnic, linguistic or religious identity is the basis upon which claims to constitutional independence are invariably set. As so often, agitation for change is a claim to "tradition", custom or, as in this case, to a "lost" nationhood that is to be "reclaimed".

Incidents of nationalist revolt in post-1707 Scotland were invariably small-scale, short-term, failed to attract meaningful levels of support, and were instigated in contexts of fiscal, economic or industrial unrest in which a nationalist banner was a secondary consideration to some other issue. Scottish nationalism is a difficult object to pin down because there has been so very little of it. Indeed, the story of the "nationalist movement" in Scot-land can be reduced to five phases. In the first during the four decades after the Union between Scotland and England in 1707, there were periodic protests at the imposition of English law in Scotland-notably fiscal measures of taxation which were seen as novel.[2] In the second, the development of the Scottish Enlightenment in the eighteenth and early nineteenth centuries – notably in the four older Scottish universities – is seen as creating a distinctive philosophical, scientific and educational regime (sometimes referred to as "the democratic intellect") which linked Scotland with international (and notably European) philosophy in advance of developments in England.[3] In the third phase during and after the Revolutionary and Napoleonic Wars of 1793-1815, Scottish radicals included amongst their demands for electoral and industrial reform references to Scottish rights, notably during the so-called "Scottish Insurrection" of 1820 in which less than a hundred men were defeated in a military operation with three ringleaders being executed for treason.[4] A longer fourth phase from the 1850s to the 1920s saw a succession of voluntary organisations with relatively small numbers of members promoting the cause of Scottish "home rule" – beginning with administrative home rule which created the Scottish Office in 1885 but which included support for a succession of failed parliamentary Bills for

---

[2]C.A. Whatley, "How tame were the Scottish Lowlanders during the eighteenth century?" in T.M. Devine (ed.), *Conflict and Stability in Scottish Society 1700-1850* (1990, John Donald, Edinburgh), pp. 1-30.
[3]G. Davie, *The Democratic Intellect: Scotland and Her Universities in the Nineteenth Century* (1961, Edinburgh University Press, Edinburgh).
[4]P.B. Ellis and S. Mac A'Ghobhainn, *The Scottish Insurrection of 1820* (1970, Gollanz, London).

devolution of legislative power to a Scottish assembly.[5] In the fifth phase, a nationalist political party came into being in 1926, but it enjoyed negligible electoral support until the early 1970s when it gained just under 20 per cent of Scottish Members of Parliament, and which since then has fallen back to less than five per cent.

Of these five phases, the first four were insignificant expressions of national consciousness in comparison to similar developments in the regions of Europe. The last, continuing phase is more important, and marks the first emergence of a coherent scheme of national self-government based on some measure of widespread popular support. Even then, nationalism in Scotland is not the mass expression of a suppressed people, likely to break out in mass demonstrations, national agitation or armed rebellion. Scotland is not akin to the former Yugoslavia, Slovakia, or even the Basque country. Nationalism is weak in Scotland, and does not have a heritage of active (or even passive) resistance to "foreign" domination – in this case, perceived to come from England. Nonetheless, home rule in Scotland is looking more likely now in the mid 1990s than at any time since 1707. The British Labour Party fears that the Scottish National Party may take some of its parliamentary seats, threatening Labour's struggle with the Conservative Party at Westminster. Accordingly, Labour has promised that if it wins the next General Election it will award Scotland a parliament with its own "prime minister".

On the threshold of this brave new world, intellectuals in the broad Scottish nationalist movement have been trawling history for the Scottish "nation" that is about to "reclaim its destiny". A cynic might suggest that what many of them are doing is to "talk up" this "nation", its "identity" and its historical consciousness. Certainly, there has been a very distinct tendency to "talk up" the putative role of religion in this matter. Religion has become a hunting ground for evidence of a national identity in Scotland during the eighteenth and more especially the nineteenth centuries. Hungry for any evidence of a nationalist movement, intellectuals for the cause have been offering highly partisan interpretations of ecclesiastical events and popular religiosity in order to portray a heritage of nationalist resistance to English encroachment on

---

[5]H.J. Hanham, *Scottish Nationalism* (1969, London); R.J. Finlay, *Independent and Free: Scottish Politics and the origins of the Scottish National Party 1918-1945* (1994, John Donald, Edinburgh).

Scottish affairs, and to demonstrate the existence of a national consciousness focussed on presbyterianism.

III

David McCrone, in his recent textbook on the sociology of Scotland, writes: "Religion has been one of the abiding cultural characteristics of Scotland which distinguish it from its southern counterpart".[6] He goes further, bringing presbyterianism more directly into the equation:

> Presbyterianism was clearly a more democratic form of church government than Catholicism or Episcopalianism, and the doctrine of predestination, the essence of Calvinism, helped confirm the equality of this elect. Its association with national identity helped it retain its hold for longer than elsewhere.[7]

McCrone is building upon an old tradition within Scottish nationalism. This tradition has perceived the struggle between Scottish presbyterians and episcopacy in the late sixteenth and seventeenth centuries as the crucible of a national identity that was to outlive the Union of 1707 with England. One source of nationalist identity has been with the Covenanters – extreme presbyterians of the seventeenth century who led armed opposition to Crown episcopacy, and who continued to oppose the "moderate" presbyterianism of the Church of Scotland after 1690. But the Covenanters are a dubious model for the modern nationalist as their nationalism was very much a vehicle for their defence of "true religion"; they harboured a violent detestation for Catholics and episcopalians, and were illiberal and puritanical to the point of anti-intellectualism. However, some modern nationalist historians still admire those who have used the Covenanters as symbols of patriotic resistance, as they offer "with our present interest in constitutional reform [i.e. home rule]... a useful bridge to the constitutional concerns of the Renaissance and Reformation in Scotland".[8]

---

[6]D. McCrone, *Understanding Scotland: The Sociology of a Stateless Nation* (1992, Routledge, London), p. 36.
[7]*Ibid.*, p. 99.
[8]C. Harvie, "The Covenanting tradition", in G. Walker and T. Gallagher (eds.), *Sermons and battle Hymns: Protestant Popular Culture in Modern Scotland* (1990, Edinburgh

The quest for a religious-based national consciousness continues amongst nationalist historians beyond the Union of 1707 and into the era of Scotland as a province of Britain. Though the Treaty of Union which merged Scotland and England preserved the distinctive presbyterian nature of the Established Church of Scotland, the Scottish church system was to undergo significant change, and the British state was to become embroiled – mostly reluctantly – in those changes. Nationalist historians tend to skate over the British state's beneficient interference – notably the granting of freedom of worship to non-presbyterians in 1708. Instead, focus has fallen upon what is perceived as malicious interference, and particularly one ecclesiastical event – the most spectacular church schism in Britain since the Reformation: the Disruption of 1843.

When in 1987 the Conservative Party won the British General Election, and refused to consider any measure of home rule for Scotland, a pressure group incorporating opposition political parties, some leading church figures and other lay figures was established to seek a consensual approach to Scottish devolution. The Scottish Constitutional Convention, as it styled itself, called its founding document of 1988 the "Claim of Right", a name borrowed from two documents of presbyterian protest dating from 1689 and 1842. The "Claim of Right" of 1842 was made to the British government in search of assurance of kirk independence from state interference. When the Claim was rejected, it instigated a mass secession on 18th May 1843 in the wake of which 37 per cent of the clergy and between 40 and 50 per cent of the adherents of the Church of Scotland walked out to form the Free Church of Scotland. It is this event more than any other that nationalist historians and intellectuals of the late 1980s and 1990s have been turning to as the greatest nationalist protest since the Union.

Until the 1980s, the religious divisiveness of Scotland was a problem for nationalist writers in search of the great "Scottish consensus" – a "national identity" which overrode party and class concerns. One such nationalist historian, Christopher Harvie, wrote in 1977 that "religion had frustrated nationalism" at many turns in recent Scottish history.[9] The Disruption of 1843, as the greatest of all Scottish church schisms, was regarded as a

---

University Press, Edinburgh), pp. 8-23 at p. 19.
[9]C. Harvie, *Scotland and Nationalism: Scottish Society and Politics 1707-1977* (1977, George Allen and Unwin, London), p. 115.

disaster for the country; two ecclesiastical historians, both Church of Scotland ministers, wrote: "Before the Disruption Scotland had a national history; afterwards she had not."[10] Harvie commented that it "destroyed the possibility of any Scottish consensus and placed the initiative in legislation securely in the hands of Westminster politicians who. . . simply did not care about Scottish affairs."[11] But by the mid 1980s, the Disruption was starting to be interpreted a little differently. One historian suggested tentatively in 1982 that it was "partly fuelled by something very close to nationalism", whilst another wrote in 1987: "A great national institution, indeed the most essential of all, was broken up and a fundamental element of Scottish identity destroyed."[12]

By the early 1990s, the Disruption of 1843 was being widely interpreted as a great nationalist event – including in a documentary broadcast by Scottish Television in 1992, presented by the Rt. Hon. Sir David Steel M.P., former leader of the British Liberal Party. Sir David also wrote the preface to a book by William Storrar, a Church of Scotland minister, in which it was argued that the essence of Scottish national identity was a vision of the "Godly Commonwealth" that was lost at the Disruption. Not mincing his words, Storrar spoke of there being a "godly vision of Scottish nationhood" until 1843.[13] He quoted another historian, Monica Clough, who had written of the events of 1843 that "what might have developed into a declaration of independence, had there been leaders more concerned with the underlying political implications than with religious ones, merely turned into the Disruption of the Kirk, and not the rupture of the state".[14]

The growth of these assertions in relation to the Disruption has not been based on substantive new research. Indeed, it is one of the characteristics of the whole use of religion in the question of national identity that a new "master narrative" has been created by those with at best only a passing research portfolio in Scottish religious history.

---

[10] A.L. Drummond and J. Bulloch, *The Church in Victorian Scotland 1843-1874* (1975, Saint Andrew Press, Edinburgh), p. 4.
[11] C. Harvie, *op. cit.*, p. 86.
[12] H.R. Sefton, "The Church of Scotland and Scottish nationhood", in S. Mews (ed.), *Religion and National Identity* (1982, Basil Blackwell, Oxford), p. 549.
[13] W. Storrar, *Scottish Identity: A Christian Vision* (1990, The Handsel Press, Edinburgh), p. 51.
[14] Quoted in *ibid.*, p. 36.

Amongst the specialists in the history of the Disruption, only two can be said to have ventured any substantive support for the "nationalist" interpretation. Church historian Stewart J. Brown, the author of the most important biography of the Disruption's leading clergyman, has recently stated:

> The Disruption was not only the break-up of the national religious establishment; it was also a disruption in Scottish national identity, a radical break from its Reformation and Covenanting past and a turning-away from the vision of the unified godly commonwealth. The Disruption undermined the Presbyterian nationalism that had shaped early modern Scotland, with its ideal of the democratic intellect preserved in its parish schools, kirk sessions and presbyteries.[15]

This is an important statement from an authoritative figure, and a judgement that must be taken seriously. However, it is not one that can go unchallenged.

For one thing, the dissenting presbyterian churches which were so influential to the religious and political life of Scotland for seventy years after 1843 would not have shared this view. Victorian Scotland was for them a venue for a new "godly commonwealth", voted in by the dissenting-dominated electorate as church representatives on the *ad hoc* bodies which exercised enormous influence on the civil life of the country: the parochial boards and parish councils, school boards and town councils. In addition, it was the presbyterian dissenters who brought Scotland close to Prohibition after 1913.[16] This was a time when Scottish presbyterian clergy urged that municipal government be viewed as the vehicle for "the realisation of the Kingdom of God on earth", and urged Christians "to be alit with civic ideals, to be alive with civic ardours, and

---

[15]S. J. Brown, "The Ten Years" Conflict and the Disruption of 1843', in S.J. Brown and M. Fry (eds.), *Scotland in the Age of Disruption* (1993, Edinburgh University Press, Edinburgh), p. 2.

[16]B. Aspinwall, *Portable Utopia: Glasgow and the United States 1820-1920* (1984, Aberdeen University Press, Aberdeen), pp. 106-84; I. Sweeney [Maver], "The Municipal Administration of Glasgow 1833-1912: Public service and the Scottish civic identity", unpublished Ph.D. thesis, University of Strathclyde, 1990; C.G. Brown, "Religion and the development of an urban society: Glasgow 1780-1914", unpublished Ph.D. thesis, University of Glasgow, 1982, pp. 93-260.

to be aglow with civic pride and patriotism."¹⁷ The "godly commonwealth" was alive and kicking – it had only modernised and democratised its presbyterian character in line with the political dominance of dissenting electors.

For another thing, the notion of a "presbyterian nationalism" is a contentious one. It is attributing a label which may well stick, if applied sufficiently, but which nonetheless would have meant little to presbyterians in their virtually unanimous support for the union with England in the eighteenth and early nineteenth centuries. The priority for them was never reclaiming a nationhood: it was staying the power of episcopacy, Catholicism and radicalism. The concept is derived essentially from a modern constitutional agenda, and not from the past.

Even Professor Brown's collaborator tends to be more cautious. Political historian Michael Fry considers the same issues in a slightly more direct way, but ends more cautiously. Of the Ten Years Conflict which led up to the Disruption, he writes:

> Scotland might have been united in a nationalist sense, against English abuses of the Treaty of Union. During the Ten Years' Struggle the spirits of Wallace and Bruce were from time to time evoked and the cry of "Scotland for ever!" had been heard. But, because of the domestic disunity, sharp lines were hard to draw between Scottish and English interests, and the conflict could thus not readily take on a nationalist colour either. Instead, it would be turned inwards, into bitter sectarianism within Scotland, and cease to cloud relations with England.¹⁸

The most fundamental flaw in Professor Brown's interpretation, however, is that it is one drawn overwhelmingly from a "top-down" view of the Disruption. His studies of the event, and of its clerical leader Thomas Chalmers, tend implicitly to emphasise the causative role of ideologues and intellectuals. Their cavils at English government intransigence, and their commentaries on the great Scottish institution – the Church of Scotland – being left vulnerable to schism, are highly coloured and exaggerated, but are the principal evidence for this interpretation. But the

---

[17] D.S. Watson, *Perfect Manhood* (1905, London), p. vii; A.S. Matheson, *The City of Man* (1910, London), pp. 196-9.
[18] M. Fry, "The Disruption and the Union", in Brown and Fry (eds.), *op. cit.*, pp. 31-2.

leaders of the Disruption were always restraining grassroots pressure for radical action against the owners of patronage, the landowners. Their commentary is based on reluctant schism, apprehension of what they might do to the Kirk, and fear of the plebeian power which could be unleashed in both ecclesiastical affairs and – in the early 1840s – in industrial and Chartist unrest. Looked at from "the bottom up", the Disruption takes on a very different hue.

IV

The Disruption is by far the leading issue in the attempt by nationalist observers to link religion with a nationalist movement in Scotland since 1707. But to understand the significance of any one incident in Scottish ecclesiastical history, it is vital to appreciate that in the long-run the desire of "true presbyterians" has not been for an *independent* Scotland but for a truly *Protestant* one. All manner of controversies arose from this – including the role of the British state in Kirk affairs.

Scotland, like England, experienced a religious-political struggle between episcopalian Protestants and puritan Protestants in the late sixteenth and seventeenth centuries. The difference is that whilst the episcopalians won in England in 1660, it was the puritans (or presbyterians) who won in Scotland in 1690. But this together with the Union of 1707 came to be regarded by "true presbyterians" as introducing the weakening of the Scottish Church. Various legislative enactments (such as the 1712 Patronage Act, which restored the right to select parish ministers to large and often episcopalian landowners) and various legal cases (such as the 1708 House of Lords decision to grant freedom of worship to episcopalian clergy), reverted ecclesiastical power to the landed classes who could now, many presbyterians came to appreciate, control the Church of Scotland whilst actually worshipping in the Episcopal Church.

The Disruption was the pinnacle of the long class-based struggle that emerged soon after the Union over patronage. The agricultural revolution of the eighteenth century made landowners – the patrons – very wealthy, and increasingly refugees from presbyterianism. They favoured episcopacy – by one estimate in the year of the Disruption, 86 per cent of the Scottish high nobility were episcopalians.[19] As the lower and middle

---

[19]J.P. Lawson, *History of the Episcopal Church from the Revolution to the Present Time*

orders suffered evictions and the rise of commercialism in farming, so they resented the patronage system and other failings of the patrons.[20] Confrontations between worshippers and "intruded" ministers, selected by patrons, occurred from the 1710s onwards, creating two large dissenting denominational groups – the Secession Church and the Relief Church dating from 1733 and 1756 respectively. In practically every one of Scotland's 943 parishes, there was already by 1843 a mature heritage of dissent, dissension and distrust between plebeians and landed elites.

Whilst the Secession and Relief Church had their origins in changing social and economic structures in eighteenth-century rural society, the Disruption had its origins in the more complex social antagonisms of the 1840s. By then, industrialisation and urbanisation had created a new middle class of small merchants, clerks, commission agents and travellers who formed the backbone of the urban Free Church which emerged from 1843.[21] At the same time, the Lowland farming areas of Scotland were at various stages of agricultural improvement, with dispossession of small tenants and cottars, and the creation of enlarged farms and a proletarianised class of farm servants.[22] Meanwhile, in the Highlands and Hebrides of Scotland's rugged north and north-west, the neo-feudal clan system was changing into a divided economy of very large estates dedicated to sheep farming and field sports on the one hand for the benefit of the elite, and of small-scale crofting and fishing on the other for the peasants. For each of these social groups, the Free Church of 1843 became a focus of class identity – especially for the 75-90 per cent of Highland crofters who joined it.[23]

So the events of the 1840s joined a long heritage of class resistance to upper--class usurpation of perceived custom and tradition in a "true" presbyterian kirk. Since the 1730s a myriad of schisms from the Church of Scotland had created a variety of sects and denominations seeking congregational home-rule.[24] They had all been products of emerging class

---

(1843, Edinburgh), pp. 432-3.

[20]C.G. Brown, *The Social History of Religion in Scotland since 1730*(1987, Methuen, London), pp. 28-44.

[21]A.A. MacLaren, *Religion and Social Class: The Disruption Years in Aberdeen* (1974, Routledge Kegan Paul, London).

[22]I. Carter, *Farmlife in North-east Scotland 1840-1914: The poor man's country* (1979, John Donald, Edinburgh).

[23]J. Hunter, *The Making of the Crofting* Community (1976, John Donald, Edinburgh).

[24]C.G. Brown, "Protest in the pews: interpreting presbyterianism and society in crisis during the Scottish economic revolution", in T.M. Devine (ed.), *op. cit.*, pp. 83-105.

ideals and values amongst both the middle and working classes. The Disruption gave further occasion for this — especially, though not exclusively, for the crofters of the Gaelic-speaking Highlands and Hebrides, for the emerging lower middle class of Glasgow, Edinburgh, Dundee and Aberdeen, for the dispossessed tenant farmers in Aberdeenshire, and for the fisherfolk of the coastal villages. And it was not just the Disruption of 1843 which represented such social changes. The 1840s was a decade in which religion was alive as the embodiment of class and occupational identities: the Mormons were recruiting tremendously in Lanarkshire and Ayrshire mining villages, the Chartist Churches were doing the same amongst the impoverished weavers of Glasgow and environs, the Catholic Church was growing by leaps and bounds with the arrival of Irish migrants, and the Scottish Episcopal Church struggled fruitlessly to decide what to do with the Irish Episcopalians flooding its Glasgow province.

The social origins of the Disruption are now quite well documented, and whilst interpretations of the nature and intensity of the social antagonisms on which it was based are still debated, there is no suggestion in this detailed literature that the defectors of 1843 saw themselves involved in a "nationalist movement" against England. To suggest in this context, as Monica Clough did, that a declaration of independence was a possible course of action for Scots in the 1830s and 1840s is ludicrous. The English did not cause the Disruption; Scots did. This is even recognised by one recent nationalist commentator. Lindsay Paterson writes:

> The disputes over lay patronage were between congregations and the Court of Session [in Edinburgh], not London. It was Scottish judges in that Court and the House of Lords who invented the concept of the absolute sovereignty of parliament to justify this in turn as a defence of the traditional national role of the Church of Scotland....The UK Parliament was thus dragged into the disputes by Scottish invitation.[25]

And what it was dragged in to adjudicate upon was a series of rifts in Scottish society in which emergent social classes sought charge of their own destiny. It is folly to argue that the Scots "nation" was doing the

---

[25]L. Paterson, *The Autonomy of Modern Scotland* (1994, Edinburgh University Press, Edinburgh), p. 57.

same. Scottish intellectuals then and now have been too eager to equate every frustration at English complicity with the Scottish landed classes with a pan-class patriotism. Even John Wolffe, an English ecclesiastical historian who carefully dissected the Disruption for evidence of "a nationalist movement", could only go so far as to suggest that within it "the distinctive spirit of Scottish religion was vigorously reaffirmed", leaving at the end of the day "little sign of a more fully developed secular nationalism".[26] In sum, the Disruption was class-driven not nationalist.-driven.

V

If it were merely the Disruption that was pulled from Scotland's social history to bolster the ecclesiastical aspects of the nationalist historian's story, then the task of the empiricist would be relatively easy. But there is a wider claim to contend with. Many writers have argued that presbyterianism and Calvinism acted as foundations of Scottish identity.[27] It has been so easy for writers over many decades to invoke "Calvinism" and declare a divergent Scottish psyche from the English. But non-ecclesiastics who tread into the arena of religious doctrine tend to do so with heavy boots, and invariably come to grief in the mud. To lay Calvinism at the door of Scotland and something supposedly opposite like "Arminianism" at the door of England, is to completely misunderstand the nature of the two, their intermingling, and the common strands of popular religious doctrine shared between the Scottish, English, Welsh and Ulster Protestants during the nineteenth and twentieth centuries.

The common ground between Scots, English and Welsh in the field of religious doctrine in the eighteenth and nineteenth centuries is sharply and empirically drawn by David Bebbington.[28] He illustrates in a very detailed manner how there is no justification for delineating Scotland in these centuries as "Calvinist" and England as "Arminian". The mixture of

---

[26]J. Wolffe, *God and the Greater Britain: Religion and National Life in Britain and Ireland 1843-1945* (1994, Routledge, London and New York), pp. 43, 102-3.
[27]McCrone, *op. cit.*, pp. 36-42; K. Burgess, "Scotland and the first British Empire", in T. Dickson (ed.), *Scottish Capitalism: Class, State and Nation from before the Union to the Present* (1980, London, Lawrence & Wishart), p. 114; A.A. MacLaren, "Introduction: an open society?" in A.A. MacLaren (ed.), *Social Class in Scotland: Past and Present* (n.d., John Donald, Edinburgh), pp. 3-5.
[28]D.W. Bebbington, *Evangelicalism in Modern Britain* (1989, Unwin Hyman, London).

the two within denominations, even within individuals, just does not allow the social historian to be so cavalier with them as labels of national religious characteristics. At maximum, we are dealing with differences in degree: the degree to which Calvinist or Arminian thought affected the main churches in each country. At minimum, we are dealing with doctrines which mixed at the practical level of preaching and common appreciation. Even the Covenanters, who by common acknowledgement were the most ardent presbyterians, were divided: in 1753, their descendants the Reformed Presbyterian Church split in two when nearly half of them adopted the doctrine of universal atonement.[29] Other examples like this abound,[30] and commentators in this field need to come to terms with them. For, they totally confound the attribution of simplistic doctrinal traits to distinguish the Scots from the English.

Even broad attempts to plant Scottish national identity in presbyterianism in the eighteenth, nineteenth and twentieth centuries should confound the nationalist historian. At its simplest, staunch presbyterians were staunch unionists (or supporters of the unifed Britain and its constitutional arrangements) at times of constitutional peril: in 1745-46, in the 1790s, in the 1810s, and in the early 1830s. Whenever Catholicism or Episcopalianism threatened, the Union with England was a "Protestant Union" to be defended at all costs: as in 1745 when staunch presbyterians formed special militias to defend the Protestant Union against the march of Charles Edward Stuart's marauding Catholic and Episcopalian Highlanders. When invasion from France threatened in the 1790s, staunch presbyterians were unwavering in their support of the Union and the "beloved Constitution", against what Scots regarded as the only nominally de-churched Catholic French. Threats from political agitation during the 1810s, 1830s and 1840s saw the presbyterian churches, without exception, solidly behind the British state and the monarchy.[31]

The rise of the presbyterian dissenting churches cannot be seen as the product of a burning "nationalist" resentment with a "national" church under foreign control. The dissenters were not being schismatic over nationhood, not even indirectly. Schisms were over power and control

---

[29]M. Hutchison, *The Reformed Presbyterian Church in Scotland: Its Origins and History 1660-1876* (1893, Paisley), pp. 194-201.
[30]C.G. Brown, *The Social History of Religion*, pp. 136-141.
[31]H.J. Meikle, *Scotland and the French Revolution* (1912, London).

295

within Scotland, especially over control of the parish state, over church resources, and over thwarted democratic ambition within the congregation. They were over who paid for and chose the minister, about church fees and taxes, and about access to a seat in a parish church. Money, class and power were at the root of the rapidly changing ecclesiastical situation in Scotland between the 1730s and the 1850s – just as they were in the rest of Britain.

The Disruption was one example of the way in which social and economic change was focussing protest and resentment into religion. It illustrates how presbyterianism could not sustain a national identity because it was constantly being re-shaped from 1733 onwards by the turbulence of evolving class identities. Religious identities and institutions were constantly realigning as a result of pressure from a people under stress from intensifying capitalism in agriculture and manufacturing, and by the erosion of custom and tradition. People as often as not took their protest with changing patterns of power to the church – in protests over who chose the minister, the level of exorbitant pew rents, the erosion of traditional customs in worship, and over the perceived decline in congregational democracy. Presbyterianism in the eighteenth and nineteenth centuries was a battlefield for class issues, but never in any consistent way for nationalist ones. Religion divided Scots – it never united them.

VI

Relatively few scholars of ecclesiastical impartiality would seriously argue that religion has played a significant role in shaping national consciousness in twentieth-century Scotland. Basically, Scotland has been secularising so rapidly since 1900 that the nation has failed to retain that national piety that has characterised Ireland, Poland or the ethnic-national groups of eastern Europe. Church-going was declining rapidly by 1914, and the membership of Protestant churches was in a gradual fall from 1905 that was to accelerate sharply from the late 1950s down to the present.[32] In Scotland unlike many European nations and regions, thwarted nationhood

---

[32] C.G. Brown, "Religion and Secularisation", in A. Dickson and J.H. Treble (eds.), *People and Society in Modern Scotland, vol. 3, 1914 to the Present* (1992, John Donald, Edinburgh), 48-79.

has not been a bulwark for the churches during this century.[33] At the same time, the division of Scotland between Protestant and Catholic sharpened in the first half of the twentieth century, and with it destroyed any hope that religion could act as a unifier of the Scots people. More profoundly, it can be argued that this sectarianism has so poisoned the culture of Scotland that – irrespective of declining church-going and adherence – it has postponed indefinitely the unity of Scots behind a nationalist banner.

The sectarianism between Protestant and Catholic that arose in the towns and cities of depressed central Scotland in the 1920s and 1930s was of some ferocity. For Protestants, a national identity of sorts was forged in a framework borrowed from the seventeenth century but given relevance by the division of Ireland in the early 1920s. Religion was at the heart of Protestant intellectualising about Scottish national identity – expressed perhaps as never before or since in a racial, ethnic tenor akin to modern Bosnia, Serbia and Croatia. From the senior law officers of Scotland and the Church of Scotland's national General Assembly down to young thugs on the streets, hatred of the Irish-descended Catholic community of central Scotland was providing a focus. A committee of the Church of Scotland General Assembly stated in 1923:

> "[Irish Catholics] cannot be assimilated and absorbed into the Scottish race. They remain a people by themselves, segregated by reason of their race, their customs, their traditions, and above all, by their loyalty to their Church, and gradually and inevitably [they are] dividing Scotland, racially, socially and ecclesiastically... [We fear] the loss of the Scottish race to civilisation."[34]

This sharpened sectarian national identity was being upheld on the streets of Glasgow by the Protestant Billy Boys gang, and by Protestant electors voting for sectarian parties at municipal elections in the 1930s. Like outbursts about the English in the 1840s, these outbursts about the Catholic Irish occurred in part because presbyterianism was in internal crisis. The presbyterian churches in the inter-war period were highly conscious of declining attendance, falling income, and the loss in 1929 of

---

[33]D. Martin, *A General Theory of Secularisation* (1978, Basil Blackwell, Oxford).
[34]*Reports of the Schemes of the Church of Scotland, 1923*, pp. 750-61.

much of the influence they had previously exercised in education and poor relief. In the same year, the two main presbyterian churches united in a prelude to ecclesiastical contraction. In this context, "Irish" Catholics became an easy target for presbyterian insecurity.

The shift which occurred in Scottish political ideology in the 1920s and 1930s has remained – though a little dimmed – through until today. Scottish popular culture became divided by the polarities of Northern Ireland – of Protestant loyalist versus Catholic republican. This has left much of Scottish identity in hock to an overseas agenda. Though much work on sectarianism in Scotland has suggested that it has diminished since the 1940s,[35] there is an important though unfashionable school of thought that the ethnic-religious identities of Protestant and Catholic in contemporary Scotland are dividing the nation, national identity and nationalism. Sectarianism is increasingly focussed for the working classes on the football rivalry of the Glasgow clubs of Rangers and Celtic.[36] Though the predominantly-Protestant Rangers supporters identify themselves as "patriotic Scots", their hostility to their predominantly-Catholic Celtic opponents makes them ardently "Unionist" in Ulster terms, and consequently "British" in the same way as Ulster loyalists. Celtic supporters, on the other hand, identify strongly with Irish republicanism but poorly with symbols of Scottish patriotism. This division, formerly limited to Glasgow and surrounding industrial towns, has become in recent decades Scotland-wide, with supporters of the two clubs travelling from all parts. In a very real sense, Rangers and Celtic are more vital for Scottish identities than the Scottish international soccer team. Every Saturday during the football season, the supporters articulate in their chants the dominant agenda which paralyses a single Scottish nationhood – an Irish agenda which makes Protestant patriotic Scots feel British and Catholic unpatriotic Scots feel Irish.

That is the vicious circle which throttles the emergence of a Scottish national consensus so favoured by nationalist intellectuals. It was brought home very forcibly in the Monklands parliamentary by-election of 1994. This community to the east of Glasgow has been since the 1830s bitterly

---

[35] S. Bruce, *No Pope of Rome: Anti-Catholicism in Modern Scotland* (1985, Mainstream, Edinburgh); T. Gallagher, *Glasgow: The Uneasy Peace* (1987, Manchester University Press, Manchester).
[36] J. Bradley, *Ethnic and Religious Identities in Modern Scotland* (1995, Avebury, Aldershot). See also B. Murray, *The Old Firm: Sectarianism, Sport and Society in Scotland* (1984, John Donald, Edinburgh).

divided between Protestant and Catholic, and the election campaign degenerated into a sectarian squabble between Catholics (who voted overwhelmingly Labour) and Protestants (who voted overwhelmingly for the Scottish National Party). Though Labour narrowly won (Helen Liddell being elected MP), the marginalisation of the SNP message of "Independence within Europe" into a sectarian dispute is indicative of the way in which religion confounds modern Scottish identity. For all its industrial decline, the West of Scotland where the by-election occurred is still the heart of the country, and a national identity must succeed there if Scotland is to feel in any sense "united".

VII

Militant presbyterianism supported the Hanovarians in the eighteenth century, the British Empire in the nineteenth century, and Union with England in the twentieth century. Religious identity in post-Union Scotland has not been a national identity but a sectarian identity. Ecclesiastical disputation has been endemic, representing regional, class and ethnic schisms. In this way, religion has divided Scotland *from* a national identity, and continues to do so despite secularisation.

Those historians who seek evidence of nationalist sentiments in ecclesiastical affairs after 1707 will not find a concerted, consistent and unifying nationalist creed. What they will find in the eighteenth and nineteenth centuries are mere outbursts of frustration with Westminster failure to grant victory to one Scottish class interest or another. In the twentieth century, they will find sectarian dispute between Protestant and Catholic. That rivalry has not disappeared, but has emerged as a blockage to the rise of both the S.N.P. and consensus nationalism. To win over militant Protestants, nationalists must show that breaching the Union with England has nothing to do with breaching Northern Ireland's union with Britain. And to win over Catholics, nationalists must be convinced that a new Scottish state will be a safe home for religious minorities. In this regard, it might have been a symbolic mistake in 1988 to name the "Claim of Right", the founding document of a consensual nationalist movement, after two earlier protests of Scottish presbyterians wishing to preserve "true Protestant religion" in Scotland.

The Orthodox and the Lutherans in Finland
1809-1923

Mika Nokelainen

In 1809 Finland, the eastern province of Lutheran Sweden, was incorporated into Russia, a country confessing the Orthodox religion. Nowadays the Orthodox church of Finland does not play any significant role in the policy of Finland but a hundred years ago the situation was different. From the end of the nineteenth century up to Finland's declaration of independence in 1917, the Orthodox church in Finland played an important role in the politics of the Czar of Russia.

This article will be divided into two main sections. The first deals with Russian policy in Finland from its annexation in 1809 to the end of the Russian empire, which forms the basis for the next section where I consider the question of Russian garrison churches during the early years of Finland's independence.

On the incorporation of Finland into Russia, Czar Alexander I of Russia summoned the Diet in the city of Porvoo in 1809. From this time Finland was united with Russia only through the person of the monarch. In his declaration Alexander I promised to maintain constitutional law and the privileges of the different estates recognised under the reign of Sweden. The Czar also promised to maintain the Lutheran religion in Finland.

Finnish autonomy meant that Finland really was an enclave within Russia. For example, Russians had no automatic right to Finnish citizenship and there were customs at the frontier between Finland and Russia.[1]

Alexander's intention was to keep the Finns peaceful. Winning their hearts by making some concessions would ensure that they would not rise against their monarch. This was also a policy directed to other European sovereigns to assure them, that while he was an autocrat he nevertheless followed a tolerant policy in territories which he had conquered.[2]

---

[1] Jutikkala & Pirinen 1962, 178-193; Seton-Watson 1967, 113-115.
[2] Seton-Watson 1967, 142-198; Jussila 1986, 207-214.

Alexander I died in 1825. His successor was his brother Nicholas I, an exacting autocrat who believed in rigorous discipline and order. In addition, he wanted to protect Russia from the influence of western countries. Sending his troops to different parts of Europe, he helped other European sovereigns to put down rebellions, which earned him the sobriquet "the gendarme of Europe".

Nicholas I gave a sovereign pledge to maintain autonomy in Finland. There was hope in Finland that the Czar would summon the Diet, but he never did so and Finland was ruled by officials. Nicholas I also pursued a strict censorship policy against Universities and newspapers. The Lutheran church in Finland co-operated with this task stressing loyalty and obedience to God and the Russian authorities.[3]

Nicholas I died in 1855 and was succeeded by his son Alexander II. His policy was much more tolerant than his father's. For example, he abolished serfdom in Russia. Nevertheless he refused to share power.

His reign was most remarkable for the Finns. He eventually summoned the Diet and gave Finns a currency of their own. Trade and shipping was developed and the position of Finnish improved because of special language legislation. Alexander II was murdered by a revolutionary group in 1881.[4]

Alexander II's successor was Alexander III, whose reign was a time of glory in Russia. The economy of the country grew, its infrastructure was developed, factories were built and the army was built up. It was also a time of colonial expansion. Russia, like the other Great Powers in Europe, conquered new colonies, for example in Central Asia and incorporated them into Russia.

Alexander III's Finnish policy was quite tolerant at the beginning of his reign, but the severe rivalry between the great powers forced a change. To come off victorious in this game Russia had to be strongly unified. There were so-called panslavic groups in Russia demanding the creation of a common Russian nationality. The symbol of this nationality was the Russian language and the Orthodox religion. The panslavic groups doubted whether the north-west borderland would be loyal to the mother country. They disliked any kind of fennomanic movement in Finland and tried to put them down.

---

[3]Jutikkala & Pirinen 1962, 194-211; Seton-Watson 1967, 199-226; Jussila 1986, 214-235. See also Lincoln 1978.

[4]Jutikkala & Pirinen 1962, 211-217; Seton-Watson 1967, 415; Jussila 1986, 235-256.

Another reason to tighten policy was that there were many revolutionary groups in Russia demanding a constitutional system of government. Russia felt obliged to tighten its grip on the peripheral areas such as Poland, the Ukraine, the Baltic Countries and Finland.[5]

Alexander III died in 1894. The new and the last Czar of Russia, Nicholas II was only 26 years old – Like his predecessors he embraced autocracy. He soon proved to be a weak Czar in that his advisers, the minister of interior and the police authorities, wielded the real power in Russia. These authorities demanded that the special regulations in Finland must be restricted which brought many administrative and legislative changes in Finland after 1891.

An example of this kind of change is the so-called Manifesto of February 1899 in which the Finnish legislative procedure was radically modified. The Finns considered these actions an oppressive policy because in their opinion they violated Finnish constitutional law. The period from 1899 to 1905 and from 1907 to 1917 came to be known as The Years of oppression, a term generally used by historians since.

The Russian Central Administration in St. Petersburg and the Finns were looking at the matter from different viewpoints. The Central Administration tried to integrate the various territories of the State, while from the Finns' viewpoint the intention was the russification of Finland.[6]

We might well wonder, whether the orthodox had something to do with these political questions in Finland. The answer is that they did. I will deal next with one action of the orthodox during the Years of oppression and the reputation they acquired as a result.

Russification was not only administrative or legislative by nature. Cultural questions including the Orthodox religion especially were also very important. There were approximately 60,000 Orthodox believers in Finland but they had no diocese of their own. Russification policy sought to strengthen the position of orthodoxy in Finland. After secret preparations, an Orthodox diocese was founded in 1892.[7]

The first archbishop, Antonij, did not agree with severe russianization, as Russian authorities supposed he would; however the situation changed after his reign. The new archbishop, Nikolaj, was

---

[5]Jutikkala & Pirinen 1962, 224-226; Seton-Watson 1967, 460-546; Luntinen 1986a, 257-280.
[6]Jutikkala & Pirinen 1962, 227- 259; Seton-Watson 1967, 547-597; Luntinen 1986b, 281-309. See also Jussila 1977.
[7]Setälä 1966, 6-7; Seton-Watson 1967, 485-505; Koukkunen 1977, 208-219.

closely associated with the governor-general, N. Bobrikov, the highest representative of the Czar in Finland.[8]

Karelia, the border area between Russia and south-east Finland, was the area where the major part of Orthodox Finns lived. The nationality of the Karelians was a controversial question. The Russians thought they were Russian because of their religion and because their language was being influenced by Russian, whereas the Finns considered the Karelians as a part of the Finno-Ugric tribes. Wanting to strengthen Russian identity in Karelia, Russian administrators built schools where the Russian language and orthodox religion were taught. A lot of Orthodox churches were also built in the cities which had Russian military congregations.[9]

The defeat in The Russo-Japanese war and the affect of the general strike in Finland in 1905 caused the russification policy to be more lenient. But soon there were conflicts again in Karelia. In 1907 the special society for russification and supporting the Orthodox religion in Karelia was founded. The rivalry was severe in Karelia. For example, the Russian schools enticed pupils with free clothes and sweets. The period from 1907 to 1917 was one of continuous strife.[10]

Finland became independent in 1917 in the aftermath of the October revolution. The young state had to create its own internal and foreign policy. That meant Finland did not want to be dependent on Russia either politically or culturally.[11]

The years of oppression had aroused provocative and violent resistance in Finland. Many Finns considered the Orthodox as representatives of Russia and as strange and harmful to Finnish culture and there was even hostility against them in Finland. The Orthodox church were called the "Russki church", a name full of antagonism and contempt.[12]

The bad reputation of the Orthodox increased during the years of oppression, provoking demonstrations against them. Some nationalist Finnish groups even damaged Orthodox church buildings and spat on Orthodox clergymen in the street. Not all action, however, was as radical

---

[8]Koukkunen 1977, 220-257; Koukkunen 1982, 11-12; Luntinen 1985b, 152-153.
[9]Luntinen 1985b, 125-159.
[10]Seton-Watson 1967, 663-669; Koukkunen 1982, 12-14; Luntinen 1985a, 206-220; Luntinen 1985b, 142-159; Sihvo 1994, 265-291.
[11]Jutikkala & Pirinen 1962, 227-259; Luntinen 1992, 160-162; Piilonen 1992, 134-139.
[12]The name is still heard nowadays but not with the same implication.

as this. We might also ask, what was the real target of these demonstrations?

We will now consider the question of Russian garrison churches in Finland and especially the debate about church in Hämeenlinna.

The Russian garrison churches in Finland

Finland's army was wholly organised by the Russian authorities and there were only a few Finnish soldiers in Finland. Since 1905 this army was wholly made up of Russian troops. During the time of autonomy the number of Russian troops in Finland varied between 55,000 and 125,000.[13]

The Orthodox religion and rituals played an important role in the Russian army. Orthodox church buildings were thus built in all the bigger cities where there were military forces, mainly for their needs. Sometimes these churches were used both by civilian and military people. There were Russian garrison churches in such places as Helsinki, Tuusula, Tammisaari, Hämeenlinna, Lahti, Kotka, Mikkeli, Viipuri, Lappeenranta, Tornio and Oulu.[14]

The intentions in building these churches were not simply religious. Governor-general N. Bobrikov noted that people in Finland associated nationality with religion, considering Lutheranism as Finnishness, Orthodoxy as Russianism and Catholicism as Polishness. During Bobrikov's governship (1898-1904) more than ten churches were built in order to strengthen russification in Finland.[15]

After the Finnish revolution in 1918, Russian troops were removed from Finland and the property of the Russian army, including garrison churches were confiscated by Finnish State.[16]

The Orthodox garrison congregations were organized and ruled by the Russian military authorities, not by the Finnish Orthodox diocese so that the Orthodox church of Finland had no legal right to own them.[17]

---

[13]Närhi 1985, 161-162, 180.
[14]VA SenA OPMA KD 6/416 1918 Hengellinen konsistori to Senate 29.7.1918.; VA VNA OPMA Ee 1Luettelo Sotasaaliskeskusosaston hallussa olevista entisistä venäläisistä sotilaskirkoista 26.5.1919; Knapas 1976, 30-31.
[15]Polvinen 1988, 182-184.
[16]VA VNA OPMA Ee 1 Luettelo Sotasaaliskeskusosaston hallussa olevista entisistä venäläisistä sotilaskirkoista 26.5.1919; See also Upton 1980.
[17]AK 15/5.8.1918 Nykyajan huolia kirkkokunnassamme; Koukkunen 1978, 17; Pispala

However, the Finnish government was asked by the General Assembly of the Finnish orthodox church to give those garrison churches used by civilians to local Orthodox parishes.[18] This was wishful thinking. The Ministry of Defence announced that Finnish troops would need these garrison churches and they would become Lutheran. The Ministry however promised to return the fittings because they had been donated by private persons. The administration of the Finnish Orthodox church was defined by the statute of 26.11.1918. The orthodox church was allowed to own all the property which had been in its possession during the autonomous period, but there was a special section in which stated that garrison churches belonged to the Finnish State.[19]

The destiny of garrison churches and conflicts between Finnish soldiers and Orthodox monasteries during the Finnish revolution in 1918 caused anxiety among the Orthodox in Finland. Some of them complained that the Finnish State persecuted them. The nationalist wing of Finnish orthodoxy – a section who wanted to create a national Finnish orthodox church with a Finnish spoken service and education – tried to calm these people. They denied that there had been any persecution of the Orthodox in Finland. They also explained that Lutherans had no reason to persecute them because Lutherans and Orthodox fought together against the Red Guard and Russian troops in the Finnish revolution.[20]

The intention of making all the Orthodox in Finland sure that they were Finnish, not Russian is apparent. The national wing of the church was between the devil and the deep blue sea. They had to assure the government that they wanted to nationalize the Orthodox church. On the other hand they had to get all the orthodox in Finland to understand that despite their Orthodox religion they were totally Finnish and had to be loyal to the Finnish government.

As we have noticed, garrison churches were built to russianize Finland. What did the Lutherans think about these church buildings at the beginning of Finland's independence? Let us take an example from Hämeenlinna.

1984, 24-25.
[18] VA SenA OPMA KD 6/416 1918 Hengellinen konsistori to Senate 29.7.1918.
[19] VA SenA OPMA KD 6/416 1918 SotT to Senate 26.9.1917; VA SenA OPMA KD 6/416 1918 Kirkollishallitus to OPM 6.11.1920; As. kok. 185/26.11.1918, § 3.
[20] AK 15/5.8.1918 Nykyajan huolia kirkkokunnassamme.

"What to do with the old Russian garrison church in Hämeenlinna?"

In the Finnish revolution of 1918 the Red Guard conquered Hämeenlinna. German troops bombed the town and freed it in 26.4.1918.[21] There were two Orthodox churches in Hämeenlinna. One was used by Orthodox civilians but the other was a Russian garrison church built by governor-general Bobrikov. After the revolution people in Hämeenlinna were very frustrated by all kinds of russianism, both tsarist and socialist.

A conservative newspaper *Hämeenlinnan Sanomat (HäSa)* wrote an article concerning the old garrison church in Hämeenlinna. The *HäSa* was ashamed that the first thing which the Germans (inhabitants of an old state with a splendid cultural history, as it was said in the *HäSa*) had to see was an eastern ruin. In the newspaper's opinion this church was in bad condition and it made the atmosphere of the city too eastern. Finally *HäSa* asked its readers to suggest what to do with this building.[22]

HäSa got a lot of feedback. Most writers demanded the demolition of the building. Some people wanted to substitute the church for the monument in honour of the Finnish civil war. A pen name "Soldier" wanted to make this church Lutheran because there would be Finnish troops in Hämeenlinna. Other suggestions were a nursery school, a market hall, a theater and a library. Not one writer demanded keeping this church unchanged. [23]

The most radical newspaper article was written by J.D. Möller, who considered Orthodoxy a heathen religion. He demanded that all the temples of paganism in Finland must be destroyed and the children of pagans must learn biblical christianity.[24]

The organ of the Orthodox church in Finland *Aamun Koitto (AK)* soon responded. AK suspected that some communists, who were impudent enough to use christian phrases in order to destroy religion, were behind these opinions. *AK* continued that no one had any right to persecute the Orthodox in Finland because the government had ratified their position in

---

[21] Koskimies 1966, 602-609.
[22] HäSa 8/12.1.1919 Mitä tehdään Hämeenlinnan venäläisellä varuskuntakirkolla; SLH 5 1988, 161.
[23] HäSa 9/14.1.1919 Mitä tehdään Hämeenlinnan venäläisellä sotilaskirkolla?; HäSa 10/15.1.1919 Mitä tehdään Hämeenlinnan venäläisellä sotilaskirkolla?; HäSa 11/16.1.1919 Mitä tehdään Hämeenlinnan venäläisellä sotilaskirkolla; Häsa 14/19.1.1919 Mitä tehdään Hämeenlinnan venäläisellä sotilaskirkolla?
[24] HäSa 10/15.1.1919 Mitä tehdään Hämeenlinnan venäläisellä sotilaskirkolla?

a statute in 1918. Moreover, the Orthodox fought together with Lutherans for Finnish independence. Finally *AK* mentioned that there were interests in incorporating Orthodox East Karelia, the territory across the eastern frontier, to Finland.[25] All the bourgeois parties of Finland were interested in annexing this territory, because Finland would thereby secure a shorter and more easily defensible border in the east.[26]

It should be obvious that no one can force them to give up their old religion, the AK continued, and demanded that some organ of the Finnish Lutheran church must explain what kind of attitude the öreal lutheran believerö take toward the orthodox in Finland.[27]

The *HäSa* answered this immediately. It wrote that people in Hämeenlinna do not hate the Orthodox but the political reasons for building this church. J.D. Möller's article was only his own opinion with no common support and, in addition, the Lutheran priests in Hämeenlinna disapproved strongly of his article.[28]

A conservative Minister and statesman, E. N. Setälä, also criticized this kind of religious intolerance. Also pointing to the territorial plans.[29] Setälä probably did not want make trans-Karelians afraid to incorporate in Finland.

Soon an unofficial organ of the Finnish Lutheran church the *Kotimaa* also wrote a general article concernig the history and contemporary position of the Orthodox church in Finland. The *Kotimaa* wrote that the Orthodox church had a long and remarkable history in Finland. Relations between two Churches had been good exclusive of the russianification period. *Kotimaa* confessed that while the Orthodox church was a very small but an equal national church with the Lutheran church in Finland.[30] The message was clear; the Lutheran church at least officially dissociated itself from the negative policy directed towards the Orthodox. This was natural because many leaders of the Lutheran church were high-rated politicians. It was not unusual at all for church policy to follow State policy in Finland.[31]

---

[25]AK 3/5.2.1919 Uskonnon vainoamiskiihko vapaassa Suomessa.
[26]Jutikkala & Pirinen 1962, 264.
[27]AK 3/5.2.1919 Uskonnon vainoamiskiihko vapaassa Suomessa.
[28]HäSa 34/12.2.1919 Hämeenlinnan venäläinen sotilaskirkko.
[29]US 46/23.2.1919 Ankarasti paheksittavaa suvaitsemattomuutta.
[30]Kmaa 23/21.3.1919 Luterilainen kirkkokunta ja kreikkalaiskatolinen kirkko Suomessa.
[31]See for example Lauha 1990, passim; Lauha 1993, passim.

An Orthodox priest, M. Michailov, and a Lutheran, B. Boxström, – both Karelian – also commented on this debate. They saw the relations between two churches as good and criticized J.D. Möller's desire to convert the Orthodox.[32]

This was the end of this debate. In 1921 the Ministry of Education handed the garrison church own to the city of Hämeenlinna. The church was changed into a library. A condition was that the eastern facade of the church had to be changed.[33] The other garrison churches were either pulled down or put to other uses. Churches in Suomenlinna (Helsinki), Lappeenranta, Viipuri, Kouvola and Mikkeli were made Lutheran. The church in Tammisaari was handed over to the prison administration and the church of Tornio was made a museum.[34]

Epilogue

From the beginning of the 20th century the Orthodox church in Finland was clearly divided into two main sections. The national group wanted to create a nationally reliable Finnish Orthodox Church. The other group consisted mainly of Russian emigrants, pastors, both ecclesiastical and State administrators, shopkeepers, soldiers, and so on, who did not believe in bolshevist administration in Russia. They were convinced that the monarchy would return to Russia and Finland would lose its independence, so that they disapproved of any attempts to create a national Orthodox church in Finland.

Naturally the government of independent Finland supported the national wing of the Orthodox church. The Finnish governments were anxious about the Russian sector of the Orthodox church because of their connections with Russia.

---

[32]AK 8/20.4.1919 Kreikkalaiskatolisten asema Suomessa luterilaisten lausuntojen mukaan.
[33]VA RHA Hl 1 OPM to YrY 27.9.1921.
[34]VA RHA Hl 1 SotT to Suomenlinnan komendantti 19.12.1919; Knapas 1976, 35-37; Koukkunen 1977, 61-63; VA VNA OPMA Ee 1 Luettelo venäläisistä sotilaskirkoista, jotka ovat luovutetut YrY:lle 8.3.1922; VA VNA OPMA Ee 1 Läänin Rakennus-Konttori Wiipurissa to YrY 23.9.1919; VA RHA Ee 1 Sotilasrakennusten intendentti to YrY 3.2.1922; VA VNA OPMA Ee 1 SotT to YrY 10.9.1919; VA RHA Hl 2 OPM to YrY 20.6.1922; VA RHA Ee 1 VN YrY:lle 7.10.1924; VA RHA Ee1 Sotilasrakennusten intendentti to YrY 18.10.1921; VA VNA OPMA Ee 1 Luettelo venäläisistä sotilaskirkoista jotka ovat luovutetut Yleisten rakennusten Ylihallituksen käyttöön 8.3.1922; VA RHA Hl 3 Oulun läänin rakennuskonttorin esimies to architect G. Sundelinille 545/12.10.1923; VA RHA Hl 3 OPM to YrY 707/ 26.2.1925; Koukkunen 1977, 61-67.

The nationalist wing got the upper hand over the Russians. It meant that the Russian Arcbishop Serafim and the other Russian leaders of the church were removed and nationalists took their place. Moreover, the Orthodox church in Finland tried to achieve autocephalism but this effort failed. It then separated from the Russian Orthodox church, joining the ecumenical patriarchate of Constantinople in 1923.[35]

Summary

Finland was incorporated into Russia in 1809. At the outset the policies of the Czar concerning Finland were quite tolerant. At the end of the 1880s that policy changed because of the rising panslavic ideas in Russia. The central administration of Russia tried to russianize Finland in order to strenghten the unity of the Russian empire. The Orthodox church in Finland also took part in this work, acquiring a bad reputation.

The Russian garrison churches were built in Finland in order to russianize Finland. Immediately after Finnish independence they were confiscated and put to other use. People in Finland hated these churches because of their political significance. The debate concerning the garrison church in Hämeenlinna shows that the question of Orthodoxy in Finland was more political than religious.

Sources

National archive of Finland, Helsinki	VA
Archive of the Senate	SenA
Archive of the Ministry of Education	OPMA
Anomus- ja valitusdiaarien asiakirjat	1918AD
Kirjediaarien asiakirjat	1918KD
Diarioimattomat asiakirjat 1918-1925	Ee 1
Archive of the National Building Board	RHA/YrY
Sotasaalistalletuskeskuksen Uudenmaan Turun,	
Viipurin ja Hämeen piirin asiakirjoja 1918-1927	Hl 1-3

---

[35] Jutikkala & Pirinen 1962, 261-285; Setälä 1966, passim; Koukkunen 1982, passim.

Code of Statutes of Finland 1918

Journals and periodicals

Aamun Koitto 1918-1919	AK
Hämeenlinnan Sanomat 1919	HäSa
Kotimaa 1919	
Ortodoksia 1976	
Uusi Suomi 1919	US

Literature

Jussila, Osmo
1977 Nationalism and revolution: political dividing lines in the Grand Duchy of Finland during the last year of Russian rule. Scandinavian journal of history 1977:2. Stockholm.
1986 Konservatiivinen imperiumi. -Venäjän ja Neuvostoliiton historia. Keuruu.

Jutikkala, Eino & Pirinen, Kauko
1962 A History of Finland. London.

Knapas, Rainer
1976 Ortodoksiset sotilaskirkot. Summary: Orthodox Garrison churches in Finland. -Ortodoksia 25.

Koskimies, Y. S.
1966 Hämeenlinnan kaupungin historia 1875-1944. Hämeenlinna.

Koukkunen, Heikki
1977a Suomen valtiovalta ja kreikkalaiskatoliset 1881-1887. Summary: The Finnish Authorities and the Greek Orthodox 1881-1897. Diss. Publications of the University of Joensuu. Series A No 7. Joensuu.

1977b　Helsingin ortodoksinen seurakunta 1827-1977. Pieksämäki.
1982　Tuiskua ja tyventä. Suomen ortodoksinen kirkko 1918-1977. Pieksämäki.

Lauha, Aila
1990　Suomen kirkon ulkomaansuhteet ja ekumeeninen osallistuminen 1917-1922. Zusammenfassung: Die auswärtigen Beziehungen der finnischen Kirche und das ökumenische Engagement in den Jahren 1917-1922. Diss. SKHST 150. Jyväskylä.
1993　Suomen kirkon kansainväliset suhteet 1923-1925. Zusammenfassung: Die internationalen Beziehungen der finnischen Kirche 1923-1925. SKHST 159. Jyväskylä.

Lincoln, W. Bruce
1989　Nicholas I. Emperor and autocrat of All the Russias. Illinois.

Luntinen, Pertti
1985a　F.A. Seyn. A political Biography of a Tsarist Imperialist as Administrator of Finland. Studia Historica 19. Jyväskylä.
1985b　Karjalaiset suomalaisuuden ja venäläisyyden rajalla. – Venäläiset Suomessa 1809-1917. Ed. Pauli Kurkinen. Historiallinen arkisto 83. Huhmari.
1986a　Keisarikunta mahtavimmillaan. –Venäjän ja Neuvostoliiton historia. Keuruu.
1986b　Vanhan Venäjän viimeiset rauhanvuodet. –Venäjän ja Neuvostoliitonhistoria. Keuruu.
1992　Autonomian vahvistamisyritys. –Itsenäistymisen vuodet 1917-1920. 1. Helsinki.
1995　Venäjän valtakunnan muotoutuminen. Alue, asukkaat, valtiojärjestys.Oppimateriaaleja 1947. Lahti.

Närhi, Matti
1985　Venäläiset joukot Suomessa autonomian aikana. – Venäläiset Suomessa 1809-1917. Ed. Pauli Kurkinen. Historiallinen arkisto 83. Huhmari.

Piilonen, Juhani
1992   Sisäinen rakennustyö. Itsenäistymisen vuodet 1917-1920. 3. Helsinki.

Pispala, Elisa
1984   Ortodoksisen kirkkohallinnon uudistus Suomessa 1883-1917. Licensiates dissertation.

Polvinen, Tuomo
1988   Riket och gränsmarken. N. I. Bobrikov, Finlands generalguvernör 1898-1904. Borgå.

Purmonen, Veikko
1981   Orthodoxy in Finland. Past and present. Pieksämäki.

Seton-Watson, Hugh
1967   The Russian Empire. Oxford University Press.

Setälä, Voitto
1966   Kansallisen ortodoksisen kirkkokunnan perustamiskysymys Suomen politiikassa 1917-1924. Summary: The Establishment of the National Orthodox Church in Finnish Politics During Years 1917-1925. Diss. Porvoo.

Sihvo, Hannes
1994   Vanhasta Suomesta autonomian ajan Karjalaan. -Karjalan kansan historia. Porvoo.

SLH 5
1985   Suomen lehdistön historia 5. Jyväskylä.

Upton, Anthony
1980   The Finnish Revolution 1917-1918. Minneapolis.

Foreign relations for nationalistic goals

The activity of Finnish theologians abroad during the years of russification between 1908-1914

Aila Lauha

Experience from the the First Period of Russification

The last years of the Russian empire crushed a great many utopias in Finland. It became clearer and clearer that the national interest of the Finns – Finnish language, culture and autonomy – could not develop satisfactorily under Russian rule. The changes in domestic policy in Russia, most of all the rise of Pan-Slavist tendencies, as well as the strained international situation in Europe, made the Russian government tighten its control over the border areas which had been incorporated into the Empire. Most of all the Russian authorities tried to be aware of any nationalistic movements appearing in those areas.[1]

This tightening of administration was extended to Finland in the 1890's. The legislative or administrative reforms started at that time concerned mostly the right of the Finns to preserve their own internal legislation and to retain and to develop the position of the Finnish language. The intention of the Russian government was to absorb Finland into the great mother country. The first implementation of this policy was the February Manifesto in 1899 which started the First Period of Russification (1899-1905). In Finnish historiography this period is generally called the First Period of Oppression.[2]

These changes in Russian policy towards Finland forced the Finns to protect their rights. It was, however, difficult to reach unanimity as to the methods and tactics in this battle for Finnish national identity. Some political groups believed that the wisest method was to emphasize the Finns' absolute loyalty. These groups were ready even to make some minor con-

---

[1] Seton-Watson 1967, 445-459, 485-498; Jutikkala-Pirinen 1984, 197-201; Hobsbawm 1990, 86-87, 106.
[2] Seton-Watson 1967, 415-416, 498-499; Paasivirta 1978, 306-315, 322-328; Jussila 1979, 28-30; Jutikkala & Pirinen 1984, 202-213; Paasivirta 1988, 14-15.

cessions to the Russians in their internal politics. This way of thinking in Finnish politics is called the policy of submissiveness.

Another group of Finns preferred a policy of passive resistance. Such resistance manifested itself mostly in Finnish internal affairs. However, it also had an international character; in fact, the resistance party wanted to make the crisis between Finland and Russia into an international question by spreading information and nationalistic propaganda abroad. The key role in this action was played by the Finnish intelligentsia, who had always had foreign contacts in the fields of the arts and sciences. Through these contacts the Finns tried to make the Finnish point of view known abroad; thus they served the Finnish struggle for the country's autonomy.[3]

Because the Lutheran Church of Finland during these years had as its members 98% of Finnish population, it was then inevitable that the political controversies infiltrated into the church as well. Most leaders and pastors of the Lutheran church, in regard to the oppression policy of Russia, preferred to be as cautious as possible. The four bishops and most of all Archbishop Gustaf Johansson intended to keep the Church untouched and to preserve its ability to act. They feared that in the case of any controversy the Russian Orthodox Church would try to weaken the position of the Lutheran confession in Finland. This had already happened in some Baltic areas.[4]

Besides their tactical goals, the bishops also held some theological points of view leading to the same conclusion. Many bishops and pastors found it incorrect to oppose the legal government, the Sovereign who had received his authority from God himself. Even Martin Luther had forbidden this in his texts, they reminded their parishioners.[5]

In spite of this the church also included individuals sympathetic to the party of passive resistance. Nevertheless, public opinion saw the entire church as representing the policy of submissiveness. Especially the young educated generation criticized the church leaders very sharply.

In doing research on Finnish church history, one finds plenty of evidence of the extreme cautiousness of the Lutheran Church of Finland in the

---

[3] Seton-Watson 1967, 499; Paasivirta 1978, 326-333.
[4] Amburger 1961, 100-103; Murtorinne 1964, 42-46, 48-49, 323; Kahle 1982, 51-52; Lauha 1990, 27-29.
[5] Murtorinne 1964, 324-327; Lauha 1990, 30-31, 48-49. On the tense relations between the Lutherans and the Orthodox Church of Russia see Koukkunen 1977, 33-35, 40-42, 170-171, 189-192; Heikkilä 1985, 353-369, 384-389, 400-411.

years of oppression. It is more difficult to find documents on activities which could be called resistance.[6]

It is therefore important to pay attention to theologians who, just as many other well-educated Finns did during the First Period of Russification, tried to carry out passive resistance by using their foreign contacts. I shall give two examples of this activity.

Among the bishops, the Bishop of Porvoo, Herman Råbergh[7], provided most of the information on Finland abroad. His target country was mainly Sweden, and the most important Swedish recipient of these communications was the Bishop of Visby, K. H. G. von Schéele[8]. It was, in fact, through this correspondence between Råbergh and von Schéele that the Finnish Church became involved with the international Lutheran cooperation organization AELK (Allgemeine Evangelisch-Lutherische Konferenz) in 1901. The international meetings of AELK opened the doors for the Finnish Church not only to Scandinavian sister churches but also to the less well-known German "Landeskirchen" and even to American Lutheranism.[9]

The emphasis on Lutheran identity evoked a natural response in the Finnish Church and its revivalist movements, not least for doctrinal reasons. However, it became especially important at the time when the activities of the Orthodox Church seemed to threaten the ruling position of the Lutheran Church.[10]

The foreign contacts of Finnish theologians were not limited only to Lutheranism. The Church of Finland had since the middle of the 19th century been enriched by some international Christian movements which mostly had their origin in Anglo-Saxon Christianity, such as the YMCA, the YWCA and the international missionary movement. Many of these movements had an ecumenical or rather a pre-ecumenical character. Just at the turn of the century many of these organisations extended their ac-

---

[6]Murtorinne 1964, 134-137 153-164, 323-327; Paasivirta 1978, 331-332, 343; Mustakallio, 1983, 33-37; Heikkilä 1985, 294-298.
[7]Herman Råbergh (1838-1920) was Professor of Ecclesiastical History at the University of Helsinki between 1872-1892 and Bishop of Porvoo in the years 1892-1920. On Råbergh's life and theology see Murtorinne 1964, 123-159, 176-177 and 1988, 148-158.
[8]Knut Herman Gezelius von Schéele (1838-1920) was the Bishop of Visby, Sweden, between 1838-1920. On the friendship between Råbergh and von Schéele see von Bonsdorff 1962, 143-146.
[9]Grundmann 1957, 141-151; Wadensjö 1971, 17-19, 46-47; Oesterlin 1972, 28-35; Lauha 1990, 34, 43-49.
[10]On the participation of the Finns in the meetings of AELK 1901-1913 see Lauha 1990, 43-49.

tivities to Finland. They found members especially among the younger generation, students or young pastors and university teachers.[11]

These activities had political side effects that were more apparent than within AELK. For instance, the Finnish representatives in the international conferences of the YMCA often managed to spread information on the oppressive policy of the Russian government. The prayers for the autonomy of Finland read in front of a world-wide conference were rather effective propaganda and still could be considered "apolitical". One result of this "resistance policy" of the Finnish theologians was that the International Council of the YMCA in 1902 gave Finland a place of its own on its International Board. After that time the Finns no longer belonged to the Russian delegation of the YMCA. In a letter sent by the Leader of the International Committee, the Finns were reminded that God can still show to his people the way over the Red Sea. The letter was read aloud at a conference of over one thousand young Finnish YMCA activists.

It is not surprising that the Russian administration very soon started observing the foreign contacts of the Finnish religious leaders travelling abroad. The leaders of the Finnish YMCA were under particularly intense surveillance.[12]

One of the enthusiasts for spreading political information was the professor in Exegetics of the Old Testament, Arthur Hjelt, who became the pioneer and long-standing key figure of ecumenicalism in Finland.[13]
Thus, even though the leaders of the Church were passive towards Russian oppressive policy in domestic situations during the First Period of Russification, in international contacts the church and other religious channels served the general intention of the politically active Finnish intelligentsia to provide more information on Finland.[14]

---

[11]Juva 1960, 227-231; Kansanaho 1960, 221-227; Franzén 1987, 35-46.
[12]Louhivuori 1915, 198-200; Shedd 1955, 365; Lauha 1990, 41-43.
[13]Arthur Ludvig Mikael Hjelt (1868-1931) was Assistant Professor of Biblical Languages 1903-1904, Professor in Exegetics of the Old Testament 1904-1926 and Professor in Exegetics of the New Testament 1926-1931 at the University of Helsinki. Murtorinne 1988, 176. On Hjelt's ecumenical activity see Lauha 1990, 37, 41-42, 375-381.
[14]Lauha 1990, 41-42.

The conditions for international sympathy during the Second Period of Russification (1908-1914)

Finland's position was immediately affected by the political developments in Russia which had begun to accelerate in 1905. Social discontent in Russia had increased and the Russian defeat in the Russo-Japanese war contributed to the deterioration of the situation. The Czar's position was at stake.

The revolutionary movement started by the strikes in October 1905 finally ended the Czar's absolute rule. The Duma became the highest legislative body. It was generally hoped that it would manage to tackle Russia's social and political evils.[15]

Russia's rebellions and strikes in October 1905 also spread among the Finns, who had ample reason for discontent with imperial policy. The Finnish General Strike ended in early November after Czar Nicholas II promised in his November Manifesto to cancel some of the administrative rulings considered illegal by the Finns. The Finns believed their autonomy had been saved. Confidence in Russia was partly restored. A parliamentary reform was also carried out in Finland, which increased the satisfaction of the Finns. Finland was given a modern parliament based on equal and general suffrage.[16]

However, the relief of the Finns did not last long. Already in 1908 it became evident that the russification of the Finnish administration and culture was to continue. A new period of russification, which in Finnish historiography is called the Second Period of Oppression, began in 1908 and continued during the First World War. It finally ended in 1917, the year of the Russian Revolutions and of the Finnish Declaration of Independence.

The new period of russification was a great disappointment to all parties and individual citizens. Attitudes towards Russian oppressive policy grew more negative, even among those who had earlier supported concessions.[17]

---

[15] Seton-Watson 1967, 598-627; Luntinen 1985, 44.
[16] Seton-Watson 1967, 610-611, 626; Jutikkala-Pirinen 1984, 213-217; Paasivirta 1988, 12.
[17] Seton-Watson 1967, 663, 668-669; Paasivirta 1978, 377-382; Jutikkala-Pirinen 1984, 217-219; Paasivirta 1988, 15-16.

The need for international sympathy was again great. However, this time the international political situation placed greater obstacles to Finnish activity abroad.

The Entente cordiale, the political alliance between Britain and France formed in 1904, was expanded in 1907 by an agreement between Britain and Russia. Correspondingly, Russia and Germany were estranged from each other. The cooperation between Russia and Britain was clearly directed against Germany from 1907 onward. Also Sweden and Russia grew closer politically, and so the position of Russia in international politics was becoming stronger.[18]

Since no foreign country had an interest in discussing Finland's situation internationally, there was no chance for the Finnish information activities to succeed as well as they had right after the February Manifesto in 1899. The Finns carried out organized and successful activity especially in Britain and the United States. The key figures in this so-called Western-oriented activism were the journalist – and later the Foreign Minister of Finland – Rudolf Holsti, and Professor J.N. Reuter and Mrs. Aino Malmberg, M. A., who were all residing in England. They tried to propagate their views through the British press, with which Holsti had achieved useful contacts. The liberal press in Britain began in particular to sympathize with the Finnish issue.[19] In 1911 Holsti's own newspaper, Helsingin Sanomat, mentioned the Manchester Guardian as one of the most important supporters of Finland.[20]

In 1912 a group of Englishmen concerned about the situation in Finland founded the Anglo-Finnish Society. Its members included many liberal politicians and journalists. It was these men especially who were responsible for British sympathy for far-away Finland and its political situation.[21]

---

[18]Seton-Watson 1967, 679-682, 684-686; Luntinen 1975, 238-239; Paasivirta 1978, 374-376, 383-394.
[19]Paasivirta 1978, 391-392; Lyytinen 1980, 46-55; Paasivirta 1984, 32-33; Pietiäinen 1986, 141-146.
[20]Helsingin Sanomat 196/27 August 1911 Suomi Englannin sanomalehdistössä; Helsingin Sanomat 199/31 August 1911 Englannin sanomalehdet.
[21]Lyytinen 1980, 53.

Church contacts in Sweden and Germany

Information activities concerning Finland involved many influential clergymen and their contribution had some significance in advancing Finland's position. Bishop Herman Råbergh had von Schéele as a secure friend of Finland to whom he could supply news about circumstances in the country. Von Schéele, for his part, ensured that Finland stayed within AELK as he thought the organization was an important lifeline for the Finns.[22]

The Second Period of Russification did not in itself prevent the continuity and development of international theological interaction. However, political conditions coloured, to some extent, even this kind of activity which in itself was quite apolitical. Also, von Schéele had to tell Råbergh that he had been warned not to emphasize the brotherhood of the Finnish and Swedish nations in international connections.[23]

Finnish theologians continued their traditional study trips abroad without disturbance during the first years of oppression. These trips offered opportunities to tell about the political situation in the country. For example, Doctor of Theology Antti J. Pietilä, who had done research work in Germany, discussed russification with religion researcher Edvard Lehmann in 1910. According to Pietilä, Lehmann had promised to influence the Theological Faculty of the University of Berlin to appeal to the Kaiser on the Finnish issue. However, this intention was rejected by Lehmann's colleague, the Professor of Systematic Theology Reinhold Seeberg. In his opinion there was no reason to interfere unless the position of the Lutheran Church was endangered.[24]

Seeberg's decision and its reasoning represented the traditional interpretation of Lutheran social ethics, according to which there is no reason for the church to interfere in government affairs. From the German point of view Finland was only a peripheral area and there was no need to take any unnecessary risks on its account. Reinhold Seeberg, who was born in Lithuania and had studied in Tartu, however, followed the russification of the Baltic countries with quite a different outlook and he was one of the most active in the group of German professors who took a stand on the Baltic issue.[25]

---

[22]HYK HR von Schéele to Råbergh 12 December 1910.
[23]HYK HR von Schéele to Råbergh 30 July 1909.
[24]Tiililä 1972, 26-27.
[25]Craig 1978, 360-361.

The Finnish clergymen teaching at the University considered Reinhold Seeberg such an interesting researcher that it was decided to invite him as a guest lecturer to the University of Helsinki in 1913.[26] The reason for this invitation was ostensibly Seeberg's being a noteworthy and versatile researcher. However, it is apparent that Seeberg's Baltic origin and his attitude towards Russian policy were well known in Finland.

On the whole, the political situation was only secondary to the relationship between Finnish and Swedish and, correspondingly, Finnish and German theologians and there were no appreciable results of the information activity.

Arthur Hjelt – promoter of Western-oriented activism

Of all the Finnish theologians it was Professor Arthur Hjelt who had the most significant international contacts. Hjelt's international circle of acquaintances was wide and he was in active correspondence with persons abroad. In his contacts with Germans, priority was given to scholarly matters, but in Britain his contacts had a strong political flavour. Because of this activity, it is appropriate to count him among the so-called Western-oriented activists.

As early as in 1907, Hjelt became acquainted with W.T. Goode who was a teacher in a London teacher training college as well as a journalist. The acquaintance was made during Hjelt's visit to England when he was participating in the World Conference of the YMCA in London in July 1907.[27]

The very same year Goode visited Finland. During this visit he also met Arthur Hjelt's brothers Edvard and August Hjelt who were important figures in Finnish politics. They were to be the last Finnish chairmen of the Finnish Senate before the russification of the Senate in November 1909. Under their guidance, Goode got to know many prominent men in Finnish cultural life.[28]

However, international relations, for example the correspondence of Finnish senators, were closely controlled by the Russians. It is no wonder that later on it was only the youngest brother, the Biblical scholar Arthur

---

[26]Gummerus 1928, 186; Rosenqvist 1913, 435-449.
[27]Louhivuori 1915, 200; Lauha 1990, 32.
[28]HYK AH Goode to Hjelt 3rd November 1907 and 19th January 1908. On Edvard and August Hjelt see Rasila 1977, 31-32, 35-36.

Hjelt, who could maintain the connection with Goode. Besides the active correspondence, Arthur Hjelt visited Goode in London at least once.[29]

W. T. Goode became one of the most outspoken critics of the official British government policy on Finland. Goode contributed to the Manchester Guardian and during the World War he became a full-time correspondent for the paper in Finland and the Baltic countries. He also later published two books which dealt with the Finnish and Baltic questions.[30]

A considerable part of Goode's information on Finland was at first provided by Arthur Hjelt. Reciprocally, Goode provided Hjelt with copies of his articles on Finland, at the same time complaining how little he could do. However, Goode's achievements were by no means insignificant. From 1907 onward, he arranged lecture series and public events concerning Finland and its political situation in his London institute, Craystoke Place Day Training College. By promoting knowledge of Finland in Britain, he hoped to change political attitudes in a direction more favourable to Finland. Through Goode, Hjelt got stimuli to debate even the possibility of independence.[31]

The correspondence between Hjelt and Goode turned more clearly political as russification restarted in 1908. Goode asked Hjelt for more detailed information on the russification activities and especially about their influence on the University and the school system. His intention was to answer Russian pamphlets which tried to influence public opinion in Britain on the Finnish issue.

At the end of 1910 there were numerous articles in the British press which reported – based on Russian sources – such stories as how badly Russians and Jews were treated in Finland. According to Goode, the rest of the information concerning Finland was coloured by Russian interests and there was hardly any news about the change in Finland's juridical status, the implementation of the nationwide legislative procedure.[32]

---

[29]HYK AH Goode to Hjelt 19 October 1910.

[30]W. T. Goode, Bolshevism at Work, London 1920; W.T. Goode, Intervention in Russia. London 1931; Lyytinen 1980, 53, 126.

[31]HYK Goode to Hjelt 3 November 1907; Helsingin Sanomat 174/2 August 1911 Englantilaisten opettajien vierailu.

[32]HYK AH Goode to Hjelt 19 October 1910. On the issue of Finland in the English press in 1910 see Pietiäinen 1986, 147-148.

Goode was concerned about this situation and again he asked Hjelt for help. Hjelt sent him a whole parcel of underground printed material concerning the Russian oppression.[33]

The next year Goode took part in arranging and leading a visit of London teachers to Russia and Finland, which, in his opinion, would also increase understanding of the Finnish situation. The Finnish press followed enthusiastically the visit, during which Goode openly spoke of his pro-Finnish propaganda work in Britain.[34].

At first Arthur Hjelt was actively arranging the programme for the British teachers.[35] However, at the same time, the newspaper Novoye Vremya, which was close to Russian government circles, began to criticize him because of his activity in international politics. Hjelt's appearance abroad as if he were a representative of an independent country was considered so aggravating that the Russian governor-general began to oppose the World Conference of the YMCA which was planned to be held in Finland and which Hjelt was organizing. In September 1911 Czar Nicholas II did forbid the conference to be held in Finland.[36]

These factors must have been at least part of the reason why Hjelt stayed in the background during the visit of the English teachers. It also made him more cautious in his correspondence with Goode. Hjelt did have good reason to be careful with his position. Deportations had terminated the careers of many activists during the First Period of Russi-fication.

Hjelt's contacts with Goode, even though not great, can be fully compared with the work done by the other Western-oriented activists in Britain – Rudolf Holsti, J. N. Reuter and Mrs. Malmberg etc. – during the Second Period of Russification. The important connecting figure in this activity was Goode, with whom all these above mentioned persons were, sooner or later, somehow in touch.[37]

---

[33]HYK AH Goode to Hjelt 19 October and 14 November 1910.
[34]Helsingin Sanomat 174/2 August 1911 Englantilaisten opettajien vierailu; Helsingin Sanomat 179-186/8-16 August 1911; Uusi Suomi 184/12 August, 186/15 August and 207/8 September 1911.
[35]HYK AH Goode to Hjelt 14 November 1910 (Itinerary for the L.T.A. Finland Trip); HYK AH Goode to Hjelt 2 and June and 9 November 1911.
[36]Novoye Vremya 9/21 January 1911, 3; Kotimaa 7/23 January and 61/23 June 1911; Uusi Suomi 206/7 September and 209/10 September 1911; Lauha 1990, 42.
[37]VA RH Malmberg to Holsti 29 May 1914, Goode to Holsti 25 February 1918. Since 1913 Goode tried together with his Finnish friends to establish in Britain a Finnish Parliamentary Committee. VA EIP 603:14a Goode's memorandum to Sir Frederick Pollock s.a. [1914]; Lyytinen 1980, 53-54.

Anglophiles Sirenius and Gummerus play their part

Two other theologians had contacts with the representatives of the Western-oriented activism. In 1909, right after arriving in London, Rudolf Holsti made friends with a Finnish seamen's missionary, Sigfrid Sirenius[38]. Sirenius was, like Holsti, also a kind of journalist as he was for years a London correspondent for several Finnish papers. Feeling indignant, Sirenius described in his articles the slavophile reports on Finland in the conservative English press, and it is apparent that during his years in London Sirenius himself, again like Holsti, spread, in his opinion, "correct" information on Finland and its political conditions.

The third Finnish theologian with significant English acquaintances was the Professor of Church History Jaakko Gummerus[39] who was one of the first anglophiles in the Finnish church. During his research travels Gummerus also came to know Rudolf Holsti and so came into contact with the Western-oriented activism. In 1910 Holsti and Gummerus were even planning to turn the Church of England officially favourable towards the Finnish political views. This plan did not seem to have had any appreciable results. However, in 1914, besides liberal politicians and journalists, there were three bishops, namely those of Hereford, Lincoln and Kensington on the Anglo-Finnish Society's list of "friends of Finland". In my opinion, it was Jaakko Gummerus who was the most important link between Finnish political activists and British church circles.

On the whole, the international political activity of Finnish theologians between 1908 and 1914 was not very far-reaching and was based only on the work of a few activists. However, it did have its own significance in forming the image of Finland abroad. The whole activity was by no means large-scale and its international obstacles were great. As during the First Period of Russification, also during the Second Period of Russification the international channels of church and theology served, besides their own special task, also nationalist goals.

---

[38]Sigfrid Sirenius (1877-1961) was a most important pioneer of the settlement work in the Church of Finland. He also had a great admiration for the work and traditions of the Church of England and published in 1917 an important work "The Church and Parish Work in English Cities" in Finnish. Murtorinne 1988, 230.

[39]Jaakko Gummerus (1870-1933) was Professor of Ecclesiastical History at the University of Helsinki from 1900 to 1920. In 1920 he became the Bishop of Porvoo (later Tampere). On Gummerus see Murtorinne 1988, 188-192; Ijäs 1993, 5-6, 502-523.

Bibliography

Archival Sources

Valtionarkisto (The Finnish National Archives), Helsinki (VA)

    The Aleksi Lehtonen Collection (AL)
    The Eino I Parmanen collection (EIP)

Helsingin yliopiston kirjasto (Helsinki University Library), Helsinki (HYK)

    The Yrjö Alanen Collection (incl. Gustaf Johansson's diary) (YA)
    The Arthur Hjelt Collection (AH)
    The Jaakko Gummerus Collection (JG)
    The Gustaf Johansson Collection (GJ)
    The Collection of Svenska Litteratursällskapet; Herman Råbergh's papers (HR)

Newspapers and Periodicals

Helsingin Sanomat (1908-1914)
Kotimaa (1908-1914)
Kristen gemenskap 1928
Novoye Vremya 1911
Teologinen Aikakauskirja 1913
Uusi Suomi 1908-1914

Books and Articles

Amburger, Erik
1961   Geschichte des Protestantismus in Rußland. Stuttgart.

Bonsdorff, Max von
1962   Herman Råbergh. En förgrundsgestalt i Finlands kyrka II. Professorsåren och biskopstiden 1. Borgå.

Craig, Gordon A.
1978	Germany 1866-1945. Oxford.

Eskola, Seikko
1965	Suomen kysymys ja Ruotsin mielipide (The Finnish Question and Swedish Opinion). Diss. Porvoo.

Franzén, Ruth
1987	Studentekumenik och väckelse. Finlands kristliga studentförbund i internationell brytning 1924-1950. (Student Ecumenism and Revivalism. The Student Christian Federation of Finland at the International Crossroads 1924-1950.) Publications of the Finnish Society for Church History 140. Diss. Jyväskylä.

Goode, W. T.
1920	Bolshevism at Work. London.

Goode, W. T.
1931	Intervention in Russia. London.

Grundmann, Siegfried
1957	Der Lutherische Weltbund. Grundlagen – Herkunft – Aufbau. Forschungen zur kirchlichen Rechtsgeschichte und zum Kirchenrecht 1. Köln – Graz.

Gummerus, Jaakko
1928	Finlands kyrka och dess mellankyrkliga förbindelser. – Kristen gemenskap.

Heikkilä, Markku
1985	Kirkollisen yhdistysaktiivisuuden leviäminen Suomessa. Virallisen jäsenorganisaation kehitys 1900-luvun alusta toiseen maailmansotaan (Religious Associations in Finland. A Study of the Development and Organisation of Official Lutheran Associations in Finland from the Beginning of the Twentieth Century to the Second World War). Publications of the Finnish Society for Church History 112. Diss. Kouvola.

Hobsbawm, E. J.
1990 Nations and nationalism since 1780. Programme, myth, reality. Cambridge.

Ijäs, Matti
1993 Jaakko Gummerus kirkkohistoriantutkijana (Jaakko Gummerus as a Church Historian). Publications of the Finnish Society for Church History 165. Diss. Jyväskylä.

Jussila, Osmo
1979 Nationalismi ja vallankumous venäläis-suomalaisissa suhteissa 1899-1914. Historiallisia tutkimuksia 110. Forssa.

Jutikkala, Eino & Pirinen, Kauko
1984 A History of Finland. Fourth revised edition. Espoo.

Juva, Mikko
1960 Valtionkirkosta kansankirkoksi (From the State Church into the People's Church). Publications of the Finnish Society for Church History 61. Porvoo.

Kahle, Wilhelm
1982 Lutherische Begegnung im Ostseeraum. Die Lutherische Kirche, Geschichte und Gestalten, Band 4. Gütersloh.

Kansanaho, Erkki
1960 Sisälähetys ja diakonia Suomen kirkossa 1800-luvulla. Pieksämäki.

Koukkunen, Heikki
1977 Suomen valtiovalta ja kreikkalaiskatoliset 1881-1887 (The Finnish Authorities and the Greek Orthodox 1881-1897.). Diss. Publications of the University of Joensuu A 7. Joensuu.

Lauha, Aila
1990	Suomen kirkon ulkomaansuhteet ja ekumeeninen osallistuminen 1917-1922 (Foreign Relations and Ecumenical Participation in the Church of Finland between 1917-1922). Publications of the Finnish Society for Church History 150. Diss. Jyväskylä 1990.

Louhivuori, Verneri
1915	Neljännesvuosisataa nuorisotyötä. NMKY-liikkeen vaiheet Suomessa vv. 1889-1914 (YWCA in Finland 1889-1914). Helsinki.

Luntinen, Pertti
1975	The Baltic Question. Annales Academiae Scientiarum Fennicae B 195. Diss. Helsinki.

Lyytinen, Eino
1980	Finland in British Politics in the First World War. Annales Academiae Scientiarum Fennicae B 207. Helsinki.

Murtorinne, Eino
1964	Papisto ja esivalta routavuosina 1899-1906 (Pfarrer und Obrigkeit in den Jahren der Unterdrückung in Finnland 1899-1906). Publications of the Finnish Society for Church History 1968. Diss. Kuopio.

1988	The History of Finnish Theology 1828-1918. Societas Scientiearum Fennicae; The History of Learning and Science in Finland 1828-1928, 1. Helsinki.

Mustakallio, Hannu
1983	Säätypapista kansalaiseksi. Papiston poliittis-yhteiskunnallinen rooli demokratisoitumisen murrosvaiheessa 1905-1907 (The Tranformation from Spiritual Estate to Ordinary Citizenry: The Socio-Political Role of the Finnish Clergy in the Critical Years of Democratization 1905-1907). Publications of the Finnish Society for Church History 126. Diss. Loimaa.

Oesterlin, Lars
1972 Lutherdomens möte i Lund 1901. – Nordisk lutherdom över gränserna. De nordiska kyrkorna i 1900-talets konfessionella samarbete. Red. Lars Österlin. Skrifter utgivna av Nordiskt institut för kyrkohistorisk forskning. Lund.

Paasivirta
1978 Suomi ja Eurooppa. Autonomiakausi ja kansainväliset kriisit 1808-1914 (Finland and Europe 1808-1914). Helsinki.

1988 Finland and Europe. The early years of Independence 1917-1939. Publications of Finnish Historical Society, Studia Historica 29. Jyväskylä.

Pietiäinen, Jukka-Pekka
1986 Rudolf Hosti. Lehtimies, tiedemies, poliitikko 1881-1919. Diss. Espoo.

Rasila, Viljo
1977 Suomen poliittisen historian vuodet 1905-1919. – Suomen poliittinen historia 1809-1975. 2 osa. Porvoo.

Rosenqvist, G. G.
1913 R. Seeberg och hans föreläsningar i Helsingfors. – Teologinen Aikakauskirja.

Shedd, Clarence Prouty
1955 Expanding Vision, 1878-1913.- History of the World's Alliance of Yuong Men's Christian Association. Aylesbury and London.

Seton-Watson, Hugh
1967 The Russian Empire. Oxford.

Tiililä, Osmo
1972 Antti J. Pietilä. Kiistelty kirkonmies. Porvoo.

Wadensjö, Bengt
1971 Toward a World Lutheran Communion. Developments in Lutheran Co-operation up to 1929. Acta Universitatis Upsaliensis. Studia historico-ecclesiastica Upsaliensia 18. Diss. Uppsala.

To Die is Gain? Religion, the Monarchy and National Identity in Britain 1817-1910

John Wolffe

> There never was an occasion of such magnitude, and at the same time of such peculiarity. It does not wear the aspect of an affair of politics at all, but of an affair of the heart; and the novel exhibition is now offered of all party-irritations merging into one common and overwhelming sensibility. Oh! how it tends to quiet the agitations of every earthly interest and earthly passion, when death steps forward and demonstrates the littleness of them all ...[1]

The year was 1817, the speaker Thomas Chalmers, then a rising star of the Church of Scotland, and the occasion the day of the funeral of Princess Charlotte, only child of the Prince Regent and second in line to the British throne, who had tragically died after giving birth to a still-born infant. Chalmers perceived the occasion as one of great significance: for him death stirred profoundly religious reflection on the vanity of all earthly aspirations and in this context the royal family was held up as a focus and a spur for national spiritual regeneration in the face of the social disorder and material insecurity of the times. When St. Paul wrote that "to die is gain"[2] he had in mind personal union with Christ beyond the grave, but for our purposes the phrase serves to introduce the hypothesis that royal deaths stimulated public and popular religiosity and enhanced the standing of the monarchy itself. Moreover grief for royalty was expressed in a language and spirit that drew heavily on Christian motifs and linked throne and altar in a powerful undergirding of patriotic impulses.

At the time of Princess Charlotte's death the nation had subconsciously come to associate the throne with immortality. In 1817 George III had been reigning for fifty-seven years, and aged and mentally

---

[1] Thomas Chalmers, *A Sermon Delivered in Tron Church, Glasgow, on Wednesday Nov. 19, 1817* (Glasgow, 1817), pp. 7-8.
[2] Philippians i. 21

incapacitated though he was, only his very oldest subjects could remember any other sovereign. The twenty years after 1817, however, saw numerous royal bereavements. The deaths of Queen Charlotte in 1818 and of George III himself in 1820 were hardly unexpected in the course of nature, but still stirred profound reflection on the ending of an era and the ultimate transience of human life and achievements.[3] Meanwhile the Duke of Kent, fourth son of George III, was struck down, also in 1820, in apparently vigorous early middle age.[4] In 1821 followed the tragic farce of the death and funeral of George IV's estranged wife Queen Caroline whose remains were shipped off to Brunswick after a ramshackle procession in which royal ceremonial merged into popular protest.[5] The deaths of the Duke of York in 1827, George IV in 1830, and William IV in 1837 rounded off a period which must have served substantially to undermine the sense of stability and continuity associated with the monarchy in the later decades of George III's reign.

In the next fifty years on the other hand, the chances of the life cycle of the royal family generated only one death of comparable magnitude and impact, that of the Prince Consort in 1861. Indeed the very novelty of Albert's death may be one important reason for the vigour of the cult of memory for him that followed.[6] At the close of the nineteenth century, however, the unexpected and the inevitable once again joined together to produce a significant cluster of royal bereavements. In 1892 the Duke of Clarence, Queen Victoria's grandson, died in his twenties shortly after the announcement of his engagement to Princess May of Teck.[7] Queen Victoria's own death when it came in the first month of the new century somehow managed to take the nation by surprise,[8] and the country seemed even more stunned by Edward VII's death a mere nine years later. By further contrast, after the three major royal deaths between 1892 and 1910, the remainder of the twentieth century has, to date, seen only two

---

[3]Thomas T. Biddulph, *National Affliction Improved* (Bristol, 1820), pp. 25-31, 49-50. For narrative accounts of the circumstances and aftermath of the royal deaths discussed in this paper see Olivia Bland, *The Royal Way of Death* (London, 1986).

[4]Anon, *Radicals and True Patriots Compared* (London, 1820), p. 59.

[5]*A Faithful Account of the Last Illness and Death of Her Late Most Gracious Majesty Queen Caroline, and the Particulars of the Procession* (London, 1821?)

[6]For details see Elisabeth Darby and Nicola Smith, *The Cult of the Prince Consort* (London, 1983).

[7]F.F. Carmichael, *Honour the King* (Dublin, 1892), p. 12.

[8]John Wolffe, "The End of Victorian Values? Women, Religion and the Death of Queen Victoria", in W.J Sheils and Diana Wood, eds, *Women in the Church: Studies in Church History*, 27 (Oxford, 1990), pp. 481-503.

equivalent occurrences, the deaths of George V in 1936 and of George VI in 1952.

Death might be the great leveller, but even among royalty the circumstances and significance of its incidence varied very significantly. Royal deaths impinged on every age group, from the youthful Charlotte to the matriarchal Victoria. Some – such as that of William IV – came at the conclusion of protracted illness; others – such as that of Edward VII – appeared very sudden. The wider context also changed. The two decades after 1817 were a period of relative unpopularity for the monarchy and of an associated sense of crisis in church and state. The evident depth and sincerity of public mourning for George IV's daughter, parents, wife, and even his brothers carried with it an implicit dislike of the reigning monarch, which was confirmed by the apparent lack of any real grief at his own death in 1830.[9] In 1837 William IV was mourned with greater respect, but little real passion. By contrast, the deaths of Clarence, Victoria and Edward VII came at a time when the monarchy was at an unparalleled pinnacle of popularity and when the Church of England was enjoying an Indian summer of prestige and national standing.

The death of Princess Charlotte was a key event in forming the nineteenth-century pattern of public response. Services were held and sermons preached in numerous churches on the day of the funeral. Some read these events as an authentic expression of national piety:

> Uncalled by any special ordinance of God – unbidden by any mandate of temporal authority – they have voluntarily, and with humble awful earnestness filled our sacred temples to supplicate the throne of mercy. A whole people thus prostrate before God, has in it something so holy, so majestical, so edifying, that we would blush for ourselves, if we hesitated to acknowledge the emotion of piety with which we are inspired. If the expression of such feelings in individuals is accounted virtue, and *the assured means of divine grace*, we may be permitted to indulge the pious hope, that it will procure us that favour.[10]

---

[9]*The Times*, 16 July 1830.
[10]*Courier*, 19 Nov. 1817, quoted Scoto-Britannus (Thomas McCrie), *Free Thoughts on the late Religious Celebration of the Funeral of HRH The Princess Charlotte of Wales* (Edinburgh, 1817), p. 41.

However, many other churches remained closed[11] and a lively pamphlet controversy broke out in Edinburgh over the appropriate means of marking the occasion. Andrew Thomson, a leading Evangelical Church of Scotland minister, was forcefully criticised for his alleged disloyalty in refusing to preach a sermon on the day of the princess's funeral.[12] He was defended by Thomas McCrie, a prominent Dissenting minister and church historian. McCrie began by noting the genuine depth of grief apparent in Edinburgh when news of Charlotte's death arrived, but argued that an excited public feeling had been manipulated by the Court and turned – at least in Scotland – in a direction "opposite to the principles and habits of the people" themselves. The public had been persuaded to take part in mock Anglican burial services, a proceeding unprecedented even in England, and wholly unacceptable in Presbyterian Scotland. An unshakeable precedent had however now been set.[13] McCrie was particularly concerned that "superstitious" English usages were being surreptitiously introduced into Scotland, but his argument had wider implications. He suspected that many who – whether north or south of the Border – gathered together in church on the day of the Princess's funeral had "no higher or more sacred end in view" than paying respect to her memory. This he thought was impious, even blasphemous, use of the outward forms of organized religion.[14]

The response to Princess Charlotte's death thus foreshadowed two significant trends in the later nineteenth-century response to royal bereavements. There was an almost seamless blending of the Christian and the national, in a manner that was disconcerting for those adhering to rigorously orthodox theological positions, coupled with a tendency for responses to become increasingly standardized across the United Kingdom.[15] The precedent set did indeed prove to be a powerful one, confirmed as it was by the similarly extensive commemoration of the death and funeral and George III three years later.[16] The acid test came with the demise of George IV, for whom, according to *The Times*, there was no

---

[11]Scotus, *Strictures upon the Letter of Lucius* (Edinburgh, 1817), p. 16.
[12]Lucius, *A Letter to the Rev. Andrew Thomson on the Respect Due to National Feeling* (Edinburgh, 1817).
[13]*Free Thoughts*, p. 34.
[14]Ibid., pp. 40-6.
[15]John Wolffe, "Secular saints: Church and civic commemoration in the United Kingdom, 1847-1910", *Hispania Sacra*, 42 (1990), pp. 435-43.
[16]Robert Southy (pseud.), *Authentic Memoirs of our late venerable and beloved monarch, George the Third* (London, 1820), p. 420.

real regret or "unmercenary sorrow". The performance of religious worship was evidently less widespread than it had been on the deaths of Princess Charlotte and of George III, and at St. James's Piccadilly the congregation consisted of only six persons.[17] Nevertheless the forms of national grief had assumed a dynamic of their own quite independent of the real depth of the sense of loss experienced. For example, Newcastle-on-Tyne on the day of George IV's funeral "presented an appearance of solemnity" and processions and church services were held.[18] Even if few, if any, tears were shed for the late monarch, the occasion provided an important opportunity to assert civic dignity and loyalty to Church and Crown.

Thus royal deaths stirred a blending of religiosity and national consciousness that was robust enough to transcend passing unpopularity. The mournful rituals of funerals evidently acquired a paradoxical appeal, a tendency confirmed in the later nineteenth century as personal veneration for deceased royalty reached new heights. Prince Albert died late on a Saturday evening and so many first learnt of this shattering national bereavement while attending church services on the following day, often through the stark action of the minister in omitting his name from the liturgy. The funeral itself on 23 December 1861 was private, with limited ceremonial, but this did not prevent the holding of numerous parallel services and commemorations. "Never before", wrote *The Leeds Intelligencer*, "was the unity of feeling in subjects and their ruler so strongly evident, so feelingly displayed." In Leeds all business was suspended at the time of the funeral and the streets were thronged as a procession wended its way to the parish church to hear an elaborate choral service and an appropriate sermon. Services were also held in other churches and in Nonconformist chapels.[19] A generation later, when the Duke of Clarence died in January 1892, the public yearning for elaborate ceremonial was revealed by disappointment when it was decided not to hold a procession through London. Services at St. Paul's and Westminster Abbey provided however a focus for expressions of grief.[20] The much more elaborate processions and ceremonial associated with the funerals of Queen Victoria in 1901 and Edward VII in 1910 moved far

---

[17]*The Times*, 16 July 1830.
[18]*An Account of the Last Moments and Death of His Majesty King George the Fourth* (Newcastle, 1830), p. 23.
[19]Bland, *Royal Way of Death*, p. 169-70; *The Leeds Intelligencer*, 28 Dec. 1861.
[20]*The Yorkshire Post*, 18 Jan. 1892.

outside the ecclesiastical context, but they still culminated in services at St. George's Chapel, Windsor, and it was through church services that their subjects in the provinces expressed their identification with the proceedings.[21]

The ritual solidarity with the monarchy mediated by the churches was undergirded by expressions of sympathy and identification in bereavement. Sentiments of this kind moved beyond orthodox Christianity, but expressed a Durkheimian sense of the royal family as a focus for national cohesion. Such reactions were most apparent in relation to the more untimely royal deaths. A Unitarian preacher on the day of Princess Charlotte's funeral claimed that "the public temper at this moment shews that Englishmen are sympathizing and confiding; that they cannot see affliction in the exalted or the humble without paying to it the tribute of *natural tears*".[22] By 1861 a sense of identification with the royal family had intensified: an Irish clergyman described the Prince Consort's death as "a kind of personal and family affliction, in every loyal household in the nation."[23] Queen Victoria's later family bereavements reinforced such ties. The death of her son Prince Leopold in 1884 struck a chord with parents who had themselves lost children[24] and when the Duke of Clarence died in 1892 he was perceived as every young woman's fiancé and every middle-aged parent's rising hope.[25] In parallel fashion Queen Victoria was to be everyone's grandmother and Edward VII everyone's father.

While reactions to death gave the monarchy the powerful legitimating support of religious and quasi-religious ritual, and the bonds of spiritualized sympathy, there were also substantial corresponding benefits for the churches. Above all, awareness that proximity to the Crown bought no exemption from the ravages of the grim reaper provided a golden opportunity for the clergy to adminster pointed reminders of mortality to those neglectful of their spiritual duties. In 1817 Andrew Thomson was thus charged with wantonly rejecting an opportunity to instruct his congregation.[26] Subsequently the allegedly

---

[21]Wolffe, "Secular saints", p. 438.
[22]Robert Aspland, *A Funeral Sermon, Preached on Wednesday, November 19, 1817... before the Unitarian Church Hackney* (London, 1817?), p. 18.
[23]Maurice F. Day, *A Sermon on the Death of the Prince Consort* (Dublin, 1861), p. 6.
[24]Charles Bullock, *"Ich Dien: I Serve" Prince Edward. A Memory*, p. 71.
[25]*In Memoriam Albert Victor Christian Edward*, British Library broadside, 1871.e.2 (46).
[26]Lucius, *Letter to the Rev. Andrew Thomson*, pp. 15-17.

miserable deathbed of the radical sceptic Thomas Paine was compared with the Christian character of the Duke of Kent and of George III. Moreover the duke's sudden death shortly after the birth of his beloved daughter, the future Queen Victoria, was a striking demonstration of the vulnerability of earthly hopes:

> Neither youth nor health, nor strength nor beauty, nor rank nor virtue, nor a nation's love, can exempt us from the stroke of death!... Happy will it be for us if, warned by such events, we seek "a habitation whose builder and maker is God:" and if like this worthy Prince, we learn to look by faith to that Saviour who hath died to make reconciliation for transgressors, brought in everlasting righteousness, and gone before to prepare a mansion in the Heavens.[27]

Four decades later the death of the Prince Consort stirred similar reflection. A Manchester minister felt that it would be "inexcusable" for him not preach on such a "dispensation of Divine Providence" and like many others he took as his text II Samuel iii.38, "Do you not know that a prince and a great man has fallen this day in Israel?" Albert's death demonstrated the vanity and transitoriness of earthly greatness: had the Prince made the present world his all it would now have availed him nothing. All men are liable to death and the grave, which are impartial and irresistible in their impact. Accordingly one should place one's confidence not in men but in the Most High. Preparedness for death should be habitual: no-one knows who may be the next victim.[28] By the end of the century, however, preachers and writers had softened the message. While the unexpectedness of death and the transitoriness of earthly achievements and status was still a popular theme, reminders of mortality became rather less pointed. The stress rather was on the value of falling back on Christian doctrine in the face of human helplessness and in looking forward to Paradise, eternity and reunion beyond the grave.[29]

---

[27]*Radicals and True Patriots Compared*, p. 60.
[28]Patrick Thomson, *Lessons Suggested by the Fall of Greatness* (Manchester, 1862?), pp. 4-9, 14-16.
[29]*"He that Comforteth" A Plain Sermon on the Death of HRH the Duke of Clarence* (London, 1892), pp. 4-6; E.F. Wanstall, *A Memorial Triplet Being Three Sermons Preached on Jan 27th, Feb 2nd and 3rd, 1901, in Reference to Queen Victoria of Blessed and Glorious Memory* (London, 1901), pp. 23-9.

Were untimely royal deaths a divine judgement on the sins of the nation? Even in the earlier part of the period answers to this compelling question were sometimes couched in cautious terms. There were preachers on the death of Princess Charlotte who straightforwardly applied a text such as Amos viii.9-10 ("And on that day", says the Lord God,"...I will turn your feasts into mourning,...I will make it like the mourning for an only son"), to speak of divine chastisement of national sins.[30] Nevertheless, such conclusions were usually balanced with the claim that seemingly negative events reflected an underlying beneficent providence: God had given great, perhaps pre-eminent, blessings to the British nation in the past and his judgement now was a call to repentance reflecting his ultimate love and mercy.[31] Moreover, a degree of circumspection was apparent in the acknowledgement of the leading Bristol Evangelical Thomas Tregenna Biddulph that the dispensation was "mysterious", even if "after mature reflection" he had concluded that it was "a manifest token of God's holy displeasure."[32] The Baptist Robert Hall, in a sermon that came to be particularly admired, considered it "highly presumptuous to attempt to scan the secret purpose of the Deity...by assigning to it *specific* moral causes." It was undeniably a general chastisement but it was arrogant and divisive to look for particular explanations of what had happened.[33] On the other hand, such reservations did not in practice prevent preachers from going on to talk of their own perceptions of the nation's moral and spiritual failings: Biddulph was particularly concerned by failure to acknowledge the goodness of God; Hall by "open impiety and profaneness, the perjury and injustice, the profanation of the sabbath and contempt of sacred things".[34]

When the Prince Consort died the debate over divine judgement was more sharply focused. The sense that God was chastising the nation was still widespread among the clergy, the cause identified variously as a failure to proclaim the gospel with sufficient energy whether at home or abroad, specific moral delinquencies in terms of intemperance, irreligion and sensuality, or general over-reliance on human strength and lack of

---

[30] For example see T.F. Bowerbank, *A Sermon Preached in the Parish Church of Chiswick, Middlesex on Wednesday, November 19, 1817* (Chiswick, 1817), pp. 7-8.
[31] Ibid., p. 7; cf. C.S. Hawtrey, *A Funeral Sermon on the Death of ...the Princess Charlotte Augusta of Wales and Saxe Cobourg* (London, 1817?), pp. 12-19.
[32] Biddulph, *National Affliction Improved*, pp. 11, 13.
[33] Robert Hall, *A Sermon Occasioned by the Death of Her Late Royal Highness the Princess Charlotte of Wales* (Leicester, 1818), p. 56.
[34] Biddulph, op. cit., p. 15; Hall, op. cit., pp. 56-7.

recognition of dependence on God.[35] Others, however, forcefully rejected such assertions, as least when they were couched in narrow and specific terms.[36] Significant support for such an approach came from John Cumming, popular as a preacher and lecturer on prophecy, who argued that while the prince's death might reflect the workings of a paternal providence, calling the queen herself closer to Christ and stirring a sympathy and contrition which removed the prospect of conflict with the United States, this did not mean that it was a penal judgement.[37] For others again, the whole thing was just deeply perplexing, even if it did serve forcibly to remind believers of their dependence on God: "This event, who can interpret? It is as yet, all darkness...It has a meaning, perhaps many, for God sent it."[38] By the time of the Duke of Clarence's death, however, even such non-specific affirmations of divine agency in the event were rare, certainly in the secular press. Even more religious comment usually stopped short of any references to judgement and emphasized rather the generalized possibility of finding God in and through sorrow.[39] Nevertheless, there were still those who saw the event as a sign of God's direct providential dealing with the nation.[40]

A further source of moral and spiritual edification to be derived from royal deaths was from the example of the deceased. Obviously there were occasions on which preachers had a delicate path to tread in this respect: for example, the vicar of Bradford acknowledged that George IV was a dignified and peaceable occupant of the throne who had at least shown religious leanings during his last illness. On the other hand,

> we do not affirm that he was faultless – faults much to be lamented. But we now feel disposed to forget them, remembering whatever faults he had, with the same leniency of

---

[35]W.L. Alexander, *A Sermon Occasioned by the Death of HRH the Prince Consort* (Edinburgh, 1861), pp. 12-13; J.W. Brooks, *The Rod of the Almighty* (London, 1861?), pp. 9-14; E.H. Carr, *The Nation Admonished* (London, 1862); T. Clarke, *A Sermon on the Death of HRH the Prince Consort* (York, 1862), p. 13.

[36]R.G.L. Blenkinsopp, *Britain's Loss, and Britain's Duty* (London, 1862?), p. 10.

[37]John Cumming, *From Life to Life. Two Sermons on the Death of His Late Royal Highness the Prince Consort* (London, 1861), pp. 18-19.

[38]Enoch Mellor, *Be Still and Know that I am God* (Liverpool, 1861), p.18.

[39]Bullock, *"Ich Dien"*, p. 30.

[40] Alex. R. Macewen, *The Distress of Nations* (Glasgow, 1892), pp. 3-10.

memory and censure, as each of us hopes they are now remembered by the great God himself.[41]

Fortunately however it was not always so difficult to reconcile loyalty and piety. A more subtle problem, though, was the recognition that, by definition, royal personages were hardly realistic role-models for the ordinary Christian. The solution was to emphasize their "domestic", personal, and spiritual qualities, an approach especially popular in relation to women, but also employed for men such as George III, the Prince Consort, and even Edward VII. Thus Princess Charlotte was held to "exemplify the Virtues of Youthful Piety and Domestic Life" while her grandmother and namesake represented those of "Female Virtue and Domestic Religion".[42] George III was held to have possessed not only only the Solomonic monarchical virtues of piety, temperance, justice, mercy, and valour, but also the private virtues of a "Husband, a Parent, a Citizen, and a Christian".[43] In the eyes of J.W. Cunningham, the vicar of Harrow, he was "the perfect Englishman", having simple tastes, sincere, loyal to his friends and magnaminous. Above all he cultivated domesticity, an example "calculated to extend and perpetuate amongst us that taste...which is one of the main pillars of our greatness and welfare – I mean *an ardent attachment to the joys of home.*"[44] When Queen Adelaide, William IV's widow, died in 1849, preachers found in her another model of royal female virtue. Christopher Wordsworth observed that "The love and tenderness of Woman find their best employment in the cause of Religion" and went on to expand on her qualities of piety, wifely duty and philanthropic endeavour.[45] The presentation of royalty as role models reached its culmination with Victoria and Albert: the Prince Consort's public virtues were undergirded by his exemplary conduct as husband and father and by his Christian piety, while the queen "exemplified in her own

---

[41] Henry Heap, *A Sermon Preached on the Occasion of the Lamented Death of His Late Majesty, George IV* (London, 1830), pp. 18-19.

[42] S. Piggott, *Female Virtue and Domestic Religion* (London, 1818), pp. vi-vi.

[43] A. Barker, *The Character of a Good King* (Taunton, 1820), pp. 13-25.

[44] J.W. Cunningham, *A Sermon Preached in the Parish Church of Harrow on the Hill on...the Death of His Most Gracious Majesty George the Third* (London, 1820), pp. 7-12.

[45] C. Wordsworth, *She is not dead but sleepeth* (London, 1849), pp.8, 10-19.

conduct the place which religion should hold both in our personal and in our national life."[46]

It is important to remind ourselves that texts of this kind provide evidence in the first instance of the views of clergy rather than revealing the sentiments of congregations. Nevertheless widespread press reports of the reverence and interest with which such utterances were heard suggest than the pulpit did have an important role in forming public opinion at times of national bereavement. This impression is confirmed by the large numbers of sermons which were published, suggesting that there was a substantial market for them.[47] The British Library catalogue lists eighty-one sermons on the death of Princess Charlotte, seventy-five on George III and seventy on the Prince Consort. However, there are only sixteen listed for Victoria and four for Edward VII, an indication that by the beginning of the twentieth century sermons had become much less central in shaping public sentiment.[48]

Even if – as so often in religious history – the depth of the beliefs of the men and women in the pews are very hard to recover, there can be little doubt about the breadth of participation. The tone of the utterances of most clergy suggest that they were aware of speaking to occasional attenders as well as to their regular congregations, an impression confirmed by newspaper accounts of crowded churches. Moreover, and this is a point worth dwelling on a little, involvement was by no means limited to Anglicans. In 1817 all but two of the Edinburgh Church of Scotland parish ministers preached funeral sermons on Princess Charlotte.[49] English Dissenters also appeared very ready to preach and to attend on such occasions. A Cambridge Independent minister in his sermon on Princess Charlotte reminded his congregation that as Dissenters they had particular cause to be grateful for the toleration they received under the Hanoverian dynasty.[50] When George III died it was

---

[46] A.E. Lord, *A Prince and a Great Man Fallen* (London, 1862), pp.7-8; C.W. Sandford, *The Queen and Mother of Her People* (London, 1901), p. 7.

[47] W. Wharry, *A Funeral Sermon written on the Death of Her Late Majesty Queen Charlotte* (Horncastle, 1818), pp. iii-iv.

[48] These figures are for sermons listed in the printed British Library catalogue under the entries for the deceased and are almost certainly an underestimate of the total numbers of sermons published.

[49] Candidus, *Observations on a Letter by Lucius to the Rev. Andrew Thomson, Minister of St. George's Church* (Edinburgh, 1817), p. 12.

[50] William Harris, *Christian Grounds for National Interest in the Death of Princes* (Cambridge, 1817), pp. 10-13.

affirmed that he had "no better or more loyal subjects" than Protestant Dissenters:

> We rejoice to think, that however sincerely our deceased Monarch was attached to the interests of the Episcopal Church of England, he entertained the most heart-felt respect for all conscientious Non-conformists, and ranked them among the earliest, as well as warmest, supporters of his government and family.[51]

In the following year, by contrast, Queen Caroline's death offered an opportunity for implicit criticism of authority under the cloak of loyalty to a member of the royal family, but this case was exceptional.[52] The subsequent extensions of religious liberty which occurred during the reigns of George IV and William IV led Nonconformist preachers on the deaths of those sovereigns to gloss over their distaste for their personal failings in fulsome affirmations of loyalty and gratitude.[53]

Significantly, by the time of Prince Albert's death, Dissenters had become less self-conscious in affirming their distinctive identity. Nevertheless the capacity of deceased royalty to be all things to almost all people was again demonstrated. A Congregational minister cited evidence that the Prince "was in the habit of attending a truly evangelical ministry, when in the Isle of Wight"; the theologically liberal George Dawson cast Albert in his own image as a man who "served his God with art and science, with modern industry and mechanism".[54] In Leeds forty-nine of the sixty-four members of the predominantly Liberal and Nonconformist town council turned out to attend a service in the Parish Church and subsequently recorded a vote of thanks to the vicar for his sermon.[55] Queen Victoria's death provided an early stimulus to ecumenical services: for example in Ipswich Church of England and Nonconformist clergy joined together to hold a service at the Public Hall. T.M. Morris, a

---

[51] John Morison, *Patriotic Regrets for the Loss of a Good King* (London, 1820), p. 20.

[52] C. Berry, *A Sermon on the Death of Caroline, Queen of England* (London, 1821), pp. 9-10, 26.

[53] J. Ritchie, *He Removeth Kings* (Edinburgh, 1830), p. 39; E. Steane, *The Eternal King* (London, 1837), pp. 27-8.

[54] A.E. Lord, *A Prince and A Great Man Fallen* (London, 1862), p. 8; British Library 1878 d.12 Newspaper cutting: *Public Service in the Town Hall. Mr George Dawson's Funeral Eloge*.

[55] *The Leeds Intelligencer*, 28 December 1861.

former president of the Baptist Union, hailed the gathering as a hopeful sign of the times and a promise of closer union in the future.[56]

In the earlier part of the nineteenth century Roman Catholics were the only significant religious group who made little formal acknowledgement of royal deaths. They contrasted in this respects with Jews, who appeared even more anxious than Dissenters to use such occasions to express their loyalty. Thus a dirge was sung in the Great Synagogue in Aldgate on the day of George III's funeral. It was subsequently translated into English and published in a beautifully produced little book.[57] One London rabbi preached a particularly flattering sermon on the death of George IV, suggesting that the late monarch was of comparable stature and worth to King David, notably in the moral rectitude of his government and his tolerance of every religion, and "proving" that he was now, like the pious and good of all religions, enjoying eternal glory. The British constitution, he suggested, was "the most excellent that human wisdom was able to frame, and probably approaches nearest to our Israelitish government".[58] Later in the period Jews were able to use such occasions to underline their own increasing status: the Chief Rabbi noted the Duke of Clarence's attendance at Passover services and his interest in Judaism; on Queen Victoria's death the political and social enfranchisement achieved during her reign was recalled.[59] Even at this date, on the other hand, Roman Catholics were reluctant to jump on the patriotic bandwagon: in 1892 a priest in Exeter expressed sympathy with the royal family, but compared the Duke of Clarence's death adversely with that of Cardinal Manning. "When they contemplated the manner of these two deaths" he went on," they [ought] to thank God that they were out of one Church and into the other." [60] Nevertheless in 1901 votive masses and singings of the miserere began to take place: a transition could be observed in Edinburgh between the "short memorial service" with "a fairly numerous congregation" held for Victoria and the "full and imposing ceremonial" in a packed cathedral offered for Edward VII.[61]

---

[56]*The Proclamation of King Edward VII. An Account of the Ceremony at Ipswich on XXV January MDCCCCI.*

[57]Hyman Hurwitz, *The Tears of a Grateful People* (London, 1820).

[58]Solomon Myer, *A Funeral Sermon on the Death of His late Majesty George IV* (London, 1820), pp. 12-15, 18, 21-5.

[59]H.M. Adler, *The Nation's Lament* (London, 1892), pp.9-10; S.A. Adler, *The Passing of Our Queen* (London, 1901), p. 9.

[60]*Exeter Flying Post*, 18 Jan. 1892.

[61]Ibid., 21 May 1910; *The Scotsman*, 4 Feb. 1901, 21 May 1910.

The solidarity of religious observance of royal deaths had thus always been impressive, but it became even more so at the end of the period. The whole process gave spiritual legitimacy, human accessibility and ritual continuity to the monarchy, sustaining it in times of relative unpopularity and giving added depth and power to the upsurge of veneration associated with the jubilees of 1887 and 1897 and the coronation of Edward VII in 1902.[62] Meanwhile the churches benefited from the opportunity to offer reminders of the transience and vulnerability of human life, to consider the providential involvement of God in earthly affairs, to direct patriotic impulses in a Christian direction, and – sometimes – to hold up deceased royalty as examples for moral and spiritual emulation. As the period went on the potential for churchmen to use such events as a platform for prophetically detached observation tended to decline, and their utterances increasingly became the religious icing on the cake of national secular consensus. Nevertheless, as institutions the churches remained an essential medium for expressing the nation's shared sense of identity and loss. In so doing they ensured that – in this respect at least – British nationalism evolved out of orthodox Christianity rather than in reaction to it.[63]

---

[62] On jubilees and coronations see David Cannadine, "The Context, Performance and Meaning of Ritual: The British Monarchy and the "Invention of Tradition", c. 1820-1977", in Eric Hobsbawm and Terence Ranger, eds, *The Invention of Tradition* (Cambridge, 1983). Also relevant to the wider context of this paper is the dangerous illness of the Prince of Wales in 1871, on which see William M. Kuhn, "Ceremony and politics: the British monarchy, 1871-1872", *Journal of British Studies*, 26 (1987), pp. 133-62.

[63] Grateful acknowledgment is made to the Humanities Research Board of the British Academy and to The Open University (Faculty of Arts) for funding the special research leave during which the research for this paper was carried out.

BIBLIOTHECA HISTORICO-ECCLESIASTICA LUNDENSIS

1. K G Hammar, *Liberalteologi och kyrkopolitik.* 1972.
2. Karl-Johan Tyrberg, *Lekmannaverksamheten och församlingens förnyelse.* 1972.
3. Göran Åberg, *Enhet och frihet. Studier i Jönköpings missionsförenings historia.* 1972.
4. Hugo Söderström, *Confession and Cooperation. The Policy of the Augustana Synod in Confessional Matters and the Synod's Relations with other Churches up to the Beginning of the Twentieth Century.* 1973.
5. Ingmar Brohed, *Prostmötet i Svenska kyrkan under 1900-talet.* 1975
6. Lars Edvardsson, *Kyrka och Judendom. Svenk judemission med särskild hänsyn till Svenska Israelmissionens verksamhet. 1875 -1975.* 1976.
7. Ingmar Brohed, *Offentligt förhör och konfirmationen i Sverige under 1700-talet. En case study rörande utvecklingen i Lunds stift.* 1977.
8. Leif Eeg-Olofsson, *Johan Dillner. Präst, musiker och mystiker. 1978.*
9. Göran Åberg, *Sällskap – samfund. Studier i Svenska Alliansmissionens historia fram till 1950-talets mitt.* 1980.
10. Kristin Drar, *Konungens herravälde såsom rättvisans, fridens och frihetens beskydd: Medeltidens fursteideal i svenskt hög- och senmedeltida källmaterial.* 1980.
11. Rhode Struble, *Den samfundsfria församlingen och de karismatiska gåvorna och tjänsterna. Den svenska Pingströrelsens församlingssyn 1907-1947.* 1982.
12. Hans Wahlbom, *Husförhöret under regressionsperioden i Lunds stift.* 1983.
13. Anders Jarlert, *Ämbete och tro. En undersökning av den kyrkliga debatten i Göteborgs stift under slutet av 1800-talet.* 1984.
14. Alvin Isberg, *Kyrkopolitik och nationalitet. Ett dilemma för minoritetskyrkorna i mellankrigstidens Polen.* 1985.
15. Anders Jarlert, *Emanuel Linderholm som kyrkohistoriker.* 1987.
16. Rune Imberg, *In Quest of Authority. The "Tracts for the Times" and the Development of the Tractarian Leaders, 1833-1841.* 1987.
17. Rune Imberg, *Tracts for the Times. A Complete Survey of All the Editions.* 1987.
18. Aleksander Radler, *Peregrinatio religiosa. Studien zum Religionsbegriff in der schwedischen Romantik. Teil 1: Die christliche Persönlichkeitsphilosophie Erik Gustaf Geijers.* 1988.
19. Kjell O U Leijon, *Reagan, Religion and Politics. The Revitalization of "a Nation under God" during the 80s.* 1988.
20. Birgitta Rosén, *Fädernas kyrka – Församlingens hus. Svenska kyrkan och gudstjänstrummet ca 1890-1930 med speciell hänsyn till Stockholm.* 1988.
21. Lars Aldén, *Stiftskyrkans förnyelse. Framväxten av stiftsmöten och stiftsråd i Svenska kyrkan till omkr t1920.* 1989.
22. Pétur Pétursson, *Från väckelse till samfund. Svensk pingstmission på öarna i Nordatlanten.* 1990.

23. Jan Carlsson, *Region och religion. En regionindelning utifrån den kyrkliga sedens styrka på 1970-talet.* 1990.
24. Samuel Rubenson, *The Letters of St. Antony. Origenist Theology, Monastic Tradition and the Making of a Saint.* 1990.
25. Rune Imberg, *Biskops- och domprostutnämningar i Svenska Kyrkan 1866-1989.* 1991.
26. Kristin Parikh, *Kvinnoklostren på Östgötaslätten under medeltiden.* 1991.
27. Alf Lindberg, *Förkunnarna och deras utbildning. Utbildningsfrågan inom Pingströrelsen, Lewi Pethrus ideologiska roll och de kvinnliga förkunnarnas situation.* 1991.
28. Thomas Björkman, *Ein Lebensraum für die Kirche. Die Rundbriefe von Landesbischof D. Moritz Mitzenheim 1945-1970.* 1991.
29. Anders Björnberg, *Teaching and Growth. Christian Religious Education in a Local and International Missionary Context.* 1991.
30. Mats Selén, *The Oxford Movement and Wesleyan Methodism in England 1833-1882: A Study in Religious Conflict.* 1992.
31. Catharina Segerbank, *Dödstanken i svensk romantik. Odödlighetstanke och uppståndelsetro hos tre svenska diktare: P.D.A. Atterbom, J.O. Wallin, E.J. Stagnelius.* 1993.
32. Kjell O U Lejon, *"God Bless America!" President Georg Bushs religiopolitiska budskap.* 1994.
33. *Resan till Continenten. Christian August Sylvans resedagbok.* Redigerad av Carl-Edvard Normann. Slutförd och med förord av Barbro Lindgren. 1995.
34. *Hilding Pleijel Symposium 1993. Ett hundraårsjubileum.* 1995.
35. Anders Jarlert, *The Oxford Group, Group Revivalism, and the Churches in Northern Europe, 1930–1945, with Special Reference to Scandinavia and Germany.* 1995.
36. *Church and People in Britatin and Scandinvia.* Ingmar Brohed (editor). 1996.